A Strong-Minded Woman

THE LIFE OF MARY LIVERMORE

Wendy Hamand Venet

UNIVERSITY OF MASSACHUSETTS PRESS

AMHERST AND LONDON

Copyright © 2005 by Wendy Hamand Venet
ALL RIGHTS RESERVED
Printed in the United States of America

LC 2005019234
ISBN 1-55849-514-2 (library cloth); 513-4 (paper)

Designed by Steve Dyer
Set in ITC Bodoni Book by Binghamton Valley Composition, Inc.
Printed and bound by The Maple-Vail Book Manufacturing Group

Library of Congress Cataloging-in-Publication Data

Venet, Wendy Hamand.
  A strong-minded woman : the life of Mary Livermore / Wendy Hamand Venet.
    p. cm.
  Includes bibliographical references and index.
  ISBN 1-55849-513-4 (pbk. : alk. paper) — ISBN 1-55849-514-2 (library cloth
: alk. paper)
  1. Livermore, Mary Ashton Rice, 1820-1905. 2. Social reformers—United
States—Biography. 3. Women social reformers—United States—Biography.
4. Orators—United States—Biography. 5. Women orators—United States—
Biography. 6. Nurses—United States—Biography. 7. Newspaper editors—
United States—Biography. 8. Women newspaper editors—United States—
Biography. 9. Suffragists—United States—Biography. 10. Temperance—United
States. I. Title.
  CT275.L5V46 2005
  303.48'4'092—dc22

                                                    2005019234

British Library Cataloguing in Publication data are available.

For Jason and Andrew

CONTENTS

ACKNOWLEDGMENTS

A S A GRADUATE STUDENT at the University of Illinois in the 1980s, I became fascinated by the topic of women in the Civil War. Surprised by how little had been written on the subject, I set out to produce a dissertation, later a book, on the role of women abolitionists in wartime. Researching that topic gave me a deeper understanding of how many women who had led traditional lives before 1861 were transformed by their experiences in the Civil War. Many became involved in the public sphere in unprecedented ways; some became feminists. My earlier work led me to Mary Livermore as a prime example of both. She was, additionally, a major figure about whom no biography had been written. When I discovered that Livermore had intentionally destroyed the bulk of her personal correspondence, I hesitated momentarily, then decided to complete the book with what evidence I could glean from surviving sources.

Although Livermore created a roadblock I did not anticipate, I have nonetheless received a lot of help with this project. Georgia State University awarded me a Research Initiation Grant that helped to jumpstart my archival research. The Department of History provided summer research money at several points along the way and the Copen Award that defrayed the costs of including photographs. My colleagues in the History Department have given moral support, especially Diane Willen, Tim Crimmins, Glen Eskew, Cynthia Schwenk, Doug Reynolds, Larry Youngs, and Hugh Hudson. I owe a debt of gratitude to Kent Hackmann, who read and commented on the entire manuscript. Over the past eight years, I have been fortunate to have the help of these talented graduate research assistants: Jeff Moore, Johanna Rickman, Jyotsna Vanapalli, Jennifer Gonzolez, and Monica Waugh.

Librarians and archivists have lent me their time and expertise. I could not have completed this book without the help of the Reference and Interlibrary Loan departments of Georgia State's Pullen Library. I would also like to acknowledge the Newspaper and Periodicals Department of the American Antiquarian Society, Worcester, Massachusetts, for preserving and making available to me the *New Covenant*, which is the single most important source in revealing Mary Livermore's life from 1857 to 1869. Librarians and archivists at the following repositories offered their assistance: Andover-Harvard Theological Library of Harvard Divinity School; Boston Public Library, Chicago Historical Society; Connecticut State Library; Houghton Library, Harvard University; Huntington Library; Illinois Historical Library; Library of Congress; Library of Virginia; Massachusetts Historical Society; Melrose Public Library; National Archives; Newberry Library; New-York Historical Society; New York Public Library; Prestwould Foundation of Clarksville, Virginia; Princeton University; Schlesinger Library, Radcliffe College; Smith College; State Historical Society of Wisconsin; Stowe-Day Library; University of Illinois at Chicago; University of Virginia; Vassar College; Wellesley College; Wichita State University.

I have made an effort to visit the places where Mary Livermore lived, and local hosts have been generous with their time during my visits. Today the North Boston neighborhood of Mary's youth bears little resemblance to the way it looked in the 1820s, and Chicago, home to Livermore and her family from 1857 to 1869, burned in the Great Fire of 1871. Other locations have been preserved at least partially the way she knew them. In 1999, I visited Mecklenburg County, Virginia, where Mary lived from 1839 to 1842, seeking to understand more about her life as a plantation schoolteacher and to unravel the mystery surrounding the identity of her employers. JoLee Gregory Spears, who runs a genealogy website, and Muncy Moore, who has done extensive work on area tombstones, helped me to succeed in naming Mary's employers. I also owe special thanks to E. E. Coleman Jr., Circuit Court Clerk, who welcomed me to the Mecklenburg County courthouse and its marvelous collection of local records, Julian Hudson of Prestwould Foundation, who allowed me to read notebooks kept years ago by a local historian, and Edna Puryear, who drove me all around the county showing me antebellum homes and the site of the plantation where Mary lived. From 1847 to 1852, Livermore resided in Stafford, Connecticut. When I visited in 2002, Isabel Zablanski of the local/historical society gave me a tour of the area and arranged for me to see the inside of the Universalist church where Daniel Livermore once preached. Mary Livermore lived in Melrose, Massachusetts from 1870 to 1905. Her house still stands, purchased from her descendants by Josephine Mutti in 1954. Mrs. Mutti resides there yet, and was gracious enough to let me see the house when I arrived unannounced one afternoon in 1996.

My experiences with the review and publication process for this book have been very positive. Jim Stewart read the manuscript for the University of Massachusetts Press, offering astute and very helpful comments. The staff at the press have been gracious, patient, and wise. Acquisitions editor Clark Dougan has been altogether supportive of my project since our first meeting at the Berkshire Conference in 2002. Copy editor Amanda Heller is a wizard with a No. 2 pencil; my writing is vastly improved because of her input. Managing editor Carol Betsch ably shepherded the manuscript through the production process.

My family has lived with Mary Livermore as long as I have, and I thank them for their support. My mother, Martha Hamand, accompanied me on research trips to Boston, New York, Worcester, and Princeton, acting as my research assistant and travel companion. My husband, Allen Venet, was always willing to listen to yet another story of research travails or writer's bloc or, conversely, the joys of finding a really good shred of evidence. Our sons, Jason and Andrew, have grown up with Mary Livermore. I dedicate this book to them, with love.

A STRONG-MINDED WOMAN

Mary Livermore and Historical Memory

WHEN MARY LIVERMORE DIED in 1905, the *Boston Transcript* called her "America's foremost woman," lauding her role as Civil War nurse, her dedication to improving her community and nation, and her work on behalf of women. Ten years earlier the *New York Times*, in reporting Livermore's retirement from public speaking, also noted that she had once been among the four most popular lecturers in America, and the only woman in this elite group. For many years she had lectured five nights a week for five months each year, traveling an astounding 25,000 miles annually on the lyceum circuit.[1] As a leader in the woman's rights and temperance movements, she edited the nation's premier suffrage newspaper and later presided over the American Woman Suffrage Association. She led the Massachusetts branch of the Woman's Christian Temperance Union and lectured extensively in support of that cause. The high praise that fell on her in 1905 was well deserved.

A century after her death, few persons recognize her name or remember her accomplishments. Her Civil War medical work and efforts to organize women in support of the Union cause are an unknown story compared to the life of Clara Barton. Livermore's support of temperance and her career as a suffragist have not captured the attention that the public has focused on Frances Willard, Susan B. Anthony, and Elizabeth Cady Stanton.[2]

Livermore's descent from "foremost woman" to relative obscurity happened over a period of several decades. During her own lifetime she was featured in books about eminent women, beginning with *Woman's Work in the Civil War* by Linus P. Brockett and Mary C. Vaughan, published in 1867. Brockett and Vaughan noted that Livermore had emerged from the war as a figure of national prominence: "Few of the busy and active laborers in the broad field of woman's effort during the war, have been more widely or favorably known than Mrs. Livermore." During the last two decades of the century, she appeared often in texts such as Phebe Hanaford's *Daughters of America; Or, Women of the Century*, in which she was the leading figure in a chapter about women lecturers. In the two decades following her death, Livermore still appeared in books about important women, including *Women Who Have Enobled Life* by Lilian Whiting and *Across My Path: Memories of People I Have Known* by LaSalle Corbell Pickett, widow of the Confederate general who led Gettysburg's famous charge. In *Women in American History* by Grace Humphrey, a book intended for students and published in 1919, a biographical sketch of Livermore appeared along with those of fourteen others, including Betsy Ross, Martha Washington, Dolley Madison, Sacajawea, and Harriet Beecher Stowe.[3]

In 1920 Livermore's hometown of Melrose, Massachusetts, honored her memory on the centenary of her birth with a public ceremony. Livermore's daughter, granddaughter, and great-grandson served as guests of honor, and a variety of reformers attended, including the daughters of her friends Julia Ward Howe and Lucy Stone. Paying homage to her role in Civil War nursing as they had fifteen years earlier at her funeral, members of the Grand Army of the Republic performed the trooping of the colors and a salute. Governor Calvin Coolidge sent a telegram saying, "Her life and work will ever remain as a great source of inspiration to our people."[4]

During the Second World War, a merchant marine "Liberty Ship" was named for her. President Franklin D. Roosevelt even mentioned Livermore in a famous news conference during the summer of 1941. Returning to Washington after a meeting with Winston Churchill, he wanted to impress on the American people the dangers posed by Nazism. Roosevelt was already beginning to invoke the spirit of the nation's most famous wartime president, Abraham Lincoln, even though the United States had not yet formally entered the war. During the news conference he produced a copy of Carl Sandburg's biography of Lincoln and read an excerpt in which Sandburg quoted Mary Livermore's Civil War memoir. The passage described her 1862 meeting with

Lincoln and the president's grim assessment of the war. It would take arduous fighting and not just grand strategy to win, Lincoln had told Livermore. Roosevelt used this episode, recorded by Livermore, as a lesson to Americans that the war with Germany might be prolonged and deadly.[5]

But by the 1940s she had begun to fade in the public's memory. Covering Roosevelt's news conference, the *Boston Herald* felt compelled to ask, "But who was Mary A. Livermore?" Adding "Boston ought to know," the article presented a brief account of her birth and girlhood in Boston, her life, and her accomplishments, including her extraordinary career as a public speaker. It concluded, "Her eloquence was universally recognized."[6]

If Livermore had begun to fade from popularity by the 1940s, she continued to fare reasonably well among Lincoln biographers and Civil War historians, who cited her memoir *My Story of the War* as an authoritative and readable source of information about the northern homefront, women in wartime, and Lincoln's interactions with female volunteers. From popular writing to academic histories, Livermore often appears in text and notes as a testament to women's role in America's greatest war. In his epic documentary about the Civil War, Ken Burns showcased Livermore, and Stephen Oates included a semi-fictional portrait of her in his book *Whirlwind of War*. A new generation of women's historians have revived Livermore's reputation in their studies of the United States Sanitary Commission, the relationship of the predominantly female volunteers with its male leadership, and its role in launching women as late-nineteenth-century public figures.[7]

Among historians of reform and woman's rights, Livermore has missed the recognition she deserves. While the legacies of Susan Anthony, Elizabeth Cady Stanton, Julia Ward Howe, Lucy Stone, and others have been preserved and celebrated, the astounding range of Livermore's accomplishments in a public career lasting forty-five years has not. Several explanations help account for Livermore's relegation to the shadows of the feminist pantheon. Unlike Stanton, Stone, and Howe, she did not have a daughter who wrote a loving memoir, thus keeping her reputation alive for future generations. Her wartime autobiography, which sold well initially, dropped out of sight when a fire at her publisher's destroyed the plates from which it had been printed; the volume would not be reprinted until the late twentieth century.[8]

Livermore was a mentor to several prominent figures in the woman's rights movement, including Anna Howard Shaw and Frances Willard, both of whom valued her friendship and appreciated her talents. Shaw believed that Livermore and her husband, Daniel, "deserved far more than they received from a world to which they gave so freely and so richly." Witty, affectionate, and generous with her friends, Livermore sometimes came across as formal, sanctimonious, even antiquated to some of the younger generation. A woman of Victorian sensibilities, she upheld the wearing of corsets and expressed shock that respectable people were reading Walt Whitman and Oscar Wilde. She certainly did not touch the majority of younger-generation suffragists the way Susan Anthony did. Anthony's tenacity and absolute dedication to woman suffrage inspired scores of young women, who carried her name and her reputation into the twentieth century. Nor did Livermore inspire the kind of loyalty that brought Frances Willard the unbounded adulation of thousands. After Willard asked the Massachusetts branch of the Woman's Christian Temperance Union to raise money for a Livermore sculpture, its president responded to Willard's secretary that fundraising was not going well. "Large numbers of people admire Mrs. Livermore," she wrote, "but very few love her."[9] Livermore's failure to inspire many early-twentieth-century activists contributed to her decline in the collective memory of the suffrage and temperance movements.

Livermore also contributed significantly to her own historical obscurity by consciously destroying personal correspondence and other sources that might have revealed her inner self. For reasons that are not entirely clear, she sought to protect herself from anyone who might become her "indiscreet biographer." Having written about herself in articles and eventually in two volumes of autobiography, she saw no reason to save her private papers. In 1881, after a serious illness, she destroyed all her letters, telling a friend, "I burned all my past behind me." After completing two best-selling memoirs, she "cremated" the manuscripts. At the turn of the century, she destroyed eighty scrapbooks containing a lifetime of short book descriptions because they also included "a record of my most intimate thoughts and feelings for many years" written in the margins. What Livermore began, her descendants completed. Several decades after her death, when the last of her relatives moved out of her residence in suburban Boston, the new owner of the house recalled seeing family members throwing books and papers out of a third-story dormer window into a truck below. "They thought they were doing me a favor cleaning out the old papers," she remembered, adding that she had rescued a few of the books.[10] The combined efforts of Mary Livermore and her kin discouraged *any* biographer, sympathetic or "indiscreet," from attempting to know more about her than already existed in published form. This biography represents the first full-length study of her life.

Despite her concerted effort to wipe out the historical record, Mary Livermore did not succeed. Beginning in 1857 she wrote regularly for a succession of newspapers, including her husband's religious weekly in Chicago, the *New Covenant*, and then for her own woman's rights newspapers, the *Agitator* and, later, the *Woman's Journal*. During a journalistic career lasting five decades, she produced stories, letters, editorials, travelogues. She wrote in a way that was thoughtful and insightful, sometimes critical or satirical, occasionally poignant, and often hilariously funny. In short, she was both a keen observer and a participant in some of the great events and social movements of the nineteenth century. These stories and essays, hundreds of which survive, are key printed sources about her life and career.

Letters to friends and colleagues constitute another important source. For the period after 1860, a reasonably large collection of her correspondence has survived, albeit a one-sided correspondence. Especially rich sources are her letters to her Universalist minister friends Phebe Hanaford and Olympia Brown in the 1860s and suffragists Elizabeth Boynton Harbert and Lucy Stone, along with Stone's husband, Henry Blackwell, and their daughter Alice Stone Blackwell in the 1870s and 1880s, and, in the last two decades of her life, to journalist Lilian Whiting and artist Anne Whitney. Small collections of her letters are sprinkled among more than fifteen archival repositories. Additionally, her two published memoirs, *My Story of the War* (1887) and *The Story of My Life* (1897), along with the poems, short stories, and articles she wrote for a variety of publications beginning in the 1840s, provide many insights into her long and productive career. Published memoirs by Livermore's friends and colleagues contribute additional pieces to the puzzle.

Her life represents a remarkable journey. Intellectually curious and rebellious from a young age, she began a lifelong quest to explore new places, new cultures, and new ideas. She experienced profound transformations at three points in her life. The first was her decision to leave her Boston home at age eighteen and become a schoolteacher to a slave-owning family in Virginia; the second was her marriage to Universalist minister Daniel Livermore and resolution of her religious doubts; and the third was her emergence as a public figure during the Civil War, undeniably the most important period in the evolution of her public career. As a volunteer and later as a paid agent of the United States Sanitary Commission and associate manager of its Chicago branch, she mobilized local women in support of the Union cause. In addition, she organized scores of local aid societies in the Midwest and planned the first blockbuster Sanitary Commission fair, a fundraiser that was so successful it would inspire women throughout the North to organize similar events. By the time the war ended, Livermore had earned a national reputation for her relief work and had met with leading figures of her era, including President Lincoln and General Ulysses S. Grant. The transforming experience of the Civil War for Livermore and for women she worked with is a major theme of this book.

Before the Civil War, Mary Livermore led a reasonably conventional life, one that was defined by her husband's professional duties and by her commitment to their daughters. Although she had begun writing poems and stories for publication as early as the 1840s, and had devoted time toward charities to help the indigent, ill, and orphaned, she certainly did not advocate rights for women, and she was appalled at the very thought of women speaking before an audience on any topic at all. The war changed that. By the time it was over, Livermore had turned her considerable talents toward the woman's rights movement. In wartime she had called on all patriotic women to support their country in its hour of need; now she called on the nation to reward women's patriotism and acknowledge their importance to public life by giving them full legal and political rights. She would dedicate the rest of her life to this cause. Her evolution as a feminist represents another important theme in this biography.

From an early age, Mary Livermore exhibited signs of being focused and determined. Throughout the four-year-long "rebellion" of the Confederate states, when she resided in Chicago, the city's leading Republican newspaper, the *Tribune*, was her staunch supporter. It applauded her efforts to help Union Army soldiers through her role with the Sanitary Commission. It cheered her for upholding the Union, the Lincoln administration's war policy, and the emancipation of the slaves. It defended her against the accusations of the Democratic press, which assailed her for accepting a salary from the Sanitary Commission while the Catholic Sisters of Mercy worked without pay. But the *Tribune* turned against Livermore after the war when she began to advocate legal and political rights for women, including the vote. In a series of articles the newspaper ridiculed her as "the Livermore" and condemned her as "selfish" and "a strong-minded woman." To be strong-minded was the very antithesis of what social norms defined as woman's appropriate persona. She was supposed to be self-effacing, deferential to her husband, and wholly dedicated to serving her children, her church, and her community. Far from shrinking from the *Tribune*'s intended insult, Livermore embraced the term and in one self-parody described herself as a "ferocious woman."[11] Once she embraced woman's rights, she never looked back.

After the war, Mary Livermore emerged as a central figure in many reform movements of her era. Her later career constitutes the last major focus of this biography. Livermore made important and lasting contributions to American life during the Gilded Age. She played a pivotal role in the emerging woman's rights movement in the Midwest during the late 1860s, publishing a suffrage newspaper and founding the Illinois Woman Suffrage Association. Returning to her native Boston in 1869, she helped launch the American Woman Suffrage Association, after a feminist schism in which she played a central role. Her public quarrels with Susan Anthony and Victoria Woodhull in the 1860s and 1870s serve as a reminder that the woman's rights movement was richly textured, often contentious, and never static. Her efforts promoting women's access to higher education and better-paying jobs underscore the fact that the nineteenth-century woman's rights movement was never about suffrage alone. Despite being a liberal Christian, Livermore played a leadership role in the WCTU, an organization dominated by evangelical women, and helped turn it into a large and powerful pressure group supporting both prohibition and suffrage. She campaigned for the Republican Party in 1872 and 1884, reminding women that while they could not vote, they could influence those who did. In addition, she worked in Christian Socialism and the club women's movements. At the same time, she maintained a highly successful career as a lyceum lecturer, speaking about rights for her gender and many other pressing issues of the day, including poverty, class conflict, and business regulation. By the 1870s and 1880s she had become a kind of civic educator to the nation, a popular speaker sought after from Maine to California.

Mary Livermore's greatest gifts lay in her ability to communicate and persuade. She used her pen and her voice during the Civil War and in her remarkably successful postwar career as an orator and a writer to persuade Americans that they could make their country better. She told women that it was their destiny to play a greater role in public life. She told them to improve themselves by seeking greater educational opportunities and more varied professional possibilities. She told them that they must use their influence to end drunkenness and sexual license, and must seek solutions to the social problems of poverty and inequality. She told them they must help their nation in wartime and become politically savvy in the postwar world. She told them that they must demand legal and political rights as both a matter of justice and a vehicle for improving society. And she told them that they could be womanly and also embrace woman's rights. Mary Livermore was not a pioneer suffragist. Her path to feminism may seem maddeningly slow to the modern reader.

And yet, by being a Civil War heroine first and then an advocate of woman's rights, Livermore became one of postwar American's most effective spokeswoman for the causes she espoused, a leading figure among the second generation and one who would bring legitimacy and respectability to the cause.

Mary Livermore was far too modest to write an epitaph for herself. But one woman from Connecticut who heard her speak in 1889 sent a glowing account to the *Woman's Journal*. Her words summarize as well as any Livermore's contributions to her gender in a lengthy and productive public career: "Who can hear her, and not be elevated in thought and carried beyond the darkness of doubt as to the future of woman?"[12]

CHAPTER 1

———— ◆•◆•◆ ————

Boston Childhood

IN HER LATER YEARS, Mary Livermore would look back on her childhood and describe it as "eminently and severely religious."[1] As a convert to liberal Christianity, she would remember the orthodoxy of her youth as cold, dreary, and comfortless. She would also recall feelings of rebelliousness and the desire to find outlets for her intellectual interests and ambition. Her childhood was a dramatic contrast between religious insecurity on the one hand, intellectual and personal growth on the other.

Mary's parents must have looked upon her birth, at 6:00 A.M. on December 19, 1820, with a mixture of joy and anxiety. Preceding her arrival, they had mourned the deaths of three infants, all of whom had died before reaching the age of one. With their fourth child born in the winter, when Boston's weather could be severe, when houses were ill heated and medical knowledge remained rudimentary, they had reason to be concerned. Yet the child they named Mary Ashton Rice would enjoy robust health and high energy from her earliest days and indeed for most of her long life. Two more daughters followed her birth: Rachel, three years younger, and Abigail, seven years younger.[2]

Mary's father, Timothy Rice, became the strongest influence on her early life and perhaps even her later professional one. The Rice family had antecedents dating back to the earliest days of colonial Massachusetts. Their fore-

9

bears arrived in 1638, less than ten years after the founding of the colony. Timothy Rice grew up on his family's farm in Northfield, Massachusetts, the sixth of eleven children. He moved to Boston as a young adult and served in the navy during the War of 1812. In her autobiography Mary described her father as "tall and large physically . . . studious and religious, . . . fluent in speech, and talking with much power." Mary's father read avidly and encouraged her to do so, and he held strong views about the importance of education. Far ahead of his time, he believed in schooling for girls, and saw to it that his daughters had the best education he could afford to give them. A man of strong will and great determination, he was both a loving parent and a strict disciplinarian. He disapproved of uncomfortable clothing and refused to allow his daughters to wear fashionable "stays," an early version of a corset held in place by a wooden busk that forced the wearer into a stiff posture. He adhered to a moral code that included abstinence from alcohol, a cause his daughter would espouse throughout her adult life. "My father was a rigid temperance man," she recalled in her autobiography, "long before the subject of temperance was discussed in public, or indeed in private."[3] Rice imparted his forceful personality and code of ethics to Mary. They would be his most lasting influence on his daughter.

Mary's mother, Zebiah Vose Ashton Rice, a native Bostonian, was the daughter of a sailor in the service of the East India Company, the corporate behemoth whose decision to ship tea directly to the American colonies helped trigger the American Revolution. Mary's grandfather remained proudly English and Anglican, alternately residing in Boston and London. Her grandmother, however, refused to leave Boston. Mary later recalled, "The law on both sides of the water gave my grandfather the right to compel my grandmother to reside in England as he desired; but he never attempted such compulsion, nor would he have succeeded if he had, for his wife was a woman with a mind of her own, and, young or old, carried her points."[4]

All the women in her family seem to have been adept at "carrying their points." Zebiah Ashton's betrothal to Timothy Rice lasted six years. Perhaps influenced by her own father's absenteeism, she would not marry him until he left the navy after the War of 1812 and renounced a maritime career altogether. While gentle and gracious, and never directly challenging her husband's socially ordained role as head of the household, she nevertheless exerted her influence quietly. Mary recalled that her father conferred with Zebiah on all matters of significance, and every family prayer included the words, "Bless the united heads of this family!"[5]

The Rice family lived in Boston's North End and appear to have moved yearly during Mary's early childhood, living in a succession of residences before settling in a house at 91 Salem Street. During Mary's childhood, the North End housed artisans and laborers. The neighborhood was also characterized by its large proportion of native-born residents, one of the highest in a city that was becoming rapidly populated by the foreign-born, especially Irish. The *Boston City Directories* during the 1820s list Timothy Rice's occupation as "laborer," a designation that reveals little about his actual form of employment. Mary makes no reference to her father's occupation and gives little detail regarding the family's economic status, saying simply that they were "neither rich nor poor." She did recall worrying about money, especially the cost of her private school education.[6]

Several houses away from Mary's childhood home on Salem Street stood Old North Church. Although this was not the family's house of worship, Mary remembered its bells with great fondness, both when they marked church services and on special occasions, such as the Fourth of July, when they rang out with "Hail, Columbia, Happy Land."[7]

During her childhood Mary felt very close to her mother's extended family of Ashtons and to the Rice family's neighbors and friends. They, in addition to her parents and sisters, gave her a sense of security and belonging. In the evenings when guests dropped by, her mother often served apples, cider, and doughnuts. In the winter, when the oysterman made his rounds, Zebiah Rice might purchase this New England delicacy to make a hot oyster stew. Mary's favorite room in the Salem Street house was the kitchen—illuminated with sunlight from four windows, its floors covered with beach sand in summer and with handmade rugs in winter, and dominated by a massive fireplace. The family cooked, ate, and relaxed in this room. Mary recalled playing house at the kitchen table set with tiny pewter dishes and porringers, dressing rag babies in home-stitched clothes, singing songs and telling stories with her two sisters and a host of cousins. But if she remembered the many comforts of her family home, she also recalled its discomforts, including the "numbing chill" of the bedrooms in wintertime and the need for a family member to get up in the night to add logs to the fire. Nevertheless, throughout her childhood Mary seems to have been irrepressible. She loved to play outdoors, and her parents encouraged such activity as good for her health. From time to time, her boundless energy got out of hand. In an attempt to keep track of his daughter, Timothy Rice trained the family dog, Hector, to follow her. On more than one occasion, Hector failed to keep track of her, and the town crier had to be summoned to locate her when she wandered off.[8]

While family and friends provided Mary with an important source of comfort and security, religion became a source of both fear and awe. Religion was the heart and soul of Timothy Rice's world, and he imparted his religious beliefs to his children with an intensity that caused his eldest daughter considerable anguish. In keeping with the creed of his Puritan forebears, Timothy Rice believed in the Calvinist notion that God decides before one's birth whether one is destined for heaven or hell. Upright behavior may provide clues as to one's future state but is no guarantee of a heavenly future. One must attend religious services dutifully, pray and read the Bible regularly, and look for signs of God's favor. At the end of each day, Timothy Rice quizzed his children as to whether they had made good use of their time. An uncommonly serious child, Mary would sometimes lie awake worrying about whether she had performed in a godly way. When each of his daughters reached the age of seven, their father insisted that she commence reading the Bible in its entirety once each year. Mary continued this practice until she reached adulthood.[9]

The Rice family attended First Baptist Church, where Timothy Rice appears to have been a figure of stature and influence. Despite his limited means, parishioners respected him for his intellect and character. The congregation at First Baptist underwent considerable change during the years of Mary's childhood. Because so many families were leaving the North End for newer neighborhoods in the city, church membership dropped below two hundred by the mid-1820s before stabilizing and growing again with the construction of a new brick sanctuary at Hanover and Union streets in 1829. Mary recalled the earlier wooden structure, built in the 1770s and located at Stillman and Salem streets. As a child of five or six, she thought it was severe and unattractive, and she could remember the apprehension with which she viewed the rigors of Sunday services. In winter, the church was very cold. Each family brought a foot stove to be filled with live coals by the sexton, Samuel Winslow, a "sour old curmudgeon" feared by children in the congregation. Mary remembered her feet feeling "half frozen." The pastor, the Reverend Francis Wayland, later president of Brown University, spoke from a pulpit reached by a spiral stairway. To Mary, he appeared suspended in midair, very much like God himself. The prayers, sermon, and hymns seemed endless to her as a young girl. Although Reverend Wayland's sermon might be incomprehensible to a young person, napping was strictly forbidden and liable to be treated with a quick slap from her father's handkerchief.[10]

The one bright spot in her weekly Sabbath ritual was the Sunday school class that preceded morning church service. Every week Timothy Rice would escort Mary and her sister Rachel to their class, where they spent the next hour and fifteen minutes with a female teacher talking about sin and how to prevent it. But Mary's Sunday school teacher spent less time dwelling on God's wrath toward sinners than on emphasizing the love and compassion of Jesus, a message that young Mary Rice found to be wonderfully comforting. She seems to have formed a special bond with her teacher, whose name she did not reveal but whose devotion to children over her many years of service at First Baptist must have been fierce. Mary later recalled that at one point during her childhood, "in consequence of an accident," she had to miss church services and Sunday school for a three-month period. Her teacher visited her at home every week, sometimes bringing a playmate to cheer her up.[11]

After morning church service, which the Rice family attended together, they walked home to eat a cold dinner, for no cooking could be performed on the Sabbath. At two o'clock they returned for a second round of services, followed by "my great dread," a prayer meeting that might continue for hours. The quiet of the church coupled with the shadows brought by encroaching sunset caused Mary to see "specters everywhere" and to beg her father to hold her tightly. The Sabbath ended with religious instruction at home led by Timothy Rice. After catechism, each child took a turn reading aloud from the Bible by candlelight or whale oil lamp.[12]

On her eighth birthday, Mary's adventuresome and rebellious spirit clashed with her father's religious creed. She had received a gift from her aunt Mary Ashton, for whom she was named: a copy of *Robinson Crusoe* bound in red leather and filled with illustrations. With books a rarity in those days, she greeted its arrival with euphoria, but because it was Sunday, she was forbidden to read it. In her excitement over the gift and her "natural tendency to persist in anything I undertook," she disobeyed her parents and continued to read. After warning her repeatedly, they seized the new treasure and threw it in the fire. Mary remembered the incident vividly seventy years later, including her feelings of outrage at the punishment she received.[13]

A bright, serious, and sensitive child, Mary pondered endlessly about future rewards and punishments. Her father constantly extolled the importance of salvation and the perils of the unregenerate. Mary wanted to please him, and so she worried about her own soul, sometimes expressing "a bitter regret that I had ever been born." She also worried about her sisters, friends, and classmates. How could God consign any of them to eternal hell?[14]

Looking back later on her religious anxieties, Mary recalled some verses taught to children in an effort to warn of the effects of bad behavior, including this one: "Oh, could we step into the grave / And lift the coffin-lid / And look upon the greedy worms, / That eat away the dead." She recalled being taken to Old North Church to view the tomb of her grandmother, who had died six months earlier. These experiences created a lifelong aversion to burial practices and cemeteries. At the end of her life she would become an advocate of cremation, at a time when many Christians viewed the practice with disapproval.[15]

If Timothy Rice did his utmost to instill in his daughters a fear of God's wrath, Zebiah Rice helped to soften the effect. "If my mother *had* a creed she never stated it," Mary recalled. An intensely practical woman, she viewed issues not from a rigid doctrinal perspective but from her personal sense of right and wrong. A nurturing and tolerant parent, Zebiah Rice encouraged her children to have fun.[16]

Sometimes Mary played at being a minister, using this as an acceptable outlet for her irrepressible spirit and growing ambition. If she lacked a congregation of her peers, she might preach to an audience of logs in the woodshed, carefully laid out in rows like parishioners. Once, when she had been punished by being made to sit in a chair, she stood on its seat, imagining it her pulpit, and warned sinners to "flee from the wrath to come," while her parents stood outside the room, bewildered by her unquenchable energy, impassioned oratory, and unladylike behavior. "If that girl were only a boy," she remembered her father once saying, "I would educate her for the ministry, for she has it in her."[17] Even in childhood, Mary exhibited signs of being a strong-minded individual.

Mary's only major source of friction with her mother was her refusal to learn how to sew despite her mother's efforts to teach her. In a moment of frustration over Mary's failure to excel at this most central of female arts, Zebiah once warned that no man would want to marry her if she remained a "shiftless" woman who could not master a neat stitch and a straight hem. Coupled with her fears over whether she might be among God's elect, Mary later recalled, this warning caused her to wonder "whether I had not been elected to . . . [a] desolate future of shiftlessness and celibacy." In this instance her father rose to her defense, assuring Zebiah that Mary would learn to sew when faced by a genuine need. Although as a young bride she made clothing for herself and her clergyman husband, Mary never enjoyed sewing or cooking and was happy to relinquish domestic tasks to others when a public career and comfortable income allowed her to do so.[18]

For Mary, formal education began in the 1820s, first at a small school led by an elderly woman and later at the larger and more prestigious Hancock Grammar School. Her father's decision to relocate the family interrupted her studies, however. Timothy Rice planned to buy a farm in Michigan. Gripped by the same "western fever" that sent thousands of Americans west, he hoped to improve his family's economic condition, and would invoke his farming heritage. Zebiah Rice had no interest in Michigan. In fact, she viewed the entire venture with skepticism, as did many women whose husbands caught the fever. No doubt unhappy about leaving her extended family in Boston, but mindful of her husband's role as head of their household, she persuaded him to compromise by purchasing a farm closer to home, in western New York State. Mary was twelve years old.[19]

The Rice family's pioneering days began with a trip to Rochester along the Erie Canal. In the 1830s the "Big Ditch" represented a wonder of new technology. Constructed between 1817 and 1825, the canal would carry 100,000 people annually when it reached its height of popularity in the 1840s. The Rice family's trip took six days. Each time the boat passed through a lock, Timothy Rice would allow his daughters to leave the packet for a chance to stretch, window-shop, and occasionally purchase sweets from the stores that lined their route. When they arrived in Rochester, he left Zebiah with the younger girls and took Mary with him to Batavia to conduct business with the Holland Land Company. He purchased a farm, located near Arcade, New York, about fifty miles southeast of Buffalo, sight unseen, an indication of both his idealism and his naïveté about farming. Mary thought the site was "desolate." When she visited the farm many years later, she still found it so.[20]

The farm's previous owner had lost his land to foreclosure but bargained with Timothy Rice for the "betterments," the improvements he had made. Once these negotiations ended, the former owner departed with his family and possessions in a small wagon. The "betterments" did not impress the Rice family. The one-and-a-half-story log home had glass windowpanes on the first floor; oiled paper sufficed for the second. The chimney, made of sticks and mud, caught fire repeatedly. The previous owner had begun building a frame house, until financial reverses ended the project. The unfinished building became the barn. "Here we remained for nearly two weary years," Mary remembered.[21]

Timothy Rice faced an uphill battle to make a profit at farming. Although a small amount of his land had been cleared of trees by the former owner, most of the property was heavily wooded and better suited to pasturage. Zebiah and the girls probably grew vegetables to feed the family, but it is unlikely that they did much field work. Zebiah's health was always somewhat delicate, and she probably did not consider working the fields part of woman's appropriate sphere. Although he had grown up on a farm, Timothy Rice had left home at a young age, lured away by city life and by naval service in the War of 1812. Lacking sons to share the work, he must have struggled. To become a successful commercial farmer in western New York, a man needed help. Those who did succeed often relied on hired hands or the assistance of migrating kin. Rice had neither. Before long, he found that he lacked enthusiasm for farming.[22]

Despite his economic tribulations, Rice was determined that his daughters' education and religious practice would not suffer for his decision to relocate. He quickly organized neighbors to construct a log schoolhouse and hire a teacher who "boarded round," rotating her residence among individual families. At age twelve Mary was more advanced educationally than the other children, and her parents kept her stimulated by having her write letters to family in Boston and read aloud several hours each day. Since the area lacked a church, Timothy Rice organized religious services in the schoolhouse, leading them himself in the absence of available clergy. The intellectual challenge of religious leadership no doubt appealed to him more than manual labor. With his family's enthusiastic endorsement, he decided to move back to Boston. Realizing that it was foolish to have bought a farm he had never seen, he was only too happy to unload the place and its "betterments."[23]

Readmission to Hancock School brought a sense of stability to Mary's life, as well as the intellectual challenge she had missed in rural New York. She quickly established a name for herself as bright, diligent, and ambitious. She enjoyed writing and once composed an essay titled "A Mother's Love" that was so good her teacher refused to believe she had written it. After confronting Mary with the accusation of plagiarism, which she vehemently denied, he offered a reward to any class member who could uncover the source from which she must have copied the piece. Meanwhile, he gave Mary an assignment to write an essay on "self-government" in order to prove or disprove her skills as a writer. Grateful for a topic about which her father had so frequently admonished her, she wrote an essay of such fine quality that the teacher was forced to admit his error. Mary's heroism in standing up to an unpopular instructor earned applause from her classmates.[24]

If she was plagued by uninspiring teachers, Mary was also blessed by gifted ones, including Peter McIntosh, her instructor in mathematics and penmanship at Hancock. "No one except my father acquired so great an influence over me as did this exceptional . . . teacher," she later recalled. Although he taught her a great deal about algebra and geometry, McIntosh also engaged the eager young woman in numerous discussions about ethics and religion. His tutelage helped Mary formulate some of the most important tenets of her Christian faith, including the belief that self-discipline and selflessness are the basis for leading a useful life and that Christians must love one another as they love God. In addition McIntosh emphasized the need for religious individuals to help those less fortunate. Their discussions would encourage her to channel her considerable energy in a constructive and fulfilling direction. A deacon in Ralph Waldo Emerson's Unitarian church, McIntosh once introduced Mary to Emerson. She later remembered his plain features and "divine" smile.[25]

At the age of fourteen, Mary joined her parents' First Baptist Church, one of fifty-three new members, including eighteen young women, to be baptized that day. Although still troubled by "the awful dread of the great Hereafter," she enjoyed the company of fellow parishioners, and felt a sense of pride when devout members of the congregation told her that she would make a good foreign missionary. Mary also felt close to the man who became their new pastor in 1837, Rollin H. Neale. A commanding presence with a gift for pulpit eloquence, he was also kindly and affectionate. Neale quickly earned a reputation within Boston's religious and intellectual communities, eventually becoming an overseer at Harvard College. Mary admired him greatly, and he in turn encouraged her studies and introduced her, she recalled, to "people whom it was an advantage for me to know."[26]

One of them may have been the Mr. Callender who ran Callender's Circulating Library, the only library Mary knew about except for that of Harvard College. A cousin who was a student at Harvard once gave Mary and her friends a tour while reminding them that the college was closed to women and girls. It came as a rude awakening to Mary that however hard she worked and however accomplished she became, Harvard would never accept her as a student. With higher education unavailable to her, Callender's Circulating Library became her intellectual lifeline. In exchange for reading privileges, Mary repaired books for Mr. Callender. Delighted with their arrangement, she began by reading the works of Harriet Martineau, completing all twenty-four in just five weeks. Mr. Callender convinced her that she could not possibly absorb so much in so little time and urged her to slow down and write a brief summary of each book. Mary remained a voracious reader throughout her life, and she continued the practice of writing precis. She added her own comments on each book's strengths and weaknesses and often included personal notes in the margins in the manner of a diary.[27]

Mary graduated from Hancock School at the age of fourteen and a half, proud of winning one of six medals given each year for scholarly achievement and good conduct. Her parents literally did not know what to do with her when she graduated. The Rice family did not believe that a leisured existence suited the virtuous individual. But at fourteen she was too young to marry, nor was she expected to find paid employment. Boston offered no publicly funded schools for girls beyond the primary level, and although there were several "female seminaries," these sectarian establishments charged substantial tuition.[28]

With her usual energy and initiative, Mary decided to learn the dressmaking trade—a curious choice for one who always claimed to despise the needle. Mary may nevertheless have wished to please her mother, and she undoubtedly knew that sewing was one of the few ways a woman might earn a living in Boston during the 1830s. Against her father's wishes but with her mother's support, she contacted a neighborhood dressmaker and agreed to a four-month apprenticeship. Although she found the work onerous, by the end of her brief apprenticeship she could "cut, fit, sew, and finish" women's clothing moderately well, including a dress she made for her mother. The accomplishment won more praise from Zebiah than the Hancock School medal, and, Mary recalled, "I never again heard her express fears lest I might become a 'shiftless' woman." The experience also gave Mary early insight into the plight of workingwomen, for she noted in her autobiography that even the most gifted seamstress earned only fifty cents for a twelve-hour workday, while the less experienced might earn as little as twenty-five cents. Thousands of women in American cities worked out of their homes as seamstresses. In New York City, an estimated ten thousand were employed in this way. In Massachusetts, eighteen thousand women made hats as piecework, and another fifteen thousand made shoes.[29] The benefits of marriage and domesticity must have been apparent to Mary Rice after this experience.

By the time Mary's apprenticeship ended, Timothy Rice had decided that his intelligent and energetic daughter must pursue her education further. Perhaps his pride was hurt when she chose to learn a trade. Whatever his motives, he made the decision to enroll Mary at the Charlestown Female Seminary. Female academies, or seminaries, as they were often called, began flourishing in America after 1790, a response to the notion that educational opportunities would make women better "Republican Mothers." In a republic, this reasoning went, mothers had a special responsibility to raise good citizens, to instill in their children (especially male children, who would become voters) the virtues of honesty, selflessness, and patriotism. In order to be good Republican Mothers, American women needed more educational opportunities than were available to their colonial mothers and grandmothers. The new seminaries taught both academic subjects and "feminine arts" such as fancy needlework, music, and painting.[30]

The Charlestown Female Seminary upheld high educational standards and Baptist precepts. Its prospectus emphasized the faculty's commitment to "a regular, thorough, and extensive course of instruction." De-emphasizing rote memorization and lectures, the curriculum focused instead on the "practicable" and "inductive." By the end of its first year, the seminary had enrolled one hundred girls and employed four teachers, two in the "solid branches," one who taught music and art, and a fourth teacher to instruct in "Penmanship, Projection of Maps, and Book-keeping." By the time Mary became a pupil in 1835, the trustees had built a handsome Greek Revival building to house the school.[31]

Mary loved the school's dedicated young faculty, and she relished the opportunity to study subjects not often available to young women, including Latin and astronomy. Many years later she would recall gazing at the heavens through a telescope as "bliss beyond compare . . . [it] set my imagination on fire." As she had at Hancock, Mary established a reputation as a bright and focused young scholar. When one of the teachers resigned following a death in the family, the seminary's trustees invited Mary to take her place for the rest of the term. She accepted, happy to relieve her parents of the financial burden of paying her tuition. At the same time, she continued her studies, completing the four-year course in two years, whereupon the trustees invited her to stay on as a full-time teacher of French and Latin. Eventually she taught Italian as well.[32]

Mary later recalled that the Baptist Church wielded a strong influence over the school. Because the seminary had the reputation of furnishing potential wives for ministerial students at nearby Newton Divinity School, students at Newton called it the "rib factory." But religion was also a serious matter at Charlestown Female Seminary, and its director, Martha Whiting, presided over the school with untiring theological zeal. A sweet-looking woman with wire spectacles and a pleasant smile, she was recalled by her students for her dignity, devotion, and a "voice of memorable cadences." She was also a

woman with a mission to save souls from the almost certain damnation she
believed they would face unless they rejected false religion and sought a conversion experience in the Baptist faith. During revivals that swept through
Charlestown periodically, Miss Whiting adopted a position of wariness, cau-
tioning her pupils against confusing "sympathetic emotion" with "true conversion." Her vehemence on this subject led some students to view her as cold
and unbending.[33]

In her memoirs Mary Livermore recorded more impressions of the seminary than of Miss Whiting, but this remarkable teacher must have been an
important early role model for the serious-minded adolescent. An innovative
teacher, she believed that girls should engage in rigorous academic study. A
forceful personality in a position of authority, she gained the title "governess"
in 1837, including control over the daily operations of the school, once divided
among four associate principals. A self-sacrificing public servant, she ago-
nized over whether to deny herself small indulgences such as a new bonnet
ribbon or to donate an additional dollar to charity. A dedicated Christian, she
regularly ministered to the poor by visiting their homes and local almshouses,
and once organized teachers and students at the seminary to create a Sabbath
school for seamen at the Charlestown naval yard. A native-born American,
she struggled to reconcile herself to the growing presence of Irish Catholic
immigrants in Boston and to abide by their rejection of her attempts to pros-
elytize among them.[34]

When Martha Whiting died of diabetes in 1853, Livermore, by then a wife,
mother, and published author, composed a poem for a memoir being compiled by one of the teachers at the seminary. She had kept in touch with
Whiting and had visited with her shortly before her death, noting the older
woman's exhaustion and poor health. Livermore's untitled poem, the first
one printed in the section "Poetical Contributions from Former Members of
the Charlestown Female Seminary," focused on acceptance of death and included the comforting refrain "angel forms awaited thee, / Upon that bright
and blessed shore."[35]

By the time Whiting died in the 1850s, Livermore had learned to cope with
death from a theological standpoint. But in the 1830s Mary was still struggling
with the Baptist concept of hell and salvation which both Timothy Rice and
Martha Whiting had imparted to her. "While I was attending the seminary at
Charlestown," she wrote in her autobiography, "I reached the pivotal point
in my history, on which my future life and character turned." When Mary was
eighteen, her fifteen-year-old sister Rachel died.[36] The tragedy threw Mary

into a personal and spiritual crisis that led to her decision to leave home and to begin a new life independent of her family.

Rachel had been sickly from birth and may have suffered from a variety of health problems, some of them undiagnosed. Mary spoke of her being "always pale." One of Rachel's problems was curvature of the spine, for which her doctor prescribed a painful form of physical therapy. For several hours each day during her teenage years, Rachel lay on an inclined plane, with a strap under her arms for support and another under her chin. Heavy weights on her ankles were designed to pull the spine into alignment. The regimen caused Rachel great suffering and failed to cure her problem.[37]

Unable to share in active play with her sisters and cousins, Rachel was a passive observer. Too frail to attend school until the age of ten, she received instruction at home. Mary became more of a mother than a sister to her younger sibling, a sort of self-appointed protector. On one occasion they took a boat trip to nearby Nahant, where a popular hotel and restaurant offered opportunities to dine, dance, and explore. Mary and Rachel stared in fascination as couples in the hotel ballroom moved to the music of the Virginia reel and basket cotillion. This was their first exposure to dancing, for in Timothy Rice's household the practice was viewed as wicked and sinful. On their return trip, a sudden storm blew in, terrifying the children on board. Remaining calm despite her fears, Mary held tight to Rachel and guided her off the boat until they found their father waiting in a hired carriage with warm shawls and reassuring hugs.[38]

For reasons the family did not understand, Rachel's health deteriorated after her fifteenth birthday. Although Timothy Rice continued to carry his daughter downstairs for family prayers and meals, and others attended her bedside, bringing sewing and books to keep her occupied, the situation looked increasingly bleak. Sharing a room and a bed with Rachel, Mary was acutely aware of her suffering, occasionally waking up in the night to the sound of her sister's crying. Compounding the family's anxieties, Rachel had never felt God's saving grace, and as her medical condition worsened, Timothy Rice accused her of "resisting the spirit." Although Rachel's health had been poor for a long time, her death in August 1839 came as a terrible shock to the family.[39]

Mary felt a tremendous sense of loss. In addition, she may have felt guilty that this sister, so "gentle, and always sweet-tempered," had never enjoyed the robust health she had always been blessed with and had been denied so many of the pleasures of childhood. And she may have felt that she had failed, ultimately, to protect the little sister who had shared her secrets and her bed throughout childhood. Rachel, realizing her impending death, had decided who should receive each of her keepsakes, instructing Mary as to her wishes. The older sister must have found this a wrenching task.[40]

Rachel's death brought Mary's religious apprehensions to the point of crisis. When the two physicians who attended Rachel in her final illness pronounced her dead, Timothy Rice gathered his family around the bed and called upon each one to accept the judgment of divine providence. Mary recalled the scene vividly in her memoirs: "Not one word was uttered of assurance that all was well with the dear sister; not one intimation that she had entered into a larger, nobler, and happier life." The funeral did nothing to allay Mary's feelings of doom. She remembered the service only as "desolate and devoid of comfort." There were no flowers, no music, no words of hope, only an exhortation to the young to be mindful of the suddenness of death, which could catapult the unregenerate into eternal suffering. As Timothy Rice prayed for signs that his child was in heaven, his eldest daughter sought comfort from her pastor, Reverend Neale, repeating to him the belief that if Rachel were "lost," then she would follow her to hell. Years later Neale expressed regret that he had not done more to reassure her. At the time, only Zebiah Rice provided solace, dismissing any possibility that Rachel might be in hell.[41]

In an effort to cope with her misery, Mary determined to study religion with new rigor, searching for answers to the questions that had troubled her for so long. She read the New Testament again, hiring a tutor to teach her Greek so that she might study texts in the original. At the end of her examination, she concluded that the New Testament contained no concept of "endless punishment."[42]

In the midst of her spiritual crisis, she received a job offer to become the teacher to a tobacco planter's children in southern Virginia. Seeking a qualified instructor, James and Helen Jones of rural Boydton had written to the trustees of the Charlestown Female Seminary and learned of Mary Rice's accomplishments. They wrote directly to her, offering a teaching position at a good salary and residence in their household. The proposition no doubt intrigued Mary, because it presented an opportunity to earn substantially more money than her salary in Boston and the possibility of travel in an area of the country she had never visited. Now eighteen years old, almost nineteen, she had been a student and teacher at the Charlestown Seminary for nearly five years. It was time to try something new. Moreover, the position would give her a chance to escape from the oppressive atmosphere of a household in mourning. As she wrote years later, "The only solace for the hopeless sorrow that enshrouded me lay in the change of scene, and the absorbing occupation this situation offered."[43]

Timothy Rice opposed the move, arguing that a daughter should reside in her father's home, enjoying his guardianship and obeying his rules, until marriage. Acceding to her father's wishes, as she had always done in the past, Mary declined the offer. But her Virginia correspondents wrote again, this time increasing the proposed salary to fully twice what she was currently earning. Mary reconsidered and finally accepted.[44]

Torn between her desire to be a virtuous daughter and her wish to escape from a household she found stifling, Mary Rice chose independence. Her journey to Virginia marked the beginning of her adulthood, for she would never again reside in her parents' home.

CHAPTER 2

——◆•◆◆•◆——

Virginia Teacher

$\mathbf{F}$IFTY YEARS AFTER she left Virginia, Mary Livermore recalled her experiences on a tobacco plantation when she wrote, "This Southern residence changed and shaped my whole future career."[1] As a teacher, she faced myriad challenges and gained new confidence. Residing in the home of a wealthy family in the South, she encountered life in a new region and confronted a new racial and class dynamic. Her hosts would introduce her to the world of literature, art, and music, a world of dances, dinner parties, and debate on subjects from religion to politics. Perhaps most important, in separating from her parents, Mary achieved both financial and emotional independence.

She devoted two hundred pages of *The Story of My Life* to the years in Virginia, about 25 percent of the entire volume dedicated to less than three years of her life. In the preface she addressed the question of why she gave so much attention to such a brief period. In addition to the importance of her Virginia experiences to her future life and career, she also recognized the public's continuing interest in the plantation South before the Civil War. During the time she lived in Virginia, Mary kept a journal and in addition wrote weekly letters to her family in Boston.[2] These provided detailed accounts and later served as the source material for her memoir.

Traveling to Virginia was the greatest adventure of her life; she had never been away from home for more than a week and had never traveled without her father as chaperon. In November 1839, Mary Rice bade farewell to her family and took a train to Worcester, then to Norwich, Connecticut, where she boarded a ship for New York. Mary was eighteen years old, tall and broad shouldered, with an oval face, large gray-blue eyes, a fair complexion, and beautiful reddish-brown hair which she wore parted in the middle, draped loosely down the sides of her face, then gathered up at the back of her neck. She was an attractive young woman, too tall to be considered classically pretty by the standards of her day, but full of energy and ambition.[3]

The journey brought her into close contact with African Americans for the first time and served as an introduction to the racial order she would find in Virginia. Sailing to New York on board the *Charter Oak* in the midst of a winter storm, Mary offered assistance to an African American chambermaid, who was attempting to help a number of seasick women lying on mattresses in the ladies' cabin. Grateful, yet sensing her inexperience as a traveler, the servant repaid Mary by finding a respectable-looking gentleman on board who helped her make rail connections to Philadelphia. Once there, Mary found other benefactors, this time a married couple, who were traveling to North Carolina. They graciously volunteered to take Mary under their wing. Continuing by train, Mary and her companions dined in Baltimore. Unlike New York, where servants were free, Maryland was a slave state. Bondspeople served her dinner. It was her first experience with enslaved African Americans. "I regarded [them] with commiseration," she later wrote.[4]

In Washington, D.C., her companions needed to stop for several days to conduct business, enabling Mary to spend several nights at the famous Giddings' Hotel, a gathering place for the capital's political elite. She saw President Martin Van Buren, a Democrat, who would lose his reelection bid the following year to a Whig, William Henry Harrison. She visited the Senate and saw the congressional giants Daniel Webster, Henry Clay, John C. Calhoun, John Quincy Adams, and Thomas Hart Benton. As a New Englander, she had heard a great deal about the oratorical powers of Massachusetts's famous senator, Daniel Webster, but when she heard all the luminaries speak, it was Kentucky's Henry Clay who filled her with a sense of awe. Seated in the gallery and listening to the famous Whig, she was "captivated by his magnificent presence, his contagious enthusiasm, and his glowing eloquence." Later she met the great man at a reception. Clay said some kind words, telling Mary that she "had the power to do anything." Only later, to her great disappointment, did she learn that Clay was given to flattering all the young ladies. She would meet Clay several more times during her Virginia years.[5]

The journey continued by boat down the Potomac River. As they passed Mount Vernon, the home of George Washington, the passengers were called to the deck so that they could pay their respects to the Founding Father, who had died nearly thirty years earlier. A group of musicians on shore played "a dirge-like air" for each boat that passed by. At Potomac Creek they began the last leg of the journey, by stage to Fredericksburg, a rough and unpleasant twelve-mile ride that took three and a half hours. The trip was made all the more memorable because the black driver urged on his team of six horses in a dialect Mary found to be both incomprehensible and amazing. Once they reached Fredericksburg, the journey resumed by railroad, much to her relief, and she traveled southward, to Richmond, and then Petersburg, and finally to Ridgeway, North Carolina, just over the state line from Mecklenburg County, Virginia, where she parted with her Philadelphia friends.[6]

At the "hut" that passed for a rail depot in Ridgeway, Mary presented her letter of introduction to "Major Rainey," a friend of her new employers, who by prior arrangement would convey her to their plantation twelve miles away. An attractive middle-aged woman named Lydia accompanied them. Mary thought that Lydia looked much like Rainey and wondered why the woman had come with them, although Lydia avoided answering her questions. Mary had lived in Virginia several months before learning that Lydia was both a slave and Major Rainey's half-sister, the product of his father's union with a bondswoman. She also learned that in Virginia a young lady must not travel without a chaperon. Lydia had been sent for that purpose.[7]

Arriving at sunset, Mary beheld a magnificent plantation house that lay at the end of an avenue of oak trees. Located on a plateau two miles from the Roanoke River, the mansion was surrounded by a cluster of whitewashed out-buildings: kitchen, smokehouse, icehouse, dairy, laundry, spinning and weav-ing house, toolhouse, general storehouse, and carriage house, and a group of small cabins for house slaves. Her new employers owned extensive landhold-ings both in southern Mecklenburg County and in neighboring Warren County, North Carolina. Immediately they emerged from the house to greet her warmly, their six children joining in the welcome.[8]

In her two autobiographies Mary Livermore disguised the identity of her employers, calling them James and Helen Henderson and assigning a different set of names to their children in each book. Without advising her readers that she had done so, Livermore chose to protect the privacy of the family that had employed her decades earlier. Two years before her first memoir appeared in print, the husband of one of Mary's former pupils entered the United States Senate.[9] As a public figure herself, Livermore knew what it meant to keep one's private life out of the public eye. Fortunately, she provided enough clues to identify James and Helen Henderson as James Young Jones and Helen Leckie Jones, who owned a plantation south of Boydton, Virginia, called St. Leon. Clues about the family's identity and both the name and location of their plantation can be found in *My Story of the War* and *The Story of My Life*. The family cemetery correctly identified by Livermore as Liberty Hill is the private burying ground of the Jones family.[10]

Mary Rice came to like and respect her new employers right away. She was especially fond of the patriarch, James Jones. She described him as "tall, portly, and commanding in figure," with curly dark hair and dark eyes. Well read and well traveled both in America and abroad, he was affectionate with his family, generous and charming with friends and neighbors. "He was one of the most attractive men I ever have met," Mary recalled many years later, hinting that as an impressionable eighteen-year-old she may have had a crush on the handsome Virginian.[11]

James Jones had achieved great wealth through a series of wise investments. Although a hot temper brought him to court after he challenged a local man to a duel in the 1820s, ultimately he settled down and began investing in land. His plantation produced tobacco and corn. He also built a mill that became a major source of income. By acquiring slaves, Jones added significantly to his wealth. In 1830 he owned thirty-three slaves. Ten years later he held twice that number. By the 1850s the Jones family had achieved a level of wealth that placed them among the richest property owners in the county.[12]

Mary Rice had mixed feelings about Helen Jones. Born to Scottish immigrant parents, she was raised in Washington, D.C., before moving to Troy, New York, to attend Mrs. Emma Willard's famous seminary for girls. Helen Jones gave birth to her last child in 1838, ending a pattern of childbearing every two years since her marriage in the mid-1820s. Before the arrival of Mary Rice, she had educated the children herself, but with her considerable responsibilities as plantation mistress, she found it difficult to continue performing all these jobs.[13]

In her memoirs Livermore describes Mrs. Jones as "entirely lacking in beauty of face or figure." With "cold" gray eyes and a "shrunken" figure, she inspired more fear than love, especially when she wielded a rawhide whip across the shoulders of errant slaves, despite the objections of her more kind-hearted husband. Mary regarded Helen Jones with apprehension, for she bore the brunt of her mistress's criticism on occasion. Mrs. Jones tolerated no insubordination from anyone, including the teacher. And yet she was a woman of myriad talents, who could converse in French, play the piano, and paint skillfully. Her oil paintings and crayon and India ink sketches adorned every room in the house. A superb housekeeper with unflagging drive, she inspired Mary's grudging respect. Mrs. Jones's "immense energy," she later recalled, "was a continuous stimulant to me."[14]

Like most homes in the area, St. Leon was a frame house painted white, with broad stone steps leading to the entrance. Mary identified the largest room in the house as the "family room." Dominated by a massive fireplace with brass andirons, the room contained bookcases, writing and sewing tables, chintz-covered settees, and several enormous rocking chairs. Maps of the United States and Europe adorned the walls, along with Helen Jones's portraits of Washington, Napoleon, and the duke of Wellington. An inventory of the estate in the 1850s reveals that the family owned material possessions commensurate with their wealth, including a carriage, a piano, watches, and gold and silver jewelry.[15]

When Mary Rice moved to Virginia, it must have seemed as if she had entered a foreign land. The presence of slaves in this household seemed odd and uncomfortable. On her first night with the Jones family, a house servant named Carline was sent upstairs to help her undress and brush out her hair. Mary declined her services. She felt awkward about having a personal servant, uncertain about a black woman touching her, and equally uncomfortable when told that black Martha would sleep in the hallway between her room and the children's in case she needed anything in the night. The Jones children's obvious devotion to another house slave, Mammy Aggy, astounded the young northerner. Mrs. Jones's chief assistant, known as Mammy Aggy within the family and as Aunt Aggy by everyone else, she made a strong impression on the newly arrived teacher. With her erect posture, turbaned head, and crisp white neckerchief draped across her chest "Quaker-style," Aggy was clearly an influential force within the household. When several Jones children "sprang to the neck and arms of Aunt Aggy, with such abandon of affection, such prodigality of caresses, and such loving demonstrations," Mary admitted to being "astonished . . . beyond measure. I was terribly afflicted with color-phobia in those days. Kissing a negro woman in that way! I was amazed."[16]

In the coming days Mary Rice unpacked, settled in, and began adjusting to the new life that she had chosen. Accustomed to the hustle and bustle of the city and a family whose social and intellectual life revolved around religious activities, she now found herself in a home whose nearest neighbor was three miles away. The Jones family received mail once a week, on Saturdays, from Boydton, and the occasion of the post's arrival was one of great anticipation and much joy, for it kept the Jones family in touch with the outside world. They subscribed to a variety of periodicals, including *Littell's Living Age* and the *Democratic Review*, which kept James Jones connected to party politics on the national level. Although Mary would later recall feeling isolated on the plantation, she also fell in love with Mecklenburg County, with the magnificence of the Roanoke River, the beauty of the woods, the astonishing lushness of southern Virginia's foliage in springtime. She began taking a daily walk before breakfast, a practice she would continue throughout her residence in Virginia.[17]

Tobacco dominated Mecklenburg economically and socially. Along with neighboring Halifax, Pittsylvania, and Charlotte counties, the part of Virginia known as Southside, it produced more than one third of the state's annual tobacco harvest. During the 1840s, tobacco farmers created two Hole and Corner Clubs, in which participants met monthly at the home of a member to discuss agricultural techniques and improvements. Each July Fourth, members of the two branches met together in Boydton, the county seat, for a recitation of the Declaration of Independence and dinner at Boyd's Hotel.[18]

Boydton remained a tiny enclave during Mary's years in the county. Founded in 1812, the town lacked a savings bank until 1851 and a newspaper until 1853, when the *Tobacco Plant* began publication. But Mecklenburg County had prospered enough to build a fine Greek Revival courthouse. Commissioned in 1838, the brick structure was completed in 1842 while Mary was residing in nearly Palmer Springs Township. With a columned portico and tin roof, the two-story structure was a graceful addition to a community steeped in rural isolation and connected to the outside only by a stage line.[19]

On days when the court was in session, planters, farmers, merchants, and members of their families often gathered in Boydton to transact legal business, visit, buy goods from peddlers, and perhaps buy or sell slaves. Mecklenburg County's population was about two fifths white and three fifths black when Mary Rice lived there, a reflection of its economic base as a community with a large stake in plantation agriculture. Although the county had a small population of free African Americans, most of its black residents were enslaved.[20]

Affluent Mecklenburg residents made money from selling tobacco, corn, and slaves, and these propertied white citizens wholeheartedly endorsed the institution of slavery. Their reaction to Nat Turner's 1831 rebellion in nearby Southampton County is revealing. Following the bloody insurrection, the Virginia House of Delegates debated the issue of abolition in Richmond. Mecklenburg's white citizens held a public meeting, and in January 1832 they passed a resolution "to support no press, and no editor of any newspaper, who advocated the emancipation of slaves." Several years later, more than four hundred men meeting at the courthouse in Boydton vowed "to take into consideration the proceedings of the Fanatics and Abolitionists of the North," promising "unyielding hostility to every encroachment on their civil rights."[21]

Upper-class southerners valued education, but Mecklenburg County offered few school choices. James and Helen Jones wanted their sons prepared for college, and they wanted intellectual stimulation for their daughters. James Jones believed that his daughters had "extraordinary minds." Although there were boarding schools in some of the larger towns, none was close enough to suit the Joneses. Hiring a teacher became the only alternative. With the increasing number of female seminaries in New England, graduates of these institutions made up a pool of potential teachers for the South's landed gentry. In nearby Warrenton, North Carolina, where Mrs. Harriet Allen operated a school, Connecticut-born Mary Cheney was hired to serve as an instructor. Cheney would soon become the bride of a young editor named Horace Greeley, who had courted her when both were living in New York at a vegetarian boardinghouse. They corresponded during Cheney's residence in the South and married July 5, 1836, in Warrenton. Twenty-two-year-old Mary Cheney Greeley left the community three years before eighteen-year-old Mary Rice arrived in neighboring Mecklenburg County. While an instructor at the Allen School, Cheney had made a strong impression on the people of Warrenton, for she refused to hide her disapproval of slavery. According to one account, her views "were not kindly received," and as a result, "school patronage decreased, and the school was closed not long after this impression got abroad."[22]

Mary Rice soon became very attached to the Jones children, who ranged in age from two adolescent girls to baby Courtney. Bright, energetic, and attractive, the children filled the house with laughter, played practical jokes, and debated at the dinner table. Geographically isolated and dependent on one another, they were an exceptionally close family which fit the mold that historian Jan Lewis described in her book about Virginia family life: "Virginians often found that their ideal of the perfect family was in fact the image of their own family." The Jones household, brimming with spontaneity and joy, must have presented a marked contrast to the home Mary had recently left in the North End of Boston. The pain caused by her sister Rachel's death began to subside.[23]

The Joneses appear to have liked Mary as much as she liked them. Indeed, they embraced her as a member of their family. When she arrived in November 1839, each child helped with decorating her bedroom, contributing books, artwork, even a collection of colored birds' eggs. Establishing rapport in the classroom would present greater challenges than winning the children's affection. On the first day of school, each child appeared with a personal slave "laden with footstools, cushions, wraps, rag babies, whistles, traps, bird-snares, books, papers, pens, inkstands, and whatever else the young masters and mistresses had bidden them to take along." Mary attempted to dismiss the servants, but the children objected vociferously, and as she later recalled, "I was not yet mistress of this situation." That night, alone in her room, she gave vent to her frustration and homesickness in tears.[24]

Life began to improve for the young teacher once she recovered her composure and approached her employers with a plan. She asked that the Joneses establish fixed bedtime and wake-up hours to ensure their children's readiness to begin school promptly each morning. Their teacher was to have "absolute control" over the children for six hours of schooling. Diversions would not be permitted. While James Jones expressed doubts about this rigorous schedule, Helen Jones agreed immediately. Mary then formulated a course of study for each student that included botany and astronomy instruction outdoors and a weekly review of their progress at a Round Table Club to meet every Saturday night in her room. Many years later Mary would recall with pride that she helped to instill a love of science in the Joneses' elder son, Robert. As a young adult he would study at Yale.[25]

Mary Rice's introduction to the social world of the Jones family began almost immediately, for within a few weeks of her arrival they celebrated Christmas. In the Baptist tradition in which she had grown up, the Rice family recognized December 25 as a religious holiday but certainly not the occasion for merriment. The celebrations shocked the serious young teacher, made her feel uncomfortable and probably homesick. Six days before Christmas she had observed her nineteenth birthday, the first such occasion away from family and friends in New England. Raised to believe that dancing was immoral, she now watched as the Joneses and their guests from neighboring plantations

celebrated Christmas by dancing to violin music, playing the piano, and im-
bibing eggnog, punch, and toddy, containing, no doubt, alcohol from the
family's "well-stocked" cupboard. In the slave quarters, whisky had been al-
located along with new sets of clothing for the coming year. Slaves danced to
their own fiddle music. Mary regarded these parties as "unnatural," and probably as an unwelcome interruption to the classroom routine she had so recently established. She expressed relief when the holiday ended.[26]

If the secular world of the Jones family bothered Mary at first, she soon
became increasingly comfortable in it. Having been raised in a rigidly religious household, where duty to God was serious business, where the family
budget was tight, and recreation was viewed with some skepticism, she came
to appreciate the relaxed atmosphere of the Jones household and the luxuries
it afforded. She appreciated the way domestic help freed her from mundane
housework. She remarked on the excellent food served at St. Leon, the special
amenities the family enjoyed, including the beautiful flowers from Helen
Jones's winter conservatory and books in James Jones's impressive library.[27]
She knew that the Joneses' standard of living, so very different from what she
grew up with, was grounded in the profits of slave-based agriculture. She understood that she too was a beneficiary of the family's affluence, and she was
realistic enough to admit this when she wrote her memoirs years later.

Mary described James and Helen Jones as "extreme radicals in religion,
with no faith in historic Christianity . . . and with no more regard for the Bible
than any other book." They had revealed this in correspondence before her
arrival in Virginia, apparently also making clear their desire that she include
religious instruction for their children in her educational curriculum. She
regarded this as odd, but the Joneses explained that they viewed religious
education as a "graceful accomplishment" that also gave individuals social
standing in the community. Mary carried out their wishes, leading the children in morning and evening prayers, with Bible study each Sunday. Her
religious training may have taken root in the Jones children. While James
Jones's last will and testament, written in 1843 when he was in declining
health, contains no reference to Christianity, that of his son James Jr., written
in 1861, invokes "our lord Jesus Christ." The young man whom Mary used to
call "Batt" and his father called "Ballade" would soon depart for war. As a
youngster, he had come regularly to Mary's room to say his prayers.[28]

Mary had lengthy discussions about religion with James and Helen Jones,
who challenged her beliefs and helped her learn how to think on her feet.
Their discussions always took place at night after the children were in bed and

asleep, for the Joneses insisted on keeping their religious radicalism a secret from their children. Often these theological debates were lively and protracted, lasting late into the night. Although Mary did not share the Joneses' perspective on religion, she respected their erudition. She also appreciated their willingness to share books from their extensive library, including works by Enlightenment thinkers such as Voltaire and Rousseau. The concept of devoting considerable time to reading for pleasure was new to the young teacher, but at James Jones's behest, she commenced reading Shakespeare's plays as well as biographies of historical figures including Napoleon and Queen Elizabeth. Mary would later write that spending nearly three years in James Jones's household "was a liberal education in itself." Other than Peter McIntosh, her teacher at the Hancock School, he was the first major influence in her life who came from outside her parents' religious circle. Associating with him taught her that character and intellect were not linked to religious creed.[29]

He also introduced her to the political world, for Jones supported the Democratic Party locally and moved in a social circle that included many prominent Democrats. In her memoirs Mary referred to her employers' friendship with local monied families, including the Goodes and Baskervilles. Congressman William O. Goode lived north of St. Leon at Wheatland Plantation. Like many southern Democrats, including James Jones, he supported states' rights and slavery, although Goode sympathized with the possibility of ending the institution through gradual means.[30]

Mecklenburg's planter class socialized often. Some traveled to Virginia's well-established communities, Richmond, Petersburg, and Williamsburg, to visit friends, shop, or attend the theater, but the county's planter elite also entertained one another locally, at tobacco shows, militia parades, July Fourth celebrations, weddings, and house parties. Mary Rice visited a number of the Jones family's friends and neighbors. According to *The Story of My Life*, one of the high points of her Virginia residence came when an aristocratic family she calls the "Blackstocks" invited the Jones family and their resident teacher for a visit. The Blackstocks planned a house party to showcase their new mansion and a dinner party to honor their cousin, "Mr. Gordon," recently elected to political office. Mary describes the Blackstocks as "the oldest and the most aristocratic family in the county, if not in southern Virginia. Their plantations were among the richest and most extensive in the state." Like the name Henderson, the name Blackstock does not appear in the Mecklenburg census or county histories, but the memoir does not provide sufficient clues about the Blackstocks and their property to identify this family.[31] The variety of experiences Mary Livermore would later recall in conjunction with the Blackstocks' party implies that she may have been combining her recollections of several house parties into one dramatic narrative.

The Jones children looked forward to the house party with great joy and anticipation. James Jones came home from a business trip to Richmond with "baskets, boxes, bundles, and trunks" filled with goods he had purchased so that his wife and daughters might be suitably outfitted. Mary viewed the event with a mixture of excitement and apprehension. Though aware of her hosts' social standing, and thrilled to have an opportunity to meet distinguished political figures, she felt insecure about her lack of experience at social gatherings and perhaps about her status in this community. Treated as a member of the Jones family, she was, nevertheless, someone who worked for a living. She does not mention new clothing for herself. Her hosts made what they no doubt considered an appropriate social judgment by seating her at dinner between James Jones and "a reticent maiden cousin of the Blackstocks."[32] As an educated woman and an employee of the Jones family, Mary was accorded the status of a spinster relation.

Dinner began early, at 2:00 P.M., since not all of the guests would be spending the night and would need to depart before sunset. It was the grandest social gathering Mary had ever attended, and she eagerly observed all that was happening around her, no doubt happy to be freed from attempting conversation with the "reticent maiden cousin" seated next to her. The gendered nature of conversations during the meal intrigued her. She noted that the men focused on crop prices, the health of their field slaves, and politics (during that period of her life, politics was "rubbish to me," she later recalled), while the women, "half-starved socially" because of their geographical isolation, focused on a limited range of subjects that included family, fashion, and local gossip.[33]

Substantial alcohol consumption contributed to an increasingly boisterous atmosphere. "Conviviality ruled the hour," Mary wrote many years later, intending the comment as a criticism. As the discussion of politics became more and more raucous, one guest blurted out, "That dastardly Adams of Massachusetts has presented abolition petitions from women and slaves!" He was referring to former president and now Congressman John Quincy Adams, who had campaigned for years to revoke the "gag rule" that had prevented the introduction of antislavery petitions in Congress. The Blackstocks' dinner guests expressed outrage at the recent effort by Adams to introduce a petition signed by 148 women in Massachusetts. Their continued insults toward abolitionists, Congressman Adams, Yankees in general, and Boston women in particular finally provoked Mary Rice, who momentarily forgot her station as a hired teacher and burst out: "Gentlemen, I am a Massachusetts woman, and was born in Boston, as were also my mother and grandmother. These women whom you would hang to a lamp-post are my country-women, my kinswomen, my friends, and the noblest women on the earth. I will not be accessory to this abuse . . . by sitting any longer at table with their calumniators, and so, I bid you good afternoon."[34] It is revealing to note that Mary's tirade represented an effort to defend her "country-women," not a direct assault on plantation slavery. Unlike Mary Cheney, Mary Rice did not harbor abolitionist views that she wished to express in the presence of her employers' friends.

Fleeing to her room after leaving the dinner table, she found solace when James and Helen Jones came to comfort her. After her abrupt departure, James Jones had defended her outburst to the assembled dinner guests, arguing that she was justified in supporting her homeland. The guests, who had not known that Mary was from Boston, evidently regarded defense of one's homeland as an honorable position. Jones attributed the slurs against Boston's women to excessive alcohol consumption, and Mary admitted that "this was my first encounter with people in that condition." Mrs. Jones then asked her, "Do you advocate women mixing up with politics? What have Massachusetts women to do with slavery?" Mary responded, "I know very little about the matter, . . . and I have no opinion to express. But I disapprove entirely of men drinking to excess." (Mr. Jones, she later noted approvingly, took wine only in moderation.) Although Mary's anger toward the dinner guests had been justifiable, James and Helen Jones would not allow her to return immediately to St. Leon. Gently they reminded her that to do so would be rude, and she admitted that they were right. [35]

The visit to the Blackstocks' ended with two cataclysmic events for the Jones family. The day after Mary had fled the dinner table in such great haste, James Jones was summoned back to St. Leon by the news that his mill had caught fire. Damage was extensive. Then, on the last evening of the house party, the eldest Jones daughter collapsed and later died of what Mary identified as "neuralgia of the heart," a condition from which the young woman had evidently suffered since birth. The family was devastated, and for Mary there were painful reminders of her sister Rachel's death several years earlier. The tragedy did bring Mary closer to Helen Jones, who appreciated her efforts in nurturing the surviving children. Because there was no church close to the

Jones plantation and no available clergy, the Joneses held a family service at St. Leon, and Mary read from the Episcopal Book of Common Prayer.[36]

Much as she liked the Jones family and genuinely mourned the loss of their daughter, Mary never approved of plantation life. At some point in her tenure with the Joneses, she reached the conclusion that slavery was morally wrong. This probably happened gradually and not because of a single impression or event. Perhaps because she lived in rural Palmer Springs Township instead of in one of Southside Virginia's villages, her antislavery views, unlike those of Mary Cheney, never "got abroad," at least not until she began publishing stories and memoirs after the Civil War.

In her autobiography, Livermore implies that when she went to Virginia she had not yet formed an opinion about the morality of slavery. Her description of the dinner party outburst at the Blackstocks' also suggests that she had not yet developed strong views on the subject. While it is true that she wanted to observe the situation for herself, she did not go to Virginia without preconceived notions about the South's "peculiar institution." Her father, a religious man with deeply held moral convictions, believed slavery to be inherently wrong.[37] He undoubtedly voiced these beliefs to Mary, and they must have made some kind of impression. Furthermore, growing up in Boston during the 1830s, at a time when William Lloyd Garrison was building a radical antislavery movement there, she almost certainly read about his activism in the newspapers.

In 1838, while a teacher at the Charlestown Female Seminary, Mary heard Angelina Grimké speak before the Massachusetts legislature on the issue of slavery. In her landmark address, the first time an American woman had spoken before a state legislature, this former member of South Carolina's plantation elite had argued that women must oppose slavery because as citizens of the republic, they had a moral responsibility to do so. According to an interview Livermore gave to journalist Celia Burleigh in 1870, she had been deeply affected by the "spiritual power that Miss Grimké exercised over her audience," and the occasion "forever fixed in her mind the conviction that women ought to be free to do whatever their powers enabled them to do well."[38] Grimké's "spiritual power," however, did not yet lead to an antislavery or feminist awakening for the young woman.

In *The Story of My Life*, Livermore criticizes the indolence of the planter class, no doubt with some exaggeration. In her book about wealthy North Carolina slaveholders and their families, Jane Censer notes that Carolina planters, like middle-class northerners, labored to teach their children values such as self-reliance, self-control, thrift, and hard work.[39] The Joneses' commitment to education was unquestionable, and Livermore admits that Helen Jones was most definitely not indolent.

Many of her impressions of plantation culture correspond with those of other outsiders visiting the upper South. She realized that plantation mistresses, including Helen Jones, held positions of great responsibility. Modern scholars, including Catherine Clinton and Elizabeth Fox-Genovese, have reminded us that plantation mistresses worked hard as managers and rarely led leisured lives.[40] In her memoirs Livermore wrote that "the average plantation household was, necessarily, a self-contained establishment." Like other plantation wives, Helen Jones oversaw all phases of food production in the household from the garden and the dairy to the smokehouse. She supervised the production of clothing for the slave population and ministered to the medical needs of black and white residents. Livermore later recalled that Mrs. Jones had a leather basket in which she kept keys to all the plantation storehouses, a basket she wore "suspended from her girdle or hanging on her arm" most of the time.[41]

Mary understood that James Jones's role as patriarch gave him managerial responsibilities for the agricultural and milling operations on the plantation, which he handled with the assistance of an overseer and a miller. As head of a wealthy household, he also had public responsibilities that social norms denied to his wife. While she stayed home, he traveled to Richmond to conduct business with the commission agents who handled his tobacco crop and to purchase household items, books, and clothing for the family. He attended political meetings in the county and probably in Richmond. From her experiences with the Jones family, Mary concluded that plantation women were far more isolated geographically than their husbands.[42]

Scholars of the antebellum South have cast doubt on the image of white masters as enthusiastic supporters of slavery and their wives as covert abolitionists. The Joneses certainly reinforce this impression. Helen Leckie Jones, reared in Washington, D.C., of Scottish immigrant parents, had little experience with plantation life before her marriage, yet she upheld the institution of slavery and defended it to outsiders such as Mary Rice. Meanwhile, her husband, a native-born Virginian, quite frequently emphasized its drawbacks. He did not share the view of a growing number of planters that slavery was a positive benefit for the entire South, including slaves themselves. Instead he saw slavery as a "burden" his generation had inherited from earlier ones. Out of curiosity, he asked Mary to have her father send a few copies of Garrison's antislavery newspaper, the *Liberator*, despite the fact that it was illegal to send the incendiary paper through Virginia's mail.[43]

When the young teacher and her employer discussed the ethics of slavery, James Jones characterized his bondspeople as "grown-up children," pathetic creatures who had been "denied everything that lifts men above brutes." He refused to have them whipped for misbehavior, but did instead sell trouble-some individuals to a slave trader. Jones may have treated his servants better than many slave owners, but he was capable of losing his temper, even though it was "not his prevailing character" to do so, Mary wrote. She recalled one instance in which a female slave accidentally spilled hot coffee, scalding Jones and staining his new linen suit. He reacted by striking her several times. And yet Jones forced Mary to understand the complicity of all of white America in what was now exclusively a southern institution. He told his skeptical young employee that slavery was once legal in Europe and all of America, and that New England gave up the institution largely because its lack of agricultural cash crops meant slavery was not profitable there. He also argued that south-ern planters' wealth would be undermined without slave labor to handle the tobacco crop. "We cannot pauperize ourselves, by freeing our slaves," he told her, "and if we could, it would be an overwhelming disaster to them, for they . . . cannot take care of themselves."[44]

In *The Story of My Life*, Livermore holds herself above the Joneses for understanding slavery's immorality, yet she falls quickly into a pattern of racial stereotyping typical of nineteenth-century whites, northerners as well as southerners. The African Americans she admired and trusted were the skilled house servants and craftsmen. She described Aunt Aggy, Helen Jones's lieutenant, as tall, dignified, even "regal-looking." Paying her what she must have regarded as a compliment, Livermore writes "Her features were not of the negro type, but as perfectly moulded as any Caucasian's of gentle blood." She presents Aggy as a model woman, committed to her own husband and children, as well as the indispensable mammy, morally superior to the Joneses because of her appreciation of the immorality of slavery while also savvy enough to realize that slaves must make the best of their situation. Livermore has equally kind words for Matt, the plantation's talented and hardworking cooper. Yet she reduces other plantation slaves to stereotypes. Slave children are "little ragged ebonies," and "black tatterdemalions," the adults "poor, simple, black men and women," "pickaninnies" and "woolly heads, with faces of every shade of duskiness." Livermore notes the presence of mulattoes and octoroons among the slave population, though with the exception of her discussion of Major Rainey's slave Lydia, she does not dwell on the subject of miscegenation in her works about Virginia.[45]

Livermore writes at length about slave social customs, such as a corn shucking that included bondspeople from five neighboring plantations. The assembled crowd proceeded to strip husks from the yellow ears, some entering into contests to see who could shuck and toss the finished ears with the greatest speed and precision. While working, the slaves sang spirituals. Then they feasted on roasted hogs, geese, and turkeys, coon stew, sweet potatoes, and pones of corn bread. Livermore also comments on the Christmas customs in the slave quarters, including the annual religious revivals sponsored by the Methodists and Baptists, the distribution of whisky rations, of which she heartily disapproved, and the slaves' practice of selling for profit to the white community the baskets, mats, and brooms constructed in their free time.[46]

Like Fanny Kemble, the famous British actress who visited her husband's Georgia Sea Islands plantations in the 1830s and later wrote about the experience, Livermore remarks in some detail on the treatment of pregnant women and small children. At St. Leon, slave mothers received two or three weeks off from field work after the birth of a child. Toddlers were cared for by Ole Betty, who ran the communal nursery. Like Kemble, she comments on the poor hygiene and dehumanizing atmosphere of the slave quarters. Mary was appalled by the way slave children were fed: "The porridge, which was the chief food of these black children, was poured into a series of wooden troughs, raised on legs, out of which each child, old enough to do so, fed itself with a wooden spoon. It was not a pleasant spectacle."[47]

She also understood slaves' vulnerability. In describing a slave wedding she attended at which an African American preacher officiated, she points out that slave marriages were not legal and could end anytime the master wanted them to. Discussing one slave who was seeking a divorce, she notes that permission was required from the master. Speaking about the corn shucking party, she mentions that all slaves needed a pass in order to leave their home plantation. She quotes James Jones in reporting that a black man could not testify against a white one in court.[48]

And like Harriet Beecher Stowe in *Uncle Tom's Cabin*, Livermore speaks of the pathos of families separated by sale. When James Jones ordered the sale of Mary Harris, a slave deemed to be both lazy and adulterous, the trader would not pay for the slave's baby, and Jones refused to give the child to the trader without compensation. Helen Jones ordered the infant to be nursed by one of the other lactating slaves, all of whom refused out of anger toward the flirtatious Mary Harris. The despondent slave was sold away from her infant. The baby later died.[49]

A skilled writer, Livermore enhances the evil image of the Joneses' plantation overseer and the visiting slave trader by giving them no first names. In *The Story of My Life*, the trader is simply "Heath," while the overseer is "Bryson." These two villains present a marked contrast to the man who runs the St. Leon mill with great competence and profitability. He is "Levi Bridgman of Troy, New York," favored with both a first name and a hometown.[50]

Appalled by the physical abuse of slaves she witnessed in Virginia, Livermore would write about this subject with emotion and passion many years later. Shortly after her arrival in 1839, she witnessed young Robert Jones striking his personal servant Pete for allegedly having "sassed" him. She regretted both the pain inflicted on the hapless slave and the tendency toward petty tyranny on the part of the preadolescent master. When she discussed the episode with the Joneses, they reported that their son had the right to treat his servant as he saw fit. During one of her pre-breakfast walks in the Virginia countryside, the young teacher happened onto a scene that both surprised and appalled her. When Matt, the cooper, accidentally burned the "grim-visaged and evil-eyed" Bryson, the overseer proceeded to whip him brutally. After the flogging finally ended, Matt's "lacerated body hung limp and seemingly lifeless." Mary Rice literally became ill. Because James Jones did not condone the whipping of his slaves, she had believed that such an abuse would not be allowed.[51]

When Jones learned of it, he condemned the whipping of one of his best workers, whom he sometimes called a "three-thousand-dollar nigger." Mary found James Jones's reaction to be illustrative. The plantation owner had more humanitarian concern for his slaves' welfare than many owners, and more than his wife, who argued that "Matt has needed to be taken down for a long time." And yet, as Livermore reveals, and modern historians have also emphasized, the bottom line for planters was that a slave was an economic investment. Ultimately, Matt's health was important to James Jones because he was worth three thousand dollars.[52]

Secretly visiting Matt sometime after the beating, Livermore tells us, she offered to help him escape by giving him money and the names of friends in New England. Matt declined, reminding her that he could not easily elude capture. Whether Mary actually made such an offer of assistance is questionable, but she later wrote, "I was at the happy age when one knows nothing and fears nothing." Matt never fully recovered psychologically from the brutal treatment and died before she left Virginia.[53]

Mary Rice completed her term as the Jones family's teacher and left Mecklenburg County in the spring of 1842. She had agreed to spend two years with the Joneses and had surpassed this obligation by six months. During her tenure, the children's educational accomplishments had impressed the neighboring planters so much that Mary had agreed to expand her school to include their children, recruiting a friend from New York, referred to in her memoirs as Fanny Codman, to assist with the enlarged school. Codman taught music, drawing, and painting.[54]

Mary needed new professional challenges, and she missed her family in New England. In making her decision to leave Virginia, she may also have considered her marital prospects. In the nineteenth century, successful womanhood was defined by marriage, home, and child rearing. In a few months Mary would be twenty-two years old, and she had few opportunities in Virginia to meet eligible men who shared her religious and social values. Yet by all indications she parted with the Joneses on amicable terms. They had welcomed her as a member of their family, and she had grown very fond of the children as well as their parents. After helping them to find replacement teachers, Rice and Codman departed by train from nearby Warrenton, North Carolina, bound for Washington, D.C. Mary later recalled, "We went away young girls—and we came home young women."[55]

She returned to Boston emotionally stronger, able now to cope with her sister's death. She had gained confidence as a teacher, and felt great pride in the educational accomplishments of the Jones children and those of neighboring children who had joined her school. She also returned home with firm antislavery convictions. She had learned that it was possible to respect and even love a southern plantation family while abhorring the labor system that sustained their wealth. Genuinely close to the Joneses and grateful for both the employment they had provided and the emotional support they had given her in a period of her life when she was grieving and vulnerable, she had nevertheless reached the conclusion that slavery was incontestably wrong. Because of her dressmaking apprenticeship, she knew that many northerners, including women, worked for little money and in poor conditions. But plantation slavery was worse—much worse. "I returned to my New England home a pronounced abolitionist," she later wrote, "accepting from no one any apology for slavery, for I had seen it for myself, in its mildest form, to be sure,

under its best administration, and in the most favorable part of the South."
She began reading Garrison's *Liberator*, joining antislavery meetings, and
giving money to the cause.[56]

Barely a year after her departure, James Jones died on July 12, 1843, at St.
Leon plantation after a short illness. He was forty-eight years old. In Massachusetts, Mary Rice received a black-bordered letter "which bore the sad tidings." She later wrote that his illness had been "short, but painful, and his
departure sudden." Grieving, Mary took comfort in her fervent belief that
Jones had, in the end, embraced the Christian concept of an afterlife when he
expressed the earnest desire to meet his wife and children again.[57] He left
behind five children and a very wealthy widow. In accordance with her husband's wishes, Helen Jones never remarried.

In the coming years, Mary would keep in touch with the Jones family until
the cataclysm of disunion and civil war placed them in opposite camps and
ended their correspondence. In wartime, Mary would not communicate with
white members of the plantation household, but instead would meet with one
of their escaped slaves.

CHAPTER 3

---·•••·---

Minister's Wife

DURING THE 1840S AND 1850S Mary Rice came to terms with competing sides of her nature. On the one hand, she aspired to the traditional life of a middle-class married woman with children. On the other hand, her keen intellect, strong personality, and vast energy led her to search for creative outlets, and her idealism and religious convictions led to a desire to help others. Ultimately she would find fulfillment as a wife and mother. Writing fiction and poetry became her public forum. She also took tentative steps toward entering the world of reform, a path that first seemed straightforward, but one that over time she found far more difficult to negotiate.

Having lived independently for two and a half years, Mary had no intention of returning to her parents' household permanently. In the fall of 1842, after a cordial visit with her family in Boston, she accepted a teaching job in Duxbury, Massachusetts. Citizens of the town hired her to conduct a private school, one that would include girls as well as boys and would prepare boys for college. Recalling the chaos that had characterized her early days teaching the Jones children, Rice insisted that she be granted complete control over this school from the beginning. She would limit its size to twenty-five pupils and would not admit students under the age of twelve.[1]

Mary Rice showed her creativity and progressivism in the classroom in both her curriculum and her attitude toward governance. As she had done in Virginia, she conducted classes in botany and astronomy outdoors. She abandoned textbooks and instead chose poetry and prose readings for individual students. Because her pupils indicated an interest in music, she organized an orchestra, selecting music each Monday to be practiced and played in the coming week. On its very first day she announced an honor code for the school. All students must obey the rules and behave like gentlemen and ladies if they wished to remain in her classroom. She created a mailbox in which letters might be sent to other students or to the teacher. Students might call on her at home during specified hours on Saturdays in order to share grievances or simply to pay a social call.[2]

Looking back later on her two and a half years in Duxbury, Mary Livermore would remember the town, located on the coast between Boston and Cape Cod, as an idyllic community. Many of Duxbury's residents could trace their ancestry to Pilgrims with last names such as Brewster, Alden, and Bradford. The local economy was based on shipping and shipbuilding. Mary quickly became caught up in the town's social as well as its intellectual life. With her students, she fished for mackerel in Duxbury Bay, attended sailing and rowing parties, enjoyed picnics in warm weather and clam chowder parties in the cooler months, sometimes accompanied by music and dancing. Increasingly, she rejected the strict social tenets of her childhood religion. She enjoyed parties, and apparently she no longer disapproved of dancing.[3]

Living in Duxbury enabled her to meet Massachusetts's most famous statesman, Senator Daniel Webster, who owned a farm in nearby Marshfield. Mary recalled a welcoming party she attended with other young people in the area who gathered annually to greet the senator upon his return from Washington. On another occasion she met him at a tea in Duxbury. She praised his willingness to speak with local people, but later pointedly recalled that "he addressed his conversation more to the men of the company than to the women."[4] Although it would be many years before she would embrace a woman's rights philosophy, from a young age Mary revealed a keen sense of awareness about gender distinctions.

Mary Rice became active in the Washingtonian temperance movement while living in Duxbury. Her work with this group marked the beginning of her career as a public reformer. She would espouse the temperance cause for the rest of her life.

In Duxbury, the Washingtonian movement "spread like prairie fire," Mary later recalled. Although the organized temperance movement had begun several years earlier, the emergence of the Washingtonians in the 1840s marked a new path for the anti-alcohol movement. It originated in Baltimore, when six moderate drinkers met in a tavern and, deciding that they liked whisky too much, took a pledge to abstain from alcohol and formed a society through which to urge others to do the same. They named their organization after George Washington. Just as he had saved the country from political subjugation, they hoped to rescue America from its subjugation to alcohol. By 1841 the movement had 200,000 members. It found fertile ground in Duxbury. Unemployment was on the rise as railroads challenged the shipbuilding industry, and alcohol abuse had become a problem in the community.[5]

In the 1840s, Mary Rice adhered to the widely held notion that women's innate nature made them more moral and religious than men, and therefore well qualified to judge men's behavior, including their drinking habits. Mary read newspaper stories and novels emphasizing the dangers to American families of inebriate husbands. Because drinking was seen as unladylike, women were more likely to be victims of inebriate men than inebriates themselves. Moreover, during the 1840s, the American legal system extended few legal rights to women. Married women could not control wages they might earn or property they might inherit. Spousal abuse was an all too common occurrence. Recognition of the destructive influence of alcohol, coupled with a belief in female moral superiority, drew women into the temperance movement in large numbers. Antislavery attracted a much smaller following, both because it was more controversial and because for women in Massachusetts, where slavery had been outlawed since the Revolutionary War, the issue seemed more remote. Her memoirs do not indicate any ties to antislavery organizations while she lived in Duxbury.[6]

Part of the Washingtonians' proselytizing effort focused on teaching young children of the dangers of alcohol abuse. As schoolteacher to Duxbury's elite, Mary "was pressed into work for the children," she later recalled. Influenced by her father's lifelong adherence to temperance, and convinced by the Washingtonians' philosophy, she embraced the movement enthusiastically. One of its tactics was to provide communities with activities that did not involve alcohol consumption. Accordingly, Mary worked with the children's Cold Water Army. Every July Fourth the youngsters would parade with flags and banners, accompanied by a band, and pledge their "total abstinence from all that intoxicates!" Years later Mary Livermore would recollect living in the same neighborhood as five men who had been boys in her Cold Water Army. Two had had inebriate fathers, two had lost their fathers, and one had lost his mother, yet despite their travails, all five remained temperate and attributed their success to their childhood experience with the Cold Water Army. While in Duxbury, Mary Rice also began to write for a Cold Water Army newspaper in Boston, and spent two years as a member of its editorial staff. The Washingtonians published a collection of her articles bound in inexpensive cloth covers.[7]

By 1844 Mary had reached an important turning point in her life. Gaining confidence as a teacher and an activist, she began to rethink the religious tenets by which she had been raised. Although she had already softened in her attitude toward parties and dancing, she had not found an alternative to the theological orthodoxy of her parents' Baptist congregation. Duxbury offered her three religious institutions: the Unitarian church (the largest congregation in town and the choice of most of the town's well-to-do citizens), the Universalist church, and the Methodist church. Mary attended the last, no doubt because it was theologically closest to the Baptist faith in which she had been raised.[8]

Mary Rice's life changed forever when she decided to attend a Christmas service at the Universalist church. Raised to disdain Christmas merriment as unseemly, she had nonetheless learned to enjoy the Jones family's celebrations during her years in Virginia. Perhaps feeling lonely, on Christmas night 1844 she went out for a walk and was drawn by the music that emanated from the church. A sexton invited her to enter, and she did. "The preacher," she later recalled, "was a young man, not more than twenty-five years old, blonde in complexion, with a good voice and a simple, earnest, prepossessing manner." His name was Daniel Parker Livermore, and his sermon that night came from Matthew 1:21, "And thou shalt call his name Jesus, for he shall save his people from their sins." The young minister preached that Christ came to earth not to save humankind from endless punishment but to teach us how to live moral, uplifting lives. Although God punishes those who sin during their lifetime, he is always forgiving, always enveloping the faithful with his love, and never consigns his children to torment in hell. Mary Rice found the sermon comforting. When she introduced herself to the Reverend Livermore at the end of the service, he recognized her immediately as the town's schoolteacher. She asked to borrow a copy of his sermon, which he gave her with an additional offer to lend theological texts from his personal library.[9]

Although Mary Rice had long believed that the Universalist Church was "outside the pale of Christian organizations," under Daniel Livermore's tutelage she began to rethink her religious views. The Universalist minister lent her many works, including William Ellery Channing's "Moral Argument against Calvinism," an essay that helped her to discount the notion that God decides before one's birth the future state of rewards and punishments. Mary felt an enormous sense of relief when she was finally able to reject the Calvinist theology that had so troubled her since childhood.[10]

While studying with Daniel Livermore, Mary learned about the history of his denomination. The Universalist Church had its start in America when the Englishman John Murray brought its message of universal salvation to the colonies in the 1770s. In its early years the church joined with other minority religious groups, including the Baptists and Quakers, to promote the separation of church and state and to end the Congregationalist dominance of New England. In 1803, meeting in Winchester, New Hampshire, Universalists adopted the "Winchester Profession of Faith," in which they agreed on a basic set of tenets: the importance of biblical revelation, the emphasis on good works in life, and universal salvation. Hosea Ballou, perhaps Universalism's most important nineteenth-century theologian, published *A Treatise on Atonement* in 1804-5 in which he attacked the idea of the vicarious atonement of Jesus for the sins of men and women. The orthodox had long believed that such atonement appeased a wrathful God for the sins of humankind. Ballou rejected the notion that any kind of vicarious atonement was necessary, arguing that a loving God forgives human failings.[11]

Universalism provided Mary Rice with a reassuring religious perspective that allowed her to reject a belief in hell. She later wrote that the concept of "*endless* punishment . . . had been the horror of my life, had darkened my childhood, and made me old before my time." Although she may not have realized it then, thousands of other Americans grappled with the same religious questions. Beginning in the 1790s, with the religious revivals of the Second Great Awakening, many Americans began to resist the orthodoxy of their parents' generation and to embrace a more optimistic theology emphasizing God's love and universal salvation. As for many others, Mary's personal religious awakening heightened her desire to help those less fortunate. Indeed, her Christian faith would be a powerful motivator for her career as a reformer. Many years later she would write, *"Those whose lives are actuated by this spirit of service to the world, best know God."*[12]

When Mary Rice embraced the message of Universalism, she also embraced its messenger. While sharing books and discussing religion, she and Daniel Livermore fell in love. It must have been a whirlwind romance. They met on Christmas Day 1844 and were married May 6, 1845. She was twenty-four and he was twenty-six. Mary recorded few details of the wedding, except to note that her sister Abby served as bridesmaid. Years later Mary would recall that the word "obey" had not been included in her marriage vows.[13]

Daniel Parker Livermore was born June 17, 1818, in Leicester, Massachusetts, the youngest of nine children of a farm family. Like his wife's family, Daniel's ancestors had arrived in North America in the early days of English colonization, with the first Livermore settling in Watertown, Massachusetts, in 1634. The Livermores appear to have been moderately well off, for Daniel's parents, Daniel and Betsy Parker Livermore, made enough money from their farm to hire outside help. In most farm families, boys helped their fathers outside and girls assisted their mothers inside. The elder Livermores insisted, however, that all of their children help in both the farm work and the housework, providing their offspring with an unusually gender-balanced and egalitarian set of work experiences. Daniel was always close to his mother, who was forty-one when he was born. Mary Livermore later remembered that at the time of their marriage, he knew a great deal more about cooking, laundry, and "household sanitation" than his bride. Betsy Livermore was also an independent thinker who decried laws mandating female inequality, and she imparted this perspective to her son.[14]

Daniel Livermore was raised in the Universalist Church, as his parents were early converts to this religious denomination. Educated at the Leicester Academy, he taught school for a few years before deciding to study for the ministry, rejecting an offer from his older brothers to join them in manufacturing. He moved to Providence, Rhode Island, where he prepared for his new profession under the tutelage of the Reverend W. S. Balch. Ordained in Georgetown, Massachusetts, in 1841, he preached there and then in Duxbury. In 1846 he made a contribution to the Universalists' growing body of promotional literature when he published a treatise called *Orthodoxy as It Is*, alleging that evangelical religion caused depression and even insanity.[15]

In the nineteenth century, selecting a marriage partner was the most important decision a woman would make in her lifetime. It was from her husband that a woman derived her social and economic status. Because American law followed English common law traditions of *feme covert*, a wife lost most of her legal identity upon marriage. She could not hold property or control any wages that she might earn. Physical chastisement of wives and children was legal in most places. Moreover, in the absence of political rights for women, men voted on behalf of their entire family.

In choosing Daniel Livermore as her husband, Mary Rice made the best decision of her life. Their marriage would last more than fifty years, and by all indications it was an extremely happy one. A fellow Universalist minister once described Daniel Livermore as "a person of unbounded geniality and tenderness. It is not easy to find a sturdier friend, a more thoughtful and devoted husband." A daguerreotype taken the day after their wedding shows a pleasant-looking young couple, he with an arm solicitously around her shoulder, his other hand holding a piece of paper, probably meant to be the text of a sermon. Tall and clean-shaven, he would soon grow a beard, a nineteenth-century fashion he would retain for the rest of his life. Mary gazes demurely at the camera, hands folded in her lap, very much the proper schoolteacher and minister's wife. Both of them have the smallest hint of a smile, conveying both their shyness and their pride in each other.[16]

Mary Livermore loved her husband very much. Once, when he was away on business, she wrote, "Life is not life without you." She described him as mild-mannered, patient, and affectionate. His gentle guidance had helped to resolve her religious insecurities, and he would support and encourage her intellectual and reform interests. For both gifts she was most grateful. In 1892 she wrote about Daniel in a letter to a friend: "Commend me to the loyal old gray-beard, who after forty-eight years of marriage, writes love-letters . . . who thinks a man shouldn't marry a woman, to absorb her, as the whale swallowed Jonah, when she would certainly disagree with him, as Jonah did with the whale, but that they may reciprocally help and bless each other, their oneness made by themselves, and not by the law."[17]

Having committed herself to a new religious perspective and a new husband, Mary Livermore faced her Baptist family and her friends in Boston. "My father was inconsolable," she recalled. A Calvinist to the end of his life, Timothy Rice never reconciled the "loss" of his daughter to Universalism. He did, eventually, come to appreciate his "heterodox son-in-law." As Mary later wrote diplomatically, "courtesy, kindness, and manliness are winning qualities, and one cannot withstand them forever." Not even Timothy Rice. Although some members of the First Baptist Church ostracized them, Mary and Daniel Livermore won the blessing of her beloved former pastor, Rollin Neale, who encouraged her to attend his services as long as he continued as minister.[18]

Typically, nineteenth-century middle-class women who were employed left the salaried labor force upon marriage, and the young bride resigned her position in Duxbury when she became Mrs. Livermore.[19] Although teaching would never again be a full-time profession, it had been her livelihood for almost ten years. She had enjoyed the work immensely and would look back on these years with satisfaction and pride, delighted when, in later years, she encountered former students and had an opportunity to become reacquainted with them.

Shortly before their marriage, Daniel Livermore accepted a position as pastor in Fall River, Massachusetts. Mary now joined him there. Fall River was a factory town with a largely native-born workforce. Although the Livermores did not have much previous experience with factory operatives, they quickly adapted. Daniel worked hard to convert the spartan hall where he held religious services–Mary called it "hideous"–into a more attractive place to worship. She assisted her husband with two reading clubs, one for young people interested in popular fiction, and the other for adult Bible study. In addition they started a current events club, attended by twelve bright young factory workers who met every other Saturday evening. Increasingly, club discussions focused on the ethics of slavery and the antislavery reform movement. A few members strongly defended slavery, while the others refuted them, with lively discussions often lasting until midnight.[20]

Despite her responsibilities as a pastor's wife, Mary Livermore enjoyed considerable leisure time during her early married life. To save money, the Livermores rented inexpensive rooms but hoped one day to buy a house. Without a child or a household to care for, and with her husband preoccupied with his duties as minister, Mary sought outlets for her energy and creativity. Daniel was always her most fervent supporter. In a letter to his sister Eliza written about the time of their first anniversary, she wrote that Daniel "is so kind and indulgent, so willing to gratify me, and comply with all my wishes, that I frequently tell him I could, if disposed to be extravagant and unreasonable, ruin him."[21] Although Mary was obviously teasing, in fact, with the law recognizing a married woman as her husband's legal appendage, he might be liable for her debts. Legal discrimination could work both ways.

During these years Mary Livermore wrote a series of poems and stories for the Boston-based Universalist Church publication *Ladies Repository* and an annual gift book published by the church, titled *Rose of Sharon*. These works revealed the comfort she found in her new religious views. In "The Look of Prayer" she explored the theme of God's everlasting love and forgiveness, writing, "How our Father's love o'ershadows, and his pitying eye looks down / And his helping hand extendeth, to uplift us to his throne." In the poem "Jesus" she wrote of Christ's suffering and crucifixion, an example of courage for humans to cope with adversity in their lives: "Jesus trod that path before you, God up-holden in the strife." When Daniel's mother, Betsy, died in 1846, Mary wrote a poem titled "The Spirit-Mother," mourning her loss, but also rejoicing to have a spirit mother "when the earthly one is dead . . . the angel came to guard me."[22]

Livermore often dwelled on the theme of universal salvation. Her short stories "Annie" and "The Picture Gallery of the Heart" focus on young women who die in the prime of life but whose families learn to cope with their loss through religious faith and the understanding that their loved ones are "fastened to the throne of God [who] encircles all the redeemed."[23]

She rarely broached controversial political or social topics during the 1840s. Now and again, however, she strayed from themes of religious awakening and turned to secular topics. By doing so within the genre of poetry and short stories, she could enter the public sphere in a socially acceptable way. "To the extent that women remained anonymous readers, or authors whose reasoned arguments appeared only in print, they could influence public debate," the historian Nancy Isenberg has written. On the other hand, "publicly and politically active women symbolized a special danger." Livermore would not yet cross that line. In 1847 she published a poem, "The Present Age," in which she referred to an era of "tumultuous strife / Where the sons of Truth enlisted." One stanza makes direct reference to slavery: "Humanity is bartered at the auction or the mart, / Whatsoe'er a chain is rusting into any human right / There, they loudest swell the conflict, hottest there they wax the fight." Invoking Jesus' love and a strong sense of optimism about the future, she speaks of "a glorious Era! never yet has dawned its peer!" and urges Christian reformers " 'Onward!,' is the Present motto, to a larger, higher life, / 'Onward!' though the march be weary, though unceasing be the strife."[24]

Mary Livermore found an opportunity to reach a larger audience when she submitted a novel for a contest sponsored by a Boston temperance society. Three prominent Bostonians constituted the prize committee. Of 250 submissions, they judged hers the best. She received fifty dollars in prize money and the satisfaction of seeing her first book-length publication in print. The novel, first printed in 1847, was republished by English temperance advocates; later, in the 1870s, after it was twenty-five years out of print, a Boston publishing house brought out a new edition. Writing with satisfaction that "the unpretentious little sketch has run quite an eventful life," Livermore noted that missionaries had translated the work into several foreign languages.[25]

Titled *Thirty Years Too Late, A True Story*, this novella tells the saga of a

family's decline into poverty, disease, and death owing to the drinking of its
male members. It focuses on the theme that all drinking, including the use of
patent medicines containing alcohol, leads to drunkenness and alcohol dependence, and it emphasizes the concept of drunkenness as a moral lapse with
excruciatingly tragic consequences for women and children. The novel concludes with the more positive theme of the redemptive power of women and
the Washingtonian temperance society.[26]

In *Thirty Years Too Late*, Livermore revealed a gift for writing the kind of
sentimental prose that appealed to antebellum readers, many of whom were
female. Her intent in reaching a female audience is obvious in the novella's
message that men, not women, develop drinking problems, and that drinking
causes difficulties for families. As principal nurturers in the home, middle-
class women had to care for sick husbands and children. They must be ever
vigilant, Livermore warned, of the possibility of dire consequences resulting
from even the seemingly benign act of taking medicine. It is interesting to
note that Livermore, who deeply resented the emotional tactics that her Baptist church had used to instill the fear of hell in children, had no compunction
about creating the grisliest of scenarios to warn Americans of the evils of
alcohol, including having the drunkard Charles Austin drop his infant daughter, who subsequently rolls into the fire and burns to death. But Livermore,
like other temperance advocates of her generation, viewed inebriety as a
moral lapse. Not until the twentieth century would medical practitioners begin to view alcoholism as a disease. Willpower alone, she believed, could keep
a man sober; there was no such thing as a moderate drinker in Livermore's
worldview, and women were always the victims of drunkards, never drinkers
themselves.

Livermore followed her first major literary success by writing a second
story, this one about winning converts to Universalism. Printed by a Boston-
based Universalist publisher along with another "prize story," Mary's tale
focused on twin sisters, raised in the Baptist Church according to rigid precepts of infant depravity and God's vengeance. One sister marries a Baptist
and sinks into depression as her beloved daughter dies unregenerate. The
other sister defies her family to marry a member of the Universalist Church,
loses a son to illness, but keeps her spirits high with the assurance of God's
everlasting love and a belief in universal salvation. Although Mary later expressed disappointment that her story failed to attract the same popular following as her temperance novel, she felt pride that her success as a writer was
now bringing in $150 to $200 a year to supplement Daniel's salary. Her in-

come allowed the Livermores to upgrade their housing. Tired of living in cramped quarters, and hoping for more privacy, Daniel and Mary decided to lease six furnished rooms in Fall River and "go to housekeeping."[27]

Having launched her career as a writer, Mary was now determined to succeed in the domestic sphere. She had little experience. In most families, mothers taught their daughters domestic skills during childhood. Curiously, Zebiah Rice appears not to have done so. Lacking a son, Timothy Rice may have shielded Mary from domestic work in order to nurture her scholarly interests, while her younger sister Abigail focused on domestic training. Mary's distaste for sewing is well documented. She probably felt the same way about cooking. But she soon attacked housekeeping with the same energy and self-confidence she applied to any new endeavor. To save money, she would forgo servants. "It must be confessed that for a few months we had a trying time," she later recalled, but both Livermores seem to have approached the process with good humor. Because Daniel had assisted his mother in the kitchen as a child, he was a better cook than Mary. Countless times she interrupted him in the midst of composing a sermon to ask how to operate an oven thermometer, how to use cream of tartar, how to tell if a cake is done. The low point in her culinary efforts came when she attempted to make her first fish chowder, a delicacy she had eaten since childhood and one so easy to create that she assumed "the stupidest person" could not possibly "blunder" in its preparation. She blundered. Using a complicated recipe calling for ingredients she had never heard of, including mushroom catsup, she prepared an enormous pot containing four pounds of fresh cod. The bottom portion became scorched while the top remained undercooked. The ever loyal Daniel buried the mess in a corner of the garden at night so that "the incompetence of his wife, as a cook, might never be discovered and bruited abroad."[28] *The Story of My Life* contains an illustration of Daniel, dressed in top hat, digging by lantern, while Mary peeks out conspiratorially from a shuttered window above.

Acknowledging defeat, Mary sent for her sister Abby, whom she admiringly called "a born housekeeper." Abby stayed several months, tutoring her older sister in the intricacies of cooking, nutrition, kitchen hygiene, laundry, "the laws of ventilation," and nursing. By the time she left, Mary had gained enough experience and confidence so that, she later remembered, "if my husband brought home an unexpected guest, it did not frighten me out of my wits." She gave several tea parties, most likely for ladies of the church. One day Daniel surprised her by attending a picture sale and bringing home oil paintings and steel engravings to decorate their spartan rooms. Mary could barely contain her delight, despite the extravagance involved. Several of the pictures would hang in every home they lived in from then on.[29]

In 1847 the Livermores decided to leave Fall River. Although they enjoyed the town's weekly lyceum series, hearing such luminaries as Charles Sumner, Theodore Parker, and Horace Greeley, they longed for more time to read and study. Perhaps a move to the country would provide peace and quiet. Daniel Livermore accepted a position in Stafford, Connecticut, a rural community on the Connecticut-Massachusetts border. They would remain in Stafford from 1847 to 1852, their longest residence in one location during the first dozen years of their marriage, and it was there that they experienced the high point in Daniel's career as a pastor and Mary's life as a pastor's wife.[30]

Universalism was well established in Stafford by the time the Livermores arrived. Many of the town's leading families had joined the congregation. Prosperous farmers and businessmen, they had contributed to the construction of a handsome new church a few years earlier. A white frame Greek Revival structure, the church was embellished by a columned portico and wrought iron railing on the outside and by stained glass windows and an ornate carved wood ceiling inside.[31] The church overlooked the town's beautiful countryside and rolling hills. It was quite a contrast to the utilitarian hall where Daniel Livermore had held services in Fall River. Presiding over such a fine congregation in such a magnificent setting, the twenty-nine-year-old pastor must have felt that he had arrived as a clergyman.

Daniel quickly set about organizing his congregation, focusing his attention on church government and finances. On October 17, 1847, the Stafford Universalists adopted a constitution and articles of faith. The following year the congregation retired the debt it had accrued in the construction of its new church. Members of the congregation clearly held their minister in high esteem, for church records during this time make frequent reference to "our beloved pastor." Moreover, Daniel soon made a name for himself among members of the state convention of Universalists, giving the keynote address at its annual meeting in 1850 and serving as its representative to the U.S. Convention of Universalists for several years.[32]

Mary also won respect in the community through her work with the Stafford Ladies Benevolent Society. Founded in 1844 by a group of Universalist women "desirous of increasing their ability to do good to *all the needy* . . . and of improving their own social, moral, and religious condition," the group drafted a constitution that allowed men to join, but only as nonvoting honorary members. At its July 1847 meeting, Mary was elected secretary-treasurer.

Her carefully recorded minutes reveal an active membership of thirty-five to forty women who met every two to four weeks in the home of one member, sewing dresses, shirts, and quilts to be given to the needy. Her notations in the treasurer's ledger book show every withdrawal for purchasing calico, cotton, or silk. The Benevolent Society also raised money to purchase items for the church, including a set of mahogany chairs with haircloth seats. Judging by its minutes, the society did not stray from its goal of helping the needy while providing a social outlet for middle-class ladies. There are no indications that they discussed temperance, antislavery, or other important issues of the day. The Stafford group, like hundreds of similar organizations around the nation, allowed women to shape their communities within the confines of a separate female sphere.[33]

In Stafford, the Livermores established themselves socially. They bought a house, a modest eight-room home, which they painted and papered. Because a minister's wife was considered part of the unofficial contract that a pastor made with his congregation, Mary dutifully participated in church picnics and Sunday school outings in addition to the Benevolent Society. But her sense of duty clashed with her sense of propriety when it came to the country parish practice of holding an annual "donation party." This custom involved members of a congregation coming to the home of their minister once a year in January, bringing food and dropping money into a box. Parishioners might enjoy a potluck dinner and dance at the same time. A large part of the pastor's income would be collected in this manner.[34] For the earnest young minister and his equally earnest young wife, the practice probably seemed untoward. Daniel Livermore was accustomed to a salary, not a donation.

In her capacity as secretary-treasurer of the Ladies Benevolent Society, Mary dutifully recorded on January 1, 1848, "The customary New Year's Meeting was held at Mrs. Livermore['s]. More than 100 ladies and gentlemen in attendance." These official minutes fail to convey the fact that the meeting wreacked havoc on her house. Proud of the effort she had made in creating a comfortable and well-appointed home, and protective of the material possessions she had struggled to acquire by selling stories and poems, the minister's wife looked on in horror as revelers broke her prized astral lamp and spilled smelly whale oil on the parlor carpet, turned Daniel's writing desk into a dinner tray, leaving a trail of mince pie, pickles, and preserves among his papers and pens, and smeared the Marseilles quilt in her guest room with cream pie and cranberry sauce. Reduced to tears after the guests departed, Mary insisted to Daniel, "I never can, and never will face another such storming of my home as this!" Winning the approval of parishioners was more of a challenge than winning Daniel over, but Mary prevailed. From then on the congregation might call on their minister and his family but not hold an annual donation party in their home.[35]

When they left Fall River and moved to rural Connecticut, Mary and Daniel Livermore had promised themselves more time for study. They launched into an ambitious plan of scholarly pursuits, rising early each morning to take advantage of a few hours of free time before Daniel's parish duties occupied him. Together they studied geometry and algebra. They read the works of Plato, Shakespeare, Swedenborg, Goethe, and Carlyle. To keep abreast of national affairs, they subscribed to Horace Greeley's *New York Tribune.*[36]

They wanted to take Gamaliel Bailey's *National Era* after learning of his decision to serialize Harriet Beecher Stowe's new antislavery story "Uncle Tom's Cabin" in 1851. But, ever vigilant of the need for "a rigorous system of self-denial till we were free from debt," they decided against it. Mary, however, found the prospect of forgoing the publication too painful. While Daniel was away in Leicester visiting his father and sister, she sewed practically non-stop for a week in order to stitch him a new pair of trousers, thereby saving three dollars on tailoring expenses, precisely the cost of the journal's subscription. Her surprised husband declared that the pants were as well made as those done by a tailor. Finally, Mary Livermore had scored a domestic triumph. And she ordered the *National Era.*[37]

In the spring of 1848, Mary took a leave of absence from her position as secretary-treasurer of the Benevolent Society, for she was in the final months of pregnancy. On June 22, 1848, she gave birth to a daughter, Mary Eliza. A second child, Henrietta White, joined the family on June 6, 1851. Marcia Elizabeth arrived June 3, 1854, while they were living in Malden, Massachusetts.[38]

Mary's pattern of childbirth represented a marked contrast to the reproductive lives of her mother and mother-in-law, who gave birth to six and nine children, respectively. Mary's smaller family exemplified a new trend in American fertility patterns. During the nineteenth century, the birthrate among white American women dropped from 7.04 children in 1800 to 3.56 children in 1900, a dramatic shift that social historians call the demographic transition. Scholars have struggled to account for this drop, which appears to have occurred primarily among native-born women. The shift is all the more remarkable because it occurred in an era when birth control was widely disparaged. Some historians believe that the drop in the birthrate reveals both the mutually supportive nature of nineteenth-century marriage and the growing influence of women within the family. Women wanted fewer children and may have insisted on sexual abstinence—or voluntary motherhood, as it was often called—as a means to achieve it.[39]

Although it is certainly possible that Mary Livermore suffered miscarriages or even a stillbirth that we do not know about, she enjoyed robust health throughout her life, and so it is also possible that she had only three pregnancies. The spacing of the Livermore daughters, all born in the month of June three years apart, would imply that Daniel and Mary Livermore, like many of their generation, wanted a small family and took necessary measures to achieve it. Fifty years later, Mary responded to President Theodore Roosevelt's call for native-born American women to have large families by defending smaller families of two or three children, a size she called ideal for "a good home . . . the first step in [a] higher civilization."[40]

Daniel and Mary Livermore would look back on their years in Stafford with genuine fondness, remembering the births of their children, the purchase of their first home, the energy and time they poured into renovating it, and the kindness of their parishioners. They had attained a level of material comfort by this time, for the 1850 census includes a seventeen-year-old female member of their household named Judith Squire, probably a live-in servant.[41] Popular with parishioners, fast becoming pillars of the community, they had achieved professional success and financial security. As Mary celebrated her thirtieth birthday in December 1850, she had found fulfillment in her roles as wife, mother, and volunteer.

She had also found fulfillment as a writer, for she continued to compose stories for publication. Motivated in part by the desire for a creative outlet but also by the desire to earn money, she later recalled proudly that by the 1850s her efforts were adding as much as $300 a year to the family's annual income. She published stories in the *Galaxy*, *Putnam's Magazine*, and *Ladies Repository*. In addition, she wrote poems and stories for an annual gift book, *Lily of the Valley*, and served as editor of the volume in 1851 and 1852. Livermore described it as a publication "in the highest style of the typographical art" and filled with illustrations.[42]

In all of these stories she explored familiar themes of illness and death, God's love and forgiveness, universal salvation, and the errancy of orthodox religion. These pieces also introduced new themes. Many focus on couples falling in and out of love. Livermore's view of women's role in these stories reflects traditional thinking about their appropriate sphere and place within marriage. In "Elliot Gray; Or, the Brave-Hearted Fireman," Livermore tells of a "poor clerk" unable to convince the father of beautiful Helen Ray that he has the proper social standing and business prospects to marry his daughter. When Elliot Gray saves the "half-suffocated" Helen from a house fire, her father realizes that he has erred in judgment. He says, "I [now have] the pleasure of owning him as a son." Helen herself is a passive figure in the story, which revolves principally around the two men. In a short story called "The First Quarrel," Livermore offers marital advice through the fictional couple Henry and Anna Hamilton. Anna is given to quick flashes of temper, while Henry, slower to anger, is also slower to forgive. In the aftermath of a terrible quarrel, Anna collapses with a fever and almost dies. With her recovery, the couple learn the lessons of "forgiveness and forbearance." While suggesting that husbands and wives must both learn forbearance, Livermore again upholds the notion of female passivity in marriage, for she has Anna Hamilton's mother counsel her daughter to practice "meekness" as part of her "daily exercise in married life."[43]

The Livermores' tenure in Stafford ended abruptly and unhappily when they faced a serious controversy with their Universalist congregation over the issue of temperance. By 1850 the national temperance movement had shifted direction away from a policy of converting individuals and toward passage of state laws to prevent the manufacture and sale of alcohol. Maine became the first state to pass such a law in 1851; other New England states soon followed. In Connecticut, the Universalist Convention passed a resolution condemning intemperance as one of "the great sins of the land."[44]

The Connecticut legislature submitted the liquor issue to voters in the state. Those who favored passage of a "Maine law" campaigned fervently, as did those who opposed it. Clergymen throughout the state supported prohibition, with Daniel Livermore an enthusiastic contributor. His congregation approached the subject with decidedly less certainty. Stafford's Universalist community became deeply divided over the issue, with the majority opposing the Maine law. Livermore's parish included wealthy men, some of whom held political office and identified with the Democratic Party, traditionally the party opposing the temperance reform movement. Although parishioners urged him not to become involved in the campaign, Daniel did not heed their advice. "Mr. Livermore had always been a temperance man," his wife recalled. "It was a matter of conscience with him."[45]

Daniel spoke to audiences night after night, agreeing to engagements as far away as twenty miles from home. Opponents of the Maine law denounced him for having "dragged the white ermine of his profession into the dirty pool of politics," especially after he preached an emotional funeral sermon for a parishioner who had died in a wagon accident while drunk. Ultimately, most of Livermore's male congregants deserted him. Their departure left his church, once the largest in Stafford, almost empty on Sundays, except for a smattering of women.[46]

Mary Livermore's role in this campaign remains unclear. Her second child was just three months old, but even if maternal duties had not preoccupied her, she would certainly never have considered giving a public speech, for to do so would be to violate the most basic tenets of conventional femininity. No doubt she provided moral support for her husband, and almost certainly she talked about the question with her woman friends. She claimed that most women in town favored the Maine law. On voting day Mary so feared for her husband's safety that she insisted on accompanying him to the polls, hoping that a female presence would ward off anyone who might want to attack him physically. Still recovering from childbirth and emotionally upset by the divisive campaign, she spoke of her "severe nervous strain." As Daniel exited the polling place, several supporters began to shout, "Three cheers for Livermore!"[47]

As a result of their temperance stance in Connecticut, the Livermores learned a painful lesson about the consequences of social activism. Although the state passed a Maine liquor law in 1853 with strong support from every region except the county where Stafford was located, Daniel Livermore's ministerial career in Connecticut ended after the local vote. Resigning from his Universalist pastorate before he could be fired, he preached his last sermon in Stafford the next Sunday, expressing regret for the divisiveness of the temperance crusade but maintaining loyalty to the cause. Church minutes record his departure without any reference to his having once been known as "our beloved pastor." The entire ordeal was extremely painful for both Livermores. As they prepared to leave Stafford, parishioners had a change of heart and asked Daniel to stay. He declined, having already accepted a position in Weymouth, Massachusetts, south of Boston. Many years later, Daniel's 1899 obituary highlighted the episode as a pivotal experience in his life. "His espousal of the Maine Liquor Law cost him the loss of the best parish he ever had, in a town where he had built a house, and established himself, as he supposed, for years."[48]

The Livermores hoped that their new life in Weymouth would provide an opportunity for healing and recovery from the emotional toll of their recent experiences. Instead, their tenure there was brief and marred by tragedy. Their daughter Mary Eliza died on May 23, 1853, a few weeks before her fifth birthday. In *The Story of My Life*, Mary Livermore discusses the deaths of her sister Rachel and of the Jones's eldest daughter at great length and includes medical details. Regarding her own daughter, she speaks only of the child's "agonizing illness" and her own excruciating sorrow.[49]

Mary and Daniel moved frequently during the 1850s. Following a brief tenure in Malden, where Mary gave birth to their last child, Marcia Elizabeth, or "Lizzie," they moved to Auburn, New York, between Syracuse and Rochester. The family resided there from November 1855 to April 1857. Although four-year-old Etta remained healthy, the baby contracted a "dangerous illness" which Livermore does not identify. She may not have known its source. Terrified the child would die, Mary poured out her fear and frustration in a poem published in the *Ladies Repository* imploring God to spare her daughters, for "I have but two."[50] Lizzie survived but in a delicate state of health, causing her mother considerable anguish.

As Mary devoted her time and energy to the children, Daniel attempted to navigate stormy political waters. The temperance question had divided his community and congregation in Stafford, while in Auburn, abolitionism inflamed public opinion. Martha Wright was a local resident who actively promoted antislavery and woman's rights in Auburn. The Livermores knew her, for in a letter written in 1886 to Wright's son-in-law, Mary recalled her friendship with the Auburn woman during this time. She also recalled that Daniel allowed local abolitionists to hold meetings in the Universalist sanctuary, claiming that his was the only church in Auburn willing to do so. Through their friendship with Martha Wright, Mary and Daniel Livermore met Wright's sister, the renowned feminist and abolitionist Lucretia Mott.[51]

Preoccupied by the demands of motherhood and concerned as always about her husband's career, Mary Livermore supported abolition philosophically but remained tentative about participating actively in the movement. Many years later, without identifying her own position, she revealed that the "great host of Anti-Slavery people were found outside the Abolitionist organizations, held back from membership by cowardice or reasons springing from social and sectarian conventionalisms, even while they fully sympathized with the reform." Having been for all intents and purposes fired from a position in Stafford for espousing temperance, Daniel Livermore and his wife were keenly aware of the consequences that social activism might bring. Mary Livermore recalled slavery's divisiveness for American churches when she wrote that

ministers "found both sides of the slavery question represented in their congregations . . . for not only were churches sundered by the anti-slavery reform, but denominations were rent in twain."[52] Torn between their need to
protect Daniel's livelihood in the ministry and their desire to be morally upright, the Livermores were deeply troubled by local and national developments during the 1850s. They worried about their future and their children's
future in these divisive times. Their experiences in the temperance and antislavery crusades speak volumes about the uncertainty and apprehensions afflicting Americans in the 1850s.

Mary continued to be deeply imbued with the nineteenth-century definition of womanhood that emphasized woman's important role as moral redeemer of the family and, by extension, of society at large. She still regarded
public speaking as inherently unladylike. A young divinity student who resided with the Livermores in Auburn during 1856 recalled Livermore many
years later as "a perfect housekeeper and an ideal mother." While she devoted
a great deal of her time to entertaining her husband's congregants and to her
own literary work, "she thought a woman's place was in the home and with
the church, but she would not speak in public." During the Civil War, when
she came to embrace public oratory as part of woman's rightful sphere, Livermore recalled her earlier reluctance to take the podium. Before the Civil
War, "nothing would have tempted me" to support the notion of public speaking for women, she told a large crowd in Dubuque, Iowa, in the spring of 1864.
"I would have deemed it something terrible, horrible for a woman to come
out before the public and talk."[53]

Woman's rights activists, including Martha Wright and others who attended the historic convention at Seneca Falls, New York, in 1848, emphasized
the rights they believed society owed to women as citizens of the republic.
This premise probably held no interest for Livermore in the 1850s. She believed that women should help the needy and morally degenerate but not
demand "rights" for themselves. Like the members of the Ladies' New York
Anti-Slavery Society so skillfully studied by Amy Swerdlow, Livermore most
likely regarded the demands of feminists as selfish. Although a small number
of women reformers moved from temperance to antislavery and then to
woman's rights before the Civil War, most, including Mary Livermore, did
not. As the historian Nancy Hewitt has warned, the path from benevolence to
woman's rights was not "straight or singular."[54]

Both Livermores ultimately embraced antislavery publicly. Daniel began
talking with sympathetic members of his congregation about the possibility of

moving to frontier Kansas to help establish a community of free labor farmers. Mary also voiced her ideas about slavery in public. In 1856 she published two antislavery poems in the Auburn newspaper in response to a story she had read in the *New York Tribune*. The *Tribune* had reported the case of a runaway slave mother named Margaret Garner, brought before a court in Cincinnati for having killed one of her children rather than allow recapture. Her trial inflamed northern abolitionists, who used the case to denounce, as the *Tribune* put it, "our Southern friends who extol the delights of servitude." Lucy Stone, a fiery young abolitionist and feminist, visited the runaway slave in jail and spoke passionately to a gathering at the Cincinnati courtroom during a recess. Like Stone, who would become her close friend during the following decade, Livermore identified with Garner, but unlike Stone, she chose a less incendiary manner in which to express herself. In one poem, titled "The Slave Tragedy at Cincinnati," sympathizing with Garner as a mother Livermore wrote, "Ay, *my* hand could ope the casket, and thy precious soul set free: / Better for thee death and Heaven, than a life of slavery!" Ultimately Garner was returned to her master in Kentucky. In the second poem, titled "Kansas," Livermore addressed the issue of free soil versus slavery along the western frontier, a developing situation that riveted the nation because of the lawlessness and bloodshed involved. She wrote, "Back, ye unleashed hounds of slavedom / For we will have Kansas free![55]

After living in Auburn less than eighteen months, Daniel Livermore decided to move his family west. The controversies surrounding temperance and antislavery agitation provided constant potential for divisiveness within his congregations. In the West, the Universalist Church was growing, business opportunities appeared to be promising, and the slavery issue might be less contentious.

Like thousands of women whose husbands yearned for a new start, and like her own mother a generation earlier, Mary Livermore viewed Daniel's migratory ambition with skepticism.[56] But he was determined to leave the Northeast, and Mary, his loyal wife, felt it was her duty to support him. The Livermores would spend the next twelve years in the West, years that would profoundly reshape their lives, their outlook, and their marriage.

CHAPTER 4

Emergence of a Public Woman

Dᴜʀɪɴɢ ᴛʜᴇ ʟᴀᴛᴇ 1850s Mary Livermore still led a traditional woman's life in many respects, supporting her husband's career, raising her children, and volunteering her time to a variety of charities. With the outbreak of the Civil War in 1861, this changed dramatically. She quickly determined that women must use their talents and energy to assist their country in its hour of greatest need. For some women, including herself, that would mean stretching and even breaking free of traditional feminine roles. The Civil War would provide Livermore with an outlet for her natural skills as a leader, organizer, and communicator. By the time it ended, she would never be the same again.

In 1857 the Livermore family left Auburn along with a group of local citizens bound for Kansas. They hoped to settle the territory and bring it into statehood without slavery. Initially, Auburn's Kansas-bound "colony" included forty-six families, a number that eventually grew to sixty-one. Mary described them as "all of the right sort" and added that most of them knew something about farming.[1] By casting his lot with the Kansas settlers, Daniel Livermore went public as an abolitionist.

Frontier life held no appeal for Mary Livermore, even though she sympathized with the mission of the Kansas settlers. As early as 1846 she told her sister-in-law, "Daniel troubles me very much by threatening every little while to go West, as far as Ohio, or Illinois." Moreover, while she supported Daniel and believed that he could be a successful farmer if he put his mind to it, she also feared that she would "utterly fail as a farmer's wife, and as a pioneer." Daniel may have had doubts of his own. While his western fever and anti-slavery convictions appeared strong, and he agreed to contribute money to the venture, he never promised the Auburn group that he would actually live in Kansas.[2]

Given Mary's doubts and Daniel's tempered enthusiasm for the Kansas venture, they compromised by traveling as far as Illinois with the Auburn group in the spring of 1857. Mary would remain in Illinois with their young daughters while Daniel continued on "to do his own prospecting." Daniel Livermore did not last long in Kansas. No doubt to his wife's great relief, he returned in a matter of weeks, with little positive to say about frontier farming but with a sense of optimism about the settlers' mission. He would make three or four additional trips to the colony, which the Auburn colonists named Cayuga in honor of their upstate New York home, to offer his advice and support.[3]

Daniel Livermore accepted a position as Universalist pastor in Quincy, Illinois, but remained only a short time before moving again to Chicago. Business interests dictated his decision to settle there permanently. Several years earlier he had purchased a mortgage on the Chicago-based Universalist newspaper *New Covenant*, along with a small publishing company and book-store nearby. Its proprietor, suffering from health problems, had sold the three concerns to Daniel, who intended to make them profitable, then sell. In Cincinnati, Universalists had established a newspaper, *Star of the West*, which had a circulation of seven thousand by the 1850s. Livermore no doubt hoped to emulate its success. The Panic of 1857 quickly ended his aspirations for an easy and profitable turnover. The national depression "plunged [him] in a struggle that was severe," his wife would later write.[4]

Mary remained preoccupied with her children, especially Lizzie, whose health was a matter of constant concern and probably a factor in her determination not to move to frontier Kansas. In Chicago she began setting up a household, and at the same time helped Daniel with writing the newspaper. From the beginning he valued her help. He gave her the title associate editor, an indication of both her importance to the publication and the egalitarian nature of their marriage. Both Livermores worked hard to make the paper a success. A clergyman acquaintance, intending his words as a compliment, recalled that "it would be difficult to find two men capable of performing the amount of labor that Mr. and Mrs. Livermore wrought during those busy and useful years."[5]

Chicago newspaperman Frederick Cook once described Daniel Livermore as "well above the average of men, both in stature and mental force, and also very active in all manner of public affairs." In addition to publishing the newspaper, Daniel Livermore played a leadership role in Chicago's Second Universalist Church, a congregation that began holding regular services in 1858 in a rented sanctuary. He served as its pastor until a permanent minister could be hired. In 1861 Universalists constructed a new church.[6] Although Daniel had abandoned the role of "settled pastor," he would continue to preach in pulpits throughout the Northwest. During more than a decade of residence in Chicago, he would travel nearly every weekend in an effort to reach groups of men and women who lived in small rural communities where orthodoxy was the only religion readily available. He found many rural people receptive to Universalism's message and believed that he could help alleviate their "religious famine." As a self-described missionary, he organized new parishes, dedicated new churches, and preached sermons, with his forthcoming engagements always printed in the *New Covenant*. When he returned from weekly trips, he shared stories with Mary. On one occasion she wrote humorously about Universalist country meetings. These sessions usually took place in a local schoolhouse "with a red-hot demon of a stove . . . burning all the oxygen out of the confined air." The sermon might be followed by "liberty to any brother to free his mind," a process that could drag on for hours. Like her husband, Mary understood the importance of these country meetings. Meanwhile, home alone with the children virtually every weekend, she managed the household and the newspaper in Daniel's absence.[7]

Daniel Livermore sought ways to make money outside the ministry. He "became interested in real estate," according to his 1899 obituary. A biographical essay about Mary Livermore written after the Civil War speaks of Daniel's "fine business ability." His name appears for the first time in Chicago city directories in 1859, where he is listed as *New Covenant* editor, and is shown as residing at 168 West Washington Street. In 1860 or 1861 the family moved to 263 West Madison Street, where they lived until the end of the Civil War, then moved to their final Chicago address at 163 Warren Street. These locations, on the city's West Side, placed them near the center of Chicago's rapidly expanding downtown and in relatively close proximity to the Universalist church on Washington Street and the *New Covenant* office on Clark Street. In all likelihood they owned these homes and probably made money in

selling each. They may have invested in other city property as well. After the
Civil War, Daniel Livermore purchased farmland thirty miles from Chicago.[8]

Incorporated for only twenty years, when the Livermores moved there,
Chicago was already a boomtown. Its population by 1857 had reached 93,000,
and would grow to nearly 300,000 residents by the time they left twelve years
later. The artist G. P. A. Healy, who had arrived in the city a few years before
the Livermores, likened it to "an overgrown youth whose legs and arms are
too long for his clothes and who scarcely knows how to dispose of his lank
awkward body. The city stretched along the lake shore and out on the prairie,
unfinished, ragged and somewhat uncouth as yet."[9] No doubt the Livermores
would have agreed. Chicago was a city of great energy and tremendous potential, but it was not sophisticated, nor was it an especially comfortable place to
live in the 1850s.

Everyone complained about the lack of amenities, and especially about the
mud. In her memoirs Mary recalled, "Mud, dust, dirt and smoke seemed to
predominate." Michigan Avenue held the distinction of being the city's only
paved street and had the only adequate sidewalks. Everywhere else, citizens
had to use makeshift sidewalks made of planks. Black slime oozed through
the cracks in wet weather, and in dry weather, dust, combined with street
litter borne aloft by wind, made walking equally challenging. Moreover, the
city lacked an adequate sewer system. Ditches running along the sides of the
streets became repositories for raw sewage. Planks laid over these ditches
allowed residents to step over the refuse when leaving their homes.[10]

For the most part, Mary took these discomforts in stride. Blessed with good
health and high energy, proud of her Yankee pluck, and grateful not to be in
Kansas, she made the best of it. She liked to tell the story of a tea party she
attended in Chicago along with other New England expatriates. Their hostess
had invited a large group of former easterners, who were much given to "tears
and the dumps" whenever they gathered and would talk about their homesickness. Determined to overcome Chicago's legendary mud, their hostess hired
a large Studebaker wagon drawn by four horses to transport the guests. Lined
with straw and containing two rows of wooden chairs, the wagon backed up to
each residence so that the women might climb in without walking through the
mud. Gentlemen also attended the party. Disinclined to complain about the
mud, they were, Mary noted wryly, "gay, even to hilarity, for, if Chicago was
muddy and dirty and comfortless, they were making money, and would have
refused to change their residence to the New Jerusalem." When the party
ended, guests returned home by the same mud-free conveyance. The only

close call occurred when the wagon became stuck in a rut, and passengers had to shift quickly to the other side to avert an upset.[11]

Despite the travails of living in what was known euphemistically as the Garden City of the West, the Livermores prospered. Even the younger Livermore daughter, Lizzie, recovered sufficiently so that her mother could devote an increasing amount of time to public endeavors. But Mary was careful to remind readers of her autobiography many years later that she had not neglected her domestic responsibilities. The Livermores enjoyed enough income to employ domestic servants to do the housework, though Mary noted proudly that she acted as her own housekeeper and "directed" their efforts. She also cared for her two daughters, and she "exercised a large hospitality towards my husband's patrons and friends, which was required by circumstances."[12]

Increasingly Mary Livermore busied herself in benevolent pursuits. In addition to teaching a Sunday school class of sixteen boys, she volunteered considerable time to a number of charities that focused on Chicago's needy women and children. Livermore helped to found the Home for Aged Women and the Hospital for Women and Children. She also assisted with the Chicago Home for the Friendless, a shelter for homeless women and children, founded in 1858, which became Mary's favorite charity. She worked well with others and, when involved with a project requiring her attention, could forgo sleep until such a time that leisure permitted her to catch up on her rest. By supporting institutional solutions to the problems of poverty and illness, Livermore became part of a national trend. In the 1840s many women reformers worked in small groups, just as Mary had done with her sewing circle in Stafford. By the 1850s, a growing number of women had come to believe that hospitals, shelters, and orphanages provided more realistic solutions to society's ills.[13]

The *New Covenant* occupied most of the Livermores' time. Daniel edited the weekly paper from an office on Clark Street, along a stretch that housed most of Chicago's newspapers. Following a common practice among editors of weekly journals, he often reprinted stories from other publications. Mary called this custom "scissoring." Both Livermores also wrote their own articles, with Mary signing or initialing those she composed. The *New Covenant* called itself "a family paper devoted to religion, theoretical and practical; social reform, literature, and news." Mary would later describe it as "a prosperous weekly paper, whose subscribers were scattered throughout the Northwest." By the time he sold the paper in 1869, Daniel Livermore claimed a readership of 25,000 to 30,000.[14] Unfortunately, few issues dating from before the Civil War survive. Like so much Chicago history, files of this publication were destroyed in the Great Fire of 1871.

Religious discussions constituted an important theme of the newspaper. Universalists were often ferocious debaters, intent on defending the doctrine of universal salvation from orthodox sects that insisted the belief would lead to immorality and even anarchy. In June 1858 Daniel Livermore refuted the recent sermon of a conservative minister who had railed against the "rapid progress of Liberal Christianity." Livermore believed that "the days of Orthodoxy are fast being numbered! An enlightened and intelligent people, accustomed to think for themselves, cannot believe that a God of infinite wisdom and benevolence will torment his own children, throughout the boundless ages of eternity, for no possible good." Mary wrote a religious editorial of her own castigating Dr. William W. Everts, a leading clergyman and minister of Chicago's First Baptist Church, for endorsing the doctrine of "endless punishment" and for his "utter ignorance of Universalism" and its doctrines.[15]

The Livermores also delved into discussions of woman's role in nineteenth-century society. Two articles published in 1859 provide insights into their position on the issue of woman's rights. A brief notice in February recommended to readers a recent article in the *Atlantic Monthly* titled "Ought Woman to Learn the Alphabet?" The *New Covenant* described this essay as "exceedingly interesting" and containing "the whole of the 'Woman's Rights question' in a nutshell" in a "clear, dispassionate" manner. The unsigned *Atlantic* article focused on the liberal spirit of the era and the need for society to allow women greater educational opportunities, better pay in the working world, and property rights if married. It endorsed traditional domesticity as woman's rightful place but also suggested that neither female suffrage nor female orators presented an inherent danger to society.[16]

A selection about Dr. Elizabeth Blackwell, unsigned and therefore perhaps written by Daniel, focused on her pioneering struggle for acceptance as a woman in medical school, her large practice among wealthy as well as poor New Yorkers, her "wisdom," and her "woman's heart." The article concludes by observing: "Her example and daily life will do more for the exaltation and progress of womanhood, than all the Women's Rights Conventions which will be holden within a hundred years."[17] These two articles suggest that the Livermores espoused a moderate degree of support for woman's rights before the Civil War. They promoted educational and job opportunities for women. They certainly applauded individual women for their heroic pursuit of professional opportunities that would enhance their ability to serve the sick and infirm.

They did not dismiss female suffrage outright, but they were not yet ready to embrace a reform movement that focused on political equality for women.

Mary Livermore articulated her views on woman's sphere in a series of fictional pieces she wrote for the *New Covenant* and reprinted as a book, *Pen Pictures*, in 1862. Most of the stories feature female protagonists. One of Livermore's recurrent themes, and indeed her personal credo, concerned women's duty to serve others, especially their children and those in need. In "The Sewing Society," Julia Bradley tries to coax Henry Marston into joining a "sewing club" that in reality has nothing to do with sewing but rather is committed to frivolous pursuits such as playing checkers, chess, backgammon, and cards, as well as singing and dancing. Henry refuses to join the society because of its failure to pursue serious work for the benefit of society. Finally, after the club spends an evening in "riotous pleasure" and "extravagance of display," Julia realizes that Henry is right. She arranges for the sewing club to meet at the home of the widow Foster, where they stitch clothing for the needy family, including tubercular little Ellen. Next the society meets at the home of the inebriate Mr. Lambert, whose "criminal self-indulgence" in alcohol has reduced his family to virtual beggary. Julia's empathy helps lead the unfortunate man down the path to sobriety. He signs a temperance pledge in her presence, indicating, once again, the redemptive power of women. Not only does Henry join the sewing society, but also he proposes marriage to Julia, reinforcing the moral that the virtuous woman who devotes herself to helping others can also make herself attractive to a desirable marriage partner.[18]

By 1860, at the age of forty, Mary Livermore appears to have been settled and happy in Chicago. In both her personal and public life she had achieved the nineteenth-century definition of successful womanhood. She had married and borne children. Her husband had stable and prosperous business interests. With a small household of two children, servants to do the housework, and a husband who supported her scholarly and charitable interests, she had established a reputation as a capable writer and a dedicated, efficient volunteer. When the Civil War broke out, she possessed the right combination of maturity, skills, commitment, affluence, and family support to contribute substantially to the wartime benevolent effort, first as a volunteer, and ultimately as leader and interpreter of woman's wartime role.

In April 1861, as Confederate forces bombarded Fort Sumter in Charleston harbor, ending months of speculation about a possible military confrontation between North and South, Mary Livermore sat by the bedside of her father in

Boston. Timothy Rice believed that he was dying, and she had been summoned by an urgent telegram. Now in his seventies and frail, Rice, like his daughter, watched the secession crisis unfold with great foreboding. He had served in the navy during the War of 1812, a member of the nationalist generation that had watched America grow from fledgling colonies to united country, only to splinter. "My God! now let me die, for I cannot survive the ruin of my country!" he said on learning of Sumter's surrender. But he did not die. Instead he rallied, insisting several days later that Mary take him for a carriage ride to Faneuil Hall so that he could watch volunteer soldiers marching through the streets of Boston. Father and daughter were both moved by the outpouring of patriotism they witnessed.[19]

For Mary Livermore, the Civil War represented the tragic culmination of many years in which the North had attempted to placate the southern states with political compromises over the slavery question. To her mind, the South had reacted intolerably, repaying northern patience and peace overtures with military aggression. Twenty years earlier she had lived in Virginia, a state that had now joined the Confederacy. Much as she liked and even respected her former employers in Mecklenburg County, Livermore had no sympathy for southern nationalism, which she viewed as being grounded solely in the defense of slavery. With James Jones she had once discussed slavery and abolition. After she left Virginia, Jones wrote a will reflecting his concern that the abolition movement might threaten his economic investment in bondspeople. He recommended that if emancipation appeared likely in Virginia, his wife should take their slaves west to Texas.[20]

Unbeknownst to Mary Livermore, Jones's son and namesake had already pledged his support to the Confederate cause. Several weeks after the fall of Fort Sumter, young James Y. Jones Jr., whom Mary had called Jamie or "Batt," left home, a lieutenant in the Boydton Cavalry. A local hotel hosted a send-off dinner, after which the soldiers began their march north toward Petersburg, and then to Richmond. Mary Jones's husband, Edward Cary Walthall, also enlisted in April 1861, joining the Yalobusha Rifles, later incorporated into the Fifteenth Mississippi Regiment. By June of that year Walthall had won promotion to lieutenant colonel.[21] Like the Livermore family in Illinois, the Jones family in Virginia and Mississippi prepared to support the war effort.

When Livermore returned to Illinois, she found a state divided in its loyalties. Southern Illinois, with its ties of trade and kinship to the slave states and its support for the Democratic Party, contained many Confederate sympathizers. Northern Illinois, including Chicago, supported the Republican Party and president-elect Abraham Lincoln. The Livermores supported the Republicans and gave Lincoln their qualified support.

As journalists, they had attended the 1860 Republican nominating convention in Chicago's Wigwam amphitheater. To ensure that reporters could hear well enough to give a reliable account of the convention proceedings, Republican organizers had allotted the best seats to members of the press–sixty in all. Dressing in black to blend in, Mary was nevertheless conspicuous as the only female journalist at the press tables and the only woman on the floor of the vast convention hall.[22]

A marshal noticed her and ordered her to "go up higher" to the ladies' gallery. In keeping with literal notions about separate spheres, women commonly sat in segregated areas in lecture and convention halls. Mary's presence on the convention floor represented a direct threat to Chicago's gendered code of political ethics. In the late 1850s Joseph Medill, editor of the *Chicago Tribune*, had told his politically saavy wife bluntly, "Women don't go" to political meetings. Mary Livermore had other ideas. She protested the marshal's order to vacate her press seat. Because the Wigwam was an immense structure, and the ladies' gallery so far from the central platform, women could not hear the speeches. "There is no use of wasting words about it," the marshal responded. "If one woman is permitted here, all the others will claim the right." While Daniel tried to intervene, other reporters, afraid of missing newsworthy proceedings, told Mary to "sit up" and the marshal to "dry up!" She stayed. Livermore found the incident somewhat unnerving, although "no one but myself seemed to remember [it] ten minutes later."[23] When writing her memoirs in the 1880s, she still looked back with great pride at having been the only woman reporter on the convention floor. At the time, she had stood up for her own rights as a journalist but had not made a stand in the name of rights for all women.

Her persistence was worth the effort. "I was well repaid for the annoyance," she would later remark, "by being a near witness of the electric scenes which followed the nomination of Mr. Lincoln to the Presidency, on the third ballot." Thousands waited outside the convention hall for news, and tumultuous celebrations followed the nomination of Illinois's favorite son. Livermore later admitted that she did not share the crowd's ecstasy over the choice, for she regarded Lincoln as an obscure, undistinguished country lawyer. Following Lincoln's election, she ventured out one blustery evening so that she might see the president-elect, hoping for some indication that this man with the "rugged, homely face" might have the judgment and strength to bring the nation through the secession crisis. While she took comfort in Lincoln's being a northerner, and one whose antislavery convictions appeared genuine, she remained skeptical of his leadership abilities until she met him personally in the second year of the war.[24]

In the early weeks of the conflict, Chicagoans enthusiastically demonstrated their support for the Union. The city held a massive rally two days after the fall of Fort Sumter. Since no hall in the city could accommodate such an enormous gathering, the overflow who could not find standing room in Metropolitan Hall assembled on Randolph Street. Republican congressman Owen Lovejoy, brother of a man martyred while trying to protect his abolitionist press in the 1830s, gave the principal speech. A new song composed for the occasion, titled "The First Gun is Fired! May God Protect the Right," was sung to resounding cheers. Governor Richard Yates immediately called for six regiments of volunteers. Thousands enlisted, including all sixteen young men in Mary Livermore's Sunday school class.[25]

Women wanted to help the war effort too, and scores of patriotic Chicagoans began to use their skills as seamstresses to make supplies for the new citizen soldiers. Livermore would recall that their good intentions often exceeded their sense of practicality, especially in the production of "Havelocks," headdresses of white linen designed to protect a soldier's head and neck from sunstroke while fighting in the South. Local soldiers ridiculed Havelocks, calling them "white nightcaps" and wearing them upside down.[26]

Women also organized "relief societies," often in conjunction with specific regiments whose nutritional and medical needs they planned to ensure. Such a system was too cumbersome to function effectively, given the massive mobilization of troops taking place across the country. Moreover, local relief agencies often packed food and supplies without proper attention to preventing breakage and contamination. As a result, railroad cars were encumbered with boxes of decomposing fruits and vegetables, improperly canned meats and soups, and broken containers of jams and jellies, all too often spilled onto new clothing, ruining everything. "Out of this chaos of individual benevolence and abounding patriotism the Sanitary Commission finally emerged," Livermore later wrote. "With its carefully elaborated plans, and its marvelous system," the commission would change the nature of wartime benevolence.[27] It would also change Mary Livermore's life.

The Sanitary Commission superseded an earlier organization called the Woman's Central Relief Association. Begun in New York in the aftermath of the fall of Fort Sumter by women eager to contribute to the Union cause, the

WCRA invited the Reverend Henry Whitney Bellows to preside at its organizational meeting on April 25, 1861. The minister of All Souls Unitarian Church in New York, Bellows showed a flair for organization, and demonstrated a desire both to channel and to dominate the efforts of benevolent women. The WCRA, which included urban and rural women, had trouble establishing a relationship with the army, which was intolerant of groups with female volunteers, even those under male leadership.[28]

In May, Bellows traveled to Washington, where he met with a committee of philanthropists to discuss issues of hygiene and medical care in the army. The committee examined the British military record in the Crimean War of 1854–56, in which an army of more than 110,000 suffered nearly 21,000 deaths, 16,000 of them from disease. The urgent need for reform had led the government to grant authority to an organization called the British Sanitary Commission. The results proved startling. Through improved sanitation and the medical efforts of nurses such as Florence Nightingale, the death rate dropped from 250 per 1,000 soldiers in 1855 to 25 per 1,000 in 1856. With the British model as his guide, Bellows organized the United States Sanitary Commission, a quasi-governmental body that would advise and assist the army and the government on matters of nutrition, hygiene, and medical care. By mid-June the proposal won the endorsement of Secretary of War Simon Cameron and President Lincoln, who appears to have given his blessing unenthusiastically, fearing that the organization might become "a fifth wheel to the coach." The president's doubts would prove to be misplaced. The USSC would become the largest philanthropic organization ever created in America. Its "scientific approach" to reform, one that emphasized organization, efficiency, and professionalism, would transform attitudes toward benevolence during and after the war.[29]

On June 12 the Sanitary Commission met for the first time, selecting Bellows as its president. Alexander Dallas Bache would be vice president and George Templeton Strong would be treasurer. Prominent Chicagoans Mark Skinner and Ezra Butler McCagg served as commissioners along with other reformers and philanthropists from around the nation. When Chicago organized its own branch of the commission, one of a series of USSC offices in major cities, Skinner would be chosen its first president. A wealthy lawyer and judge, Skinner had already earned a reputation as one of the city's leading philanthropists. McCagg, himself a wealthy man and patron of the arts, became secretary. Eliphalet W. Blatchford was elected treasurer.[30]

Gradually, local aid societies founded in the initial weeks of the war started to affiliate with the U.S. Sanitary Commission. Mary Livermore's association with the commission began when a local group she directed merged with it. "Thenceforth," she wrote, "until the bells rang in the joyful news of peace, my time and energy were given to its varied work." The Chicago Commission opened its first offices for receiving and shipping supplies at 41 Wabash Street. Immediately, aid societies throughout the Northwest began sending all manner of items to this office. Volunteers unpacked boxes, separated food from supplies and clothing, stamped packages with the name "Chicago Sanitary Commission" to discourage theft, and packed the reorganized boxes. When hospitals sent word that they needed food, supplies, or clothing, the Chicago office sent boxes south. The Chicago Commission would later change its name to the Northwestern Sanitary Commission and move to more spacious quarters in J. H. McVicker's Theatre on Madison Street.[31]

One of Livermore's earliest contributions to the Chicago office was to organize a fundraising festival, along with Jane Hoge. At this week-long event, held in December 1861, Chicagoans were invited to purchase handmade gifts and culinary delicacies donated by patriotic citizens, eat meals cooked by volunteers, and attend a "Grand Operatic Concert" performed by Madame Matilda Crevelli. The festival raised the modest sum of $675.17, to be used for western hospitals. Along with their draft, the women sent the commission this note: "Accept it as our Christmas gift; we regret that it is not larger. We shall condense into a permanent organization for active hospital service, and hope to aid you in a small way, through the war."[32] More important than the modest sum it raised, this fair marked the beginning of the wartime collaboration between Livermore and Hoge, a partnership that would last until the end of the war and would be one of the most remarkable in Sanitary Commission history.

Jane Blaikie Hoge was born in Philadelphia in 1811, and, like Mary Livermore, graduated from a female seminary at the top of her class. At age nineteen she married Abraham Hoge of Pittsburgh and moved with him to Chicago in 1848. A devout Presbyterian and mother of thirteen children, Hoge somehow found time for benevolent work. In 1858 she helped to found Chicago's Home for the Friendless, and through this and other benevolent projects she worked with Mary Livermore. Nearly a decade older than Livermore, with two sons serving in the Union Army, Hoge was a forceful personality who did not hesitate to use her influence in helping her sons secure commissions as officers. In Jane Hoge, Livermore had a friend and mentor who was not the least bit intimidated by male authority figures. Chicago journalist Frederick Cook characterized her as a "Matron-General" with a very strong personality and "executive talent of a high order." Mary Livermore praised Hoge as a talented public speaker.[33]

Mary Livermore and Jane Hoge shared a sense of devotion to the war effort, a commitment to helping those in need, and unflagging energy. They did not share a common religious perspective. Indeed, the genuinely close professional and personal bond that developed between the two women is remarkable given their religious differences. Jane Hoge and her husband were members of the Presbyterian Church, one of the orthodox sects of which Livermore heartily disapproved. And yet Livermore was consistently loyal to Hoge, even writing an article in the *New Covenant* supporting a fundraising oyster supper which Hoge helped to organize for her church. In her article Livermore wrote that although "we have no sympathy with the theology of the [Presbyterian] church," Universalists would enjoy a "delicious supper [and] exquisite music" at the festival. Their religious differences may have helped make Livermore and Hoge a particularly effective team, as Livermore appealed to Chicago's liberal Christians and Hoge to more traditional sects. But Frederick Cook spoke of Livermore's skill as a leader of women regardless of religious affiliation. Despite her "heretical belief in ultimate universal salvation," he wrote, Livermore's combination of competence and personality made her a natural leader even among evangelical women.[34]

Although both Livermore and Hoge devoted an increasing amount of their time to the Sanitary Commission, Livermore still managed to write two to three articles each week for the *New Covenant*, which she used as an organ through which to define woman's wartime role and promote the commission's work. In May 1861, only a few weeks after the outbreak of hostilities, she reminded women of their obligation to support their country in its time of trial, urging them to abandon an interest in fashion and other frivolous pursuits and devote their efforts to sewing for the soldiers. In December, Livermore advertised the Soldiers' Festival she organized with Jane Hoge, emphasizing that the proceeds would support hospitals that cared for soldiers from the Northwest.[35]

The year 1861 drew to a close with little for Chicagoans to cheer about on the military front. The Confederate rebellion, which many had predicted would last only a matter of weeks, now seemed likely to extend into the coming year. Early in 1862, however, the Union Army's prospects began to improve. In the first two weeks of February, General Ulysses S. Grant's soldiers captured Fort Henry and Fort Donelson, strategically important Confederate strongholds in Tennessee that controlled access to the Tennessee and Cumberland rivers. When news of Fort Donelson's surrender reached Chicago on February 17, the city erupted with joy. A sizable number of Illinois troops under the command of General John A. McClernand had fought there, and the commanding general, Illinoisan Ulysses S. Grant, had made himself a national hero by demanding "unconditional surrender" from the fort's Confederate commander. "No one of the later or larger victories of the war, not even the fall of Richmond, awoke the enthusiastic delight of the Northwest like the fall of Fort Donelson," Mary Livermore would recall. Chicagoans rang church bells and fired cannons in celebration. Passengers cheered as they drove past the Sanitary Commission headquarters in omnibuses and wagons. At night, citizens lit bonfires against the winter cold as thousands thronged the streets. More circumspect citizens met in churches to give quieter thanks for this military victory that seemed to portend an end to the nearly year-long war.[36]

In the aftermath of Union victory, interest in the Sanitary Commission and its efforts grew. The Chicago office had now developed an efficient system, supplying its southern Illinois depot in Cairo at a rate of a thousand dollars' worth of food and medicine per day. Medical treatment of wounded soldiers remained uneven. At Fort Donelson, the battle had raged for several days, with many of the wounded unable to be removed until the fighting stopped. Some of the injured froze to death. Others were frozen into the ground and had to be cut out of the earth when the firing ceased. There were not enough ambulances, not enough hospitals, not enough beds, not enough doctors. Once soldiers could be moved, the army had facilities in St. Louis and other cities that were well staffed and clean. But field hospitals clearly did not perform their duties adequately.[37]

To address this situation, the Chicago Sanitary Commission directed Mary Livermore and Jane Hoge to visit Union hospitals in the West and report about these facilities, with the idea of improving medical care before the next major battle might take place. The decision to send the two women resulted from the resignation of Elizabeth Porter, who had acted as superintendent of the Chicago office since its inception, and who now moved to Cairo in order to coordinate nursing efforts there. Although Livermore and Hoge did not yet hold titled positions with the Chicago branch, their initial inspection tour would afford them considerable visibility with local authorities.[38]

Leaving their husbands and children, Livermore and Hoge boarded a train heading south. After meeting with Governor Yates in the state capital, Springfield, they traveled to St. Louis, the principal city in the slave state of Missouri. The army kept St. Louis and the rest of Missouri in the Union through a kind of uneasy neutrality, for the state had many Confederate sympathizers. In Springfield, Livermore had noted the difference between raw recruits and experienced soldiers. After "seeing the elephant"—a slang term for a first battlefield experience—a soldier would never be the same again. Civil War nurses also experienced their own kind of trial by fire when they gained their first exposure to badly wounded soldiers. For Livermore this experience came in St. Louis. "I cannot recall a single cheerful or humorous event connected with the visit," she would later write. "There was gloom everywhere." The city was filled with wounded men. Relatives of the sick and the dead poured into the city searching for their loved ones.[39]

Mary Livermore and Jane Hoge paid their first hospital visit to the Fifth Street Hospital in St. Louis, where they were led into a ward containing eighty badly wounded men from the Fort Donelson battlefield. The sickening smells nearly overwhelmed Livermore when she entered, but she was determined to stay. A surgeon requested her assistance in helping change the dressings on the face of a young man. When the old bandages came off, revealing that the man had lost much of his jaw along with his tongue, Mary reacted with revulsion. It was "worse than anything I had imagined," she would later write. She nearly fainted and had to be assisted out of the room. Returning to the ward, she soon succumbed to nausea and had to be led out again, unable to bear the smell and the horrifying disfigurements of the men around her. After her third exit from the ward, a surgeon told her bluntly, "A great many people cannot stay in hospitals, or render any service in them, they are so affected by the sights and smells. . . . I would not try to do anything here were I in your place." Livermore, furious with herself for being weak, refused to surrender in the face of such a challenge. Exercising "iron control," she reentered the ward, determined to overcome her faintness and nausea. Like scores of other nurses, she would teach herself to cope with the most frightful situations. Mary Livermore vowed never again to flee a hospital.[40]

That evening, alone in her room, she again confronted the horrors she had witnessed while reflecting on her introduction to a military hospital in war-time. Before the day ended, Livermore had interviewed a soldier who had spent two days and nights on the frozen battlefield before being removed following Fort Donelson's surrender, examined a delirious Confederate prisoner on the threshold of death moaning for his mother, and comforted a dying Union soldier who feared he had sinned too much to go to heaven. After

returning to her hotel, she could not eat, sleep, or even talk about her experiences. All night she paced around her room, unable to prevent herself from
thinking about what she had seen, worrying about whether she was up to the
task of nursing the wounded. But the long night finally passed. Her ordeal at
Fifth Street Hospital might have prompted a hasty retreat to the relative security of the Chicago office, but instead it had the opposite effect. Mary confronted and conquered her fear of the wounded soldiers and came away with
an even more passionate commitment to the Sanitary Commission. She continued her hospital tour with renewed determination.[41]

Livermore and Hoge spent several weeks in St. Louis visiting a number of
hospitals. They also watched soldiers march out from Benton Barracks and
down alongside the Mississippi River on their way to face the rebel army again
in Tennessee. Many regiments departed without doctors to accompany them,
without medical equipment or pharmaceutical supplies of any kind. Next, the
women traveled to Cairo, Illinois, where they visited regimental hospitals
established in private houses, carriage houses, even sheds. Dirty and poorly
staffed, these hospitals housed soldiers felled by camp illnesses, including
measles, typhoid fever, dysentery, and erysipelas. Some of the men suffered
from wounds as well. Sick soldiers often appeared even more dejected than
injured ones, for a wound bestowed a certain badge of valor that a case of
dysentery obviously did not. Patients in regimental hospitals were often cared
for by soldiers who were themselves convalescents. Livermore described these
men as "wholly worthless as nurses."[42] She believed in women's inherent
power to nurture the sick and dispirited. Convalescent soldier-nurses had
neither the God-given powers of nurturance nor the stamina of healthy female
nurses. However well intentioned male nurses might be, they were no substi-
tute for female volunteers.

Cairo's only well-run hospital was the General Hospital, or Brick Hospital,
as it became known, run by the Sisters of the Holy Cross. The nuns impressed
Livermore with their dedication and efficiency in the creation of a clean, well-
ordered, well-staffed facility. At Mound City, Illinois, Livermore also inspected a hospital staffed by Sisters of the Holy Cross, where she described
the mother superior of the order as "a gifted lady, of rare cultivation and
executive ability." Much as she admired the sisters, Livermore resented military surgeons' widespread prejudice against the use of Protestant nurses, a
bias that was well known within the army and the Sanitary Commission. When
she asked one physician why he disliked Protestants, he responded, "Your
Protestant nurses are always finding some mare's -nest or other . . . that they

can't let alone." Moreover, Protestant volunteers "all write for the papers, and the story finds its way into print, and directly we are in hot water." Doctors believed that nuns obeyed orders unquestioningly and never wrote for publication.[43]

Wounded and sick soldiers did not care whether their nurses wrote for the papers. Livermore, who was both a Protestant and a journalist, quickly learned nursing skills, those involved in both assisting doctors and dealing with the other needs of soldiers. She knew how to establish an easy rapport with these men, who expressed great appreciation for all that she did. Disabled or even illiterate soldiers often asked Livermore to write letters to their loved ones, a service she provided hundreds of times during the war. Frequently she spent time simply talking with lonely young men, who wanted nothing more than a sympathetic person to converse with. On occasion she chatted with Confederate prisoners. While in Mound City, she encountered a young Confederate officer, who remembered her as the Jones children's teacher in Mecklenburg County. As a ten-year-old child he had been a playmate from a neighboring plantation.[44]

Early in the war Livermore also learned how to cut through red tape to find relief for individual soldiers in need. In one instance she interceded on behalf of a patriotic young man, a member of the Livermores' Universalist congregation, who had joined the Chicago Mercantile Battery despite physical infirmities that should have kept him out of military service. Hospitalized in St. Louis, he could not win a discharge because of problems with his paperwork and a recent moratorium on furloughs of any kind. After revealing to a clerk that the soldier's first name had been misspelled on an official form, Livermore next sought permission for a discharge from his commanding officer. In order to facilitate her request, she considered bribing the lieutenant who handled his appointments, noting, "I had had previous experience in this line." While the lieutenant "sat smoking in the office, with his heels higher than his head," she used contacts with another officer to secure a conference with General Samuel Curtis, whom she knew personally. Curtis granted the discharge and gave her permission to take the sick man home. As the historian Nina Silber has pointed out, Sanitary Commission volunteers, because they had no formal relationship with the army and no concerns about currying favor or seeking promotions, could operate as independent and often effective advocates for Union soldiers.[45] While careful not to offend high-ranking officers, Mary Livermore never seemed overawed by them and did not hesitate to seek their help when she needed it.

Returning home in early April 1862, Livermore wrote a report with Hoge concluding that sincere efforts were being made to care for Union soldiers. Although they had found medical care to be uneven, there was no evidence that sanitary supplies from Chicago were failing to reach their intended destinations. They were able to reassure the public in this regard.[46]

When Livermore arrived in Chicago, she found the city in an uproar over news of the recent battle at Shiloh, Tennessee. Although Shiloh culminated in Union victory, the battle was a bloody one. Confederates, led by Generals A. S. Johnston and P. G. T. Beauregard, had surprised Union forces in Tennessee with a massive attack that began literally as General Ulysses S. Grant was breakfasting. In several days of intense fighting, Grant rallied his soldiers and finally beat back the Confederate offensive, but appalling casualties on both sides tempered northern enthusiasm for the victory. "There was scarcely a hamlet in the whole Northwest that was not in mourning," Livermore would recall. Newspapers printed lists of the dead, including many young men from the Chicago Light Artillery. After a local committee raised money to bring their bodies north for burial, coffins began to arrive in Chicago, a grim and personal reminder of the cost of war. Moreover, General Grant, once hailed as the man who would quickly crush the Confederates, emerged from the battle with a tarnished reputation, for the northern public viewed the Confederate surprise offensive as a sign of his weakness. The Republican *Chicago Tribune* advised its readers to withhold criticism of Grant "until the facts are known." The city's mood presented a marked contrast to its celebratory spirit only weeks before when Fort Donelson had fallen.[47]

The battle of Shiloh drained supplies and cash from the Chicago Sanitary Commission, but the city rallied to support the commission's work with additional contributions of food, clothing, and money. The commission stationed a distributing agent at Pittsburg Landing and dispatched another agent to travel with the army as it approached Corinth, Mississippi. The U.S. Sanitary Commission outfitted five hospital steamers to evacuate the wounded from Shiloh, with some of the surgeons, nurses, and supplies coming from the Chicago branch. The Chicago Board of Trade donated $2,000 to outfit two ships to transport wounded Illinois soldiers home.[48]

By the summer of 1862, patriotic fervor had begun to wane in Chicago and elsewhere in the North. In the warm weather, thousands of soldiers suffered from camp diseases. Even worse, the military situation appeared bleak in both the eastern and western theaters during the summer and fall. The battle of Antietam brought unprecedented slaughter and "no substantial advantage,"

Livermore would recall. In the West, "military movements were not crowned with the success the public had expected from previous rapid victories." After Grant's victory at Fort Donelson, many in the North had predicted that the Mississippi River would fall quickly under Union control. Instead, the Confederacy held fast to Vicksburg, creating a bottleneck that General Grant seemed unable to break. Responding to the rising death toll and poor morale, Daniel Livermore published a book titled *Comfort in Sorrow: Token for the Bereaved*, which he hoped would provide solace to families in mourning by emphasizing God's everlasting love and the immortality of the soul.[49]

As the Confederacy experienced its high tide of military success, tragedy befell the Jones family of Mecklenburg County, Virginia, when young James Jr. died in the spring of 1862. In May of the previous year he had accepted a commission as captain of Company E, First Virginia Infantry Battalion, where he earned a reputation for strict adherence to military regulations and for his adeptness in drilling the men of his company. He was also known to brag about his military ability, for a fellow officer complained in a private letter that "Captain Jones is a man a little cracked on military matters, [and] expects to be a Major General before the war is over."[50]

The First Battalion fought in Stonewall Jackson's Shenandoah Valley campaign. On March 23, 1862, as part of a diversionary strategy, Jackson sent his Confederates against federal soldiers at Kernstown, Virginia. They attacked boldly but sustained heavy losses. James Jones was one of the more than seven hundred Confederate casualties at Kernstown. Displaying the braggadocio for which he had become known, Jones, according to one fellow officer, was last observed "to get upon a stump and wave his sword, cheering his men forward, and then fall headlong to the earth." Severely wounded, he died in a military hospital two days later.[51] Mary Livermore did not learn of Jamie's death until later in the war, but she no doubt read about the ultimate success of Jackson's Valley Campaign, representing another setback for the Union cause.

Confederate military success and declining morale in the North led to a drop in contributions to the Sanitary Commission. To address this problem, the national leadership called a meeting of female representatives from the major branch offices in Washington. Mary Livermore and Jane Hoge would represent Chicago. Mired in the same sense of gloom that afflicted many of her countrymen and women, Livermore recalled leaving for the Woman's Council meeting in November 1862 with a heavy heart.[52]

Gatherings of the Woman's Council served a variety of purposes. They allowed the national commission a means by which to learn about the collection of money and supplies on the local level, and they provided women representatives from throughout the North a chance to meet, share ideas, and support one another. At this first gathering of the Woman's Council, members hoped to find better and more efficient ways to keep federal troops equipped with food and supplies. When Livermore and Hoge were called upon to report about activities of the Chicago branch, they shared their belief that the Northwest regarded itself as independent and "impatient of strict rules." They asked for and received permission for their branch to have considerable latitude to carry out business in its "own way," while also following national guidelines.[53]

At the conclusion of the meetings, Livermore and Hoge, along with other women of the Sanitary Commission, met with President Lincoln at the White House. Many years later Mary Livermore would recollect the president's demeanor that evening. "A deeper gloom rested on his face than on that of any person I had ever seen," she wrote in her memoirs. Jane Hoge agreed, remembering Lincoln's sad expression and stooped posture. "He seemed to be literally staggering under a nation's burden," she recalled. Frederick Law Olmsted, secretary of the USSC, introduced each member of the delegation, and Lincoln shook each woman's hand in a mechanical and awkward manner, until he was introduced to the Chicago women. His expression brightened. "So you are from Chicago!" he said, adding, "You are not scared by Washington mud, then; for you can beat us all to pieces in that." Livermore and Hoge chatted amicably with the president about Chicago, its weather, and its recent news until the conversation turned back to the larger group and the subject of war. Lincoln's gloom returned.[54]

Hoge asked the president if he might offer some encouragement about the army's prospects. *"What if I have none to give?"* he responded. After an uncomfortable silence, another woman asked the source of his discouragement. Lincoln replied that the army had been depleted by an excessive number of furloughs and by desertion. The women were shocked by the president's words, for, Mary later wrote, "in our glorifying of the soldiers we had not conceived of *our* men becoming deserters." Was the president enforcing the death penalty against such a crime, the women asked? Lincoln replied that "if I should go to shooting men by scores for desertion, I should soon have such a hullaboo about my ears as I haven't had yet." Lincoln also told the Sanitary Commission women that the northern public lacked resolve, "the determination to fight this war through." Mary Livermore recorded Lincoln's belief that "the army, like the nation, has become demoralized with the idea that the war is to be ended, the nation united, and peace restored, by *strategy*, and not by hard desperate fighting." The hour-long session apparently ended on a somewhat upbeat note with Lincoln urging the women, "Go on in your good work! God bless you!" The women agreed among themselves not to discuss their meeting with the press, fearful of how it might be reported in the newspapers, but Livermore and Hoge both later wrote about the episode in their memoirs.[55]

Upset by the president's words, Mary did not sleep much that night and neither did Jane Hoge. The following day the two women returned to the White House for a private meeting with Lincoln. Livermore did not record the reason for their second visit. In daylight the president's face revealed even more gravely "the ravages which care, anxiety, and overwork had wrought," an appearance that did nothing to reassure the sleep-deprived women. Admitting "timidly" that they had been depressed by his words the previous evening, they asked if he regarded the national situation as hopeless. Lincoln responded, "Oh, no! . . . our affairs are by no means hopeless, for we have the right on our side." He spoke of the preliminary Emancipation Proclamation, issued a few months earlier, which had freed slaves in parts of the Confederacy unoccupied by the Union Army. But the northern people and their army must be prepared for continued "agony and suffering," he said, before the war could end. Livermore and Hoge left the White House feeling that the president had given them only a "morsel of hope." Once outside, weary and dejected, they walked down Pennsylvania Avenue but could not speak to each other. Both dissolved into tears. Ultimately the experience would galvanize Livermore and Hoge much the same way that Mary's first hospital experience in St. Louis had done a few months earlier. She recalled: "We were women, and could not *fight* for the country. But the instinct of patriotism within our hearts, which had lain dormant when our beloved land knew no danger, was now developed into a passion."[56]

While in Washington the two women also met with Dorothea Dix, federal superintendent of women nurses. In June 1861 Secretary of War Simon Cameron had appointed Dix to head the nursing program, thereby making her the first woman in America ever to hold a position of executive authority in the U.S. government. At first, Dix wielded complete control over the selection and hiring of nurses and considerable power over their placement in individual hospitals. Early in the war she had appointed Livermore and Hoge her recruiters in the West. Livermore looked forward to the interview, for she admired Dix's prewar career as an advocate of improved conditions in institutions for prisoners and the mentally handicapped.[57]

Livermore grew to like Dix personally, describing her with somewhat mixed praise as attractive and graceful, having "very winning manners when she chose to use them," and complete dedication to the cause of nursing. She also appreciated the difficulty of Dix's position. Surgeons resented her, and often bypassed her authority. As Livermore put it, "[Many] surgeons in the hospitals did not work harmoniously with Miss Dix." As an unmarried woman and one whom many came to resent, Dix became a lighting rod within months of taking over the nursing position. At times Livermore defended her. Complaining about army gossip and its tendency to slander women, Livermore wrote in 1865, "I have been told by army officers that they had seen Miss Dix drunk in the army–which has about as much truth as if they had told me they had seen the Virgin Mary drunk in the army."[58]

At other times Livermore joined the critics, censuring Dix for insisting that all nurses be "over thirty years of age, plain almost to repulsion in dress, and devoid of personal attractions." One of Dix's biographers has claimed that Livermore and other critics have overstated the case, that Dix allowed more flexibility than many realized. According to this defense, Dix adhered to theoretical restrictions based on age, fashion, and physical appearance, but did not make it a practice to reject nurses for being too young or too pretty. Nevertheless, because of her preoccupation with protecting the reputation of army nurses, Dix probably did reject some applicants who were well qualified, and Mary Livermore found this intolerable. After inspecting countless hospitals with inadequate medical personnel, Livermore had little patience for nursing shortages that were grounded in irrelevant rules. Whether she communicated this sentiment to Dix at their November meeting is not known. Livermore probably faulted Dix as well for her failure, throughout the war, to engage in nursing patients herself.[59]

Before they left Washington, Hoge and Livermore toured the Soldiers' Home, an institution designed to provide a place for soldiers to eat, sleep, or seek medical attention while traveling between their hospitals or regiments and their homes. Volunteers also helped soldiers with personal needs such as purchasing railway tickets or processing paperwork to request back pay. Several months later Livermore and Hoge would join a committee in Chicago to create such a home in their community. The city's first Soldiers' Home would open in July 1863.[60]

On December 8, 1862, following their return from Washington, Mary Livermore and Jane Hoge were named associate managers of the USSC's Chicago branch, now receiving annual salaries of $1,000 for work they had previously performed as volunteers. Their status as professionals marked a new direction for Livermore and Hoge as individuals and a significant trend in the history of female benevolence. "Once branch women became paid professionals," the historian Judith Giesberg has written regarding the Chicago office, "women's political culture had taken a very important step away from its antebellum dependence on the strictly voluntary labor of middle-class women."[61] Livermore and Hoge had proved themselves to be dedicated, efficient, and cooperative public servants. Their administrative abilities were beyond question. Moreover, they worked well with the national and local commission power structures, with the army, and with the business and political communities in Chicago. As the dreary fall and winter of 1862 gave way to a new year, Livermore and Hoge made ambitious new plans to involve western women more fully in the war effort.

CHAPTER 5

---◆•••◆---

God's Missionary Work

T WENTY-FIVE YEARS after the Civil War ended, Mary Livermore wrote a letter to a friend in which she reminisced about the Confederate rebellion and its meaning to her life and to the nation. "War is hell," she said, quoting General Sherman, but war can also be "God's missionary."[1] By 1863 the Civil War had become a moral and religious crusade for Mary Livermore. Casting the war in religious terms helped inspire her to work harder and do more. It inspired her to advocate the abolition of slavery openly and even courageously. And it allowed her to accept her new role as public figure. By the end of 1863, Livermore was ready to challenge her old notions about separate spheres and embrace a more dynamic vision of female activism.

As the momentous year began, Livermore and Jane Hoge, as newly appointed associate managers of the Chicago Sanitary Commission, faced a daunting task. The Union Army had lost a major battle at Fredericksburg, Virginia, in December 1862, leaving people in the North with new anxieties and questions about the direction of the war effort. Public morale had never been lower. On January 1, 1863, President Lincoln had signed the long-awaited Emancipation Proclamation, adding antislavery to the northern war aim of reuniting the states. Lincoln's move played well with progressives like

Livermore and Hoge but troubled many in the Northwest and throughout the nation, for slavery remained a controversial subject.

With military casualties high and civilian morale low, Livermore and Hoge became convinced that women could, indeed must, participate in the war effort more fully. Persuading women of this would be challenging, however. Accustomed to working in small local benevolent efforts, some women would be reluctant to cede authority to the large, bureaucratic, male-led Sanitary Commission, to embrace a public and "scientific" approach to benevolence. The Sanitary Commission, historian Paula Baker has written, "moved women's traditional roles of support, healing, and nurturance into the public sphere."[2] Moreover, Livermore and Hoge were asking their countrywomen to give at least tacit endorsement to a political and military agenda, a concept that was foreign to their traditional sphere. Together they would act tirelessly as leaders, organizers, and, ultimately, inspirational speakers for the Sanitary Commission.

To give herself the flexibility to travel when commission business demanded it, Livermore decided to hire additional household help. Good domestic help was not easy to find in wartime Chicago. When scores of laundresses left the Garden City to take jobs as farm hands, replacing men who had joined the army, Livermore quickly devised a solution. Along with fifty other women, she helped to create a cooperative laundry. Though cumbersome at first, the laundry ultimately cut members' expenses in half. In addition, she relied on relatives to assist with child care. By 1863 her daughters Lizzie and Etta were nine and twelve years of age, old enough to be left with their father. The girls' adult cousin Adelaide Livermore stayed with them when both parents traveled.[3]

By all indications, Daniel Livermore fully supported the war effort and his wife's increasing activism. Mary later wrote, "My husband was very desirous that I should enroll myself regularly in the work of the Commission." Theirs had always been an unusually egalitarian marriage. He began to play a more central role as the children's caregiver, often taking a night train home from his ministerial travels in order to be present for a birthday party or a school program. Although she dropped all other public work, including her many charities, Mary continued to help Daniel by writing articles for the *New Covenant*, now as "regular contributor" instead of associate editor. The *New Covenant* supported the war policies of the Lincoln administration unwaveringly.[4]

With her children cared for and her husband in full support of her activities, Mary Livermore began to implement an ambitious plan for the Chicago Sanitary Commission. In January 1863 she wrote a letter to Dr. John S. Newberry, a highly regarded official who headed the Commission's Western Department, headquartered in Louisville. She informed Newberry that she and Jane Hoge "have decided to organize an aid Society in every county town [or county seat] in the Northwest where one does not exist, which shall be pledged to organize auxiliary societies in every town of the county." Through correspondence she had already assisted in the creation of forty-three aid societies in localities throughout the Northwest.[5]

Now she and Hoge envisioned a more systematic form of organization that involved plans to travel extensively so that they might assist in the organization of new societies. Several local societies had already been started in the vicinity of Chicago, including one in Ottawa, the La Salle County seat. With Hoge in Mississippi with the army, Livermore visited Ottawa in order to study the local society's organization and tactics. A man she identified as Major Moreau accompanied her and lectured to patriotic Ottawans about the importance of the commission's work. The next day the pair would travel to Aurora, seat of Kane County, to encourage incipient local aid efforts there. Again, Moreau lectured; Livermore organized. Mary Livermore had not yet accepted the idea of speaking in public. Throughout her life she had adhered to the notion that men should be public speakers and women should work behind the scenes. When the activist Jane Gray Swisshelm visited Livermore in Chicago that same month, she noted Livermore's unwillingness to move beyond a traditional outlook. "I visited Chicago early in January '63 [and] met Mrs. Livermore," Swisshelm wrote to a friend. "[I] found her very much opposed not only to woman suffrage but to women meddling in politics or otherwise getting out of their sphere."[6] Events in the coming months would cause Livermore to modify her position.

Much of Livermore's time continued to revolve around the Sanitary Commission's rooms at McVicker's Theatre on Madison Street. The commission occupied several large offices under the theater, with sewing rooms above tended by seamstresses working thirty to forty machines all day. Theatricals–some with racy titles like *The Female Gambler*–ran at night. Livermore almost certainly disapproved of Mr. McVicker's entertainments, while at the same time heartily endorsing his patriotism, for he leased rooms to the commission at a nominal rent. Livermore and Hoge worked in an office, nine by fifteen feet, to the side of the front door. A bank of windows faced the main supply room, while a single window looked out on the street. Because of the volume of people and supplies passing through McVicker's on a daily basis, the commission rooms were rarely quiet. "The whole impression was one of labor, noise, and confusion," according to Sarah Henshaw, who wrote an official history of the Chicago branch.[7]

Account books provide some indication of daily arrivals at the Chicago office. On a typical day in November 1863, for example, the office received 59 barrels of vegetables; 5 barrels of apples; 25 barrels, 32 bags, and 6 boxes of onions; 4 kegs and 1 barrel of pickles; 5 boxes of potatoes; 4 boxes of dried fruit; 1 box of beets; and 2 barrels of "Sour Kraut." These items would be quickly inspected, repackaged, and stamped with the Sanitary Commission's label to discourage theft, then sent south through the Louisville office. The atmosphere in the McVicker's Theatre rooms often bordered on frantic, a frenzy Jane Hoge illustrated when she wrote to John Newberry in August 1864, "We are moving heaven & earth to fill your requisition of vegetables, are purchasing & begging all we can."[8]

Although notable Chicago men held positions of authority in the commission, led by Judge Mark Skinner and later Ezra McCagg as president, and E. W. Blatchford as treasurer, four people ran the day-to-day operations of the main commission rooms. Livermore called them "constant habitues of the little office." John Freeman acted as shipping clerk, coordinating the deliveries and packing and repacking boxes. Livermore appreciated his "keen sense of the ludicrous," which helped keep the entire office laughing. William Goodsmith, whose duties included purchasing and paying for supplies and transacting business with banks, provided a counterpoint to Freeman, for he was serious and precise, but, like Freeman, reliable and trustworthy. When the commission could not supply a hospital with enough of some item it needed through donations, Goodsmith would purchase extra food and supplies in order to fill the order. Hoge and Livermore coordinated activities of the local aid societies with the Chicago branch. They tried not to be absent from the city at the same time, so that one of them was available to handle any problem or crisis that arose. "I have every confidence in her ability," Livermore said of Hoge, calling her "a noble, faithful, honorable woman."[9]

Mary Livermore wrote an account of a "typical" day in the life of the Chicago branch which was published as a U.S. Sanitary Commission bulletin. The essay provides a fascinating glimpse of this important regional office and the range of activities that she and Hoge juggled. On days when she did not travel on commission business, Livermore's workday began before 9:00 A.M., when she sent her children to school and then boarded a streetcar for the theater. The first shipment of articles would have been received, with the ever-dedicated John Freeman counting, sorting, stamping, repacking, and shipping its contents to hospitals in need. Her first duty might be to meet with ladies of an "Aid Society in another State" who came with news of their most recent fundraising activity and who sought reassurance that the commission was indeed a reliable organization and the best means of coordinating local efforts.[10]

Next, Livermore dealt with the mail. One letter announced the impending arrival of a shipment of hospital stores. A second carried complaints about an unanswered letter; the copying book revealed a reply has been sent, though apparently lost in the mail. A third related a "mythical story" of medical incompetence by doctors and nurses in the field, while a fourth came from a woman urgently seeking appointment as a nurse. Letter number five was from a widow desperate for news of her only son. Number six came from a distant town requesting direction for the creation of a patriotic society. Seven was penned by a group of nine-year-old girls who had earned and collectively donated five dollars for the sick soldiers. In number eight the writers begged Livermore or Hoge to visit their town and "re-kindle the flagging zeal" of townswomen. Nine brought the tragic news of a nurse's death, just a few months after the commission had sent her to Tennessee. While attempting to answer each letter, Livermore also received callers at the Madison Street rooms: parents searching for news of their soldier sons; men from city hospitals in need of shirts, slippers, or combs; nurses about to depart for Memphis, requesting advice and direction; a twelve-year-old messenger boy from Admiral David Porter's gunboat with a personal note from the admiral requesting that the boy be taken to the Soldiers' Home for the time being. At any given time, from two to three hundred letters might be awaiting Livermore's attention.[11]

After long hours of contending with inquiries, favors, services, complaints, and donations, Livermore's workday ended, usually between 6:00 and 7:00 P.M. More often than not, despite John Freeman's efforts to create an atmosphere of levity, she would be emotionally and physically spent. "Wearied in body, and saturated, mentally, with the passing streams of others' sorrows," she would again board a streetcar for home, where the "cheerful companionship" of her children, an exchange of news with Daniel, and a hearty meal prepared by Martha, her Norwegian immigrant cook, brightened the end of her day. Monday through Friday belonged to the commission, while Saturdays and Sundays were reserved for the family, church work, and the *New Covenant*.[12]

Increasingly Livermore acted as both organizer and public defender of the Sanitary Commission. Traveling frequently to mobilize groups of local women, she showed a marked talent for inspiring volunteers. In one instance she visited an aid society with a membership of eight to ten. As a result of her organizational efforts, its membership quickly jumped to forty. One USSC colleague likened Livermore's work to that of a bishop ministering to his diocese, asking on one occasion, "What happy women are now enjoying Mrs. Livermore's apostolical ministrations?" Livermore also put her pen to use as propagandist for the commission. She often used the *New Covenant* as a vehicle through which to advertise the USSC's activities as well as fend off criticism of the organization. She posted routine notices about the arrival of supplies from local societies. For example, one article in 1862 announced the efforts of ladies in Whitewater, Lake Maria, and Rubicon, Wisconsin. In another she refuted charges that Sanitary Commission supplies had failed to reach soldiers in the field because dishonest medical and military personnel appropriated items for personal use.[13]

Mary Livermore also defended the Sanitary Commission against what she regarded as a serious competitor: the United States Christian Commission. Begun in 1861 as an extension of the YMCA, the Christian Commission focused some of its attention on the physical needs of soldiers but for the most part concentrated on their spiritual needs. Like the USSC, the USCC operated through the assistance of many local societies. Both organizations maintained that a sturdy Christian character made for a strong soldier. But there were also significant differences between the two groups. The Sanitary Commission was organized according to well-defined rules and regulations and used a paid staff of traditional Protestants, while the Christian Commission's operations were run by evangelical volunteers. In Chicago the USCC's leadership included the powerful and charismatic Dwight Moody, whose Civil War revivalism would propel him into a national career as one of evangelism's late-nineteenth-century titans. Following the battle of Shiloh, during a religious service for medical volunteers near the battlefield, Moody had clashed with Sanitary Commission agent Robert Collyer, a highly respected Chicago Unitarian minister. While reminding listeners of divine mercy, Moody had also railed against sin. Collyer refuted him, winning applause from Sanitary Commission volunteers.[14]

Mary Livermore, a friend of Robert Collyer, shared his disapproval of the

Christian Commission's approach to religious proselytizing in army camps. Although she avoided public disputes with USCC agents, she believed with Collyer that dying soldiers needed to be told of God's love and forgiveness, not God's wrath. In *My Story of the War*, Livermore recounted a humorous episode that illustrates her views about evangelism in the army. On one of her many trips to visit soldiers and hospitals in the western theater, she heard a Chicago soldier mimicking an evangelical preacher to an audience of fellow soldiers. As the young man harangued his listeners for their sins, they would shout out other alleged sins and appropriate punishments. At first Livermore feared that the soldiers were being irreverent, but then someone noticed her presence and called out, "I say, Harry, you'd better wind up your gospel yarn, and see who's behind you!" At that point Livermore realized the joke and joined in the merriment "raised at the expense of the counterfeit chaplain."[15]

If Livermore felt uneasy about confronting members of the Christian Commission in public, she did not hesitate to state her objections in writing. In 1865, after consulting Senator Lyman Trumbull of Illinois, she wrote first to Secretary of War Edwin M. Stanton and then at his direction to Colonel James A. Hardie, inspector general of the War Department, about a problem troubling the Army Mission of the Northwestern Conference of Universalists, founded eighteen months earlier. Its goal was to send religious reading material and missionaries to camps and hospitals throughout the Union Army. She claimed that the Christian Commission, which disagreed doctrinally with this group, "regards these missionaries with disfavor and hinders their work, where it has the power, shutting them from hospitals, even when sick and dying men have asked [for] their visits." Livermore continued, stating emphatically, "Soldiers of Freedom should have liberty of conscience," and concluded by asking that the Universalists' mission be given "equal powers" with that of the Christian Commission.[16] Although Livermore sent this letter just a few weeks before the war ended, and may not have received a response, its tone conveys her strong belief that liberal Christians must take a stand against orthodoxy.

As a Sanitary Commission official, Livermore also feared the Christian Commission's potential to rival the USSC in the search for volunteers and the collection of supplies. Jane Hoge shared her concern, writing to John Newberry in the summer of 1863 about the "increasingly popular" USCC and its potential to raise supplies "that we should have received." But she had recently met with Dwight Moody, who assured her that the majority of the Christian Commission's supporters "heartily endorse the San. Com., & desire to act through it." In 1864 Livermore was still troubled by the evangelical group, complaining in a letter to Robert Thorne about the USCC's "pretending friendliness and yet all the while seeking to undermine us."[17] Livermore and Hoge would continue to seek ways of ensuring that their organization remained the premier volunteer agency in the Northwest.

Two events in 1863 contributed to Mary Livermore's growing self-confidence and emerging importance as a leader. The first was a trip she took to Vicksburg with the Sanitary Commission, the second a fundraising fair that started small and became a national sensation. The year would represent a major turning point in her life.

In March 1863, she departed down the Mississippi River with a delegation of Sanitary Commission volunteers and 3,500 boxes of supplies, including large shipments of vegetables for the "scorbutic patients"–those who suffered from scurvy. The delegation would visit every hospital from Cairo, Illinois, to Young's Point, near Vicksburg, the last Confederate stronghold on the Mississippi River. Already a veteran of several lengthy inspection tours, Livermore knew what to wear and what to bring. Her most useful accessory was a pair of knee-high rubber boots as protection against the mud. She also brought crackers, Japanese tea, a teapot and small oil lamp to heat water, condensed milk, and sugar to be used both for herself and for needy soldiers. As she always did before leaving on a trip, Livermore placed notices in Chicago newspapers, volunteering to take messages or small parcels to soldiers along her route. She would return to Chicago bearing messages from soldiers to their families, the saddest ones, of course, from those near death. Her experiences as a Civil War nurse enabled Livermore to empathize with the wounded and ill men. They would also help make her a phenomenally popular interpreter of American culture and life in her postwar career as a lyceum lecturer. As she traveled, giving speeches across the nation, soldiers or their families would sometimes approach Livermore because they recognized her name and remembered her many acts of kindness. In most instances she would not recall the specific cases, both because there were so many sad stories and because she had learned to keep a certain emotional distance. "Hospital and army life," she wrote, "after the first few weeks, mercifully bred a temporary stoicism, that enabled one to see and hear any form or tale of horror without deep emotion."[18]

During her 1863 trip she would have ample opportunity to employ her skills in dealing with military personnel. By the midpoint of the war, Livermore had become adept at "reading" the personalities and temperaments of individual officers in order to discern the best way to approach them to get what she wanted for the sick soldiers. Whenever possible, she chose a nonconfrontational approach, although she could be forceful when necessary. A sanitary agent who accompanied her between Memphis and Young's Point noted that "Mrs. L. was quite exacting in her demands upon the time and services of the Boat." She was even more forceful when she encountered an inebriated officer, for drunkenness was something she could never abide. Livermore could be ferocious in seeking disciplinary action or removal of the offending officer. One such instance occurred at Milliken's Bend, near Vicksburg, when she toured a regimental hospital housing two hundred sick men. With no one to care for them except a surgeon "dead-drunk in bed," Livermore set forth to cheer up the dispirited and ill soldiers by ministering to them with her assortment of tea, milk, and crackers. Then she sought out Surgeon General E. B. Wolcott, a Wisconsin man, to whom she related the sorry story of the hospital, which, coincidentally, housed some Wisconsin soldiers. In due course Wolcott ordered the soldiers' transfer to better facilities in Nashville, and the drunken surgeon was sent home "in disgrace."[19]

Livermore also learned how to confront military authorities from her friend and fellow Illinoisan, Mary Ann Bickerdyke. Livermore and Bickerdyke had a common first name but very different backgrounds and temperaments. While Livermore was well educated, ladylike, respectable, and precise about administrative duties, Bickerdyke was uneducated, blunt, earthy, and oblivious to rules and regulations. She was also fiercely dedicated to helping soldiers in need, and her unflagging energy and total dedication impressed many, including Livermore. Unwilling to be dominated by anyone, including nursing superintendent Dorothea Dix, Bickerdyke acted as an independent operator, holding no title and receiving no pay. Eventually she became a sanitary commission agent. Even then, her unorthodox practices alienated many. On occasion Bickerdyke purchased supplies and sent the bills to the Sanitary Commission, a clear violation of the USSC's standard procedures. Mary Livermore and Jane Hoge quietly raised the money to settle these debts from among their friends and Bickerdyke's admirers. Even Livermore fussed at Bickerdyke for her carelessness about paperwork, reminding her in one instance to thank a group of Milwaukee ladies for their contribution, "and do it *immediately*. Now, don't delay it." Willing to travel with the army and dedicated to serving wounded and sick men wherever she found them, Bickerdyke was repaid by the adoration of soldiers who called her "Mother Bickerdyke." On rare occasions when Bickerdyke left "her boys" for a brief furlough, she stayed with the Livermores in Chicago.[20]

While residing in Memphis, Bickerdyke introduced two plans to improve hospital conditions. Angered at the prospect of having to buy what she regarded as substandard milk and eggs from Confederate-sympathizing civilians, Bickerdyke used one of her Illinois furloughs to organize a campaign to encourage the donation of cows and chickens, at one point turning the commission rooms in McVicker's Theatre into "a huge hennery." Accomplishing her mission within her thirty-day furlough, Bickerdyke arrived in Memphis at the head of a column that included one hundred head of cattle and one thousand hens, proudly announcing, "These are *loyal* cows and hens." For the next several months, Livermore sent Bickerdyke money from patriotic citizens in the Northwest to purchase additional cows and hens.[21]

When Livermore visited Bickerdyke in Memphis at Gayoso Hospital in March 1863, "Mother" had developed a new procedure for recycling hospital linen. Instead of destroying used hospital gowns and sheets, she would wash and reuse them. Requisitioning washing machines from the Sanitary Commission, she employed between fifty and seventy contrabands, or former slaves, to do the labor. She eventually applied this system to all the hospitals in Memphis, which cared for close to ten thousand patients. Although Bickerdyke had long since earned the admiration of leading generals, including Ulysses S. Grant, who had given her a pass that allowed her to travel wherever she pleased, and William T. Sherman, who was her personal favorite, she occasionally found herself at loggerheads with other officers. The medical director in Memphis was a young man, dedicated, efficient, and anxious to be regarded by all, including Bickerdyke, as "in charge." Livermore would later recall that "he disapproved of Mrs. Bickerdyke's laundry; chiefly, it seemed, because he had not organized it." Moreover, as a Catholic, he preferred that nursing duties be handled by the Sisters of Mercy.[22]

Although Bickerdyke did not care what anyone thought of her so long as she was left alone, the medical director took it upon himself to dismantle Bickerdyke's laundry. One evening, on returning from a visit to a nearby hospital, she learned that he had ordered her entire workforce returned to a contraband camp by 9:00 the following morning. Immediately she decided to pay a visit to General Stephen A. Hurlbut's headquarters, telling Livermore, "If Dr.——is going to be ugly, he'll find two can play at that game, and a woman is better at it than a man." She added, "Get yourself ready, Mary

Livermore, to go with me!" At first Livermore hesitated, suggesting to Bickerdyke that her nocturnal visit to the general might be ill advised. It was
raining torrentially, the streets of Memphis had been wrecked by departing
Confederates, and the city lacked street lighting. Bickerdyke responded with
characteristic brusqueness, accusing Mary of being a coward and announcing
that she would take a driver and go without her. As usual, Bickerdyke prevailed. Livermore agreed to make the trip.[23]

They arrived at General Hurlbut's headquarters, only to learn that he had
retired for the night. Probably recognizing Bickerdyke's reputation for persistence, the general agreed to leave his bed for a meeting and, on hearing her
story, signed papers allowing her to keep the contraband workers and her
laundry. The women returned to their hospital in triumph in the pouring rain.
The following morning the medical director angrily confronted Bickerdyke
and threatened to have her expelled from Memphis for failing to honor his
authority. She responded, "And, doctor, I guess you hadn't better get into a
row with me, for whenever anybody does[,] one of us two always goes to the
wall, and 'tain't never me!'" Apparently the young man saw the humor in the
situation and overcame his anger. Livermore recalled the episode in her memoirs as another example of a "clever man . . . dominated by the inborn belief
that all women were to play 'second fiddle' to him."[24]

More often than not, Livermore preferred to cajole rather than confront,
firmly convinced that a more traditionally "female" approach worked well
with military men. With some, she drew on her contacts within the Sanitary
Commission or within the political, business, or reform elite of the Northwest.
Chicagoans, in particular, felt a strong kinship with others from their region.
By mentioning a mutual acquaintance, she was often able to break the ice with
an unfamiliar officer. With others, she employed what she called her "amiable
woman" routine, combining small talk and sunny smiles with mild obsequi-
ousness. From her years working in benevolent reform movements, she knew
that such deference often yielded results.[25]

Although she prided herself on an ability to establish rapport with military
men, Livermore had a difficult time communicating with General Ulysses S.
Grant, commander of the western theater of the war. The first time she met
him, as part of a group of USSC women, she found him laconic and ill at ease.
"We would as soon have undertaken a *tête-à-tête* with the Sphinx itself" than
with this quiet man, she wrote. But if Grant did not want to chat, he did seem
willing to offer passes, escort, and transportation, when possible, on his dis-

patch boat, the *Fanny Ogden*, known to be the fastest boat in the western service.[26]

Livermore had occasion to visit with Grant privately a few days later. As a Sanitary Commission employee, she received numerous requests to intervene with generals on behalf of soldiers, especially those who believed that they had been wrongly punished. These men thought that a woman would have a better chance of pleading a case successfully with military officers. Knowing Grant's preoccupation with the Vicksburg campaign, Livermore did not want to ask a personal favor of the general unless she felt it to be absolutely necessary. Such a case presented itself when Livermore learned of twenty-one desperately ill soldiers whom the surgeons believed to be incurable. Because of bureaucratic difficulties–lost paperwork, problems with the mail, forbidden furloughs, or lack of escorts–none could win a discharge through the normal channels. Livermore decided to champion their case with Grant. "Having 'got the hang' of the General on the first interview," she knew how to approach him. One morning after breakfast she went to his office alone and requested an audience. She was told to pass up the line. Livermore then negotiated her way past several layers of staff, relating her mission to each. Finally, she reached Grant himself. She found him alone.[27]

The general sat at a table, one foot perched on a chair, surrounded by maps, reports, and letters. Startled to see a woman before him early in the morning, Grant gazed at her through his cigar smoke, then fumbled around to find her a chair, took off his hat, removed the cigar, and then, evidently without thinking, replaced both. Livermore chose to stand, no doubt emphasizing to Grant her intention not to take much of his valuable time. She repeated her well-rehearsed story in support of the ill soldiers, and Grant listened to her in silence. While keeping her recitation short, she also used "the earnestness that women felt in these sad cases during the war." He then asked why she had not approached his medical director, and she replied that if the "red tape" were not cut quickly, the men might die. She offered to accompany all twenty-one soldiers north and see that they were released to family members. Grant looked over the documents she had brought and promised an answer by the following day. The next evening a member of his staff arrived with the necessary discharge papers.[28] As she had done so many times already in this war, with junior and senior officers, Livermore had used her position as a Sanitary Commission woman to plead the cause of enlisted men successfully.

Even though Livermore found it more expedient to cajole than to confront

military men, she was willing to engage in verbal combat with a woman secessionist at her hotel in Memphis. The hotel's guests included many southern
sympathizers, among them a group of women waiting for permission to return
to Confederate lines. Livermore recorded their petty insults, which consisted
of leaving parlors when northern women entered, holding handkerchiefs over
their noses in the presence of Sanitary Commission women, and making loud,
derisive comments about "Northern white trash."[29]

One afternoon, a Confederate congressman's wife from Louisiana deigned
to speak with Livermore. She proclaimed that southern soldiers were gentlemen, on whose behalf women were sacrificing fine silks and jewelry in order
to devote all their money to their soldiers' care. Yankee soldiers, by contrast,
were guttersnipes, drunks, and barbarians whose womenfolk did not care
enough about them to nurse and nurture them properly. She complained
bitterly about her home being ransacked and her possessions burned by "*your*
soldiers." Livermore responded by defending northern women. Since "the
war is not impoverishing us as it is you," she noted disingenuously, women in
the North could still wear fine clothes and "provide everything needed for the
soldiers." She then matched the southern woman's invective with scorn of
equal severity. Given the woman's "unbearable" manners during the last two
weeks, Livermore expressed surprise that the soldiers had been generous
enough to spare her life instead of consigning her to "cremation with your
villa and furniture." Livermore added, "It is astonishing clemency that allows
you to be at large in this city, plotting against the government and insulting
loyal people." The conversation ended with the southern woman insisting that
England's intervention would be the South's salvation.[30]

By debating with this woman and others, Livermore demonstrated a willingness to engage in political discourse in a public setting. For more than two
decades she had expressed her views in writing about woman's appropriate
role as nurturer and redeemer of her family and community. Now, increasingly, she would broaden her focus to the political world and would express
those views in public. Her confrontation with a congressman's wife also illustrates her growing self-confidence as a public figure.

If Livermore remained unwavering in her belief in reunion of the states
and the abolition of slavery, she did, ultimately, find praise for Confederate
women on one level, admiring their complete commitment to their cause,
wrong though she thought it was. The congressman's wife she had so heatedly
debated in Memphis won permission to travel to Vicksburg, where she stayed
until that city surrendered in July 1863. Livermore later wrote that this woman

had "evinced courage as unyielding, and tenacity of purpose as unflinching, as any officer who wore the Confederate gray."[31]

Livermore's increasing willingness to engage in public discourse may also be seen in her experiences speaking to groups of soldiers. At Milliken's Bend she stayed in a "shebang," a hut constructed out of boards with a canvas roof. In the evening, groups of soldiers would crowd around her, especially the Chicago boys, eager to hear stories about home. A few were members of her Second Universalist Church. After she exhausted all the news she could think of, soldiers often pressed her to "draw on imagination" to keep them entertained. On a more serious note, Livermore encountered thousands of men ill with "miasmatic diseases" in the army's hospitals. Feeling a special affinity for sick and dejected men, whose lack of a war injury robbed them of claims to valor, she nursed more of these soldiers than those with battle wounds, and always tried her best to lift their morale. When time and numbers prevented her from speaking with soldiers individually, she would stand in the middle of a room and address them collectively. She had brought Sanitary Commission supplies to ease their suffering, she told them. These donations represented the nation's commitment to and pride in their soldiers, and the loyalty and sacrifice of the women they had left behind. She reminded the soldiers, too, of the righteousness of the cause for which they fought and of a loving God who was always nearby. She might then distribute crackers and brew tea in her little pot.[32] Her performances seemed to resonate with the soldiers. Although she did not regard this as public speaking, she must have sensed her ability to reach people with her voice just as she had learned to connect with her audiences by writing short stories and newspaper articles. Her trip to Vicksburg was yet another step toward Livermore's emergence as a public figure.

Livermore and her Sanitary Commission colleagues began their long journey back to Chicago during the last week of April 1863. Before she left, Mary enjoyed a trip by rowboat through one of the small creeks near Vicksburg, where she used Colonel Josiah Bissell's fieldglasses to view the city of Vicksburg, which had become the object of so much attention in the war. She could see soldiers, nurses, and servants at a military hospital there, standing in doorways, walking around the grounds, some on crutches.[33]

The Sanitary Commission delegation traveled home on an old three-decker boat called the *Maria Denning*. Its lowest deck held mules and horses bound for sale in St. Louis. The second deck housed contrabands, also destined for St. Louis, along with soldiers being furloughed or discharged, including the twenty-one men released to Livermore's care by General Grant. The top deck was reserved for officers and passengers such as herself. Livermore felt great sympathy for the freed slaves on board, some three to four hundred in number. At one point along the journey, a group of African Americans on shore waved white flags in an attempt to stop the boat and gain passage north. The captain of the *Maria Denning*, fearing a trick to ambush the vessel deep in enemy territory, refused to stop.[34]

Although Livermore could do nothing to help those stranded people, she did intervene to assist one slave child during her return journey. When the *Maria Denning* made a stop to pick up a large cargo of cotton at Lake Providence, she saw Ford Douglass on shore, an African American abolitionist she had known before the war. Born in slavery, Douglass had run away and settled in Chicago, where he earned a reputation as an antislavery orator. When the war began, he enlisted in the Ninety-fifth Illinois Volunteers. Before Livermore's arrival, Douglass had seized a young slave boy named Ben Morris from a plantation near New Orleans. The child's mother, who lived in Chicago, had implored Douglass to locate her son, and he was now awaiting an opportunity to send him on to Chicago. Douglass viewed Mary's appearance as providential.[35]

Livermore's friends aboard the *Maria Denning*, including an Illinois legislator, warned her of the risks. The state's Black Laws prescribed fines and imprisonment for anyone bringing a black person into the state. Moreover, in Cairo, at the southern tip of Illinois, the provost marshal made certain that every train was searched for African Americans as well as military deserters. Livermore decided to take the child despite the risks.[36] By helping to liberate Ben Morris, she made a tangible contribution to the antislavery movement she had supported philosophically in the past.

The first leg of the trip presented no problems. The child was whisked on board ship, where he remained in the company of contrabands on the middle deck. At Cairo, where the passengers boarded a train, the stakes rose. Fortunately, the train's porter, an African American whom Livermore knew from previous railway journeys, sympathized with her mission. He suggested that she hide the child in her sleeping berth under some blankets. Livermore would not hear of it, for the boy was filthy and covered in vermin. Always the proper lady, she would risk criminal prosecution to liberate him, but refused to jeopardize her personal hygiene and sense of propriety. The porter then assisted her in hiding Ben under her berth, in a space large enough to accommodate a suitcase but small enough not to be a likely target for inspection.[37]

The child fell asleep and immediately began snoring loudly. Livermore was aghast at the thought that such unladylike noise might be attributed to her, but, fearing that Ben might be discovered, she leaned back against the pillow and affected a snore, a pretense she kept up throughout the night. In Centralia, where the train changed crews, a friend tipped off Mary that the new conductor had once served on the "underground railroad," helping to emancipate slaves. As she later recalled, "my black boy's perils were over." They arrived in Chicago at midnight. The following day, a Sunday, Livermore searched the city's black churches, finally locating Ben's mother and reuniting her with her son. The story of Mary's role in smuggling Ben Morris to Chicago would be told and retold in the Livermore family for years.[38]

The boat and train trip to Chicago tested Livermore's physical and emotional endurance. Although the rescue of Ben Morris ended happily, two of the soldiers she accompanied home did not make it, one dying in Memphis, the other in a Chicago hotel room before his family could arrive to meet him. A despondent Mary Livermore succumbed to illness and took to her bed for several days. Among the Sanitary Commission workers in Tennessee and Mississippi, she had been the only one to escape "swamp fever" during their spring tour. Now it was her turn.[39]

On July 4, 1863, the city of Chicago held a celebration to inaugurate its new Soldiers' Home. Modeled after the institution Mary Livermore and Jane Hoge had toured in Washington, D.C., it would house soldiers while they traveled between their regiments and home on furlough or medical leave. Both women now served on its executive board. Chicago soon had reason to celebrate again, as news quickly reached the city that Vicksburg had formally surrendered to General Grant.[40] The Mississippi River was now under federal control and the Confederacy had been sliced in half. Because so many western soldiers had fought in the Vicksburg campaign, and because the Chicago office had supported their efforts so successfully, the city had much to cheer about.

Shortly after this pivotal victory, Mary Livermore suggested a fundraising fair to be held in Chicago. Although morale surged in the Northwest following the fall of Vicksburg, the military campaign and the construction of the Soldiers' Home had drained the commission's cash reserves. In addition to raising money for the Sanitary Commission, a fair would bring people together in defense of the Union and in support of the abolition of slavery. Livermore explained the goals succinctly in a letter to a potential participant: "We mean to make [the fair] not only a money-making agency, but a great moral demonstration, rebuking disloyalty, and upholding Freedom."[41]

Livermore and Hoge probably had several other implicit goals in mind. If their fair attracted crowds, drew significant donations of merchandise, and netted impressive proceeds, it would focus national attention on the city of Chicago and the Northwest. By extension, it would bring recognition to the Northwest's own Abraham Lincoln and his Republican Party. Although the two women had to be careful to appear nonpartisan, they certainly opposed the "peace Democrats," who advocated a negotiated settlement of the war with southern independence and the continuation of slavery. Whether or not they chose the fair's dates with politics in mind, the event would coincide with off-year elections in the city.[42] Additionally, if their fair succeeded on a large scale, it would help to boost the Sanitary Commission as the premier wartime benevolent organization, perhaps at the expense of the Christian Commission. Finally, the fair would allow Livermore and Hoge to plan and execute a large-scale undertaking. Although they would seek the approval and support of Sanitary Commission officials, politicians, and business leaders, they would direct it. They would draw women into the war effort more fully by convincing them that this type of public activism was both necessary and patriotic.

Livermore later recalled that the Sanitary Commission's elected officers in Chicago "languidly approved" their plan. The fair "was pre-eminently an enterprise of women, receiving no assistance from men in its early beginnings. The city of Chicago regarded it with indifference, and the gentlemen members of the Commission barely tolerated it." Perhaps remembering the paltry sum of $675 that Livermore and Hoge had raised at the small fair they had organized in 1861, the Sanitary Commission's elected officials had reason to be skeptical when the two women announced their goal of collecting $25,000. Jane Hoge recalled that the men were "startled" by that figure. But if branch president Mark Skinner and others appeared doubtful about the ability of these women to raise such an ambitious sum, they did not try to dissuade them from attempting it. From the time of their appointment as managers of the Chicago branch in December 1862, Livermore and Hoge appear to have exercised considerable freedom in directing the office, with little interference from either the national commission office in New York or the elected male leadership in Chicago.[43]

Fundraising fairs, based on medieval European fairs, had existed in America since the 1820s. Wives of prominent citizens often organized them to raise money for a charitable cause, such as an educational or religious institution, or for construction of a patriotic monument. After 1830, antislavery fairs in northern cities became effective fundraisers for a controversial cause. During the Civil War, fundraising fairs took on new importance as vehicles through which to support either the Unionist or the secessionist side. Although several southern cities hosted fairs, notably Richmond, Savannah, Charleston, and New Orleans, the most financially successful fairs were those held in the North.[44]

Livermore and Hoge envisioned a fair that would attract visitors from throughout the Northwest. They hoped to draw crowds to exhibition halls displaying an array of donated items, from artworks to patriotic artifacts to machinery. They also planned a range of entertainments including lectures, concerts, and "tableaux." None of the other Sanitary Commission branches had ever attempted an undertaking on this level. One scholar has written, "This fair created a stir throughout the Union and functioned as a turning point–a kind of sea change–in the way women's fairs were perceived and operated in the nineteenth century."[45]

Beginning in late July, the two women held a series of planning meetings for the fair. At the first one they created an executive committee and agreed to work with Protestant, Catholic, and Jewish congregations in the city. (There are no indications that Livermore and Hoge made efforts to recruit African Americans via religious or fraternal organizations.) Next, they organized a meeting to recruit women from throughout the Northwest. One hundred fifty women from around the region attended the meeting in Chicago, held September 1-2, with Jane Hoge presiding. Hoge was careful to introduce the proceedings in such a way that her leadership would not offend those with traditional notions of woman's sphere. She noted that although women lacked political power and did not seek it, they had considerable "moral and benevolent power and [their] influence is great." The organizers' political intent for the fair was apparent in their choice of speakers. Two of them were abolitionists, including Congressman Owen Lovejoy of Illinois, who condemned the "accursed rebellion," called slavery a "crime," and praised Lincoln's Emancipation Proclamation. "The Nation will be preserved, and become the home of universal freedom," Lovejoy declared to great applause. Clearly Livermore and Hoge now viewed the Sanitary Commission as far more than an organization that helped with the medical and nutritional needs of northern soldiers.[46] They had embraced the war as a crusade for liberation.

Following the early September meeting, Livermore and Hoge would be designated as co-managers of the fair. With momentum building, they quickly organized a canvassing campaign, soliciting funds to defray construction, decoration, and advertising costs. They also sent out twenty thousand circulars advertising the forthcoming fair and requesting help from throughout the region. Additionally, they wrote letters to governors, members of Congress and state legislatures, miliary officers, postmasters, ministers, and teachers. On one particularly fruitful day, they posted "*seventeen bushels of mail matter,* all of it relating to the fair." Their efforts paid off. "In every principal town of the Northwest 'fair meetings' were held, which resulted in handsome pledges," Livermore wrote in her autobiography. "The whole Northwest was ransacked for articles, curious, unique, *bizarre*, or noteworthy." Hoge and Livermore used their connections in the East to solicit additional unusual items for the fair.[47]

At a meeting of fair organizers held in Chicago on October 3, Hoge announced a possible lineup of speakers for the event. In order to appeal to northwestern women, Livermore had contacted the Pennsylvania abolitionist and Republican orator Anna Dickinson. A young Quaker whose fresh and innocent demeanor contrasted with a dynamic and often acerbic speaking style, Dickinson drew large audiences in support of antislavery and the Republican Party. She had campaigned successfully for the party in New Hampshire and Connecticut, earning as much as $400 for a single speech. Because Dickinson would be forgoing potentially remunerative speaking engagements in the East, she apparently requested $600 for two lectures. After consulting with other members of the executive committee, Livermore agreed to "accede to your terms." She knew, however, that the commission was taking a calculated risk in spending so much money to bring a relatively inexperienced young orator to Chicago. "*We shall depend on you for two evenings. . . . Don't fail us!*" she warned Dickinson.[48] By choosing an abolitionist as their keynote speaker, Livermore and Hoge made their own philosophical position known. And by choosing a female speaker, they emphasized that this two-week function was to be preeminently a women's fair.

Chicago's business community was slow to show its support for their project. In an article published in the *Chicago Tribune*, Livermore and Hoge appealed to the city's sense of destiny and regional pride, noting that their hometowns of Boston and Pittsburgh had contributed generously to the fair, and praised women's "busy hands" engaged in the creation of "fancy and useful articles of the most elegant description." Apparently their efforts at gentle persuasion failed. The following week Livermore and Hoge used stronger language, chiding Chicago's manufacturers for underestimating "the importance, as well as the *immensity* of the forthcoming Fair." They noted that one of the city's most "successful manufacturers," a man who had spent $100,000 on new buildings in the past year, and whose business interests were "second to that of no other concern in the West," had donated "skinchingly," giving only two dollars to the fair. They were equally scathing about a doctor with a lucrative practice in "lung complaints" who had failed to donate at all, citing his British citizenship and his nation's official position of neutrality in the war. Publicly shaming prominent men whose identity might be easily discerned by the *Chicago Tribune*'s readers was a somewhat risky tactic, but their tone reveals a high level of frustration. Midwestern women had donated thousands of small items for sale, but businessmen were not forthcoming with large items. Livermore and Hoge ended their article on a conciliatory note, announcing the railroads' offer of half-price fares into the city during the fair.[49]

Their efforts to secure and display large pieces for the fair proved to be one of the biggest headaches that Livermore and Hoge faced. As part of their initial planning, they had decided to build an addition to Bryan Hall, the fair's main building. This temporary wooden structure east of the main hall would house "heavy and bulky machinery." They secured a building permit from the city and found a businessman willing to donate the lumber. Lastly they hired a builder, who drew up a contract and met with them to sign it. "Who underwrites for you," he asked. "What?" they responded in apparent confusion. "Who endorses for you?" he asked. "We wish no endorsers," they replied. "We have the money in the bank, and will pay you in advance." "You are married women," he replied, "and, by the laws of Illinois, your names are good for nothing, unless your husbands write their names after yours on the contract."[50]

When Mary Livermore described the incident twenty-five years later in her autobiography, her anger was still palpable. "Here was a revelation," she wrote. "We two women were able to enlist the whole Northwest in a great philanthropic, money-making enterprise in the teeth of great opposition. . . . But by the laws of the state in which we lived, our individual names were not worth the paper on which they were written. Our earnings were not ours, but belonged to our husbands." Although Livermore implied that this incident represented her first realization that married women lacked property rights in Illinois, this was not the case. She had published *Pen Pictures* the previous year, and Daniel's name had appeared on the copyright. Just six months earlier on her trip to Vicksburg she still regarded an obsequious approach as the best way to deal with powerful men.[51]

But by the fall of 1863, Mary Livermore had emerged as a more confident and independent leader. She had organized dozens of aid societies, written hundreds of letters, met with the president of the United States and with his generals. She had begun to regard the legal strictures directed at married women to be unacceptable, even intolerable. While resenting the insult and the delay necessitated by the contractor's demands, Livermore and Hoge had no choice but to comply. They sent for their husbands, who duly signed the document and thereby gave legal weight to it. The building was constructed and christened. But Livermore did not forget the incident. "I registered a vow," she wrote later, "that when the war was over I would take up a new work–the work of making law and justice synonymous for women."[52] She would keep her promise, but the war would first have to come to an end.

Mary and Daniel Livermore at the time of their marriage, May 6, 1845.
(From *The Story of My Life*)

Mary Livermore as she looked in the Civil War.
(Library of Congress)

The Chicago Sanitary Commission had its offices in J. H. McVicker's Theatre on Madison Street.
(A. T. Andreas, *History of Chicago*)

Mary Livermore and Jane Hoge organized two blockbuster fundraising fairs for the Sanitary Commission in Chicago. The simplicity of the first is pictured here with its procession of farmers bringing contributions of food on opening day.

(Frank Goodrich, *The Tribute Book*. Courtesy, Chicago Historical Society)

The second Sanitary Commission fundraiser was an ostentatious affair depicted here by the interior of Union Hall, part of an immense building constructed for the occasion.

(*Frank Leslie's Illustrated Newspaper*. Courtesy, Chicago Historical Society)

Livermore's wartime colleagues included Jane Hoge (upper left) *and Mary Ann Bickerdyke* (upper right). *After the war she befriended Lucy Stone* (lower left) *and her husband Henry Blackwell, who became her closest friends in the suffrage movement.*

(Hoge, Stone, and Blackwell images: Library of Congress; Bickerdyke photograph: Frank Moore, *Women of the War*)

By 1870 Livermore was regarded as one of America's "Representative Women."
Clockwise from top: *Lucretia Mott, Elizabeth Cady Stanton, Mary Livermore,*
Lydia Maria Child, Susan B. Anthony, and Grace Greenwood. The figure
in the center is Anna Dickinson, whose career as a public speaker Livermore
helped to promote.

(Library of Congress)

In the 1870s and 1880s, Mary Livermore was the most popular female public speaker in the nation, known as "queen of the platform."
(Princeton University Library)

As editor of the nation's leading suffrage newspaper, the Woman's Journal, *Livermore grappled with the emerging scandal over the antics of Victoria Woodhull. Cartoonist Thomas Nast caricatured Woodhull as "Mrs. Satan" in* Harper's Weekly.
(Library of Congress)

For more than fifty years, Daniel Livermore (above) *was Mary's husband, her closest friend, and her adviser.*

(Mary Livermore, *The Story of My Life*)

Their daughter Lizzie (left) *lived with them, while daughter Etta* (right) *lived nearby with her husband and children.*

(Princeton University Library)

In her post–Civil War career, Mary Livermore projected an image of unassailable propriety while also advocating progressive reforms. Here she is included among a group of literary figures titled "Eminent Women" (1884) and distributed by the Travelers Insurance Company. Livermore is standing at left. Her close friend Julia Ward Howe is seated, center, with white cap.

(Boston Athenæum)

CHAPTER 6

Fair Mania

M ARY LIVERMORE and Jane Hoge seemed to be everywhere during the final hectic weeks before the fair's inauguration. They organized groups of women into committees to handle the preparation of meals. They answered correspondence. They kept up a steady stream of announcements to the newspapers showcasing the arrival of items for sale or exhibition. Secretary of War Edwin M. Stanton's contribution of a collection of rebel battle flags generated local publicity, but the gift that gave Livermore and Hoge the greatest joy was the one provided by President Lincoln.[1]

On October 11, 1863, Mary Livermore wrote to the president. After describing the forthcoming fair and the efforts of volunteers throughout the region to make it a success, she asked for Lincoln's help: "The Executive Committee have been urgently requested to solicit from Mrs. Lincoln and yourself some donation to this great Fair. . . . It has been suggested to us from various quarters that the most acceptable donation you could possible make, would be *the original manuscript of the Proclamation of emancipation*." Livermore explained that the proclamation would be auctioned off, with proceeds going to the Sanitary Commission and the purchaser strongly encouraged to donate the document to the state of Illinois or the Chicago Historical Society.[2]

The president responded on October 26. Addressing his letter to "Ladies having in charge of the North-Western Fair," he wrote: "The original draft of the Emancipation proclamation is herewith enclosed. . . . I had some desire to retain the paper; but if it shall contribute to the relief or comfort of the soldiers that will be better. Your obt. Servt. A. Lincoln."[3]

In the final days before the fair opened, Chicago manufacturers finally began to make significant donations. Responding to persistent entreaties from the fair's managers, publicity about their letter to the president, growing public interest in the event, and perhaps the realization that it was actually going to succeed, they contributed "liberally," according to the *Chicago Tribune*. As Mary Livermore later recalled, businessmen gave an "avalanche of gifts." Sewing and knitting machines of the highest quality and newest technology, a "beautiful steam engine" as well as a steam boiler, and two $500 pianos came in. Chicago's most renowned entrepreneur, Cyrus McCormick, gave "one of his very best" reapers. (McCormick may well have been the businessman who had previously given "skinchingly.") Potter Palmer, another giant among the city's business elite, visiting New York at that time, mailed checks totaling $5,500, representing personal gifts and those of wealthy friends. Palmer also showed his support by advertising his dry goods business in the *Volunteer*, a daily newspaper published during the fair that was designed to showcase forthcoming events as well as raise revenue by selling ads.[4]

After working continuously for thirty-six hours, Mary Livermore returned home at 2:00 A.M. the day the fair was to open. Exhausted and eager to rest a few hours before the festivities began, she quickly opened a note from the printer of the *New Covenant*, only to learn that he needed two more columns of material for page two and one for page three. He would stop by the house at 5:00 A.M. to collect the copy. Daniel was out of town on business, and no one else could be summoned to help her at that ridiculous hour. Light-headed from lack of sleep, Mary found humor in the situation and wrote about her frantic quest for copy. As she often did when writing for the *Covenant*, she referred to herself as "we."

> We have frantically torn open the papers and letters of the mail which, providentially, we thought to call for, and have "scissored" till we can find nothing more scissor*able*. Never were papers so barren of news, or interesting matter—never were correspondents so provokingly reticent—the editor is in Canada and will not be back until too late for the printers, and there is nobody and nothing for us to fall back upon. So the appalling fact stares us in the face, that

there is a column yet to provide for–and that something must be written to fill it. With a feeling as if a special rheumatism were detailed to every separate joint in our weary body, sleepy, head-ache-y, and longing to hurl an anathema at the printer who *dares* to want copy during *the* Great Soldiers' Fair, which we have carried in our arms, as the man did the calf, from the earliest day of its inception, until now, it has become such a mammoth, that it requires the whole Northwest to move it, we address ourself to the task of writing a column. Patience, dear readers.

Livermore then proceeded to fill the columns, describing the forthcoming fair "for our country readers" who had not seen the nearly continuous coverage in Chicago's daily newspapers. "The promise of the Fair is magnificent," she concluded enthusiastically.[5] The next two weeks would sustain her optimism.

The fair began on October 27, 1863, with a procession that stretched three miles long. People began gathering in Chicago's streets well before 8:00 A.M. Schools, banks, courts, and the Board of Trade all closed in honor of the occasion. By 9:00 "the city was in a roar," with groups participating in the procession gathered at designated locations. At 10:00 the "mighty pageant" began. Marching bands alternated with groups called "divisions," beginning with police in platoons, two regiments of Illinois state militia, and a detachment of soldiers from the Invalid Corps at Camp Douglas. Convalescing men from the Soldiers' Home traveled in wagons. The next set of divisions included fraternal organizations, workingmen's groups, and temperance societies, many of them immigrants representing Chicago's sizable German American and Irish American populations. Professional men and politicians came next, joined by elected officers of the Sanitary Commission, students and faculty from Chicago University, and, last, the Ladies' Executive Committee and Committee of Arrangements for the fair. Behind them, schoolchildren riding in wagons waved little flags while singing "John Brown's body lies a-mouldering in the grave!" The Lake County Delegation brought up the rear of the procession. One hundred wagons decorated with flags came loaded with produce representing the bountiful harvest of the Northwest and intended as a donation to the Sanitary Commission.[6]

At one o'clock the procession ended at the courthouse. After the bands played a series of patriotic songs, businessman Thomas B. Bryan gave an opening address. Aware that tradition forbade women from being orators on occasions of civic celebration, Bryan nevertheless wanted their efforts in planning this fair to be publicly recognized. "It is an enterprise born of woman," he said, "and nursed to maturity by her skill, her taste and untiring zeal." Following Bryan's speech, the firing of a cannon signaled the fair's official opening. The day's events, the *Chicago Tribune* gushed, represented a sight "never seen before in the West upon any occasion."[7]

For the next twelve days, an estimated 100,000 people attended the fair. Soldiers in uniform were admitted to all events without charge. For everyone else, payment of twenty-five cents bought a single admission, while one dollar bought a "season ticket" admitting the bearer to all functions in Bryan Hall for the duration of the fair. The art gallery and Metropolitan Hall, where evening functions were held, required an additional fee. Each afternoon, young women distributed free copies of the *Volunteer* containing news of the fair's progress and showcasing evening events. In the final days of October, poor weather, including rain, sleet, and snow, caused outdoor temperatures to plummet and created problems with the city's ubiquitous mud, but spirits remained high inside the fair buildings. In Bryan Hall, sale booths were arranged on the lower level in two semicircles around a two-story octagonal pagoda, and on the upper level a band played music to create a festive mood. Mary Livermore later recalled that "the national flag was festooned, and clustered in all appropriate places."[8]

Donated articles for sale continued to pour in, listed individually in the pages of the *Volunteer* and the *Chicago Tribune*. Manufacturers donated a variety of items, including a "patent horse-power pitch fork" from W. C. Palmer of Chicago and silver-plated tableware from Blair & Parsons of Milwaukee. Authors Henry Wadsworth Longfellow, Oliver Wendell Holmes, and William Cullen Bryant sent autographed copies of their works. Women continued to create their own handmade contributions. A Mrs. Simonds of Jefferson, Illinois, donated one hundred tumblers of homemade jelly; seventy-year-old Mrs. Brewer of Sterling, Illinois, gave one dozen "ironing holders"; and the German ladies of Davenport, Iowa, sent a "highly ornamented screen of worsted work." Mrs. Doggett of Chicago gave an album with photographs of antislavery leaders. Some loyal citizens sent cash. Women of the Milwaukee Aid Society contributed $1,000; patriotic citizens of Kankakee County, Illinois, donated $100; and General John A. McClernand sent a letter regretting his absence but contributing $50. The fair began to bring in receipts of $5,000 per day.[9]

The fair's restaurant, art display, and Confederate relics also attracted visitors. The Ladies' Dining Hall in Lower Bryan Hall served 1,000 to 1,500 meals daily, with a prominent Chicago matron presiding over every table and six young women acting as servers. The art gallery, run by the sculptor Leonard Volk, showcased more than three hundred artworks on loan from private collections for viewing by culturally minded midwesterners. While the collection drew disappointing profits, the "Curiosity Shop," displaying a variety of captured Confederate flags and weaponry, more than made up for it. Its focal point was the bloodstained flag that General Grant had selected as the first to be flown over Vicksburg's courthouse when the city fell into Union hands. Mary Livermore later wrote that "the assistants in this department daily talked themselves hoarse and weary in reiterated explanations of their storied collections." Fair organizers also taught moral lessons by displaying relics of slavery, including a three-inch-wide iron band worn by a slave who had been liberated by the Eleventh Wisconsin at the Battle of Port Gibson. The *Tribune* advised that donations of clothing intended for freed slaves might be dropped at the Sanitary Commission offices.[10]

Mary Livermore must have been dismayed when she read a critical review of the accommodations for the Mechanical Department, housed in the structure she and Jane Hoge had struggled so mightily to have built. The *Chicago Tribune* described it as a "rude shed . . . not large enough to contain all the machines which have been received and are on their way to the Fair." Nevertheless, whether out of patriotism or the sudden realization that the Great Northwestern Fair afforded enormous advertising potential, manufacturers of farm machinery kept sending large pieces to Chicago until the closing days. Livermore later recollected that "the contributions to this department . . . were sufficient in number and importance for a good-sized State Fair."[11]

In the midst of success, Mary Livermore faced criticism from the *Chicago Times*, the city's leading Democratic newspaper. The *Times* had begun sniping at the fair's managers before the event even started, publishing a series of articles about the planning meetings which insinuated that Mary Livermore and Jane Hoge were overbearing and unladylike. In a particularly damning editorial, the *Times* compared the two unfavorably with the Catholic Sisters of Mercy, declaring that while the nuns volunteered their efforts to help the soldiers, "there are several ladies who draw a thousand dollars" in annual salary though "they scarcely raise a finger," an obvious reference to Livermore and Hoge. The *Times* went on to accuse the Sanitary Commission of being an abolitionist organization. Livermore and Hoge did not respond to this accusation, although they must have been gratified when the rival *Chicago Tribune* praised "their energy, devotion, and ability." They answered the

Times only by denying that they had gone to "extravagant expense" in creating the exhibition hall for the fair, pointing out that most construction costs were covered by donated money.[12]

By the time the fair started, the *Chicago Times* had silenced its editorial cannons, though not for long. During the fair's second week, the Democratic newspaper published a story under the headline "The Sanitary Commission: An Insight into Its Secret Workings, A Startling Exposure." This time identifying Livermore by name, the *Times* alleged that Mrs. Benjamin H. Chadbourne, a Sanitary Commission volunteer and wife of an infantry captain in the Fifty-seventh Illinois, had been rudely treated by Chicago branch associate manager Mary Livermore. Mrs. Chadbourne had written to the Chicago branch requesting help in securing nurses and had then journeyed to Chicago from Tennessee to escort the new nurses back to the South. She had been detained several days while final arrangements were being made and had asked the Chicago USSC to refund the cost of her hotel bill.[13]

According to this account, Livermore had refused, claiming, "We have no funds for such purpose," and telling Mrs. Chadbourne, "Go and take the nurses and begone with them." Then, fearing that she had angered the woman, she called her back, telling her, "You must not go away in this manner and report us, *it will ruin us.*" Livermore gave Mrs. Chadbourne ten dollars to pay her hotel bill, saying that she and Jane Hoge *"put our hands right into the treasury and take what we want."* Livermore allegedly urged Mrs. Chadbourne not to volunteer her time but to become a salaried employee of the Sanitary Commission so that she, like Livermore, could receive $100 per month plus expenses. Mrs. Chadbourne responded, "I voluntarily gave my services and now labor in the cause for principle and patriotism, and not to gratify vanity and make money."[14] As in the earlier editorial comparing Livermore and Hoge unfavorably to the Sisters of Mercy, the *Times* implied that "true women" worked only as volunteers and deserved no pay.

The *Chicago Tribune* reported several days later that "Mrs. L[ivermore] has not taken any notice of the infamous attack, believing, as she stated, that Mrs. Chadbourne would herself publish a denial." Chadbourne did so in a letter to the *Tribune*. Calling the *Times* "a *contemptible secession sheet,*" she stated emphatically, *"I pronounce the whole statement as set forth in the Times false!* No such scene ever transpired between Mrs. Livermore and myself." According to her account, Livermore had sent Chadbourne to branch president Mark Skinner's law office to seek reimbursement for her hotel bill. It was Skinner, not Livermore, who had refused to pay the bill, claiming that there was no money for such expenses. Mrs. Chadbourne had then returned to the Sanitary Commission rooms and appealed to Livermore, who responded, "Your bill must be paid–I have some money given to me for sanitary purposes, and I shall feel justified in paying it out for your expenses." Livermore had also assisted her in obtaining transportation on another occasion. The *Tribune* added its own condemnation of the *Times*, accusing the Democratic newspaper of attempting to drop "a bombshell in the midst of the great Sanitary Fair, which would at once blast its prospects, [and] stop further contributions. . . . The attempt has miserably failed." The *Times* printed a rejoinder, noting that Chadbourne's letter to the *Tribune* "sustains and strengthens" its earlier charges in "several important respects."[15] Indeed, both versions referred to Livermore's use of discretionary funds.

Although Mary Livermore refused to debate the *Times*, she did note in a descriptive article about the fair for the *New Covenant*, "Disloyalists have assaulted both it and its managers, frantically, and almost fiendishly." She regarded her use of USSC money to fund contingencies such as Mrs. Chadbourne's travel expenses and Mary Ann Bickerdyke's projects as both necessary and appropriate. The historian Glenna Matthews has written that the willingness of Livermore and other wartime women to see their endeavors written up in the newspapers connotes both "a significant departure from traditional norms of decorous feminine conduct" and an indication that the image of public womanhood was changing.[16] Livermore's refusal to be intimidated by the *Times* reveals, in addition, an acceptance of her new role as a public woman.

The *Chicago Times* would continue its assaults in the coming days by attacking Anna Dickinson, who came to the fair at Livermore's behest and delivered public lectures on November 4 and 6. Speaking to capacity crowds, Dickinson praised the Union war effort and embraced the record of African American soldiers, but also condemned the Democratic Party and its "sneaking and lying" members for disloyalty to their country. The *Times* complained that she had been paid $300 per speech to "preach the abolition gospel" and the "theory of negro superiority."[17]

The high point of the fair came on November 7, when Livermore and Hoge arranged a dinner for eight hundred to honor northwestern soldiers. It was an emotional evening for everyone who attended. An effort was made to include every local soldier able to walk on his own or be carried to the hall. Many had suffered wounds, amputations, and a variety of illnesses. Mary Livermore recalled the scene in an article for the *New Covenant*, concluding, "Never have we witnessed a more touching sight." Dickinson's speech on this occasion added solemnity and dignity, but Livermore made the closing remarks at the banquet herself. She promised the assembled soldiers that women of the Sanitary Commission would look after their needs until the war ended, while those who had died would remain always in their hearts.[18]

Her speech appears to have been brief, its text unrecorded by the city newspapers, but it represented a milestone in her career. A woman who had once believed that public speaking did not constitute appropriate female behavior now stood before an audience of eight hundred and spoke of her patriotism and her convictions. In the past year she had withstood the condescension of politicians, the indifference of manufacturers, and the scurrilous attacks of newspaper reporters. She had emerged from the ordeal a respected public figure and an unabashedly strong-minded woman. Now she was a public orator as well.

She even sparred with an ally, the *Chicago Tribune*. In writing about the soldiers' banquet, the paper gave its candid assessment of women's recent visibility in the public sphere. Although it had defended Livermore, Hoge, and Dickinson in print, the newspaper wanted to assure its readers of its overall opposition to any change in gender roles. "Society at large has an honest horror of the assumption by women of the functions which belong strictly to men," one reporter wrote. Moreover, "of late years there has [been] . . . a dissemination amongst us of exaggerated notions concerning woman's sphere, rights and duties."[19] Livermore responded in a letter to the *Tribune* using only her initials, M.A.L. Friends and colleagues would recognize her identity from these initials, as would subscribers to the *New Covenant*, who knew that she wrote for the Universalist weekly using that abbreviation. Nevertheless, this device afforded her some anonymity with the general public.

In order to come to Chicago, Livermore wrote, Dickinson had turned down a series of ten lectures in the East for which she would have been paid $100 per speech. Her two lectures in Chicago had brought in proceeds of $1,300, and the commission had paid her the agreed upon fee of $600, an acceptable rate of return. Moreover, Livermore argued, "Anna Dickinson is a fatherless girl . . . [who] earns her own living and supports her mother." During the six months of the year when she did not lecture, Dickinson worked as a volunteer nurse in Philadelphia's military hospitals. Livermore's indignation toward Dickinson's critics was apparent when she wrote: "Her youth, beauty, grace, impassioned fervor, wonderful eloquence, thorough knowledge of national and political events, all rendered her fully the peer of male lecturers, and a mighty power in battling with the meanest and most dangerous enemies of the country–traitors at home." Then Livermore added a comment that revealed her own emerging feminism: "May not a woman receive all [the pay] that she can?"[20]

The Great Northwestern Fair was a huge success. "No other Fair held for purposes of benevolence has ever yielded similar results," the *Chicago Tribune* exulted. In the weeks after the fair ended, cash contributions continued to pour in. As Livermore and Hoge had predicted, the most valuable single item had been Abraham Lincoln's copy of the Emancipation Proclamation, which was purchased by businessman Thomas Bryan for $3,000 and later donated to the Chicago Historical Society. Proceeds from the fair exceeded everyone's expectations, including those of the co-managers. By the end of the last day, receipts totaled $60,000, and by the time the final contributions rolled in, the fair had cleared $86,000, more than three times what Livermore and Hoge had hoped to raise. Publicly and privately, members of the Sanitary Commission sang the praises of the fair's organizers.[21]

The Great Northwestern Fair started a frenzy of fair mania throughout the North. Referring to this trend, Jane Hoge wrote, "The brave prairie pioneer little dreamed of its brilliant successors in the good cause." Within the next year, Sanitary Commission branches staged fairs in Boston, Cincinnati, Cleveland, New York, St. Louis, and Pittsburgh. The Boston fair, held in December 1863, raised $146,000, while the New York metropolitan fair the following April brought in astounding profits of $2 million. Livermore visited the Cincinnati fair in December 1863 and, while praising its efforts and its profits of $280,000, also noted that it lacked the "white-heat earnestness and enthusiasm" of Chicago's fair. In her autobiography she wrote proudly and a little defensively that none of the later sanitary fairs "were characterized by the enthusiasm, originality, earnestness, and contagious patriotism that glorified [the Chicago fair] and made it forever memorable." Nor was any subsequent Civil War fair so closely associated with women, according to the historian Beverly Gordon. Livermore pointedly noted that the Cincinnati fair "was inaugurated and planned by gentlemen."[22]

Mary Livermore emerged from the Sanitary Commission fair with rekindled energy, renewed commitment to the organization, and a growing sense of self-confidence. But there was little time for self-congratulation. Although news from the military front appeared promising, a great deal of work still needed to be done, for in addition to the thousands of soldiers requiring care, the families of enlisted men in Chicago and elsewhere suffered from wartime conditions, including spiraling inflation that drove food and fuel prices to all-time highs. But first she would have to deal with a squabble involving the Sanitary Commission in a neighboring state.

Livermore traveled to Des Moines a few weeks after the Chicago fair to help resolve deep divisions between the state's feuding sanitary agents and the factions that supported them. Early in the war Annie Wittenmyer, a wealthy widow, had founded the Keokuk Ladies' Soldiers' Aid Society. Several months later, Iowa's governor established the Iowa State Army Sanitary Commission as an auxiliary of the national Sanitary Commission and appointed a minister named A. J. Kynett to be its corresponding secretary and general agent. Wittenmyer viewed this as a threat to her society and to local female control of benevolent work in the state. A resolution of sorts was reached when Wittenmyer was appointed a sanitary agent, but tensions continued as Kynett sent sanitary stores to the Chicago office while Wittenmyer sent hers to the Western Sanitary Commission in St. Louis, an organization completely independent from the U.S. Sanitary Commission. According to Wittenmyer's supporters, delegates at the Des Moines meeting hoped to eliminate her influence entirely.[23]

The Des Moines meeting was contentious to say the least. Livermore sided with Kynett, publicly praising his "valuable service" in contributing to the Chicago office and privately slamming Wittenmyer in a letter to John Newberry. Her apparent dismissal of Wittenmyer's stand in favor of local female control might appear surprising, but Livermore had long since become convinced that the Sanitary Commission was the most efficient means of caring for wounded and ill soldiers. Moreover Kynett, not Wittenmyer, supported the Chicago commission. Livermore made a presentation touting the efficient bookkeeping and overall effectiveness of the Chicago branch. A motion was made, then withdrawn, to send all Iowa sanitary stores to Chicago. At one point Wittenmyer interrogated Livermore as to whether she could supply vouchers for her itemized expenses in Chicago. Livermore replied that she could have them telegraphed immediately. Wittenmyer responded that she could do likewise. After two days of discussions "at times stormy and fierce," Livermore wrote in the *New Covenant*, governor-elect William Stone stepped in to resolve the impasse, brokering a compromise that led to the formation of the Iowa Sanitary Commission, which would be auxiliary to both the U.S. and the Western Sanitary Commissions. Livermore later admitted to John Newberry that her efforts in Iowa had been "the severest labor of my life. I would not do anything of the kind again, for even the Sanitary Commission."[24]

Whether or not Livermore was disappointed in this outcome, she spent little time ruminating about the situation. When she returned from Des Moines in late November, she threw herself into efforts to help Chicago's impoverished citizens, whose precarious existence was threatened by the advent of winter and by soaring food and fuel prices caused by wartime inflation. Her special concern lay with the families of rank-and-file soldiers serving in the Union Army. The winter of 1863–64 would be "long, cold, and dreary," she wrote in the *New Covenant*, and warned that the war was producing "famine prices" that threatened many. Together with Jane Hoge, she launched a new initiative to provide assistance, including coal and firewood, for the families of enlisted men in Chicago. They held an organizational meeting on December 6, less than one month after the Great Northwestern Fair had ended. The group decided to associate itself with the Young Men's Christian Association, probably because the YMCA had money to contribute, quickly gathering $8,000 for this relief effort. In addition to families, soldiers also needed warm clothing for winter. The Sanitary Commission offered to supply cotton batting and calico to any woman in Chicago willing to make blankets for the soldiers.[25]

The following week, a group calling itself the Society for the Relief of Soldiers' Families met, electing Jane Hoge president and naming Mary Livermore to the executive committee. The *Chicago Times* sent a reporter to cover the meeting, angering those present who resented the paper's ill treatment of Livermore and Hoge during the recent fair. One woman suggested that the reporter should be expelled from the room. Livermore opposed the motion but lambasted the *Times*, charging that it "continue[s] to abuse women, which seems to be the food on which it thrives." But, she added, "be assured it can do us no harm. . . . The Chicago *Times* is without influence among the respectable people in the community."[26] Livermore was no longer willing to be silent in the face of hostile newspaper reporting.

After drafting a constitution, members moved on to consider the logistics of setting up a depository where needy soldiers' families might find assistance obtaining fuel, clothing, and even employment opportunities. Questions arose over whether to seek volunteer or paid help, igniting a debate over the status of women as wartime volunteers. When the discussion turned to the question of hiring a "a reliable, competent lady" to staff the depository, a member of the group asked whether all the work of the organization might not be accomplished by volunteers. "When we can find men and women who can live in Chicago without cost, then we may expect them to work for nothing," came the response from an unnamed participant. It was a sentiment with which Livermore and Hoge no doubt agreed. By late December the Society for the Relief of Soldiers' Families had hired a Mrs. Edgeton at seven dollars per week to serve as "matron" of its depository, located at 73 State Street. Patriotic Chicagoans might donate used clothing, secondhand furniture, food, or fuel to the depository or the Sanitary Commission offices. The society then organized a strategy to solicit contributions from churches throughout the city and a system of canvassers to identify families in need of immediate help.[27]

Livermore did canvassing work herself on the weekends when she was not at the Sanitary Commission offices. Her work with the poor gave her a visceral sense of the hardships of poverty and influenced her attitudes and her writing about the war. "If there had ever been a time in my life when I regarded the lowest tier of human beings with indifference or aversion, I outgrew it during the war," she later recalled.[28] She became aware that soldiers were poorly and sometimes irregularly paid and their families lived close to the edge of complete destitution. With no government agencies to help them, it fell to churches and charitable organizations to provide needed relief.

One Sunday morning Livermore visited eight families in whom she had taken a special interest and whom she had helped in the past. A Methodist clergyman named Charles McCabe accompanied her. Their first stop was at the household of a German woman whose husband had served in the Twenty-fourth Illinois, but whose hospitalization made his ability to provide for the family precarious. His wife supported seven children by cleaning houses, washing, and picking rags. On at least one occasion Livermore fed several of the children in her own kitchen. She helped other families by drawing on her contacts within the benevolent community. One family she visited lived in a ramshackle building on Wells Street divided into nine rat-infested apartments. The family had no wood or fuel of any kind to provide light and heat. When the widowed mother, whose husband had served in an Ohio regiment, died, along with one of her children, Livermore arranged for the surviving child to move to the Home for the Friendless and the grandmother to live at the Old Ladies' Home, charitable institutions she knew well from her prewar work. Her final visit was to an African American woman with four children who had received no money from her husband, a soldier in the famous Massachusetts Fifty-fourth Regiment. The woman suffered from typhoid fever. After learning that the husband had never been paid, Livermore wrote to Governor John

Andrew of Massachusetts and received his assurances that relief would be provided immediately for families of these soldiers now living in Chicago.[29]

The Home for the Friendless remained near and dear to Livermore's heart. In 1864 this institution was turned into temporary housing for hundreds of needy Chicagoans, many of them children. The home accepted individuals regardless of race or nationality. Adoptions were an important goal, with 121 children finding new residences in that year. Livermore praised the home's general agent, a Methodist minister named E. M. Boring, calling him "acceptable to all sects" and recommending the institution as a charity worthy of Universalist patronage.[30]

On occasion, Livermore placed ads in the *New Covenant* seeking adoptive parents for children whose mothers could not care for them. Keenly aware of ethnic distinctions in the city, she always made a note of the children's backgrounds. In the January 30, 1864, issue, for example, she sought a "home and a kind and good mother" for a three-week-old baby of Norwegian parentage. In all of these ads, Livermore stressed the physical health and comeliness of the children, their developmental "promise," and their birth parents' extreme poverty which necessitated the adoption. At times she struggled to maintain a sense of emotional detachment. In March 1864 Livermore admitted to *New Covenant* readers that helping impoverished mothers through the ordeal of giving up their children constituted "the most painful scenes . . . [I] have witnessed."[31]

The problems of the poor and vulnerable weighed heavily on Mary Livermore. Working tirelessly on behalf of the Sanitary Commission and a variety of agencies designed to help the indigent, she had little patience with those affluent Chicagoans who, she believed, might and should do more to help. In a series of editorials in the *New Covenant*, she explored a favorite topic, women's role in wartime, and incorporated the theme of their need to be self-sacrificing until the national crisis had ended.

In an article titled "Woman's Extravagance," Livermore condemned the New York fashion world and Chicago's attempt to emulate it. She reminded readers that while self-indulgent members of the privileged classes were buying unnecessary finery, the city's streets were "filled with limping soldiers," and enlisted men's families had been reduced to "semi-starvation."[32]

In another article, "Employment for Women," she explored the plight of women forced by necessity to find jobs, an issue of increasing importance given the rising death toll from the war. There were not enough jobs for women, and few paid a reasonable wage. Although educated women might work as teachers, there were twenty or more applicants for every position that came open in Chicago. A growing number of women had become trained as bookkeepers, but few had found employment in a profession many regarded as exclusively male. Women with literary talent might pursue careers as writers, but this profession provided "a precarious livelihood," as Livermore well knew after her own twenty years' experience. Women of the laboring classes faced even bleaker prospects. Livermore called the sewing trades a situation of "suicide or starvation," while other types of work, including domestic service, taking in washing, shopkeeping, nursing, and accepting boarders offered only minimal improvement. Moreover, many women seeking employment also had small children to support, making wage earning even more difficult. "We do not pretend to say that plenty of remunerative employment for women would remedy all the evils and wrongs existing among them," Livermore wrote, "but it would do very much towards it." Women themselves also bore some of the blame. They must reject long-held beliefs that working for pay was "dishonorable" and that working leads to "lost caste," she urged. For Livermore, financial independence was the key to female advancement. "Could we have granted for women to-day, the boon we most crave for them," she concluded, "it would not be the right of suffrage" nor "higher educational advantages" nor even "a revision of the laws for their benefit—none of these— but simply free access to any and every department of labor, unhindered by the opposition of man, and untramelled by legal statutes."[33]

In 1864 Mary Livermore began speaking before sizable audiences. Although she was not yet a polished orator, nor was she ready to advocate women's economic advancement in this venue, she was willing to raise her voice in support of the Sanitary Commission. On March 10 she addressed a large crowd at a Congregational church in Dubuque, Iowa, where a group of local women hoped to organize a sanitary fair to benefit the Chicago office. Following a musical number by the Union Glee Club, she began somewhat tentatively, telling the audience that she "made no pretensions to oratory" but preferred to speak informally. She then warmed to the topic, discussing the necessity of continued support for the Sanitary Commission, whose many important functions she related in detail. As she had on so many previous occasions, Livermore tackled the issue of the alleged diversion of sanitary stores, using humor to deflect criticism of the USSC by noting that some local aid societies would send "half a dozen cans of peaches" and then expect "every soldier in the Grand Army of the Union . . . to bring home tidings of having shared therein." She believed that many erroneous stories of USSC mismanagement were "inventions of disloyal men . . . circulated by such papers as the *Chicago Times*" and Dubuque's own disloyal newspaper, which she declined to identify by name.[34]

Finally, Livermore faced the issue of female public speaking, acknowledging the controversy over its propriety but justifying it as an act of wartime patriotism and predicting that once peace arrived, women would return to the domestic sphere and "let the men be Lords of creation." At the beginning of the war, she declared, "nothing would have tempted me" to support women speaking in public. "I would have deemed it something terrible, horrible for a woman to come out before the public and talk." But after witnessing the suffering of Union soldiers in camps and hospitals, "*I can't be still, and* I WON'T *be still.*" Livermore's long and rambling speech lasted two hours. A sympathetic newspaper described it as "exhaustive." Although she had much to learn about public speaking, her early attempts at oratory resonated with audiences. The *Dubuque Times* reported that her address had been followed by "immense applause" and praised her for speaking "elegantly and eloquently." More important, the address raised money for the Sanitary Commission–$1,000 from this speech alone. Iowans also voted to organize a Northern Iowa Sanitary Fair to take place in June 1864. It would raise $76,494, most of it going to support the Chicago office.[35]

By the latter half of 1864, the Confederacy's days appeared to be numbered. Ulysses S. Grant now commanded all of the northern armies, and Confederate forces, defeated at Vicksburg and Gettysburg, suffered from depleted numbers, lack of supplies and ammunition, and the deaths of many leading generals. But the northern public, anxious for the conflict to end, grew impatient with the continued killing and the economic dislocation of war. Mary Livermore worked hard to sustain morale in the Northwest. "Our cause is just, and must succeed," she wrote in the *New Covenant* in August 1864. "There can be only ultimate success, if the people stand firm in the determination to put down the rebellion, and preserve the national life. It is a war in which freedom is struggling with slavery–democracy with aristocracy–right with wrong–and who can doubt which will win?"[36]

One way she attempted to lift morale was through inspirational stories about the efforts of individuals and communities. In the pages of the *New Covenant* she described "potato processions" in some rural communities, in which farmers would bring their vegetables to the county seat or railroad town on an appointed day, then celebrate their donation to the Sanitary Commission with music and a communal dinner. But she also preached the gospel of self-sacrifice and the need for a "systematic method for raising funds." She wanted every midwesterner to donate the proceeds of one day's labor to the Sanitary Commission, one "365th part of the gifts of Providence." In a letter to John Newberry of the Sanitary Commission's Western Department, Jane Hoge called this effort "[our] new plan of 'Labor, Income, & Revenue.' "[37]

Mary Livermore respected children's efforts to support the Sanitary Commission, and she went out of her way to encourage them. When schoolchildren in Trempealeau, Wisconsin, organized a "school exhibition" in the spring of 1864 and contributed twelve dollars in proceeds to the Chicago office, Livermore wrote them a lengthy letter praising their success. Believing that children could and should understand the political and military dynamics of the war, Livermore carefully described the Union Army's successful campaign to drive Confederate general James Longstreet and his men from Knoxville, Tennessee. She explained to the children that the Army of the Cumberland, successful in the field, had nevertheless suffered greatly during the past winter from scurvy, the "great cure" for which was to provide a variety of vegetables to the soldiers. The money the children had raised would be used to purchase fifteen or sixteen bushels of potatoes. She also praised the efforts of children who organized their own Sanitary Commission fairs. During the school recess in July and August 1864, "fair mania" struck Chicago's youth, especially children between the ages of nine and fourteen, who held fairs in their parents' yards and contributed $300 to the Chicago office.[38]

In late October 1864 Mary Livermore and Jane Hoge decided that the best way to rekindle patriotism and raise money for the Sanitary Commission was to organize another fair. They would share proceeds of the second fair with the Soldiers' Home, which was now serving at least one hundred additional meals per day to feed a new constituency, southern refugees fleeing the Confederacy. Livermore and Hoge agreed to donate $25,000 in proceeds to that institution. The executive committee for the Sanitary Commission and Soldiers' Home Fair would consist of officers of both organizations. Initially they planned the fair to be held in early 1865, from February 22 (George Washington's birthday) through March 4, when President Lincoln's second inauguration would occur. They had little doubt that he would be reelected. Later, as plans became more elaborate, they would postpone the starting date to May 30. Proud of the fair mania they had started, Livermore and Hoge seemed determined to show the country again what Chicago could do. They set an ambitious fundraising goal of half a million dollars and decided that they must persuade the president to attend. Lincoln had traveled in June to Philadelphia for its Sanitary Commission fair, a wildly popular event that had raised more than $1 million. If the president had been willing to help the Philadelphia Sanitary Commission, surely he would do the same for his home state.[39]

Setting off for Washington in February 1865, Livermore and Hoge made a visit with President Lincoln their first priority. Lincoln received them "kindly." He already knew about the proposed fair and seemed receptive to the idea of attending. Jane Hoge suggested that a trip to Chicago would provide him with a change of pace and an opportunity to rest. Lincoln responded with laughter, relating his experiences at the Philadelphia fair in June. The crowds had been so large and so enthusiastic that "he actually feared he should be pulled from the carriage windows." He had shaken hands incessantly and had returned to Washington the following day "worn out worse than before I went."[40]

Mary Livermore told the president that he must be prepared for even more people in Chicago, for the entire Northwest would turn out to greet him. Petitions currently being circulated would contain the signatures of ten thousand Chicago women begging him to come. "What do you suppose my wife will say, at ten thousand ladies coming after me in that style?" Lincoln had protested. Livermore and Hoge assured him that Mrs. Lincoln would be invited to join him, and the president "promised attendance, if State duties did not absolutely forbid. . . . It would be wearisome . . . but it would gratify the people of the Northwest." Jane Hoge pledged that they would do everything they could to protect his privacy, proposing a steamer trip on Lake Michigan up to Mackinaw Island. It would be *"a season of absolute rest,"* she vowed.[41]

In 1860 Mary Livermore had had a lukewarm reaction to Lincoln's presidential candidacy. By now she had come to admire him greatly. After attending a public reception at the White House and observing the kindly and dignified manner in which he interacted with guests, she wrote: "It is impossible not to love the President. Awkward, homely, he yet finds his way to all hearts, and is to-day, we verily believe, the recipient of more affection than any living man." Although she did not criticize the president's wife in print, Livermore's dislike of fashion excess in wartime contrasted with Mrs. Lincoln's well-known penchant for elegant clothes. Livermore attended the White House reception in part so that she could meet Mary Todd Lincoln and invite her to the Chicago fair. While pleased that Mrs. Lincoln seemed interested in the idea, Livermore made a point of telling *New Covenant* readers that she had forgotten to notice the First Lady's attire and therefore could not write about it.[42]

Before returning home, the two women visited Philadelphia, Boston, and New York, where they held meetings with local volunteers and solicited aid for their forthcoming fair. In New York, USSC president Henry Bellows held a meeting in their honor. Bellows praised Chicago for having begun "the splendid series of Sanitary Fairs," and he predicted that the next fair would exceed expectations. After their visit, commission treasurer George Templeton Strong came away impressed, confiding in his diary that "Mrs. Hoge and Mrs. Livermore of Chicago . . . are fearful and wonderful women, whose horsepower is expressed in terms of droves of horses."[43]

After their month-long trip, Livermore and Hoge returned to Chicago with renewed dedication. As they had with the first fair, the two women encouraged the participation of all of Chicago's major religious denominations, each of which would be offered an opportunity to set up a display booth. Livermore had been appointed to head the Universalist department of the fair, and she intended the booth to be an appropriate showcase for her denomination. She reminded readers of the *New Covenant* that the Northwest's largest denomination, the Methodists, "are up and doing," and the Congregationalists were similarly active. Daniel agreed to help by serving as one of several corresponding secretaries. The Livermores offered to print the names of people who gave money toward this effort in their newspaper.[44]

In the midst of preparations for the fair, General Robert E. Lee surrendered his Army of Northern Virginia to General Ulysses S. Grant. The news reached Chicago a few hours later, on the evening of Sunday, April 9, 1865. Daniel was in Michigan preaching a sermon, but Mary was in Chicago, and she wrote about the city's reaction for the *New Covenant*. Her article, "The Dawn of Peace," captured Chicagoans' sense of relief and celebration: "Just as the church services of the Sabbath evening were ended, the bells clanged out the glad tidings, and the story they told was instinctively understood by every heart. All were waiting for it–all knew it would not be long delayed. Then the iron-throated cannon took up the jubilant tidings, and thundered it from a hundred guns–bonfires blazed . . . rockets flashed . . . huzzas and songs of the people rolled out from the heart of the city to its suburbs, and the quiet of the Sabbath night was broken by universal rejoicing." Few Chicagoans slept much that night, and the following day celebrations continued as businesses closed, bells peeled, cannons thundered anew, and a spontaneous procession of people began to form, many singing "Glory, Glory, Hallelujah." Mary offered thanks to God for the return of peace.[45]

Although Daniel and Mary Livermore had suffered wartime hardship, struggling financially to keep the *New Covenant* afloat, their family had been spared the loss of close relatives in military service. The same was not true of Mary's friends the Jones family in Mecklenburg County, Virginia. She had connected with a member of their household in a chance meeting during the war. On one of her trips to Washington, Livermore toured a contraband camp in nearby Alexandria, Virginia. Her entourage, which included Jane Hoge and other Sanitary Commission women, stopped first to see the house where Elmer Ellsworth had been slain. An Illinoisan and an early martyr to the Union cause, Ellsworth had led a group of Zouaves, flamboyantly dressed soldiers who often staged elaborate drills for adoring northern audiences during the early weeks of the war. Marching through Alexandria in May 1861, Ellsworth had spied a Confederate flag flying from the top of a house and determined to seize it. Shot and killed in the act, he became an immediate hero. Livermore described him as brave and foolish.[46]

The contraband camp fascinated the Sanitary Commission women, many of whom had no firsthand experience with slavery. For Livermore, the experience was particularly memorable because there she encountered Aunt Aggy, the Jones family's former housekeeper, now an escaped slave. Although it had been two decades since Mary had left Virginia, the elderly African American woman recognized her immediately because of her tall stature and erect posture and approached her in the camp. Aggy told Mary of the death of Jamie Jones, whom she correctly identified as a Confederate captain but incorrectly identified as having died in North Carolina. Livermore rejoiced in Aggy's freedom, while no doubt lamenting the deaths of Jones family members.[47]

Like thousands of families in the South, the Joneses had suffered greatly in the Civil War. James Jr. had been killed during the Shenandoah campaign in 1862. Son-in-law Benjamin Watkins Leigh, regarded as the most talented junior officer in Virginia's First Battalion, had transferred to the staff of General A. P. Hill; he died at Gettysburg during that battle's pivotal second day. Leigh left behind a widow, Courtney Jones Leigh, and three young children. Edward Cary Walthall, husband to Mary Jones Walthall, had a distinguished military career, ending the war a major general. He was the only family member to wear a Confederate uniform who survived the war.[48]

In the next few years the older generation of plantation residents would succumb to illness, infirmity, and death. After emancipation, Aggy appears to have returned to Mecklenburg County and adopted the surname of her former owner, for the 1870 federal census lists Aggy Jones, age eighty, black, and a resident of Palmer Springs Township, near St. Leon. Helen Jones, Mary's former employer, continued to reside at St. Leon until her death in 1870, which led to the sale of the family land.[49] The Joneses' once prosperous to-bacco and milling empire came to an end more than fifty years after the ambitious, enterprising young James Y. Jones had first bought land along the Roanoke River, their family saga a microcosm of the rise and fall of the nineteenth-century planter class in Virginia. For twenty-five years Mary Liv-ermore's life had intersected with that of the Jones family. Now, as their fortunes declined, hers would continue to rise.

CHAPTER 7

———◆•◆•◆———

Emergence of a Suffragist

"WOMEN DID LITTLE WORK of a public nature before the war," Mary Livermore told the *Boston Post* in 1890. "It was there that we found out we could do something more than our housework, charitable and church work. The Sanitary Commission carried women to the front at last and they have kept some hold upon affairs ever since." Livermore was a leader in the wartime process that challenged the place of middle-class women in public life. After the war, she kept hold on affairs by finding new outlets for her considerable talent, energy, and drive. One was to see the second Chicago sanitary fair to a conclusion. By the end of the decade she had discovered a new cause: political rights for women.[1]

Creating interest in the second fair presented a challenge, for the northern public seemed more interested in celebrating the end of hostilities than in caring for the thousands of sick and wounded soldiers who remained in military hospitals. Livermore hoped that President Lincoln's attendance would galvanize support for the event. On Friday, April 14, six weeks before the May 30 opening, Chicagoans learned from the *Tribune* that the president and Mrs. Lincoln planned to attend. A few hours later, Lincoln was assassinated at Ford's Theater. The *Tribune* received word of the tragedy in a telegraphic report at 4:00 A.M., and stunned Chicagoans awoke to read the details in the Saturday edition.[2]

Mary covered the arrival of Lincoln's funeral train for the *New Covenant*. She found the funeral cortege and the sight of Lincoln's body lying in state "solemn and imposing" and immensely sad. Recording her thoughts with uncharacteristic emotion, she wrote, "Not thus, Oh beloved President, did Chicago hope to receive thee. A month longer, and the great Northwest would have prepared for thee a joyous and brilliant welcome." As she filed past the casket to pay her respects, she recalled her meeting with Lincoln only six weeks before his death and Jane Hoge's promise to the president: *"When you come to Chicago, you shall have a season of absolute rest."* Now, "God has given His beloved a rest that we thought not of."[3]

Responsibility for the second fair slid from Livermore's and Hoge's hands to those of local men. Although the first fair had failed to yield support from the business and civic communities until the last two weeks before its inauguration, the second fair was the object of enthusiastic participation by public men right from the beginning. More than fifty subcommittees representing professions and fraternal organizations helped to plan the fair. Thomas Bryan of the Soldiers' Home presided at weekly meetings of the executive committee. Perhaps chafing under this arrangement and what she may have perceived as women's diminished role, Livermore introduced a resolution that "the ladies of the Executive Committee be authorised to act, in all matters pertaining to the interests of the Fair, as their own judgment may dictate, except, in cases where the expenditure of money is concerned." Minutes of the committee do not record whether her resolution was adopted. Revealingly, Livermore and Hoge each received the official title "Corresponding Secretary"; they had been "managers" of the first fair. Thomas Bryan would serve as "Permanent Chairman" and Eliphalet Blatchford as "Secretary & Treasurer," a role similar to the one he had played at the earlier fair. Major General Joseph Hooker accepted the honorary position "President of the Fair."[4]

With the war over and the nation feeling patriotic, Chicago's Democratic press displayed none of the hostility that had characterized its coverage of the first fair. Indeed, the *Chicago Times* appeared generally supportive of the entire affair, editorializing that while citizens may have had "differences of opinion respecting the prosecution of the war," they were now united in backing an event to help soldiers and their families. Nevertheless, Mary Livermore found herself compelled to use her skills as negotiator and consensus builder in dealing with a potentially explosive issue. Three weeks before the fair was to start, the U.S. Christian Commission threatened to withdraw its support if it did not receive a share of the proceeds. If evangelicals throughout the region stayed home in solidarity with the USCC, the fair was doomed to fail. With great reluctance, Livermore joined other members of the executive committee in agreeing to give the USCC $50,000 and at the same time to raise the Soldiers' Home allotment to the same figure. The official statement issued by the executive committee spoke of "removing all occasions for unseemly rivalry or unchristian spirit."[5]

Friction between the Sanitary Commission and the Christian Commission had persisted throughout the war. According to the *New Covenant*, the two organizations had achieved a kind of uneasy peace by the fall of 1864, in order to avoid the open hostility which had characterized the two organizations in the East. In Chicago, the Christian Commission agreed to send sanitary stores to the USSC, and the Sanitary Commission had agreed in turn to let the USCC draw on its stores on an "as needed" basis. By 1865, however, the *Covenant* reported that the relationship between the two had deteriorated. In a series of articles in January of that year, Daniel Livermore explored this theme. He alleged that the USCC had been "inaugurated by orthodox religionists in opposition to the Sanitary Commission," and further stated that the Christian Commission directly threatened the USSC by gaining control over individual ladies' aid societies and local sanitary fairs.[6]

Given the vituperative tone that the *New Covenant* had taken toward the Christian Commission during the early months of 1865, Daniel and Mary Livermore had some explaining to do when they asked northwestern Universalists to support the forthcoming fair despite the Christian Commission's new role in it. Mary tackled this highly charged topic in an editorial on May 20, just ten days before the fair was to open. Acknowledging the tension between the USSC and the USCC in recent months, she reminded *New Covenant* readers that turning over a modest portion of the fair's proceeds was a relatively small price to pay for "a cessation of hostilities" between the rival organizations. The Sanitary Commission and Soldiers' Home deserved Universalists' support. Privately, Livermore revealed her anger in a letter to John Newberry. "Our Fair progresses gloriously," she wrote, "despite the malignant efforts of the Chris. Com. to hinder it."[7]

In the weeks before the fair commenced, Mary Livermore worked on preparations at a furious pace. She fed a constant stream of descriptive copy to Chicago's daily newspapers, providing updates about financial contributions, donations of fancy goods, and construction of the headquarters. Projected to cover an entire acre at Washington, Randolph, Michigan, and Park streets, the "Mammoth Building" would be the largest public hall ever built in Chicago. The fair's executive committee quietly canceled plans for a public ceremony to lay the cornerstone, on hold since Lincoln's assassination, and ordered the building's construction without preliminary fanfare.[8]

The Great Soldiers' Fair, as the *Chicago Tribune* called it, commenced on Tuesday, May 30, 1865, a bright, temperate, nearly perfect day. Although the crowds were not as large as those gathered for the 1863 fair, the *Tribune* characterized the local audience as "earnest." Two corps of veterans led the way, the Eighth Veteran Reserve Corps, which excited onlookers with its "marching and wheeling," and the Fifteenth Veteran Reserve Corps, with its colors still draped in black to honor the president in whose funeral procession the veterans had marched less than one month earlier. Dignitaries and elected officials rode in carriages interspersed with marching bands. The Northern Illinois Coal and Iron Company joined the procession with twelve wagons of coal. In another wagon a young woman, shielded from the sun by a canopy of American flags, operated a Grover & Baker's sewing machine, a not inconsiderable feat in a moving vehicle. The last wagon carried members of the Colored Masonic Fraternity. The presence of African Americans in this parade represented a marked contrast to the 1863 affair, where they were conspicuously absent. Nevertheless, black participation may have been limited to the parade. African American religious and fraternal organizations were not represented among the booths inside the fair's main building.[9]

Mary Livermore and Jane Hoge undoubtedly rode in a carriage with other members of the executive committee, and, immediately after the procession, adjourned to the Tremont House, where dinner was served to military, civic, and fair officials. Governor Richard Oglesby then gave a speech that set a caustic tone for the fair. "Every man in rebellion against the United States is guilty of treason, and deserves the punishment of death," Oglesby intoned, though he also suggested that "those most prominent in guilt should be made to suffer most." The governor's speech resonated with a crowd that was still recovering from war and still mourning the death of a beloved president. He "retired amid loud applause," according to one report.[10]

Union Hall was a temporary wooden structure of immense size, divided into large halls, the center dominated by an enormous Gothic arch. For the price of fifty cents per day, or three dollars for a "season ticket," spectators gained admission, with additional fees required for special exhibits in other sites, including the floral displays in Horticultural Hall, the art, arms and trophy displays at Bryan Hall, a mammoth ox nicknamed "General Grant" housed in an outdoor pen, and a miniature replica of the Civil War naval battle between the *Monitor* and the *Merrimack* assembled in what the *Tribune* called "a kind of aquatic amphitheater" near the lake shore. Each afternoon the historic battle was reenacted several times, complete with firing artillery. Ladies of the Baptist church took charge of the fair's principal restaurant. Housed in the Soldiers' Home, the "New England Farm House" dished out home-cooked meals in a setting designed to invoke nostalgia for colonial days, including immense kettles and pots placed over an open fire, and spinning wheels and an old musket as authentic props.[11]

Many churches and organizations offered war-related materials for display. Chicago's German Americans unveiled an oil painting of General Philip Sheridan leading a cavalry charge. The Public School Department exhibited a wreath constructed of seeds from Abraham Lincoln's Springfield garden. The city of Liverpool, England, had a booth that showcased a painting depicting the sinking of the rebel ship *Alabama*, presented by an American diplomat. The Congregationalists paraded a kitten "born . . . under the rebel flag" and taken from Fort Sumter when federals captured the South Carolina fortress. It would be sold at auction to the highest bidder. The Episcopalians displayed a wreath said to be made from the hair of various celebrities, including President Lincoln and one of his sons. Not to be outdone, Mary Livermore's Universalist booth offered a glass case filled with Confederate bonds collected by her friend the Reverend William Ryder on a recent trip to Richmond. She had hoped to display the petticoats that Confederate president Jefferson Davis was rumored to have been wearing at the time of his capture in Irwinville, Georgia, a few weeks earlier.[12]

In an effort to obtain the undergarments, she had telegraphed her friend Senator James Harlan of Iowa, who forwarded her telegram to Secretary of War Edwin M. Stanton. Stanton consented, ordering someone to fetch the "crinoline" from Fortress Monroe, Virginia, where Davis was being held. Although northern newspapers widely trumpeted Davis's alleged attempt to elude capture by wearing a woman's dress and undergarments, thereby depicting him as an unmanly coward, in fact the beleaguered Confederate had never worn such a disguise. Urged by his wife to escape, he had grabbed a raincoat, which turned out to be hers, and she had thrown a shawl over his head and shoulders. The ruse had failed, and the entire Davis family was captured. There was no "crinoline" for a disappointed Livermore to display.[13]

Fairgoers were presented with dramatically different images of Davis and

Lincoln. In Bryan Hall's arms and trophies department, huge crowds gathered around a life-sized caricature of Jefferson Davis made out of wax, lent by the proprietor of Colonel Wood's Museum. *Voice of the Fair*, the official organ of the festival, crowed: "Let no one fail to see her. A sight of this blatant rebel, fugitive president, and disguised old lady, will amply repay the investment of a quarter." The *Chicago Tribune* expressed regret that the city had not been able to display the *real* Davis, for surely "none but crocodile eyes would weep over his fate." Visitors also enjoyed the chance to see Davis's pistol, loaded and capped just as it had been when the Fourth Michigan Cavalry captured the fleeing Confederate. It was a great favorite of soldiers who came to Bryan Hall. The fair paid tribute to President Lincoln in a variety of ways. Visitors might see a plaster cast of Lincoln's hand by Chicago sculptor Leonard Volk. They could also inspect a variety of funerary artifacts, including the catafalque used for Lincoln's coffin when he lay in state in Chicago. At the corner of Randolph and Wabash streets, Lincoln's relatives John and Dennis Hanks had reassembled the log cabin once owned by Lincoln's father near Decatur, Illinois. The price of twenty-five cents allowed admittance to the cabin and a chance to hear the Hanks men discuss the early life of its former occupant, who had helped his father build the cabin in 1830. For Chicagoans, the modest log structure symbolized Lincoln as the simple, rustic rail-splitter and man of the people and made an appropriate contrast to Davis, condemned by the *Chicago Tribune* for his "Jesuitical cunning . . . [and] heart of Satan."[14]

During the fair's second week, the United States Sanitary Commission celebrated its fourth anniversary with an afternoon program in Chicago. Henry Bellows, the national president, gave a speech to an estimated audience of ten thousand at Union Hall, praising women's roles in the Union victory.[15] But the high points of the fair came with the visits of William T. Sherman and Ulysses S. Grant, whose respective appearances occurred immediately before and just after the Sanitary Commission anniversary. Both received rousing welcomes and public accolades.

Traveling to Chicago with his wife and children, Major General William T. Sherman appeared at Union Hall on June 8, greeted on the platform by Mary Livermore and Jane Hoge. Introduced to the huge audience by Mayor John B. Rice and received by deafening cheers, Sherman gave a speech that was short and to the point. "I am not a man of words," he began, "and deeds can only be recorded by others." He praised the men in his army, "your brothers and your sons . . . men of Chicago" who had fought the war to its victorious conclusion. Sherman's speech was also marked by a degree of magnanimity toward the Confederacy that had been notably lacking in the fair's proceedings thus far. Ironically, the man so closely associated with the destruction of the South made the fair's most impassioned plea for reconciliation between the sections. "Now all is peace from here to the gulf," Sherman declared. "Instead of destroying you must build up; instead of insulting you must conciliate."[16]

Grant's appearance at the fair brought an even more boisterous public response. In March, Livermore and Hoge had written to the commanding general at his headquarters in City Point, Virginia, inviting him to attend the Chicago fair and suggesting comically that he "hurry up [taking] Richmond" so he could do so. Grant had responded formally: "My duties are such as to make it impossible for me to promise anything ahead except continued efforts to suppress the existing rebellion, and to render needless, as soon as I can, the humane offices of the Sanitary Commission." With the war now over, Grant seemed eager to honor his soldiers, raise money in their behalf, and accept the accolades of the public.[17]

The general and his wife, Julia, arrived in Chicago on Saturday, June 10. He delighted the crowd at the train station by mounting Jack, the horse he had left behind when he went east to fight Lee in 1864. Grant then rode through Chicago's streets responding to cheers by bowing and tipping his hat. Later he donated the horse for auction. Grant made several visits to the fair buildings, appearing with Sherman at Union Hall, where he accepted the cheers of the crowd but declined to speak, attending Methodist church services Sunday morning and greeting a steady stream of well-wishers, and appearing one last time at Union Hall on Monday morning. He was quickly surrounded by young women volunteers hoping to show their affection. Mary Livermore told the commander, "These girls are dying to kiss you–but they don't dare to do it." Grant replied, "Well, if they want to kiss me, why don't they? Nobody has offered to since I have been here." A hundred young women then converged upon the blushing commander.[18]

The Soldiers' Fair continued for several more weeks, although popular interest in the festivities declined with Grant's departure and Sherman's decision to cut back his public appearances. By the time it ended, the fair had raised $325,000, a successful profit by any estimate. And yet, despite the excitement over Sherman's and Grant's appearances, Livermore and Hoge had fallen short of their goal to raise $500,000, the amount Livermore had told John Newberry in February was "the smallest sum which will content us." They were hampered in their efforts by the difficulty of convincing people of the necessity to sustain the commission's treasury after the cessation of hostilities, as well as by the refusal of some religious liberals to support an endeavor that included the Christian Commission. Writing in the *New Covenant*, Livermore could not hide her disappointment. She believed that the Northwest could and should have been more generous. The fair's proceeds represented "not a third of what they would have been had the war continued," she believed, noting that thousands of men remained in Union hospitals while thousands more were being disgorged from Andersonville Prison and "other Southern hells." Livermore did offer praise for Universalists, whose department had raised $6,000, nearly as much as the Methodists and Presbyterians, whose denominations had far more adherents in the Midwest.[19]

In writing about Cincinnati's Sanitary Commission fair held in December 1863, Livermore had noted that it lacked the "white-heat earnestness and enthusiasm" of Chicago's 1863 fair. Although she did not come right out and say it, the same was true of the 1865 Chicago fair. The earlier fair had inspired a sense of public unity and moral rectitude that seemed somehow missing in the later event, with its wax image of Jefferson Davis and its jingoistic condemnation of a defeated enemy. While the 1863 fair had ended with a series of patriotic banquets, with speakers promising a brighter and better future, the 1865 fair simply faded out, crowds declining until, by June 27, the *Chicago Tribune* called it "an ignominious end to a great enterprise." Symptomatic of the fair's troubles, two Lincoln manuscripts put up for auction failed to solicit adequate bids, surely an embarrassment to the fair's executive committee.[20]

Livermore's discussion of the 1865 fair in *My Story of the War* is as revealing for what it does *not* say as for what is included. While she devoted several chapters to a detailed description of the earlier fair, she relegated the 1865 event to a few pages. Noting that "at no time were the wants of the soldiers more pressing than then," she recalled that the proceeds were to be divided between the Soldiers' Home and the Sanitary Commission, failing to mention the Christian Commission's role at all. Beyond that, she confined her discussion to General Grant's visit and a lengthy description of "Old Abe," the live eagle mascot of a Wisconsin regiment, whose popularity was so great that the fair raised money selling its photograph. Livermore made no reference to the wax image of Jefferson Davis or her own role in attempting to obtain Davis's nonexistent petticoats.[21] Perhaps Livermore's relative silence on the 1865 fair revealed her understanding that an occasion that should have been a celebration of peace, national unity, and emancipation of the slaves had become, in some respects, a tasteless attempt to pillory an already vanquished foe. African Americans, whose liberation had been a crucial achievement of the war, had been given only a peripheral role to play at the fair.

Although the second fair did not live up to her expectations, Mary Livermore could look back on her wartime career with pride. In October 1865 she resigned her position with the U.S. Sanitary Commission just as the commission was in the process of disbanding.[22] She had been a volunteer during the first year of the war and co-manager of its Chicago office since December 1862. Throughout the war she served as a tireless spokeswoman, promoter, and defender of the commission. At no other time in her life would Livermore direct so much energy toward the benefit of those in need. Through her work with the commission, the Universalist Church, the Soldiers' Home, the Home for the Friendless, and the Society for the Relief of Soldiers' Families, she had given of her myriad talents, her indefatigable energy, and her indomitable will. If service in wartime has a tendency to bring out the best in people, it had brought out the best in Mary Livermore.

After her resignation Livermore needed to spend time with her family, help Daniel with the *New Covenant*, and rest. She supported a favorite charity, the Home for the Friendless, and found employment for her wartime friend Mary Ann Bickerdyke as housekeeper there. With Jane Hoge, Livermore maintained a cordial relationship, although the two women went their separate ways. After the war, Hoge moved to Evanston, north of Chicago, and helped raise money to found Evanston College for Ladies, which later became part of Northwestern University. In 1867 she published a memoir, *The Boys in Blue*, which Livermore recommended to readers of the *New Covenant*.[23]

Mary Livermore's postwar editorials in the *New Covenant* focused on religious and domestic themes. She spoke of the need for more passion in Universalist sermons. She also criticized Chicago's Protestant denominations for constructing new, unnecessarily ostentatious churches with high pew rentals, which she regarded as undemocratic and liable to discourage religious participation by the masses. On occasion Livermore wrote humorous essays about the vicissitudes of coping with railroads, hotels, and restaurants. In January 1869, for example, she recounted her experience journeying to Dubuque, Iowa, for a meeting relating to her work with the Universalist Church. On the return trip she spent an unrestful night in a rail car occupied largely by men going to Chicago to attend an army reunion. Several men snored loudly and others responded by swearing at them. "The vocabulary of profanity must have been exhausted before morning," Livermore wrote, "for every species of profane epithet was hurled at the unconscious [men], who notwithstanding, slept as soundly, as they snored profoundly." At 3:00 A.M. a weary Mary Livermore noticed that a sleeping berth nearby looked vacant. Believing that its occupant, a former Union general, had left for a hotel, as was often the practice in those days, she climbed into the vacant bunk. She recorded what happened next, using "we" to mean herself:

> Judge of our horror, when a sepulchral voice issued from under the blankets whereupon we were sitting–"Madam, this is altogether too much of a good thing!" If we had found ourself sitting on a bombshell, with the fuse lighted, we should not have beat a speedier retreat. . . . We watched the papers for two or three days, anxious to know if any harm came to the white-haired General from the crush he received. We could not have forgiven ourself it there had. But as we saw that he, with his comrades, were able to do a great deal of talking at the Reunion, and a vast deal more of *drinking*, we concluded that we were more scared, than he was hurt.[24]

The chatty, informal articles Livermore wrote in the 1860s reveal her sense of closeness to *New Covenant* readers. She wrote as though addressing a group of friends. These articles also reveal an ability to laugh even about issues she took seriously, such as propriety, temperance, and profanity. Without a doubt, Daniel viewed her as an asset to his paper. In his first editorial of 1867 he promised that "Mrs. Livermore will continue to write extensively for every number of the paper," clearly believing that her writing increased its circulation.[25]

By 1866 the Livermores had returned to serious political engagement, taking an editorial position on the issue of Reconstruction of the South. Their sympathies clearly lay with the Radical wing of the Republican Party in its efforts to create a more egalitarian racial order in the former Confederacy. They praised Congress for its passage of the civil rights bill, a measure designed to protect the legal rights of freed slaves from vicious segregation and vagrancy laws being passed in southern states. At the same time, the Livermores began publishing a series of articles that were scathing in their criticism of President Andrew Johnson, whose veto of the civil rights bill ended in congressional override. Johnson's attempts to thwart this and other congressional initiatives infuriated the Livermores. They endorsed efforts to remove

Johnson from office by impeachment, urging Congress to send Johnson "back [home] to Tennessee, to ignominy and obscurity."[26]

When Mary's anti-Johnson editorial elicited the response that "women have no business to meddle in politics," the Livermores found themselves having to make a choice between appeasing the more conservative members of their denomination and being true to themselves. Daniel's leadership in the Connecticut temperance crusade had cost him his job in Stafford fifteen years earlier. In Auburn, New York, their views on the slavery question had ultimately caused them to leave in order to pursue a new life in the West. Now they found themselves again in an uncomfortable position. Daniel's uneasiness can be sensed in his annual "New Volume" editorial for January 1867. He acknowledged that the *New Covenant* was "the recognized organ of our denomination in the Northwest," but also reminded readers that the *Covenant* "is our individual property, and we must determine what articles to admit into its columns."[27]

Optimistically predicting that Johnson would be found guilty and removed from office, the Livermores had nothing to say when the opposite occurred. Indeed, they stayed curiously quiet about national political affairs during the remainder of their *Covenant* ownership. In February 1868 they did print a story reporting rumors that Republican presidential candidate Ulysses S. Grant had become a "hard drinker." They called for investigation: "Let the *people* set their faces like flint against the election of another drunkard–be he who he may–into the presidential chair."[28] These were harsh words about a man Mary had greeted in Chicago as a national hero eighteen months earlier. The Livermores did not comment on Grant's election or inauguration. It is possible that they succumbed to pressure from denominational brothers unhappy with their editorial policy and deliberately refrained from taking a position on presidential politics. It is also possible that they had further misgivings about Grant but chose not to express them publicly, given the lack of a more virtuous candidate on the national political scene. It is likely that, with the impeachment crisis over, they moved on to other reform issues of importance to both of them.

Woman's rights became Mary Livermore's central focus. While she had always believed that women should serve those in need, now she emphasized the political dimension. In *The Story of My Life* she recalled: "During the war, and as the result of my own observations, I became aware that a large portion of the nation's work was badly done, or not done at all, because

woman was not recognized as a factor in the political world." She truly believed, as she once wrote to a friend, that the war had been "God's missionary." "At Appomattox, the Republic had its new birth," she told an audience
in 1880, "baptized a second time in the blood of patriots" and cleansed of the
"stain of slavery." For the rest of her long and productive career, she would
invoke the war as a transforming experience for herself and her gender. Any
doubts she had once had about being a public activist were now gone.[29]

Although her thoughts may have been developed on this subject by war's
end, her actions toward the goal of woman's rights were part of a gradual
process. One of the first steps she took, even before speaking out about Reconstruction, was to promote a greater role for women in the Universalist
Church. Her religious views clearly played an important part in her evolution
as a feminist. Universalism, with its emphasis on the equal potential of all
people to achieve salvation, provided Livermore with an egalitarian framework through which to pursue her goals. In a letter to a friend she would write
of her "new realization of what Christianity does for women."[30] Universalism
also gave Livermore a venue through which to take her first steps as a public
activist in support of expanding woman's sphere.

In an editorial printed in the *New Covenant* in August 1865 titled "What
Shall the Women Do?" she criticized "Liberal Christianity" for failing to employ the talents and energies of women more fully. To date, women's work in
the Universalist Church had been "spasmodic, and transitory," mostly confined to fundraising festivals. Although women had attended regional meetings and conferences, they did so mostly as passive spectators, while men did
the serious talking. Livermore issued an appeal, being careful to use language
designed not to alienate Universalist men: "Will it not be possible for our
brothers to assign to woman a place where she may work with them in fur-
thering their place and purposes?" Apparently the Northwestern Conference
of Universalists agreed with her, for in a meeting held in Chicago in November, they encouraged women, as Livermore put it, "to organize for the fur-
therance of denominational purposes," leaving it up to women themselves to
define this role. The conference's executive committee selected three women,
including Livermore, to inaugurate the "Woman's Missionary Movement."[31]

The three women quickly decided to raise money throughout the Northwest and to use their proceeds to sustain Universalist missionary efforts, including assistance with the costs of printing denominational literature. They
also planned to help struggling Universalist societies troubled by declining
membership or debt, and finally, they wanted to subsidize the educational

pursuits of "worthy but indigent theological students." Throwing herself into the effort with her usual indefatigable energy and focus, Livermore began giving public addresses in favor of the Woman's Missionary Movement, traveling sometimes with a delegation of Chicagoans as she did at Tecumseh, Michigan, in January 1866, and sometimes with Daniel, who accompanied her to Marshalltown, Iowa, in May of that year. In 1867 she wrote to her friend Olympia Brown, "I have been 'stumping' the North West this last year for the Missionary cause–and have found no opposition anywhere to the cause of woman." The *New Covenant* printed periodic updates about the fundraising efforts of the Woman's Missionary Fund.[32]

In part because the new organization funded theological studies for deserving students, Livermore found herself embroiled in a controversy among Universalists over the propriety of admitting women to the ministry. Rather than positioning herself in a way that would preclude dialogue, she took a stance that combined morality with pragmatism.

Mary Livermore understood the difficulties faced by female clergy, for many Universalists had made it clear that they were not ready to embrace the idea of having a female minister. Until such a time as opposition had abated somewhat, Livermore believed that women should not be encouraged to enter the ministry in large numbers. In addition, in order to succeed personally and help break the resistance to female clergy, women ministerial students must be "above mediocrity in point of talent," thoroughly educated, and, like all ministers, morally upright. But Livermore also recognized that there was an ethical issue at stake. The ministry was a sacred calling, and no talented woman called by God should fail to answer. "No power, ecclesiastical or other . . . has a right to hinder her," she editorialized in February 1868.[33]

In the late 1860s relatively few female Universalist ministers had pulpits, and Livermore went out of her way to support those who did, praising their talents and accomplishments. She described Augusta Chapin, who held a pastorate at Portland, Michigan, and later Mount Pleasant, Iowa, as "modest, lady-like, quiet and unassuming . . . [with] a most resolute will, [and] a solemn conviction that God sent her into the world for the very work she has undertaken."[34] Olympia Brown, who became a close friend of Livermore's, held a Universalist pastorate in Weymouth, Massachusetts, but wanted to move west. A Michigan native, Brown had graduated from Antioch College in 1860 and from St. Lawrence University theological school three years later. When the Northern Universalist Association ordained her, Brown became the denomination's first woman minister. Livermore tried to find employment for Brown in Chicago, for her own congregation was seeking a new pastor. Evidently Brown did not receive an offer, for in 1870 she left Weymouth for Bridgeport, Connecticut. Mary and Daniel Livermore did help to secure speaking engagements for Brown and for Phebe Hanaford, another friend and East Coast Universalist.[35]

The Livermores also supported a successful effort to found a theological seminary affiliated with Lombard College in Galesburg, Illinois. Traditionally, northwestern Universalist clergy trained at St. Lawrence in Canton, New York. Mary Livermore endorsed the proposed school because she believed that it would boost Universalists' presence in Illinois and also because she hoped that the new school would be receptive to female students. Women divinity students were so unwelcome in Canton, she reminded Olympia Brown, "that it is useless to send them." Livermore began fundraising for the new institution, soliciting donations at the same time she asked for money for the Woman's Missionary Fund. "*I am determined*, with God's help, to have a better Theo. School at Galesburg than that at Canton," she promised Brown. Meanwhile, in the *New Covenant*, Daniel Livermore launched a fundraising campaign in which he asked one hundred individuals to pledge $100 toward Lombard's $10,000 endowment campaign. Livermore promised to give $100 himself.[36]

In addition to her work promoting Universalist female clergy, Livermore herself became more visible within the denomination. In June 1868 the Northwestern Universalist Conference's nominating committee selected four women to become vice presidents of the conference, including Mary Livermore to represent Illinois. The *New Covenant* predicted that these four "will exhibit an interest in the Church Extension enterprise that will excite our wonder." Livermore gained even greater distinction when she traveled with Daniel to Providence, Rhode Island, that fall to attend a national meeting of the Universalist Church. To the best of her knowledge there had never been a woman delegate to the national convention, but when one of Illinois's lay delegates failed to appear, Livermore's name was substituted. She was duly elected and took her seat. "I claim the honor, therefore, of being the first woman delegate to the U[nited] S[tates] C[ouncil] of Universalists, and I wear it somewhat proudly," she wrote home to *New Covenant* readers, adding, "I hope nobody will try to 'take me down a peg,' by reminding me that, like [President] Andrew Johnson, my honor came through an accident, for I intend to ignore this fact."[37]

In 1868 Livermore began writing articles for the Universalist monthly magazine *Ladies Repository*, reestablishing ties with a publication she had written for in the 1840s and 1850s, before moving to Chicago and assuming her editorial role with the *New Covenant*. Livermore's friend Phebe Hanaford now edited the magazine. The January 1868 issue of *Ladies Repository* led off with a biographical article about Livermore written by the Reverend J. S. Dennis and accompanied by her likeness in a steel engraving. Dennis praised her "energy and courage" during the Civil War, including her organization of two major fairs, and spoke of the hardship and danger she endured at the front, even within range of Confederate fire. He proclaimed, "Thousands in our land . . . have learned to admire and love her."[38] Clearly the Universalist Church had embraced Mary Livermore as a heroine.

Over the next eighteen months Livermore published many articles in the magazine, most of them focused on the patriotism of northern Unionists, including Abraham Lincoln and Mary Ann Bickerdyke. Some of these stories had already appeared in the *New Covenant*, although others were original essays. She also wrote about her experiences on a Virginia plantation, which she did not identify as St. Leon. Apparently this was to be the first in a proposed series exploring the antebellum South.[39]

She never completed the series. In April 1869 the Universalists' Boston-based North East Publishing House fired Phebe Hanaford as editor because she had promoted the right of women to preach and did so herself. Although Hanaford had edited the *Ladies Repository* since 1866, she was not ordained in the denomination until 1868, the same year that Livermore started contributing to the journal. Livermore expressed her outrage to *New Covenant* readers. "Our women clergy have been slandered, caricatured, insulted, and persecuted," she complained. Blasting the publisher for its part in this deplorable situation, she charged the company with playing a central role in attempts at "crushing out half a dozen good and gifted women, whose sole crime is that they feel called to God to preach the gospel of a world's salvation, and *are* preaching it, with a success that verifies their claim." Adding insult to injury, Hanaford had not even been allowed to give a "valedictory" in her last edition. Livermore did not publish in the *Ladies Repository* after Hanaford's dismissal. Presumably the decision was hers and not the new editor's, since, as late as January 1870, the magazine still claimed that Livermore intended to finish the Virginia sketch. Although Livermore believed that the Universalist Church had made important strides during the late 1860s, she also felt a sense of frustration over her denomination's unwillingness to move more quickly to incorporate women into its leadership structure.[40]

Increasingly Mary Livermore devoted her attention to the issue of female advancement. Impatient with those who questioned women's interest in national affairs and their ability to make contributions to civic and religious life, she would hold back no longer. The former Sanitary Commission leader who had acquiesced to male domination of the second fair, the church activist who had used conciliatory language to appease male Universalists, gave way to a feminist of unyielding determination. The strong-minded woman finally won out over the traditional one.

Central to Livermore's vision of female advancement was economic independence. As a young woman she had read Margaret Fuller's *Woman in the Nineteenth Century*, first published in 1845. In this landmark text Fuller advocated women's "self-reliance and self-impulse," not because she believed that women did not need men, but because their "excessive devotion" to men through the ages had prevented them from living up to their full potential.[41] During the Civil War, Livermore had editorialized about the need for women to reject old taboos against paid labor and called on society to allow women greater financial opportunities. She returned to that subject in a series of editorials for the *New Covenant*.

A workingwoman since the age of fourteen and "desirous to be known as such," Livermore believed that a woman's professional advancement should be limited only by her capacity. Moreover, she should be paid "the same wages as men are, for doing the same work." In the *New Covenant* office, the Livermores showed their support for women workers by hiring female typesetters exclusively. They placed "Miss Mary Tomlin" in charge of the presses and instructed her to hire and fire subordinates. The results had been very satisfactory. Tomlin and her staff of four handled all printing, folding, and mailing of the weekly newspaper and quickly established a reputation for competence and reliability. Hiring women typesetters had the added benefit of freeing their office from tobacco smoke and profanity. By calling attention to their own success, the Livermores hoped that other employers would follow their example. Mary Livermore's sympathy for workingwomen was also manifested in articles praising the creation of a "Sewing Women's Home," opened in the fall of 1865 to provide housing for the city's many seamstresses and a Woman's Home founded three years later to provide room and board at reasonable rates for up to eighty-four workingwomen.[42]

In 1867 Mary Livermore publicly endorsed women's right to vote. Although the issue had seemed less important to her than empowering women economically, the vote was clearly emerging as a central concern of leading women reformers, including Elizabeth Cady Stanton, Susan B. Anthony, and Lucy Stone. As national debate over the enfranchisement of African American men grew in intensity, woman suffragists actively lobbied for inclusion of women in legislation being considered by Congress. It was an issue that seemed to resonate with women. "The Civil War was a time when middle-class women came to believe that they had an acknowledged stake in a national ordeal of overwhelming importance, a personal stake in national politics," the historian Lyde Cullen Sizer has written. When the state of Kansas began debating universal enfranchisement, Stanton, Anthony, and Stone went west to campaign in its favor. With attention thus focused on the West, and Chicago as its de facto capital, Livermore realized that it was time for her to take a stand. By doing do, she would position herself to lead the new movement in the West. Writing a letter of introduction to Susan B. Anthony, she referred to her *New Covenant* editorials about women's economic advancement, then acknowledged the national focus on voting rights. "I have announced myself as henceforth committed to the cause of woman suffrage," she told Anthony. Three weeks later she wrote a suffrage editorial for the *New Covenant* defending female voting as a right of citizenship and a safeguard to protect life and property. Livermore knew that her editorial would arouse controversy among the newspaper's more conservative readers. She received five disapproving letters right away.[43]

Two years after her public declaration as a suffragist, Mary Livermore organized a woman's rights convention in Chicago, the first ever held in the city. Her efforts would provide a forum for woman's rights in the Midwest and would bring her into contact with some of feminism's leading national proponents.

Although she was not a key player in the national feminist movement before 1869, Livermore followed developments in the newspapers. At the end of the Civil War, feminists and their abolitionist allies founded an organization called the American Equal Rights Association, in order to advance the interests of both women and African Americans, notably toward the goal of universal suffrage. The group quickly became embroiled in acrimony when it divided over the question of whether to support the Fourteenth Amendment, which granted civil rights to black men and demanded that southern states enfranchise them or face the possibility of a reduction in congressional representation. Elizabeth Cady Stanton and Susan B. Anthony alienated many of their colleagues by denouncing the amendment for defining citizenship in purely male terms, but it won ratification by the requisite number of states in 1868.

Stanton, Anthony, and other feminists had already turned their attention toward the Kansas universal suffrage campaign, an effort that went down to
resounding defeat.[44]

It was in this context that Livermore issued her call for a convention to be
held in Chicago in February. Her meeting aroused controversy even before it
began. The previous year she had helped to found a Chicago branch of the
women's club known as Sorosis. According to the *Chicago Tribune*, its goals
would be "to promote the welfare of both sexes–the female sex especially."
Woman suffrage quickly emerged as a central focus of the new organization,
and Livermore, along with other leaders, began making plans for a convention
to promote this cause. Later that year disagreement over priorities and procedures led to a split within Sorosis, with one faction led by Mary Livermore
and the other by Delia Waterman and Cynthia Leonard. Both groups moved
forward with plans to hold separate woman suffrage conventions.[45]

Mary Livermore appears to have made some attempts to bring the two
groups together. Portending a philosophical position she would take in the
future, she believed that the woman suffrage conventions should focus exclusively on women's issues without being sidetracked by other reform causes,
however worthy they might be. The Waterman-Leonard faction, which
claimed use of the name Sorosis, found her terms unreasonable, and the two
groups continued to plan competing conventions. When Sorosis members
wrote letters to Chicago newspapers defending their interest in a broad range
of issues and blaming Livermore for the schism, she did not respond. According to the sociologist Steven Buechler, Livermore knew that she had succeeded in recruiting the most important reformers in Illinois's incipient suffrage movement, and for that reason she may have chosen to ignore Sorosis
after her reconciliation efforts had been rebuffed. Livermore did share her
view of Sorosis in a letter to Olympia Brown. Complaining about the preva-
lence of spiritualists among them, she told Brown that she had tried her best
to bring the members of Sorosis under her suffrage umbrella. "We are compelled to go on without them," she wrote one week before her convention
began. "Sorosis has not an educated, executive, intelligent, or influential
woman among them–only they are *women*, and we would like all women to
pull together."[46]

Mary Livermore gaveled to order the first woman's rights convention ever
held in the city of Chicago on the morning of Thursday, February 11, 1869.
Participants filled Library Hall to capacity. Livermore persuaded some of the
city's leading citizens to attend, many of them individuals she had worked

with in the Sanitary Commission, including Robert Collyer and James Bradwell and his wife, Myra, who in 1868 had started a newspaper called the *Chicago Legal News*. She publicized the convention in its pages. From Galesburg,
the Reverend Edward Beecher arrived to join the proceedings, a respected
clergyman and brother of Harriet Beecher Stowe. The former slave and noted
abolitionist William Wells Brown, from Boston, represented African Americans. But Livermore's greatest coup had been to induce the feminists Elizabeth Cady Stanton, Susan B. Anthony, and Anna Dickinson to travel from the
East. Stanton and Anthony had spoken in Chicago in late 1867, when Livermore heard them for the first time. Deeply impressed by Stanton's intellect
and oratorical powers, she had described her to *New Covenant* readers as
"superior to any woman we have heard[,] even to Lucretia Mott in her best
days." The appearance of all three women at the February 1869 meeting attracted widespread public interest and equally widespread journalistic attention. Chicago's newspapers reported the proceedings of the convention almost verbatim, followed by articles relating to the Sorosis meeting being held
simultaneously in Music Hall.[47]

Elected president of the proceedings, Livermore chaired the two-day meeting. According to the *Chicago Tribune*, Livermore claimed that "she was not
very good at talking, but was pretty good at working, and should do all she
could." Livermore insisted that parliamentary procedures be followed and
that the proceedings be conducted in a manner that would be "Christian and
moral in every respect." Clearly, she wanted her first convention to be a
success. Because she was serving as president of the convention, Livermore
did not make a major speech. After announcing that the object of the meeting
was to further the cause of female suffrage in Illinois and then appointing a
committee to draft resolutions, she introduced a parade of speakers.[48]

Elizabeth Cady Stanton and Susan B. Anthony both gave speeches supporting woman suffrage and denouncing universal manhood suffrage, a cause that
was gaining momentum and would eventually lead to passage of the Fifteenth
Amendment, extending the vote to male African Americans. William Wells
Brown rebutted their position by reminding the audience that slaves had suffered more profoundly than women. He argued that the "negro question"
held the greatest importance to the nation at that time. Naomi Talbert spoke
next on behalf of "the colored women of Chicago," declaring that "woman
was needed to help in political affairs as well as in private and domestic affairs." Anthony brought the crowd into an uproar by proposing a resolution
suggesting that the Republican Party, by sponsoring the Fourteenth Amend-

ment, had acted in a manner that was "invidious and insulting to woman, and suicidal to the nation." A variety of speakers quickly expressed their opposition to Anthony, whose resolution was summarily rejected.[49]

The convention ended with more oratorical fireworks, passage of resolutions, and the creation of a new organization. Anna Dickinson drew applause and laughter when she debated a conservative clergyman who had argued that women's God-ordained work as nurturers of their families and guardians of their homes precluded their political participation. She pointed out that many women, herself included, had no husband, while many other women were trapped in marriages to drunken and abusive men, reason enough that women should be able to vote. Judge Charles B. Waite of the Committee on Resolutions submitted a report including a call for universal suffrage to be added to the Illinois constitution, justifying its passage as beneficial to "a happy home, a refined society, and a republican state." The report also called for educational opportunities for women along with new avenues of remunerative industry, a resolution that clearly reflected the sentiments of Mary Livermore.[50]

The convention concluded with the formation of an organization called the Illinois Woman Suffrage Association. Its goals would be to secure the elective franchise for Illinois women and to lobby against any "distinction [being] made in the laws relating to personal liberty, the custody of children, education or property on account of sex." Delegates elected Mary Livermore president and chose the Reverends Collyer and Beecher among the vice presidents. Myra Bradwell would serve as corresponding secretary. Although Livermore briefly objected to being elected president and thought that the organization might be better served by a male executive, she agreed to take the post, and also to represent the IWSA at the American Equal Rights Association anniversary to be held the second week of May, along with Myra Bradwell and Kate Doggett, a Chicago public school official.[51]

Livermore was very pleased with her convention. It was the first woman suffrage meeting she had ever attended. She had organized it, she had led it, and now she would lead its permanent organization. Although some newspaper reports had been hostile–the *Chicago Evening Journal* claimed that the new woman's movement "is evidently on the John Brown Trail"–others were complimentary. The *Burlington (Iowa) Hawkeye* sent a reporter, who wrote: "The meeting has created a great sensation. It is the theme of conversation and comment everywhere." Noting the "remarkable" audience in the *New Covenant*, Livermore praised Elizabeth Cady Stanton as "the most eminent woman of our country," commended Susan Anthony's earnestness, and applauded Anna Dickinson for having vanquished her clerical opponent. Livermore was equally proud that "the Convention did precisely what it set out to do, steering clear of all isms, and ologies and outside questions, and discussing the question of Woman Suffrage, right through the entire sessions, and no other." She admitted it was an "honor" to be asked to serve as president of the Illinois Woman Suffrage Association, an organization that she promised would promote not only suffrage but also employment opportunities for women and equal pay for equal work.[52]

Although she did not comment about Sorosis in her *New Covenant* editorial, Livermore must have been relieved to learn of the rival organization's less than stellar convention performance. Some of its delegates had accepted Judge Bradwell's invitation to join the Livermore convention, while others forged ahead despite their decreasing momentum. Although Sorosis created its own Universal Suffrage Association, the organization lasted only a few months. The Illinois Woman Suffrage Association remained in existence for more than fifty years, until passage of the Nineteenth Amendment granting women the vote at the national level.[53]

On March 3, 1869, Mary Livermore wrote a letter to Olympia Brown in which she characterized her new role as suffrage activist. "You see where the tide has carried me–clear out to sea. I am in for the [suffrage] war, now."[54] Livermore had begun lecturing two to four times a week in favor of the vote for women. Convinced that female enfranchisement would win acceptance in the West before it was embraced elsewhere in the country, Livermore threw herself into the cause with considerable energy and enthusiasm. She would devote the rest of her life to this crusade as a tireless organizer, speaker, and writer in support of woman's rights. Unfortunately, the "war" would take longer than she anticipated.

CHAPTER 8

The Agitator

D URING THE CONVENTION proceedings in February, Mary Livermore had hinted that a newspaper would soon be published to promote the interests of women in Illinois. On March 13, 1869, she started that newspaper, called the *Agitator*, assisted by Mary L. Walker as associate editor and by Daniel Livermore, who handled the business side of the operation. The *Agitator* would provide her with a vehicle through which to promote her new interest in feminism.

At the same time that they prepared the *Agitator*'s inaugural issue, the Livermores negotiated the sale of the *New Covenant*. Their decision was based in part on Daniel's reaching several milestones in his life, celebrating his fiftieth birthday and thirty years as a Universalist pastor. The Livermores had talked about scaling back their public work and perhaps moving out of the city to enjoy a quieter life in the countryside.[1]

Mary's newfound interest in woman's rights altered their plan and marked a formal change in their relationship, one that had been evolving since the beginning of the Civil War. For more than two decades of their marriage, Daniel's career had defined their lives together. Now, Mary's career took precedence over her husband's. Daniel Livermore believed his wife to be a woman of extraordinary ability. Comfortable with his marriage and with his masculine identity, he encouraged her to pursue a public role as woman's rights advocate, confident that she would have a "great career." He told Mary, "For twenty-five years . . . you have stood beside me, and merged yourself in my work, rendering me invaluable aid. . . . Now it is your turn."[2]

In the April 3, 1869, issue of the *New Covenant*, Daniel Livermore announced the newspaper's sale to the Reverends J. W. Hanson of Dubuque, Iowa, and Selden Gilbert of Bridgeport, Connecticut, effective May 1. In their final issue as owner-editors, the Livermores each wrote a valedictory column. Daniel admitted feeling "a sort of paternal regard" for a paper he had purchased when it was declining in subscribers and floundering financially. He now claimed a readership of 25,000 to 30,000. In her valedictory, Mary spoke of her interest in woman's rights, mentioning that "our own children are daughters, just entering womanhood, so that the question appeals to our motherhood," a rare public reference to Etta and Lizzie. She hoped to work in the cause of woman's rights for two to three years before retiring from the public spotlight. Both Livermores pledged their continued support for and activism in the Universalist Church.[3]

The *Agitator*'s first issue appeared on March 13, 1869. Its masthead announced that the weekly would be "Devoted to the Interests of Woman," and included this motto: "Healthy Agitation Precedes All True Reform." Although Livermore hoped to attract a respectable readership by emphasizing the paper's "high moral and Christian ground," she was now a committed feminist and did not intend to equivocate. "[My] position has been taken deliberately, after years of thought and investigation," she wrote, adding that she would not "be driven from it by opposition, nor laughed out of it by ridicule." No longer constrained by the need to consider the *New Covenant*'s more traditional readership, Livermore felt free to explore and express her feminist views on a variety of topics.[4]

Like the *New Covenant*, the *Agitator* was published once a week on Saturdays. The Livermores printed 1,500 copies each week, 800 to 900 of which went to subscribers and the rest to newsdealers, an initial readership well below the *Covenant*'s long-established regional base. At eight pages per issue, the *Agitator* was twice the *New Covenant*'s length. The last page often contained advertisements for a range of goods and services including women's clothing, household products, doctors, and private schools. A six-line ad cost $1.50, with a quarter column selling for $8, a half column for $12, and a full column for $25. The Livermores invested $3,000 of their own money to launch the publication.[5]

As they had with the *New Covenant*, the Livermores employed female type-setters. In one article Mary referred to the *Agitator*'s "excellent little fore-woman." In another she mentioned a visit from a man who represented the local Typographical Union, who evidently objected to her use of non-union typesetters. Undaunted, Livermore gave him two minutes to leave her office.[6]

Mary Walker appears to have been part owner of the *Agitator*. Although she held the title of associate editor, her role in the paper's production is unclear. A promotional column for the newspaper identified her as "Mrs. Mary L. Walker, late of the *Sorosis.*" Whatever Walker's initial function might have been, Livermore's editorial association with her was not a happy one. Within six weeks of the *Agitator*'s debut, she complained to Olympia Brown that Walker "is not competent—*entre nous.*" By July Walker had ceased to be affiliated with the newspaper, and Daniel Livermore's name began to appear beneath his wife's with the title "publisher." Mary served as sole editor for the newspaper after that. In a letter to suffragist Elizabeth Boynton she expressed relief that the partnership had ended, adding, "Mrs. Walker leaving did not increase my work—it diminished my anxiety and responsibility."[7]

If the *Agitator* provided her with unanticipated headaches, Livermore did find success on another front. Her newly formed Illinois Woman Suffrage Association sent her along with James and Myra Bradwell to Springfield to lobby the state legislature in favor of a bill to grant married women the right to control their own property. After the Civil War, with national attention focused on the meaning of freedom for the former slaves, feminists argued that working wives of all races should cease to be enslaved by their husbands. They suggested that control over property was woman's inalienable right and noted that drunken and dissolute men all too often misappropriated their wives' wages. James Bradwell and Mary Livermore, joined by Elizabeth Cady Stanton, spoke at the Springfield Opera House to a large audience that included many members of the legislature. They met with immediate success. On March 24, 1869, Illinois passed legislation giving a married woman the right to "receive, use and possess her own earnings, and sue for the same in her own name, free from the interference of her husband or his creditors." Myra Bradwell had been instrumental in drafting the legislation and publiciz-ing it in her *Chicago Legal News*. It was also a sweet victory for Livermore, who remembered vividly her rude treatment by the builder who had demanded her husband's signature and Abraham Hoge's on the construction contract for the fair in 1863. In the *Agitator* she praised Bradwell's role in passage of the legislation and described its "practical benefit" to Illinoisans, especially in protecting women from drunkard husbands, who could no longer "squander" their wives' earnings.[8]

Although suffrage would be a major theme of the *Agitator*, the newspaper reflected Livermore's equally strong commitment to educational and professional advancement for women. During the late 1860s women throughout the nation were demanding admission to public and private colleges, an issue Livermore endorsed with unbounded enthusiasm, at one point recalling her own dismay when, at age thirteen, she learned that she was ineligible to attend Harvard College. In the *Agitator* she reported unsuccessful attempts by women seeking admission to Wabash College in Crawfordsville, Indiana, and the "unhandsome treatment of women students" at the University of Wisconsin. Livermore urged women to "persist in their efforts" to receive educational parity with men. In Michigan, she reported, an organization called the Woman's Education Association was lobbying for female inclusion in higher learning by bringing this subject before the public. She also reprinted an article from the *Boston Commonwealth* about an initiative before the Massachusetts House to deny funding to any public college that refused women admission. Attempts to found women's colleges in the East also received Livermore's editorial attention. She printed numerous stories about Vassar College, begun in 1865, including its unique astronomy program organized by the noted scientist Maria Mitchell.[9]

Because of her commitment to women's economic advancement, Livermore explored the subject in many articles. Hoping to encourage women to enter professions other than the sewing trades, she devoted considerable attention to alternative forms of employment. Medicine provided career opportunities that an increasing number of women were seeking in the late 1860s. Livermore wrote about the Woman's Medical College of Cleveland, which hired Hannah Tracy Cutler, a prominent Illinois woman with a history of abolitionist and feminist activism, as a professor in 1869. She also showcased the New York Medical College for Women by printing a letter from Elizabeth Cady Stanton that described its recent graduation ceremonies, urged women to "crowd into the colleges and professions," and entreated wealthy philanthropically minded women to cease donating money to Harvard and Yale and start redirecting their efforts toward female education. Stanton signed the piece as editor of the *Revolution*. In January 1868 she and Susan Anthony, along with their good friend Parker Pillsbury, had begun publishing a woman's rights newspaper by this title in New York. A shared interest in journalism gave Livermore a further bond with the New York feminists and, in addition, opportunities for an exchange of ideas, letters, and occasionally articles.[10]

Although the *Agitator* never championed issues of racial equality to the same degree that it focused attention on education, employment, and suffrage, the paper did take a stand in support of civil rights. Livermore wanted the *Agitator*'s readers to know that six hundred women worked as government clerks in Washington, most of them in the Treasury Department. They earned $900 per year, a decent salary though considerably less than their male counterparts. She reported that an African American woman from Philadelphia, Miss E. J. Ketcham, had been hired as a Treasury clerk, proudly touting her accomplishment in breaking through the department's color line. She also included a story about the courage of a female teacher in Howell, Michigan, who stood up to the school director's attempt to oust a black pupil from her classroom. Livermore applauded the tenacity of the student's father in defending his son's cause, and noted that Howell's school now had an increasing population of African American students.[11]

After the Civil War, a growing number of women sought federal patronage jobs in local post offices. These positions, which carried good salaries, attracted Livermore's editorial attention, and she printed several notices about the appointment of women as postmistresses around the nation. One aspiring postmistress aroused her special interest, Angie King of Janesville, Wisconsin. For Livermore, King's travails came to symbolize the barriers women faced in postwar America and the limitations of the separate spheres doctrine. She wrote about King's story in the waning days of her affiliation with the *New Covenant* and showcased King's cause in an article on the very first page of the *Agitator*'s inaugural issue.

Angie King applied for the job of postmistress at Janesville after being nominated by the local YMCA. She had four years' experience as postal clerk there. According to Livermore, seven men also sought the job, which carried a handsome annual salary. The local congressman, Benjamin F. Hopkins, who would be making a recommendation to President Grant about whom to appoint, suggested an election in which the citizens of Janesville might make their wishes known. King defeated her nearest rival by forty-three votes. Immediately, disappointed local men made an effort to prevent her from winning a presidential recommendation and Senate confirmation, using as their rationale the argument that King had no brothers who had fought in the recent war, had not volunteered her time with the Sanitary Commission, and therefore did not deserve the position. Livermore expressed outrage at this denial of the democratic process. She also sharply criticized the Janesville men for their refusal to accept women's professional ambition. "They all seemed to regard it as the very acme of impertinence, the grand climacteric of presumption, for a woman to aspire to an office worth $3,000 a year, when there were seven men hungering and thirsting for it," she wrote, urging Janesville's women to contact to Congressman Hopkins and make their outrage known.[12]

The following week, acting on information received from a "correspondent" in Janesville, Livermore reported triumphantly that King's Unionist credentials were impeccable, including having a brother who served in Sherman's army and a stepfather who died in Richmond's Libby Prison. Moreover, wishing to deflect criticism that King did not "need" the salary, Livermore reported that Angie King, like "many another woman, now-a-days," supported a household, including an invalid sister. The Civil War's devastating impact on families meant that old notions about men as breadwinners and women as domestic partners had become anachronistic. Livermore called upon President Grant to act courageously and appoint Angie King as postmistress. While she was at it, Livermore also suggested that the president grant Mother Bickerdyke a federal pension.[13]

Although Livermore held out hope that Grant would appoint King–he had recently selected a woman as postmistress of Richmond, Virginia–he disappointed her. Already building a reputation for rewarding his army friends and cronies, the president reappointed the incumbent postmaster, Thomas J. Ruger, who was the father of a high-ranking army officer. Although the *Wisconsin Journal* editorialized favorably about the decision, relieving Congressman Hopkins from the "trial of passing judgment on the question of woman's rights as represented by Miss King," Livermore wrote a blistering commentary condemning Ruger's incompetence, which had led to Congressman Hopkins's decision to call for a vote in the first place. Ruger had not even been a candidate. "This shabby affair can't be whitewashed," she concluded. "Angie King's election was ignored because she is a *woman.* "[14]

Two weeks later Livermore reported that King had been fired as clerk by postmaster Ruger. Livermore again called for justice in the case, and King evidently tried to effect her reinstatement by disseminating a petition locally. Although Livermore moved on to other causes, the King episode reminded her of the obstacles all women faced. It also soured her view of Ulysses S. Grant. Determined to avoid being sidetracked from women's issues, she did not use her editorial voice to express her views on national politics, but she did occasionally let slip a comment about the president. In one instance she criticized his appointment of a few postmistresses as a token gesture to women; in another she cited the *Chicago Tribune* in calling him a "*blunder*buss."[15]

To her credit, Livermore did not focus all of her attention on middle-class women and their employment struggles. She also published stories showcasing jobs for those who lacked the educational background to be clerks, teachers, and doctors. One profession that she thought might provide opportunities for women was that of florist or horticulturalist. She believed that the commercial cultivation of shrubbery or fruit trees could offer women remunerative employment without the drudgery of heavy agriculture. In an article that appeared in the *Agitator* on April 17, titled "A Hint to Working-Women," she told the story of a widow forced to seek employment to support her children. With a minimal cash outlay, she had begun marketing plants grown in her home garden and had built up a business that yielded an annual income of $2,000 per year. The woman had published a book which Livermore recommended to her readership. Livermore also explored the plight of working-women in American cities, reporting about efforts to create boardinghouses for single women in New York and Chicago, and a convention in Boston that focused attention on the plight of charwomen, washerwomen, and seamstresses. Giving her newspaper an international focus, she published articles about workingwomen and woman's rights in England, France, Belgium, Austria, Germany, Sweden, Russia, and India. In an article titled "What Is Being Done for Women, in Europe," for example, she reported on the creation of Female Industrial Colleges in Belgium, evening schools in France, and Working Women's Colleges in England.[16]

Mary Livermore believed that women's traditional work in the home was undervalued and underappreciated. When a woman married, she took charge of an entire household, frequently assisting her husband in his employment as well, and yet receiving no compensation and little appreciation for her labors. Moreover, newly married women were often ill prepared to assume their role as housekeepers. Twenty-five years earlier, Mary Rice certainly had been. An early edition of the *Agitator* reprinted an article from the *Boston Journal* advocating the creation of a school of Industrial Home Science to instruct young women in the mechanics of homemaking. Livermore also explored a variety of ideas about communal housekeeping, including a series of articles about communal laundries written by Kansas feminist Helen Starrett.

Livermore felt a special regard for this topic since she had started her own cooperative laundry during the war.[17]

Dress reform had been one of Mary Livermore's favorite topics for some years, and she discussed this subject several times in early issues of the *Agitator*, at one point declaring, "When will women learn that *simplicity* is beauty? . . . When will they learn to put health and intelligence before fine clothes?" She also supported the temperance cause with an occasional article, including one titled "A Year's Worth of Dramselling," in which she blamed liquor consumption for the deaths of 60,000 and the imprisonment of 100,000 Americans annually. She avoided the issue of divorce, probably regarding it as too controversial even to discuss in the *Agitator*.[18]

Along with education and employment, suffrage became the central focus of Livermore's newspaper. She reported on regional and national developments and printed a variety of articles defending woman suffrage and refuting those who opposed it. She wanted her readers to understand that the nation's most upstanding men and women supported female enfranchisement, that the movement was gaining momentum, and that the eventual inclusion of women in the electorate had become "inevitable."[19]

Livermore hoped that her Chicago convention in February 1869 had created interest in the suffrage cause throughout the West. She reported on local and state conventions and debates being held in midwestern legislatures that spring. In March, for example, she traveled to Milwaukee to attend a suffrage convention and assist in the creation of a Wisconsin state suffrage association. As part of a delegation that included Elizabeth Cady Stanton, Susan B. Anthony, and six Wisconsin women, she then proceeded to Madison and lobbied in favor of suffrage before the legislature. In April she visited Janesville to attend a woman suffrage meeting and to confer with Angie King, at that point still employed as postal clerk. Later that month she proudly announced the formation of the Northern Iowa Suffrage Association, founded at Dubuque. In May suffragists held a meeting in Mendota, Illinois. Emphasizing the momentum in favor of suffrage, Livermore wrote, "Let each town and hamlet imitate this movement." In an editorial titled "A Word to Women," she reminded readers of the *Agitator* that "women of the West who are with us in this movement should not content themselves with mere *words*. They should put their sympathy into *deeds*." She also reported news about suffrage efforts in other states, including Ohio, Minnesota, New York, and Massachusetts.[20]

The *Agitator* attracted both favorable and unfavorable press in the Midwest.

Some newspapers praised the feminist publication, including the *Des Moines Bulletin*, which editorialized, "It inspires us with a confidence in woman's capacity to elevate her own condition." The *Detroit Herald* wished the *Agitator* "and the cause it advocates abundant success." The *Centralia (Illinois) Sentinel* applauded Livermore and her newspaper with the words, "It should be considered a privilege by every woman to come forward with her subscription and sustain and strengthen this valuable laborer in her cause."[21]

Other newspapers criticized the *Agitator* and its editor. Livermore spent much of her time answering these critics, demonstrating a willingness to challenge hostile press with sharply worded rejoinders. Responding to the *Minneapolis Tribune*'s argument that women did not deserve the vote until it could be demonstrated that a majority of them desired it, Livermore echoed the views of Elizabeth Cady Stanton and others by contending that America could never be a true democracy without female enfranchisement. Pointing out that young men under age twenty-one were regarded as "minors," she asked whether women were to be regarded as "life-long minors." When the *Bloomington (Illinois) Pantagraph* raised biblical arguments, notably citing the apostle Paul, in opposing female suffrage, Livermore reminded readers that the Bible had been used for years to justify slavery and before that to uphold duty to kings and lords. Because men and women were equal in the sight of God, they should have equal rights under the law.[22]

The *Chicago Tribune* had been Livermore's ally in support of the Sanitary Commission, but it did not share her belief in woman's rights. The paper often disparaged suffragists, implying that they were aggressive and strident "strong-minded women." The *Tribune* assigned a reporter named George Putnam Upton to comment on Chicago's incipient woman's movement. Upton, who had been a war correspondent with the *Tribune* and became its drama and music critic in 1868, often wrote under the pseudonym "Peregrine Pickle," the ne'er-do-well hero of Tobias Smollett's 1751 novel.[23] It must have galled Livermore, who was trying so earnestly to make feminism respectable, that the mighty *Tribune* had sent a cultural reporter who used a silly nickname to cover her reform.

At first Upton, writing as "Peregrine Pickle," addressed specific issues about woman's rights in a serious manner, objecting to arguments raised at the Library Hall convention in a two-column article. He questioned whether, even if enfranchised, intelligent and moral women would vote, and whether enfranchisement would raise workingwomen's compensation or assist the disadvantaged. Quickly, however, he dropped all pretense of serious discussion and began to make fun of suffragists. Caricaturing the battle of the sexes as a contest between "Lovely Woman" and "Tyrant Man," Upton disparaged Chicago's leading suffragist as "the Livermore" and claimed that he did not know how women could possibly inform themselves about political issues of the day when they were so consumed with interest in the latest fashions. "I would like to see hand-to-hand conflict between Livermore and the Goddess of Fashion," he suggested, adding that women might learn to support themselves by selling their votes for profit. Even the *Tribune*'s fashion critic, Mrs. M. A. Rayne, writing under the pseudonym "Vic," joined the fray. In an article titled "Reflections on Spring Bonnets and Strong-Minded Women," she wrote, "I think almost any man would prefer a band-box to a ballot-box for his wife," and expressed relief that "there are women left yet, thank Heaven, who . . . are truly[,] purely feminine."[24]

The newspaper seemed to regard Livermore as a kind of turncoat—once a patriotic, benevolent woman, now a firebrand leader. "No woman ever could have had a better opportunity to gain the admiration and love of the people than Mrs. Livermore," the newspaper editorialized. Acknowledging Livermore's talent, including her pleasing speaking voice and "commanding" presence, the newspaper nonetheless concluded that she had failed to sway Chicagoans with her woman's rights philosophy because "she is governed so entirely by the caprice of selfishness." To condemn Livermore as selfish was perhaps even more grievous than to use the epithet "strong-minded." To be a selfish woman in the nineteenth century meant to violate the most cherished aspect of woman's socially assigned role. A woman was expected to be helpful, nurturing, and selfless. Livermore, the *Tribune* charged, had rejected the very traits that made her gender worthy of being what Upton called "Lovely Woman." Indeed, the newspaper suggested, Livermore was suddenly looking ten years older. Apparently the woman's rights movement robbed a woman of her looks just as it sapped her femininity.[25]

A few years earlier Mary had been reluctant to respond to hostile press. Now she did not hesitate. She answered the *Tribune* on numerous occasions. She accused "Mr. Pickle" of attempting to harass those seeking the "elevation of women." She charged the Republican newspaper with refusing to discuss the serious issues raised by the *Agitator*, including the fact that legally defenseless women were often the victims of drunken and abusive men. She also created a fictional July Fourth oration given by "Mr. Tell-lyes" to lampoon those who felt threatened by woman's expanding role. Mr. Tell-lyes railed against women whose interests lay beyond the kitchen and the cradle, suggesting that the next step would be both white and black women voting, and then white men marrying black women. By introducing the notion of interracial mixing, Livermore boldly confronted one of white society's most deeply held fears. She hoped to show the absurdity of such far-fetched reasoning. Linking votes for women to miscegenation was as ridiculous to tying it to free love, something its critics increasingly tried to do.[26]

Not even the *Chicago Tribune*'s "Peregrine Pickle" angered Mary Livermore as much as the *New Covenant*'s owner-editor, J. W. Hanson. Printing a letter from a Minnesota writer who claimed that "none but ambitious, unsexed women, and petticoat men are engaged in the Woman's Rights cause," Hanson commended the writer's "plain common sense." Mary Livermore had once believed that Daniel's successor sympathized with the Livermores' religious and reform perspective. Now it was painfully obvious that he did not. Her fury with Hanson is evident in two July editorials. In the first she pointed out that the previous March, the Reverend Hanson had attended a woman's rights meeting in Galena, Illinois, and then had allowed a feminist to speak from his pulpit in Dubuque, making him the very sort of "petticoat man" he now condemned. In the second, responding to Hanson's entreaty that activist women speak in "a low sweet voice" and that men treat them with "courtesy," Livermore offered this rejoinder: "It is not 'courtesy' that 'the sex' asks of him—but *justice.*" The *New Covenant* continued to print articles and editorials critical of feminism.[27]

Although Mary Livermore tried her best not to show it, negative press stung her deeply. Daniel was always her greatest comfort at times of controversy. Looking back on her early career as a feminist, she recalled: "We . . . sacrificed; it has cost us a good deal. If anybody supposes it is a pleasant thing to be the voice of one crying in the wilderness, I would like to have him or her try it in dead earnest for a couple of years and see what they think then." Paying homage to Daniel, she added, "I should have backed down long ago if I had not had my husband, a woman suffragist long before I was, standing behind me, saying: 'Never mind, wife; you are right; let them say what they please.' "[28]

Livermore's willingness to challenge male opponents in a public forum reveals her remarkable evolution as a public figure since the Civil War. As a Sanitary Commission official she had more often than not avoided open confrontation. Now, with the war over and Livermore an "agitator" instead of the representative of a charitable organization, she felt free to debate her opponents openly. She had also acquired the confidence to do so. In the *Agitator* she even attacked her old nemesis from the wartime Christian Commission, Dwight Moody. During the war she had been forced to withhold criticism of the popular evangelist, much as she disliked his style of proselytizing. She would hold back no longer. In May 1869 she condemned him for casting a tiebreaking vote against allowing women to become members of the Young Men's Christian Association of Chicago. "Revolutions never go backward," she wrote in a stinging editorial, "and if one-half of the Association–counting out Brother Moody–is willing to admit women as equal yoke-fellows in Christian work, the conversion of the other half is inevitable."[29]

Mary Livermore left Chicago to attend the anniversary of the American Equal Rights Association with high aspirations for the future of woman's rights. Proud of the many suffrage conventions and societies being launched in the West, she believed that the movement had gained tremendous momentum, especially with the number of leading citizens who now lent their names and reputations in support of the cause. Later that year she wrote to William Lloyd Garrison about her own commitment. "My heart is in it," she said. "The limitations, subjection, deprivations, ignorance, sufferings and sorrows of women lie on my soul like personal griefs. I want this movement of women for freedom to go forward."[30] But Livermore's optimism would soon be tested, for the incipient woman's movement faced major disagreements over philosophy and tactics, and she would be forced to take sides. When it was over, she would emerge as a major player in the creation of a new national organization.

The annual meeting of the American Equal Rights Association convened in Brooklyn's Steinway Hall on May 12, 1869. The audience was large, but not as large as the crowd Livermore had attracted to Chicago in February. She traveled east with a group from Illinois, Iowa, and Wisconsin who knew her well, but many eastern feminists would be seeing Mary Livermore for the first time at this three-day meeting. She made a strong first impression through her physical presence. Tall for her era, she towered over many women delegates. A reporter for the *Chicago Evening Post* described her "grand head and queenly form, and a countenance that speaks at once of kindness and of power." Livermore also caught the public's attention with a deep, melodic speaking voice that enabled her to project into a crowded hall and to be heard by large numbers of people. And by now she had become a skilled debater, willing to challenge the opinions of those with whom she disagreed with quick rejoinders and an array of arguments.[31]

From its inception the AERA convention was chaotic and at times quite fractious. After it was over, Livermore would report in the *Agitator* that "Mrs.

Stanton, the President, ineffectually strove" to keep the convention together. It was "rudderless, leaderless, everywhere," including efforts by one activist to focus on rights for Native Americans. Much of the debate centered on the question of universal versus manhood suffrage, a topic that had divided Stanton and Anthony from many delegates at the Chicago convention in February. Stephen Foster set the tone for the meeting by suggesting that Stanton withdraw from the AERA because of her condemnation of the Fifteenth Amendment and her support for an educated suffrage instead of universal manhood suffrage. Foster also criticized Stanton for accepting monetary support for the *Revolution* from financier George Francis Train, a notorious racist who had long offended advocates of civil rights. Livermore made clear her own view of Train when she questioned his being allowed to sit on the platform.[32]

Mary Livermore ignited a controversy of her own by introducing a resolution that repudiated "Free Loveism as horrible and mischievous to society, and disown[ing] any sympathy with it." Western delegates, angered by efforts to discredit their movement by linking it with scandalous sexual ideology, believed that suffragists should take an official position condemning free love. Phebe Hanaford spoke in favor of Livermore's resolution, but others did not, with Lucy Stone, Susan Anthony, and Ernestine Rose arguing that such a resolution would imply that efforts to link suffrage activists with free love had some credibility. The resolution failed.[33]

Livermore had several additional opportunities to address the convention. In a speech that one writer described as "the weightiest address she has yet made," she emphasized the need for the woman's movement to give its highest priority to three issues: equal educational opportunity, equal job opportunity, and equal political rights. After Lucretia Mott heard Livermore speak, she wrote to her sister Martha Wright, saying she could hardly believe that "the renowned Mrs. Livermore" who spoke so well in Brooklyn "was that Universalist Minister's wife at Auburn" whom she had met in the mid-1850s.[34] The woman Mott barely remembered from fifteen years earlier was now a rising star.

The convention concluded with passage of a series of resolutions, including one that endorsed the Fifteenth Amendment while expressing "profound regret that Congress has not submitted a parallel amendment for the enfranchisement of women." Although Livermore's philosophical position on the suffrage issue had prevailed, she found the three-day meeting frustrating, assuring to her *Agitator* readership, "We have solemnly resolved, never again to be mixed up in the *olla podrida* of an Equal Right's Meeting, which undertaking to do everything, succeeds in doing nothing, but re-producing Babel on a small scale." Livermore and others who would be participating in a Boston suffrage meeting then departed, while Stanton and Anthony remained in New York, where they hosted a lavish party paid for by a wealthy patron.[35]

Happy to escape from the tumult of the Brooklyn meeting, Livermore journeyed to Massachusetts to give a series of woman's rights lectures. She spoke in Hingham and then in Waltham, where several audience members approached her and identified themselves as former pupils from Duxbury whom she had known twenty-eight years earlier. She lectured in Rockport to "earnest, listening people," and then at Salem, where she was joined by Julia Ward Howe, president of the New England Woman Suffrage Association. In Boston's Tremont Temple, Livermore shared the platform with a variety of luminaries including Lucy Stone, Julia Howe, and William Lloyd Garrison. She listened in awe to the speech of Wendell Phillips, an orator of legendary eloquence, and was proud that the western delegation had been well represented by lectures from two young attorneys, Phebe Cozzens from St. Louis and Lily Peckham of Milwaukee. Her own hour-long speech won accolades from Garrison, who pronounced it, "one of the best he ever listened to–worth coming all the way from Chicago to Boston to deliver." Livermore became reacquainted with more old friends after the Tremont Temple address when she met three women who had been girlhood companions at the Hancock School. As a young adult she had been a bridesmaid for one of the three.[36]

Livermore's eastern tour in the spring of 1869 would be a watershed in her life, both professionally and personally. The trip marked her debut before a national audience as the West's most illustrious female orator, and she believed that she had acquitted herself well. Audiences had responded to her with enthusiasm. She found herself drawn to the New England feminists, with whom she shared an interest in supporting the Fifteenth Amendment and a commitment to winning support for woman's rights by holding meetings characterized by limited focus, sound arguments, stirring oratory, and platform decorum. Once convinced that woman's rights had more adherents in the West than elsewhere, Livermore was pleasantly surprised by the degree to which Massachusetts audiences seemed receptive to the suffrage issue. She also found herself drawn to her native state, with its beautiful scenery, its educated and refined citizens, and its ties to her childhood.

Livermore had even more reason to detach herself from Stanton and Anthony when she learned that, following the departure from Brooklyn of herself, Lucy Stone, and others, the two had created a new organization called the National Woman Suffrage Association, seizing the initiative in setting up their own suffrage society and installing themselves in leadership positions in the absence of those who disagreed with them philosophically. Livermore and Henry Blackwell had both heard rumors in Brooklyn that Stanton and Anthony intended to break away. When Livermore asked Anthony directly if she proposed such a national organization, indicating that she would remain in Brooklyn if plans were to be discussed, Anthony replied that she and Stanton "had no purpose doing anything of the kind." A short time later, the two women formed the NWSA.[37]

Hearing about this development, Livermore composed a letter to Anthony right away. She was careful to affect a conciliatory tone, but the widening split between New York and Boston feminists disturbed her. Stanton and Anthony were leaders of enormous stature. When Lucy Stone wrote to Livermore suggesting the possibility of forming a Boston-based national organization that would rival the New York–based NWSA, Livermore advised caution.[38]

During the summer of 1869 Mary Livermore edited the *Agitator*, attended woman's rights meetings in Indiana and Illinois, and planned a convention of western suffragists to take place in Chicago in September. She also continued to build support for woman's rights by giving public lectures in Chicago. On June 22 she addressed a large audience at the First Congregational Church, a speech that received extensive coverage from the unsympathetic *Chicago Tribune*. In this address she attacked many tenets of the doctrine of domesticity, so widely revered by nineteenth-century Americans. Having once subscribed to this doctrine herself, Livermore was determined to show women the need to move beyond restrictive notions of their sphere. She spoke of women's unjust exclusion from colleges and universities and their relegation to the lowest-paying jobs in the economy. She stated that the vote would help to elevate women's status nationwide just as it was doing for African Americans in the South. Women wanted the vote "not as an end, but a means," for they desired to achieve status independent of men, not to be protected by them. Careful to emphasize that women would never neglect their domestic responsibilities, Livermore spoke of husbands and wives being "united in the political as in the home partnership." And she spoke of the Civil War's effect in altering socially defined gender roles. Given the sacrifices women had made in wartime, she stated, "women grew to the stature of men. They could not be what they [once] were."[39]

By late summer 1869 Livermore was deeply embroiled in the politics of the woman suffrage movement. She met with Susan Anthony in Buffalo to discuss the possibility of western women affiliating with the National Woman Suffrage Association. In the *Agitator* she endorsed and publicized the efforts of the NWSA, printing the text of a suffrage petition it promoted and reporting on the activities of its members, including Anna Dickinson, now a vice president. Livermore still hoped that divisions within the feminist ranks could be healed instead of widened. Admitting to Lucy Stone on August 9 that "Mrs. Stanton makes herself obnoxious by her opposition to the 15th amendment," she also wanted Stone to know that the NWSA had many friends in the West who admired Stanton and Anthony for their commitment and hard work. Rather than forming a rival organization, Livermore hoped to reform the NWSA from within, suggesting that perhaps Julia Ward Howe might be elected president to replace Stanton at the next annual meeting. Livermore believed that Howe might provide unifying leadership and heal the break between New England and New York feminists. Nevertheless, Livermore made clear that her allegiance was with Stone and not with the New Yorkers. "My heart is with the New England people, and their dignified and effective methods," she wrote, but also expressed her determination not to be drawn into a public quarrel. If necessary, western suffragists could continue to operate independent of any national organization.[40]

Two hundred woman suffrage delegates assembled at Chicago's Library Hall on Thursday, September 9, 1869. They represented different constituent groups from those Livermore had called together in February. At the earlier convention she had gone out of her way to recruit both women delegates and men of stature who represented the legal, ministerial, and academic professions. At the September meeting she wanted the focus to be on western women, including representatives of the younger generation. Although she had hoped to create interest in woman's rights among Chicago's German American community, a group traditionally hostile to her efforts, she was unable to persuade a leading German American feminist, Mathilda Anneke of Milwaukee, to attend.[41]

The September convention lacked the oratorical fireworks that had characterized the February meeting, when Elizabeth Cady Stanton had discoursed in her inimitable style and Anna Dickinson had delighted the audience by debating a conservative clergyman. Neither woman attended the second Chicago convention. William Lloyd Garrison also declined Livermore's invitation, citing his wife's poor health, though he did send a letter of support, which was read aloud to the delegates. Much to Livermore's delight, Lucy Stone and her husband, Henry Blackwell, made the trip west, and so did Susan

Anthony. Livermore again served as president of the convention, much of which revolved around reports from western states about their progress in securing women's political, legal, and educational rights.[42]

Livermore hoped to avoid acrimonious discussions about the Fifteenth Amendment. Nonetheless, Susan Anthony raised the issue by stating that she "was not sorry that black men could vote, but she was sorry that they had the right to tyrannize over women." Anthony felt that the convention "had better endorse the Fifteenth Amendment openly [rather] than sugar coat the matter." The convention heeded her advice and adopted a resolution of support. The convention also adopted resolutions calling for woman suffrage, female participation in the drafting of a new state constitution, an end to legal discrimination, and women's admission to institutions of higher education. Although copies of the National Woman Suffrage Association petition were passed around during the proceedings, the convention did not consider affiliating with any organization, including the NWSA, despite Livermore's pre-convention letter to Anthony suggesting this possibility. The *Chicago Tribune* wasted no time in excoriating Livermore, her colleagues, and her convention. Alluding to the Sorosis schism, the *Tribune* opined in March, "Chicago has barely recovered from the late war of the Roses, or rather So-roses, yet it has been determined to have another convention."[43]

At some point during or immediately after the woman's rights meeting, Mary Livermore decided to cast her lot with the New England suffragists. In all likelihood her decision was the result of private discussions in Chicago with Lucy Stone and Henry Blackwell. A few days after the convention, she traveled to Cincinnati to address a suffrage convention, along with Susan Anthony. After she returned, Livermore penned a letter to the New England Woman Suffrage Association offering to give the *Agitator* to the New England group. Henry Blackwell accepted her offer with the understanding that she would become editor of a new journal representing both her own publication and the New England Woman Suffrage Association. "Your name will aid us materially in establishing the paper and your editorial supervision will be at first almost essential," Blackwell wrote, adding that he hoped she would begin editorial duties in Boston as early as November 1. She would receive a salary of $125 per month.[44]

Livermore's decision to side with the New Englanders and break formally with Anthony and Stanton's National Woman Suffrage Association was made after what must have been considerable soul-searching and long discussions with Daniel. Ever since February, when she heard Stanton and Anthony discuss their views on the Fifteenth Amendment, but especially after the events revolving around the Brooklyn meeting and the shadowy circumstances under which the NWSA had been founded, Livermore had found herself at odds with the New Yorkers, much as she admired their long-term commitment to a movement she had embraced only a few years earlier. At the same time, she clearly shared with the Boston reformers an ideological perspective and similar views about tactics. Leaving Chicago would involve trade-offs, and Livermore must have recognized the risks. In Chicago she held the distinction of being the undisputed leader of the woman's rights movement. In moving to Boston, she would become one among many. New England reformers included men and women who had won widespread recognition for many years' service as advocates of antislavery as well as woman's rights.[45]

In all likelihood, personal considerations played a role in Mary Livermore's decision. In their *New Covenant* valedictory, Mary had written that she and Daniel wanted to scale back their work and possibly move to the country, yet the *Agitator*'s inaugural year had been anything but relaxing. With the resources of the New England Woman Suffrage Association to back her in a new journalistic endeavor, many of the financial headaches associated with running a newspaper might be alleviated. Lucy Stone had spent months working assiduously to raise money for the new publication, forming a joint stock company to fund the project. In their conversations and letters, Stone probably assured Livermore of the sound financial base from which she would launch the newspaper.[46]

Family considerations weighed in the decision as well, for the year 1869 would be one of family transition. With the death of Daniel's elderly father in August, Eliza Livermore, Daniel's unmarried sister, came to live with them. Mary's mother also died in the latter half of that year. A widow since 1865, Zebiah Rice had moved to Illinois in 1868 to be closer to her daughters, Mary and Abby Coffin, both of whom now lived in the state. Sometime after Zebiah's death, Mary's sister and two nieces also joined the Livermore household, although the circumstances that prompted them to do so are unclear.[47] What is clear is that the Livermores found themselves with two additional adults and two young girls to support, along with their own daughters. The possibility of earning a steady income must have seemed appealing, especially in that Mary no longer earned money from the *Ladies Repository*.

The Livermores' elder daughter, Henrietta, graduated from high school in the spring of 1869. Her parents hoped that she would attend college. But at the recent convention in Chicago, Mary had complained that her daughter would not find a single college in the city open to her and would have to be "sent away to get an education, for which she had as much capacity as the boys she had graduated with."[48] Recalling her own anger as a young woman when she realized that Harvard College would not take her no matter how hard she studied, Mary wanted to provide Etta with opportunities denied to earlier generations of women. By moving to Boston, she and Daniel could find a college for Etta close to home.

For many years their younger daughter, Marcia Elizabeth, had caused her parents considerable anguish. Lizzie nearly died as an infant and suffered from poor health during the early years in Chicago. The 1860 census indicates that Lizzie, then age six, attended school. By the postwar period, Mary was instructing the child at home. Although Mary and Daniel Livermore never revealed the details of Lizzie's condition in any surviving letters during the 1860s, it appears that she was mentally handicapped. In a letter to Olympia Brown in the spring of 1868, Livermore wrote, "I am still compelled to devote three hours a day to teaching Lizzie, because I can find no one who can do for her what I can—and what somebody must, to perfect her cure, and develop her mind." At that time Lizzie was thirteen years old. In a letter written in the 1870s Mary used the word "feeble" to describe Lizzie, a nineteenth-century term that referred to mental slowness. It is possible that Eliza Livermore and Abby Coffin joined the household with the understanding that they would assist with Lizzie's care, along with the domestic duties that Mary had always found so tedious.[49]

On November 24, 1869, delegates from twenty-one states assembled at Case Hall in Cleveland, Ohio, to form a new national suffrage organization. They would call it the American Woman Suffrage Association and would select the Reverend Henry Ward Beecher as president. During the convention's final evening, Lucy Stone told the delegates that Mary Livermore's Chicago-based *Agitator* would move its operations to Boston and would now be published under the title *Woman's Journal*. The newspaper would be the new mouthpiece of the American Woman Suffrage Association.[50] Clearly, Livermore's decision to join the new organization gave weight to the AWSA. Not only did the Chicago editor bring her name and reputation, along with her friends, but also she brought editorial expertise that would lend considerable stature to the fledgling publication.

News that the Cleveland convention had abandoned the New Yorkers angered Susan Anthony, who attended the meeting without Elizabeth Cady Stanton. Anthony kept her composure during the meeting but lost it afterwards.

Before the convention she had told a friend that Boston feminists would never "throw Susan Anthony overboard" in favor of Mary Livermore and her newspaper. Now that they had done so, Anthony blamed Livermore personally. She checked herself into the sanitarium in Dansville, New York, for a period of rest. In January she wrote a heated response to Daniel Livermore after he asked her to publish an article about the founding convention of the AWSA in the *Revolution*. Anthony declined to "waste printers ink" by publishing his article and proclaimed, "In this great age of ours, the question is not whether one is of *Royal descent*, or even of legitimate birth;–but whether he or she is really possessed of *genuine merit*." Although the Cleveland convention damaged Mary Livermore's relationship with Susan Anthony, she remained on polite terms with Elizabeth Cady Stanton. While disagreeing over philosophy and tactics, they respected each other and exchanged letters occasionally.[51]

In May 1870, unable to keep the newspaper afloat without the financial backing of George Francis Train, from whom she and Stanton had split, Anthony relinquished control of the *Revolution* to a wealthy socialite. The paper ceased publication eighteen months later. The *Revolution*'s failure left Anthony with a personal debt of $10,000, which she labored for years to pay off. In Anthony's view, she and Livermore had both been struggling editors valiantly carrying on the cause of female emancipation despite financial reverses. She believed that Livermore had capitulated to the Boston reformers solely to resolve her shortfall, leaving Anthony and her newspaper with no chance of success. The rift between the two women never entirely healed. Although Livermore did not appear to hold Anthony in the same low regard, Livermore, unlike Anthony, came out of the Cleveland convention in a stronger position, for she had been promised editorial help with the *Woman's Journal* and a salary.[52]

In the absence of surviving records it is impossible to know the extent to which the *Agitator* was losing money. To the end of her life Livermore claimed that it did not generate debt. In her autobiography she wrote, "I conducted the paper for a year, and with the help of my husband, who took charge of the business, made it a success, and lost no money."[53] The Livermores ran the newspaper on a shoestring budget. Mary did all the editorial work while Daniel handled business affairs. Their only overhead came from the rental of their modest office at 132 South Clark Street and the costs involved in purchasing paper and ink, along with salaries for the typesetters. Each issue of the newspaper contained many advertisements, further evidence of the publication's viability. Because the Livermores invested only $3,000 of their own money, it is entirely possible that they had broken even by the time production of the newspaper ceased in November.

If the *Agitator* did not incur the kind of debt that the *Revolution* did, its long-term prospects probably looked less rosy to the Livermores than they once had.[54] Without a doubt, Anthony correctly identified financial concerns as one of Livermore's motives in becoming the AWSA's new propagandist, but she was wrong in suggesting that money alone was the motive. Ideology, personnel, and family considerations also played a role. Moreover, by 1869 Livermore had begun to demonstrate a new level of self-confidence and ambition. She was ready to embrace the role of "agitator" on the national stage, and the *Woman's Journal* would provide her with that platform.

The suffrage schism in 1869 forced feminists around the country to choose sides. The choice was often a painful one, especially for midwestern women who had been previously unaligned. Milwaukee activist Mathilda Anneke, whom Livermore had tried unsuccessfully to lure to the Western Woman Suffrage Convention, chose the NWSA. In a letter to her husband, Anneke described the Cleveland convention as a "swindle" and characterized Mary Livermore as "intriguing," while also admitting that she was a "smart politician" who would become "the soul of this new society" by editing its newspaper. Anneke indicated her continuing support for the New York feminists while bemoaning her estrangement from Lily Peckham, the young Milwaukee attorney who had recently cast her lot with the AWSA. Just as Anneke and Peckham found themselves on opposite sides, so too did Livermore and Anna Dickinson, the young orator whose career Livermore had supported for more than six years.[55]

The schism went beyond the personal. The divisions between the two organizations involved substantive differences. The NWSA, headquartered in New York and lacking a newspaper after the *Revolution* folded, allowed male membership but insisted that women hold leadership positions, believing that women too often lost out to men. The NWSA's distrust of men followed from the Republican Party's refusal to consider woman suffrage and the decision of male abolitionists, once allies of Stanton and Anthony, to support the Fifteenth Amendment despite its exclusion of women. The NWSA endorsed a sixteenth amendment enfranchising all adult Americans and focused its organizing on the national level. The National group showed a degree of sensitivity to class-based issues including workingwomen's rights. It also championed divorce reform and occasionally other causes as well.[56]

The AWSA, headquartered in Boston, supported the idea of a national amendment but preferred state-by-state action. Its membership and leadership included men, and AWSA organizers clearly believed that it was in their best interest to position prominent men in high offices within the organization. The American group revealed its sympathy toward racial issues through its support for the Fifteenth Amendment. It promoted educational and professional advancement for women in addition to suffrage but otherwise avoided the kinds of "isms and ologies" that Mary Livermore and others believed would damage their public image and weaken their cause.[57]

The 1869 schism almost certainly hurt the suffrage crusade. By supporting two groups, suffragists wasted labor by duplicating organizational and petitioning efforts. By failing to present a united front, they opened the door to criticism from new recruits hesitant about which group to join, and the general public, still skeptical of breaking down traditional barriers to female advancement. By separating Stanton and Anthony, the movement's most brilliant orator-philosopher and its most indefatigable organizer, from the New Englanders, the schism divided a talented pool of reformers. The two organizations would become effective pressure groups. Their combined talent would have been phenomenal.[58]

Throughout her life Mary Livermore looked ahead and not back, but it is hard to imagine that she did not feel a twinge of regret about closing the *Agitator*'s Chicago office. She was proud of her newspaper. Much as she had enjoyed the twelve years she spent helping Daniel with the *New Covenant*, his newspaper had always reflected denominational interests first and foremost. Although the financial and institutional support of Boston reformers would ease her burdens as an editor, the *Woman's Journal*, like the *Covenant*, owed an allegiance to others. More than any other publication for which she wrote in her long and productive career, the *Agitator* had been Mary Livermore's operation. It provided her with unparalleled opportunities to explore the myriad facets of woman's rights that interested her. Despite the headaches involved in running the paper herself, Livermore clearly found the work fulfilling. She imparted a sense of focus and optimism about the future even during the stressful summer of 1869. In one editorial titled "What Is the Aim of the Woman Movement?" she answered, "It is a movement to give to woman possession of herself . . . and the power of deciding for herself what she can do.[59]

Mary Livermore did not create the woman's rights movement in the West, but she was one of the most effective early proponents of the emerging cause. Since 1865, and especially after April 1867, when she stepped up her support for the movement in both speeches and editorials, Livermore helped to give the movement new energy and momentum, organizing two conventions in Chicago, founding the Illinois Woman Suffrage Association, speaking publicly at well-attended lectures, and traveling extensively to encourage women in smaller communities to join the cause. She also gave the movement a voice by publishing the *Agitator*. At the same time, she became Chicago's most visible target for those who opposed the cause. Not only did she accept the label "strong-minded woman," she embraced it, and in one self-parody published in the *Agitator* even branded herself a "ferocious woman."[60] She was willing to face conservative clergy, hostile members of the press, and angry male union members who opposed women entering nontraditional professions. She never wavered, and she did not flinch.

Livermore's experiences with the Sanitary Commission had shown her what women could accomplish with the right combination of leadership, dedication, and planning. The Sanitary Commission had also convinced her that the best way to achieve goals was through a well-organized national association. In 1869 she became convinced that the AWSA would propel the woman's rights cause to new heights. In the late fall Mary Livermore took a train to Boston, rented a room, and began her new career. Her family would remain behind until Daniel had fulfilled his long-scheduled preaching engagements and sold the family home.[61]

Chicago would forever hold a place in Mary Livermore's heart, for in this city her children had grown up, her career as a journalist had been established, her work with the Sanitary Commission had gained her recognition, and her first efforts as a woman's rights reformer had begun. But in 1869 she became a New Englander again. She would spend the rest of her life in the state where she was born.

In October 1871 much of Chicago burned to the ground in one of the most tragic urban conflagrations of the nineteenth century. Most of what had been the Livermores' world for twelve years was destroyed: their neighborhood on the city's West Side, their church, the offices, printing presses, and files of the *New Covenant*, the membership lists of the Illinois Woman Suffrage Association. Chicago would astound the nation with its determination to rebuild. On the Sunday morning after the fire, the Livermores' friends Robert Collyer and William Ryder preached sermons while standing in the ruins of their Unitarian and Universalist churches. The *New Covenant*'s editors, escaping with only their subscriber list, resumed publishing the Universalist paper in Milwaukee just two weeks later. Myra Bradwell never missed an issue of the

Chicago Legal News. "Her enterprise was superior to the circumstances," Livermore wrote proudly in the *Woman's Journal.*[62]

Admitting to a friend, "I have a constant heart-ache over Chicago," Mary did what she could to help her favorite charities in the city. She spoke before an audience at the New England Woman's Club urging contributions for the Chicago Hospital for Women and Children. From readers of the *Woman's Journal* she solicited donations for the Chicago Home for the Friendless. In another editorial she reminded *Journal* readers that New England was allied to Chicago "through the noble young men and women it has sent thither, who have helped to build and shape it." Mary and Daniel Livermore had once been "sent thither" from New England to help shape the Garden City of the West. Now, in their mature years, they had returned home to help shape New England.[63]

CHAPTER 9

-◆◆◆◆◆-

Two Newspapers
and a Scandal

B Y THE TIME SHE MOVED back to Boston, Mary Livermore had embraced
a well-defined blueprint for women's role in postwar America. Education,
employment opportunities, and political empowerment through voting rights
were all fundamental to her vision. Once women were empowered politically,
Livermore believed they could both enrich their own lives and use their influence to end the nation's most serious problems: poverty, drunkenness, and
the physical abuse of women and children. At the outset of her tenure as
Woman's Journal editor, Livermore was irrepressibly confident about the nation's future. She could already see women making strides in the realms of
education and employment. With black men receiving the vote through the
Fifteenth Amendment and with a growing number of prominent Americans
now talking about female suffrage, Livermore believed that enfranchisement
was a realistic goal for women. Convinced that the war had liberated Americans from old ways of thinking, she became a full-time crusader for woman's
rights, using her newspaper and her public speaking voice to reach a national
audience. Eventually her outlook would be tested, for the publication of a
rival newspaper advocating both suffrage and free love would challenge Livermore's optimism.

On April 25, 1870, Mary Livermore wrote a letter to Henry Blackwell in which she described her feelings of closeness for her friends in the American Woman Suffrage Association, especially those who helped her in writing the *Woman's Journal*. After praising Blackwell's "Executive talent," she described the contributions of the four other friends who made up Livermore's group of associate editors—Lucy Stone, Thomas Wentworth Higginson, William Lloyd Garrison, and Julia Ward Howe. "Lucy is its *conscience*, Higginson its literary apostle, Garrison its pet lion, Julia Ward Howe its goddess Minerva," and, she added, "I, its maid-of-all-work."[1]

Livermore loved her work and quickly developed friendships with all five associate editors. Julia Howe became one of her closest companions, "the *darlingest darling* of all my women friends," as she described her in a letter to a colleague. Like Livermore, Howe was a published author in the 1850s but rejected feminism. During the war she wrote "Battle Hymn of the Republic," the most stirring anthem of the war. The mother of five children, Howe lived in Boston with her husband, Samuel Gridley Howe, a well-known reformer who did not share her postwar interest in woman's rights. Like Livermore, she often recalled the Civil War in her speeches and writing, and in her inaugural editorial for the *Woman's Journal* called upon her sex to form a peaceful "Grand Army of the Republic of Women" in order to achieve their legal and political rights.[2]

With Lucy Stone and her husband, Henry Blackwell, Livermore and her husband developed strong professional and personal bonds. Stone and Blackwell lived in Boston with their daughter Alice Stone Blackwell, born a few years after the Livermores' youngest daughter, Lizzie. Unlike Howe and Livermore, Stone embraced a reform career well before the Civil War. She had attended Oberlin College, paying her own expenses by working several jobs and graduating in 1847, the first woman from Massachusetts to earn a college diploma. She became interested in William Lloyd Garrison's American Anti-Slavery Society and lectured on its behalf. By 1850 Stone had joined the emerging feminist movement and helped to organize the first national woman's rights meeting, held in Worcester, Massachusetts. With her petite stature, melodic speaking voice, and feminine demeanor, Stone helped to deflect criticism of those who argued that the woman's rights movement unsexed women. In 1855 Lucy Stone married Henry Blackwell after a two-year courtship and Blackwell's promise that she would be free to continue her career as reformer. Thomas Wentworth Higginson officiated at the ceremony, which included a "Marriage Protest" decrying laws that discriminated against women. Lucy Stone shocked many Americans by keeping her maiden name.

For the next century the term "Lucy Stoner" referred to the rare and unorthodox practice of a woman keeping her family name. Livermore described Stone
as "gentle, sweet-voiced, winning, persuasive, and withal persevering and
undaunted."[3]

Stone, Howe, and Livermore were nearly the same age; Stone was born in
1818, Howe in 1819, and Livermore in 1820. Frequently the three traveled
together when attending suffrage conventions around New England. In Burlington, Vermont, in March 1870, one wag composed a poem titled "Three
Old Crows" as a parody of the trio. Sung to the tune of "When Johnny Comes
Marching Home," the lyrics compared Lucy Stone to an "old she Crow . . .
gnawing a bone" and called Mary Livermore a "loyal Crow, to guide the
Corps." The individual who composed the song did not intend it kindly. Julia
Howe called the piece "vulgar and silly."[4]

Phebe Hanaford used more charitable words when she called Livermore,
Howe, and Stone "the three divinities of the *Journal* office." Livermore must
have chuckled at being included in such a designation. Tall and big-boned,
she dwarfed both Howe and Stone, who stood barely five feet tall. In her
memoirs, Julia Ward Howe recalled an instance when she and Livermore
attended a suffrage meeting "somewhere in New England." Howe traveled
alone at night, by train, and as she emerged into the bracing cold of a frigid
morning, she spotted Livermore, who, unbeknownst to her, had journeyed in
a different car of the same train. "Oh, you dear big Livermore!" she cried
upon seeing her friend. Livermore quickly took Howe under her wing, found
a hotel porter to take Howe's luggage, and accompanied her to their hotel.
With members of her family and among her close friends, Livermore would
always be a generous, loyal, and understanding companion.[5]

In addition to being their physical opposite, Livermore also differed from
Julia Howe and Lucy Stone in that she enjoyed a happy and stable relationship
with her husband. Howe and Stone each had experienced marital travails that
included lengthy separations and emotional reconciliations with their husbands. Shortly before he died in 1876, Samuel Gridley Howe admitted to Julia
that he had had an extramarital affair, and at one point Henry Blackwell had
an emotional relationship, possibly a sexual one, with a married woman identified in his correspondence with family members as "Mrs. P." Livermore may
not have known about these difficulties. If she heard rumors about them, she
may well have disregarded them, for she often refused to believe unpleasant
tales about those she liked. Although she apparently did not know Howe's
husband well, Blackwell was her good friend and Daniel's too, for he chose

Harry Blackwell to serve as witness when he wrote his last will and testament. In the decades following his marriage to Stone, Blackwell had struggled to establish an identity apart from that of his more publicly acclaimed wife. He tried a variety of business endeavors, none of them very successful, but he was indispensable to Mary Livermore in publishing the *Woman's Journal*. Once, when he was out of town, she wrote, "I would give more for you, Henry Blackwell, as far as Executive talent goes, than for all the rest of the American Woman Suffrage As'sn. put together."[6]

William Lloyd Garrison and Thomas Wentworth Higginson completed the sextet of *Woman's Journal* editors. Livermore had known Garrison for many years, had attended his lectures in Boston during the 1840s and visited with him socially while she lived in Auburn, New York, during the mid-1850s. Although he had ceased to publish his antislavery newspaper, the *Liberator*, in 1865, Garrison remained active in a variety of reforms and wrote a weekly column for the *New York Independent*. He contributed infrequently to the *Woman's Journal*, though he supported the AWSA enthusiastically and rebuffed efforts of NWSA leaders to woo him into their camp. Higginson, an antislavery activist and Unitarian minister before the Civil War, served as colonel of an African American regiment during the war. Friends continued to call him "Colonel Higginson" in recognition of his wartime contributions. A strong proponent of woman's rights, he presided at the founding AWSA convention in Cleveland.[7]

Sometime in the winter of 1870, Mary Livermore's family, along with their cook Martha, left Chicago and moved to Melrose, a suburban community north of Boston. The Livermores chose to live outside of Boston because of their desire to escape the noise and congestion of city life. They purchased a house at 21 West Emerson Street, on one of the town's major thoroughfares. Behind their home was Ell Pond and beyond it a park, which lent a certain pastoral flavor to the neighborhood. With the advent of spring, Etta and Lizzie Livermore enjoyed rowing a boat on the pond.[8]

For Mary and Daniel, their new location seemed ideal. A few blocks from their house in one direction was the Melrose business district. A few blocks in the other direction brought them to the Universalist church and to the train station, where Mary took the Boston and Maine Railroad to the *Woman's Journal* offices on weekdays. Daniel took the train each Sunday to the town of Hingham, south of Boston, where he had accepted a position as minister to the Universalist congregation there. The Livermores' friend Phebe Hanaford had recently left Hingham and moved on to an appointment in New Haven,

Connecticut, thereby creating this vacancy. The position appears to have been
part-time, possibly involving Sunday preaching only. Daniel filled the rest of
his week reading, managing the household finances, and writing suffrage articles, some of which appeared in the *Woman's Journal*. Fondly, Mary Livermore described her middle-aged husband to *Journal* readers as "a stout gentleman . . . with whom we have had an intimate acquaintance for a quarter of
a century, and whom we like better and better the more we know him."[9]

The Livermores' new house was a three-story white frame Italianate structure, solid and spacious enough to accommodate a family of eight without
being overly ostentatious. On one end of the first floor was a double bay
window, and a single bay on the second. Bracketed cornices under the roofline
and dormer windows on the third floor provided additional ornamentation. A
porch ran across the front of the house, surrounded by rose bushes. Cherry
and locust trees adorned the backyard. Although a carriage house stood behind the house, the Livermores appear to have walked or taken public transportation, just as they had in Chicago. Mary and Daniel Livermore would live
in this house for the rest of their lives, along with their daughter Lizzie and
their sisters, Abby Coffin and Eliza Livermore. In the early 1870s their daughter Etta and nieces Sara and Helen also resided there.[10]

Mary Livermore's activism in the Universalist Church began to wane after
she moved to New England, for her work with the AWSA and the *Woman's
Journal* limited her time for other pursuits. She did support the Women's
Centenary Association, a fundraising effort by Universalist women, giving a
speech on its behalf. In the fall of 1870 she spoke at "the great Gloucester
jubilee" festival held to honor the denomination's centenary in the hometown
of its American founder, John Murray. Universalist women held their own
session intended as a "quiet business meeting." The crowd, however, quickly
became impatient with this mundane format and demanded speeches. Livermore gave an address characterized by the *Ladies Repository* as "inspiring."
Although she continued to identify herself as a member of the Universalist
Church and to speak in the pulpits of her Universalist husband and friends,
her denominational identity became a far less important aspect of her life.
Instead, Livermore poured her time and energy into the cause of woman's
rights.[11]

The *Woman's Journal* office, located at 3 Tremont Place in Boston, shared
a suite with the American Woman Suffrage Association headquarters and the
New England Women's Club. The *Journal*'s offices consisted of two rooms: a
back room, where the paper was folded and prepared for mailing, and a front

room, where the editors wrote, corrected, and polished articles for the paper. Mary Livermore worked there on weekdays and received guests each Monday from 10 A.M. until 2 P.M. In keeping with her philosophy as editor of the *Agitator*, she hired female staff to assist with the newspaper.[12]

The *Woman's Journal* consisted of eight pages and cost three dollars for an annual subscription. Its initial circulation of eight hundred copies increased to several thousand within a few years. The five associate editors wrote articles under their initials, while Livermore saved space on page four of each edition for her own thoughts. Henry Blackwell and Thomas Wentworth Higginson wrote nearly every week. Lucy Stone, Julia Ward Howe, and William Lloyd Garrison contributed essays as time permitted. Livermore had final editorial control over the newspaper's content. Higginson explained the situation this way: "The editor of this journal is Mrs. Mary A. Livermore; and the 'associate editors,' as they are called, claim no control, and exercise no responsibility as to anything which does not bear their initials."[13]

Mary Livermore's contributions as a writer to the *Woman's Journal* reflected her experiences in the Civil War and her belief that the war had altered gender roles irrevocably. In the inaugural issue, her first article took its title from Ulysses S. Grant's orders to his generals as they were poised to take Richmond in the spring of 1865: "Push Things." Like Grant at Richmond, Livermore hoped that suffrage sympathizers would "push things" in support of the vote for women. She appealed to the patriotism of Bay State residents by reminding them that they had always played a role in leading the nation, beginning with the battles of Lexington and Concord, which had launched the American Revolution. She concluded: "Let us join hands in a partnership of work and devotion that shall never know divorce; and let us 'push things' with such unanimity of energies, such persistence of purpose, such wisdom of effort, such buoyant and uplifting faith in our sure ultimate victory, that not only Massachusetts, but every State in the Union shall speedily surrender to the advocates of woman's equality and elevation."[14]

Livermore was never a one-issue activist. She worked hard to make sure the *Woman's Journal* was not "too proper, too sober," and she used her platform as editor to "push things" in a variety ways. Education and employment opportunities remained central to her view of women's advancement. As she had in the *Agitator*, Livermore argued that for the vast number of American girls, education was largely superficial, confined to "a little smattering of French and Italian," along with embroidery and other ornamental arts. Such an aimless education created a class of young women subjected to "grinding dependence" and forced to choose a marriage partner for economic security instead of companionship and love.[15]

Livermore wanted greater educational opportunities for women, especially at the college and university level. During her years in Illinois she had supported the idea of women's colleges, writing frequently about Vassar College, for example. Now she championed the cause of female admission to men's schools, believing that the superior resources and more highly credentialed faculty of those institutions made them a better choice for women. The *Woman's Journal* turned its editorial sights on Harvard College because of its long and distinguished history and its location in nearby Cambridge. Although Harvard allowed women to attend a series of "University Lectures," the school remained steadfast in its opposition to admitting women to its degree-granting programs. Livermore urged qualified women students to keep submitting applications and never to be discouraged. Repeated attempts might ultimately pry open Harvard's ancient gates. At the same time, she showcased the success of midwestern state universities where coeducation had succeeded "admirably." The University of Michigan was one example. The Ann Arbor campus had graduated one female student as doctor of medicine and another as bachelor of laws in 1871. Moreover, the best scholar of Greek among the entire student body was a Miss Stockwell, the first woman admitted to the campus, who had previously spent her time preparing male students for college.[16]

Although she never made racial equality a centerpiece of her activism, Mary Livermore did follow the educational progress of African Americans. In May 1871, for example, she wrote an article about the academic success of Fisk University, an educational institution founded for blacks in Nashville, Tennessee. The previous year Livermore had noted approvingly that Boston had hired its first African American woman teacher. But the *Woman's Journal* also documented the continuation of pervasive racism against black students. In Quincy, Illinois, trustees of Female High School at first agreed to allow a young African American woman to attend, but when thirty-seven white girls walked out in protest, the trustees backed down and expelled the black student, whereupon the white students returned. Livermore characterized the episode as an example of "white stupidity."[17]

As she had in the *Agitator*, Mary Livermore focused considerable attention on the issue of female employment. She urged educated women to bypass low-paying teaching jobs and enter the traditionally male workforce as lawyers, doctors, and ministers. Livermore understood the barriers these women faced. Her friend Myra Bradwell had been rejected by the Illinois Supreme Court when she applied to become a licensed attorney. Although the governor of Massachusetts appointed Julia Ward Howe a justice of the peace, the state's high court overturned the appointment because of her gender. In Pennsylvania, physicians at the State Medical Society meeting in Philadelphia rejected female membership. "The poor scared doctors forgot everything–quacks, Homeopathy, patent medicines, vaccination, which they had commenced discussing, everything–and rushed pell-mell to bar out the incoming women," Livermore wrote sarcastically after one doctor had made a recommendation to allow women members. And yet Livermore saw reason for optimism. In Wisconsin, Lily Peckham completed her legal studies and joined her brothers' law practice. Peckham was also a rising star in the suffrage movement. In Illinois, the Woman's Hospital Medical College began its second year in 1871 with an impressive list of qualified students. Women played increasingly visible roles as preachers in a variety of religious sects, including the Quaker, Methodist, Unitarian, and Universalist denominations, and Congregationalists, Baptists, Presbyterians, and Episcopalians appeared more receptive to the idea of female deaconesses "whose office is only one remove[d] from the ministry." She believed that Protestants had a great deal of work to do in catching up with the Roman Catholic Church, which had learned at a much earlier date how to capture the "vast moral power" of women.[18]

Mary Livermore drew attention to the poor working conditions and low pay received by women in many traditional forms of employment. Domestic service and the sewing trades continued to employ thousands of female workers in post-Civil War America. In an article titled "The Wrongs of Sewing Women," she pointed out that in New York and Brooklyn alone, 35,000 women earned their living in this manner, often doing piecework at six cents per shirt. Underfed and unhealthy, they eked out a miserable existence. In another article, "Women's Labor in Massachusetts," she quoted statistics gleaned from a state report about the salaries of store clerks, chambermaids, waitresses, and nursery maids.[19]

Livermore believed that there were several remedies for the problems of workingwomen. First, she wanted readers of the *Woman's Journal* to know that enlightened employers existed. When possible, women should seek them out. A subscriber sent in the story of a Mrs. Flynt, a dressmaker with shops on Chauncy Street, who employed twenty seamstresses, paid them well, and housed them in large, sunny workrooms with a separate dining room for their meal breaks. Second, Livermore publicized efforts to provide affordable housing for women, such as the Young Woman's Boarding House in Philadelphia, which made bedrooms with bathrooms available for two to three dollars per week, thanks to the charitable efforts of Protestant women in the city. The Woman's Club of Brooklyn established a similar residence. In certain circumstances, Livermore believed, workingwomen needed to be more demanding. For example, St. Louis paid female teachers and principals dramatically less in salary than their male counterparts. She hoped that negative publicity and female protest would force school districts to equalize salaries. In St. Louis the saga ended happily when, by a vote of eleven to eight, the Board of Education agreed to stop discriminating against women in its pay scale. Livermore commended St. Louis while criticizing Chicago for its failure to take a similar approach. In another article the *Woman's Journal* noted that Boston had only one female principal, who received $1,700 per year while her male colleagues received $3,000.[20]

More than any other strategy, Livermore wanted women to consider nontraditional forms of employment as a way to improve their lives. As she had in Chicago, she showcased horticulture as a remunerative profession. She noted the opening of the Horticultural School for Women in Newton, Massachusetts, remarking on the school's high professional standards and successful placement of its graduates. In September 1871 Livermore published a story, "Women as Short-Hand Writers and Reporters," which included the advice that women might become proficient after only eight months of study. Telegraphy was another field that showed great promise. New York's Cooper Institute now offered a free course of study for women who passed an entrance exam. Forty women had already graduated from this program. Livermore also published stories about women in the printing trades, including a notice about the admission of a woman to the Philadelphia Typographical Union.[21]

The struggle for women's legal and political rights was Livermore's principal focus. In numerous editorials she and Lucy Stone emphasized the lack of legal protection for women, especially those who were married. In an editorial titled "Fourth of July," written in 1870, Stone wrote that "women of this country are in a far more abject position, legally and politically, than were the handful of men who, ninety-four years ago, signed the Declaration of Independence." Mary Livermore called marriage a "Penal Institution" in an editorial she published September 16, 1871. While acknowledging that laws varied from one state to another, she pointed out that in most states a wife could not sell property, go into business, make contracts, sue or be sued without her husband's consent. Moreover, he had absolute legal control over their minor children. In another article, "Wife-Whipping Legal in This Country," Livermore examined laws in several states and revealed that some courts upheld a husband's "right" to "chastise" his wife. Women's physical safety, she saw, was integrally linked to their demands for legal and political rights.[22]

For Mary Livermore, suffrage was a means to achieve women's legal rights and to ensure equality of opportunity in the spheres of education and employment. In one editorial she wrote: "We ask the suffrage for women as a *means*, not an *end*. We repeat what we have said a score of times–the ballot in this country, organized as it is, is the symbol of equality. American women are degraded while it is withheld from them."[23]

By 1870 the issue of woman suffrage had gained considerable popular attention. The states of Massachusetts, Vermont, New Hampshire, Illinois, Michigan, and Iowa had suffrage bills under consideration, and Wyoming led the nation when its territorial legislature passed a bill enfranchising women. In the *Woman's Journal*, Henry Blackwell trumpeted the victory in an article titled "Welcome, Wyoming!" In subsequent articles the *Journal* touted the presence of women on territorial juries and the appointment of Esther Morris as justice of the peace, including her role in officiating at the marriages of several couples.[24]

During her two years as *Woman's Journal* editor, Mary Livermore traveled thousands of miles across New England and the western states speaking in support of suffrage and publicizing suffrage conventions' proceedings in her newspaper. If, in hindsight, it appears that she overestimated the degree of public support for this cause, she did not misjudge the number of Americans who were interested in the subject. Her audiences were large and for the most part sympathetic. In April 1870, for example, she traveled thirty-six hours by train from Boston to attend a series of meetings in Ohio, a state that appeared to hold great promise for woman suffrage. After speaking in Dayton, she addressed an enthusiastic audience in Oberlin. "Never before, at the close of a lecture, have so many people met us with the gratifying avowal that they were converted to a belief in Woman Suffrage," she wrote in the *Woman's Journal*. To a friend she wrote glowingly of the "tremendous excitement" she had found at Oberlin.[25]

Mary Livermore had become one of the most popular suffrage orators in the nation. Not only did her speeches attract large crowds, but also on those rare occasions when she had to cancel a speech, rumblings of disappointment might be heard, as when, in October, she had to disappoint a crowd in Lowell, Massachusetts, in order to attend the state Republican convention. Even when troublemakers or hecklers appeared, her commanding presence seemed to subdue them. In the spring of 1870, when she traveled to Burlington, Vermont, to appear along with Lucy Stone, Henry Blackwell, Julia Ward Howe, and William Lloyd Garrison, rowdies threatened to gain control over the meeting. The song "Three Old Crows" had been distributed. At the podium, Livermore simply stood up and stared at the audience without saying a word. Julia Howe recalled the scene this way: "[She] looked the audience through and through. Silence prevailed, and she was heard as usual with repeated applause. I read my paper without interruption. The honors of the evening belonged to us."[26]

Because she spoke extemporaneously, Livermore's addresses were not tightly organized, but she more than compensated with a combination of logic, pathos, anecdote, and humor, coupled with an articulate and seamless delivery. When the AWSA met for its spring convention in 1870, Livermore was given a position of honor as the closing speaker in the first day's proceedings, following AWSA president Henry Ward Beecher. Her speech is typical of the suffrage addresses she gave during this period.

After joking with the audience that voting women would not neglect domestic duties because the polls were not open "three hundred sixty-five days in the year, and twenty-four hours each day," she provided an array of arguments in favor of woman suffrage. First, she asserted that women needed the vote in order to protect themselves. Disfranchised women could never protect their earnings or, more important, their children. Next, Livermore advanced an argument that postwar suffragists frequently used: by voting, women might improve the nation. Livermore reassured her audience that feminists accepted, even rejoiced in, the inherent differences between men and women. They sought not to minimize these differences, she argued, but rather to emphasize the ways in which the sexes complimented each other. Specifically, by voting, women could use their moral sensibilities to end "licentiousness and drunkenness." Briefly she paid lip service to nativist sentiments that were building among suffragists that women's political influence was needed to enlighten recent immigrants. Livermore often concluded her speeches by invoking the Civil War. In this instance she argued that women deserved the vote because of their wartime contributions. She spoke of nurses who had served and even died for their country, and she spoke of her own activism. Before the conflict she had doubted women's readiness for the vote, but the war had changed all that. "It was not Lucy Stone who converted me to Woman Suffrage, nor even my own husband, who had been talking [of] it to me for fifteen years," she declared. "It was the war and the strength of character which it developed in our women."[27]

With her reputation as an orator firmly in place and her newspaper successfully launched, Mary Livermore still had to contend with the divisions and hurt feelings within the two branches of the suffrage movement. She had hoped that the rift between Boston and New York suffragists might be healed or at the very least narrowed. She did what she could by printing notices about activities of the National Woman Suffrage Association and its members. She reported on Susan B. Anthony's speeches, and in Dayton appeared on the same platform with her. The New Yorkers appeared to respond in kind. On January 22 Livermore reprinted a greeting from the *Revolution*, which offered the *Woman's Journal* a "hearty welcome," calling Livermore's newspaper a "valiant auxiliary."[28]

But the rift neither healed nor narrowed. Instead it widened. On March 31, 1870, Theodore Tilton, editor of the *New York Independent*, published a "card" in which he proposed a possible merger of the AWSA and NWSA. Two days later William Lloyd Garrison fired off a response in a letter, also signed by Julia Ward Howe, Henry Blackwell, and Mary Livermore, which was published in both the *Woman's Journal* and the *New York Tribune*. Garrison described Tilton's effort as "extraordinary" in its claim to have been " 'commissioned'–by whom is not stated." He went on to recount the secretive way in which the NWSA had been founded, the "discreditable alliance" of Stanton and Anthony with George Francis Train, and their repudiation of the Fifteenth Amendment. By contrast, the AWSA had been formed with "the confidence and support of all sections of the country." Although representatives of the two organizations did hold a meeting in New York, the AWSA blocked efforts to merge with the NWSA.[29]

The AWSA's momentum appeared to be building, while the NWSA's did not. In January 1870 Livermore helped to found the Massachusetts Woman Suffrage Association, which quickly became an AWSA affiliate, and assisted with its first fundraising fair. The Massachusetts society would become one of the largest state suffrage associations in the nation. Then in August Livermore announced the merger of the *Woman's Journal* with the *Woman's Advocate*, based in Dayton, Ohio, heretofore the mouthpiece of the Ohio State Woman Suffrage Association. The newly combined newspaper had nearly twice the circulation of any other suffrage newspaper in the nation. Hannah Tracy Cutler and Miriam M. Cole, who had previously written articles for the *Woman's Advocate*, now contributed to the *Woman's Journal*.[30]

On January 7, 1871, Mary Livermore proudly announced that the *Woman's Journal* had begun its second year. The paper now had subscribers in every state and territory from California to Maine. With the new year, the *Journal* hoped to improve its appearance by using larger and better-quality paper stock and increasing its number of columns from thirty-two to forty. While not formally allied with any organization, it was nevertheless "identified with the interests and in harmony with the principles" of the AWSA. The newspaper remained committed to the advancement of women and especially to their enfranchisement.[31] Shortly after completing this anniversary editorial, Mary Livermore left town for an absence of two months. She had launched a new career as a lyceum lecturer, one that would dominate her professional life for the next twenty years.

By the time Livermore became a professional public speaker, the lyceum circuit was already immensely popular in the United States. Men with established reputations such as Ralph Waldo Emerson and Henry Ward Beecher earned considerable income by traveling, for weeks at a time, to towns and cities across the nation. Typically, speakers developed a repertoire of lectures, and local organizers selected one topic for presentation. In her inaugural season as a lecturer, Livermore's audiences chose woman suffrage for every address with one exception, an oration about Queen Elizabeth. The Boston Lyceum Bureau booked Livermore's lectures. Led by James Redpath, who had a reputation as the best booking agent in the business, the bureau represented only those speakers who had a proven ability to attract audiences of considerable size.[32]

When she left on her first lecture tour, Mary Livermore had several goals in mind. She would use her powers of persuasion to sell woman suffrage, as well as literally selling subscriptions to the *Woman's Journal*. Additionally, she would write lengthy letters back to her readers describing the progress of the suffrage movement and highlighting the advancement of women in education and the professions. Finally, she would earn income to supplement her relatively modest annual salary as a newspaper editor. The first of her trips, in January and February 1871, began in Rochester, New York, and took her through Ohio, Indiana, Michigan, Missouri, and Kansas. The next trip, in April 1871, began in Foxboro, Massachusetts, and included lectures in Pennsylvania, Kansas, and Iowa.[33]

Away from home several months at a time, Livermore filled long hours in hotel rooms and railroad cars by reading novels and newspapers, and by writing lengthy columns for the *Woman's Journal* each week. She admitted missing "home and its dear ones" and "my pleasant co-workers" in the newspaper office. She also admitted having stage fright before each and every lecture. In one of her columns she wrote, "I wonder if anybody ever goes before an expectant audience without an awful dread, a momentary dying out of all self-confidence . . . that inclines one to beat an undignified retreat from the platform to the ante-room and to renounce the lecture-field forever?" Once each speech began–"the dreaded plunge taken"–Livermore would dive into her subject, and "all else is forgotten."[34]

She spoke in large cities, small hamlets, college towns, and state capitals. In Cleveland she attended a meeting of the local woman suffrage association, where she debated, and bested, an anti-suffragist judge. In Lansing, Michigan, with the state legislature in session, Livermore addressed an attentive crowd on the topic "The Reasons Why" women should vote. Scores of men and women stayed afterward to talk. She offered high praise for Lansing and even commended members of the state legislature for their sobriety. Livermore's "keen olfactories" detected "no signs of intoxication" among members of the legislature staying at her hotel.[35]

In a number of instances she spoke in small towns where local people had never heard a woman speak, let alone a speech of any kind advocating the enfranchisement of women. In hotel parlors before her lectures, Livermore would sometimes overhear men talking about the forthcoming address, unaware that she would be the speaker. In Lawrence, Kansas, for example, she heard a group talking about the novelty of a lady lecturer and their curiosity to "see the fun." With her powers of persuasion, Livermore invariably earned the respect of most audiences, if not their support for suffrage. The *Dubuque Herald*, a Democratic newspaper hostile to woman's rights, offered its grudging admiration when it concluded, "If she can't convince, she at least commands respect."[36]

To readers of the *Woman's Journal*, Livermore confided one of her funniest experiences with a small town audience. Tiny Humboldt, Kansas, population 1,600, was the western terminus of her first lyceum tour. After giving her lecture on Queen Elizabeth, she stayed at the local hotel, which she characterized as "primitive," with its unheated sleeping rooms. Livermore had hoped to warm herself by the parlor fire before bed but found the seven-by-nine-foot parlor already crowded with men sleeping on the floor. Retiring to her frigid room, "vainly trying, half frozen, to coax sleep to my bed of straw," she heard four men enter a room next to hers, and through the paper-thin walls eavesdropped on their conversation. They proceeded to carry on a lengthy discussion about whether the evening's speaker could have composed her lecture without help. Three of the four concluded that she could not possibly have written it. Somewhere they had discovered that her husband was a "smart man – a 'presiding elder' " – and they reckoned that he had written the speech, which she had "learnt by heart." "Who says that women monopolize the gossip of the community?" Livermore wrote home to the *Woman's Journal*. At least, she noted dryly, "it was some consolation that they allowed the credit of the lecture to reside in the family." But then the fourth unknown occupant of the room guessed that she had indeed written the speech herself, for though he was illiterate, his wife could "read an' write anything." The next morning, while eating an "unpalatable breakfast," Livermore watched her fellow diners closely and listened for the voice of her unknown defender, but he had apparently left the hotel.[37]

By every indication she loved the public lecture circuit despite the inconveniences, loneliness, boredom, and frustrations involved in traveling to far-flung destinations. Not only did she find enormous satisfaction in winning converts to women's enfranchisement and vanquishing opponents of suffrage in public debate, but also she loved meeting new people, experiencing new situations and adventures. In East Hamburg, New York, a village fifteen miles from Buffalo, it was so cold and snowy when she visited in January 1871 that she had to travel by sleigh. Wrapped in cloaks, furs, blankets, and buffalo robes, her feet warmed by hot soapstones, Livermore and her party drove home through a blinding storm, laughing and joking the whole way. "I dropped ever so many of my weary fifty years while in that big, closely-packed sleigh," she wrote in the *Woman's Journal*. "I shall always remember East Hamburg with pleasure."[38]

When Livermore returned from her second lyceum tour in late April 1871, the suffrage movement had reached another crisis point. After the Tilton merger flap ended, Livermore had hoped to avoid publicly criticizing members of the National Woman Suffrage Association, not just to encourage cooperation between the two groups, but because she knew that the public and the newspapers did not necessarily differentiate between suffrage societies. What one group did might easily be attributed to another. But it had become increasingly difficult to avoid taking a public stand against the NWSA. In 1871 the New York feminists appeared to be losing the battle to maintain their leadership role in the suffrage movement. Two years after the schism, thirteen state associations had allied with the AWSA but only two had become NWSA auxiliaries. While the *Revolution* ceased publication, the *Woman's Journal* expanded its length and its subscription list.[39] Hoping to attract more public attention and perhaps wishing to make her organization more competitive with the AWSA, Elizabeth Cady Stanton recruited the flamboyant, articulate, and attractive Victoria Woodhull, who now took center stage as the NWSA's spokeswoman. She brought public attention and also notoriety to the entire woman suffrage movement. By the time Woodhull faded from the public stage, controversy surrounding her activism had brought the movement to the brink of catastrophe.

Born in rural Ohio to parents who were fortune-tellers and con artists, Victoria Claflin Woodhull grew up as one of ten children traveling in a family road show that hawked the Claflins' own special elixir of life. Married at fifteen to Dr. Canning Woodhull, she bore two children. Then in 1864, at age twenty-five, she moved to Chicago, having apparently been abandoned by her alcoholic husband. Believing that she had clairvoyant powers, she opened an office, where she saw patients seeking her "magnetic healing" and advice on a variety of topics. Ultimately various members of her colorful and disreputable family joined her. In the autumn of 1865 Victoria left Chicago after the spirits advised her to relocate to St. Louis. There she met and fell in love with a Civil War veteran named Colonel James Harvey Blood, whose distress over the loss of fallen comrades had led to an interest in spiritualism. Blood abandoned his wife and children and ran away with Woodhull, earning a living by running a traveling fortune-telling show that capitalized on her alleged clairvoyant powers. Back in Chicago, rumors abounded that Victoria's father was operating a prostitution ring out of the family home on Wabash Avenue centered on his four unmarried daughters. With a lifetime interest in the art of blackmail, he ran a con game in which he would claim that a male visitor had "ruined" one of his daughters and then demand money in return. Neighbors fed up with the scandal filed several lawsuits. Ultimately the Claflin family's landlord canceled their lease and told them to get out. One of the daughters, Tennessee, or "Tennie," fled to the relative security of her sister's household.[40]

In 1868 Victoria Woodhull had a vision in which the spirit of Demosthenes told her to move to New York City. There she and Tennessee befriended the millionaire shipping and railroad magnate Cornelius Vanderbilt, whose interest in spiritualism gave the sisters an entree and whose vast fortune helped establish them as real estate investors and stockbrokers. Vanderbilt was rumored to have formed a romantic liaison with Tennessee Claflin. Victoria lived in Manhattan with an entourage that included Colonel Blood, her two children, her former husband, who was now financially dependent on her, and a variety of others. With her growing success in the traditionally male world of business, she next turned her attention to reform and politics. Befriending Stephen Pearl Andrews, a spiritualist and proponent of free love, Woodhull was soon advocating these and other causes in the pages of a newspaper called *Woodhull and Claflin's Weekly*, which she began publishing in May 1870. Her paper shared with the *Woman's Journal* an interest in suffrage, but its advocacy of spiritualism and free love created the kind of publicity for woman's rights that Livermore abhorred.[41] Indeed, the appearance of Woodhull on the national scene threatened to destroy the carefully crafted cocoon of respectability in which Boston feminists had wrapped the issue of woman suffrage.

In the spring of 1870 Woodhull announced that she was running for president of the United States. Mary Livermore ran a brief notice in the *Woman's Journal* in which she compared Woodhull to George Francis Train, whose notoriety had helped turn Livermore and others against Elizabeth Cady Stanton, Susan B. Anthony, and their efforts to lead the emerging suffrage movement. The NWSA, by contrast, quickly welcomed Woodhull as its rising star. In the words of the historian Richard Wightman Fox, "She took suffrage reform circles by storm in 1871." Woodhull had won national publicity in January of that year when she appeared before Congress arguing that women already had the right to vote based on existing definitions of citizenship under the Fourteenth and Fifteenth Amendments.[42]

In Mary Livermore's view, Victoria Woodhull was precisely the kind of person the woman's movement should avoid, not embrace. Probably aware of the Claflin family's reputation in Chicago, and certainly aware of rumors regarding Woodhull's scandalous lifestyle and her newspaper's advocacy of free love and licensed prostitution, Livermore wrote a strongly worded editorial in the *Woman's Journal*. She contended that Woodhull's newspaper represented "a damage to the cause" of woman's rights, for it promoted issues that were "simply abominable . . . we are ashamed of almost every issue." Livermore also expressed uncertainty about the validity of arguing women's right to vote based on the Fourteenth and Fifteenth Amendments.[43]

Woodhull responded in the April 1 issue of her newspaper by denouncing the *Woman's Journal* for its misgivings about her suffrage tactics and for placing undue emphasis on the character of those who espoused woman's rights. While claiming reluctance to criticize the newspaper's "talented lady editor-in-chief," Woodhull nevertheless condemned Livermore and her colleagues for their sanctimoniousness: "The editors of the *Journal* are those perfect ones whom the Lord hath appointed and sent to Boston to judge the earth, and let no rash woman lift her voice for any right she may think herself possessed of until she shall have journeyed to Boston, been tried, found pure, and thus labelled by these holy and wise (?) judges." Livermore had left town on a lyceum tour, but Miriam Cole responded to the piece by asserting that if suffragists continued to claim that women's votes were needed to purify politics, then "pure hands" among its promoters were indeed necessary.[44]

On May 11, 1871, Woodhull addressed the NWSA's New York convention in a speech that captivated her audience. She declared war on marriage as an institution that enslaved women sexually and legally. To the cheers of women and men seated in Apollo Hall, she declared: "We mean treason; we mean secession, and on a thousand times grander scale than was that of the South. We are plotting revolution; We will overslough this bogus republic and plant a government of righteousness in its stead." Paulina Wright Davis read a series of resolutions written by Stephen Pearl Andrews. One condemned "the inquisitional impertinence" of those who questioned the legitimacy of "women who are able and willing to cooperate in the movement," in other words, Woodhull. Another declared that "all laws shall be repealed which are made use of by Government to interfere with the rights of adult individuals to pursue happiness as they may choose," an obvious reference to free love. Delegates did not vote on these resolutions.[45]

While the NWSA was holding its convention in New York's Apollo Hall, the AWSA was meeting in New York's Steinway Hall. In the absence of Hannah Tracy Cutler, who had succeeded Henry Ward Beecher as president of the organization, Mary Livermore presided. Reacting to Woodhull's efforts across town, the AWSA passed a resolution condemning "recent attempts in this city and elsewhere to associate the Woman Suffrage cause with the doctrines of Free Love," calling it "an outrage upon common-sense and decency, and a slander upon the virtue and intelligence of the women of America." As the delegates debated the resolution, Livermore added her own endorsement, declaring that "this great movement was not responsible for the freaks and follies of individuals," an indication of her fear that Woodhull would drag down the entire suffrage movement. The resolution was carried by a large majority. Emphasizing the success and respectability of her convention, Livermore's self-congratulatory article in the *Woman's Journal* noted, "Thus closed one of the largest and best Conventions ever held in this country," and one that had been attended by "the best people of New York." During these proceedings, Missouri's state suffrage association sent a telegram announcing its decision to become an AWSA auxiliary.[46]

Although Susan Anthony assured a friend that the furor would soon subside, in fact the tensions between New York and Boston suffragists remained
at a fever pitch. Enraged by criticism of Woodhull, Elizabeth Cady Stanton
complained about the "respectable" men and women in the AWSA whose
personal lives did not match their public pronouncements about marital sanc-
tity. She repeated to Woodhull gossip about the personal lives of AWSA reformers, including Henry Blackwell's alleged affair, rumors of a relationship
between Henry Ward Beecher and one of his parishioners, and Phebe Hanaford's decision to accept a pastorate in New Haven, where she moved without
her husband. Mary Livermore was reported to be considering a separation
from her husband as well. While Anthony and Stanton discussed suffrage
politics in private letters, Woodhull took her case to the public. In the words
of her biographer, she "retaliated in the way she knew best—the Claflin way."
In the pages of her newspaper she struck back. In an article printed on June
17, 1871, she had this to say: "Really, Mrs. Livermore, it is a rather delicate
thing for the 'pot to call the kettle black,' or for those 'who live in glass-houses
to throw stones,' and you very well know that most people do live in these
brittle tenements." Woodhull added that Livermore "has one merit at least—
She is consistent in her determination to be unjust." Livermore did not reply
to Woodhull in the *Woman's Journal*.[47]

The following year Susan Anthony turned against Victoria Woodhull. While
on a lyceum tour in the West, Anthony picked up a copy of Woodhull's newspaper and learned that a new "People's Party" would be launched at the
forthcoming NWSA convention with the intent of nominating Woodhull for
president. She was astounded to see her own name along with those of Elizabeth Cady Stanton and Isabella Beecher Hooker listed as backers. It was now
apparent to Anthony that Woodhull was using the NWSA for her personal
gain. Moreover, Woodhull claimed to have compiled a series of "slips" containing evidence of the sexual indiscretions of AWSA members. She intended
to mail these documents to the individuals in question and threatened to
publish them unless her detractors ceased criticizing her and made a contribution to her presidential campaign. Anthony viewed Woodhull's blackmail
scheme as reprehensible. Nevertheless, Stanton and Hooker continued to support Woodhull and her presidential bid. At the May meeting of the NWSA,
Woodhull moved to allow the People's Party to hold center stage the following
day. Anthony, who objected vociferously but could not sway the majority of
delegates, stood by as Woodhull took over the podium and launched into an
impassioned political oration. Stunned by this turn of events, Anthony took

matters into her own hands. She found a janitor and commanded him to cut the lights in the convention hall. The meeting dissolved into chaos as delegates searched for the exits in total darkness. The NWSA lay in shambles, and so did Susan Anthony's twenty-year friendship with Elizabeth Cady Stanton.[48]

Victoria Woodhull had one card left to play. With her presidential candidacy going nowhere and her ability to garner national press in decline, she appeared before the American Association of Spiritualists in Boston in September 1872. Falling into a trance, she gave a speech that, in the words of one witness, "poured out a stream of flame." In it she exposed the alleged sexual indiscretions of her opponents. She accused Henry Ward Beecher of having an illicit ongoing affair with the wife of Theodore Tilton, of having fathered several of Mrs. Tilton's children, and, in a follow-up article in *Woodhull and Claflin's Weekly*, of having staged "terrible orgies." Woodhull's claims were so incendiary that most newspapers refused to print them, the *Boston Journal* noting that she had made charges against individuals of "impeccable reputation."[49]

Several years later Theodore Tilton sued Henry Ward Beecher for adultery and alienation of affection. Beecher's civil trial, which began in January 1875 and lasted six months, riveted the nation, as thousands followed court testimony in daily newspaper reports. Everyone had an opinion about the trial, and the court of public opinion was as divided as the hung jury that failed to reach a verdict.[50]

Like other members of the American Woman Suffrage Association, Livermore did not believe that Beecher had committed adultery with Elizabeth Tilton. While she did not know him well, she read Beecher's weekly column in the *Independent*, shared the lecture platform with him occasionally, and vacationed at the same New England resort. She accepted his public denials. By contrast, she found Victoria Woodhull to be discreditable in every regard, including her sensational accusations against a respected clergyman. Herself the victim of scurrilous charges by Woodhull, Livermore saw no reason to believe anything the flamboyant spiritualist said. Although she had ceased to be editor of the *Woman's Journal* by the time Theodore Tilton formally charged Beecher, she wrote a letter to Henry Blackwell, complimenting him on his articles for the newspaper and adding, "I have a theory about the whole matter." Believing that "the whole truth isn't told yet," she suggested that Beecher was covering up to shield his wife, Eunice. "Mrs. Beecher is as much to blame in this matter as almost anybody–and it is she and Mrs. Tilton– but the former especially, whom Beecher is seeking to *screen*." Livermore apparently did not want to commit the details of her theory to paper, but by positioning Beecher as his wife's defender, she tried to recast damaging insinuations as husbandly virtue.[51]

Ironically, the only person to serve jail time during the scandal was Victoria Woodhull, whose speeches and articles about adultery caused her to be prosecuted under the newly enacted Comstock law. Although a jury acquitted her based on a judge's ruling that the law exempted newspapers, Woodhull's career as an American reformer was over. After his own trial ended, Henry Ward Beecher returned to his faithful congregation at Plymouth Church, Elizabeth Tilton lived out her life in obscurity, and Theodore Tilton moved to France, his promising career as a writer considerably diminished. Abandoning Colonel Blood, Victoria Woodhull went to England, where, after denouncing the free love precepts she had previously championed, she married a proper English gentleman. Expressing relief that the suffrage movement was finally free of Woodhull, Livermore wrote to a friend, "A more stupendous fraud than Mrs. Woodhull never lived."[52]

Suffrage leaders lamented the public fallout over the Woodhull-Beecher-Tilton scandal. Alice Stone Blackwell, the daughter of Lucy Stone and Henry Blackwell, wrote: "The effect upon the movement was devastating. The cause was overwhelmed with a weight of odium which took many years to wear away." Mary Livermore had been warning about the potentially damaging impact of free love since 1869. Now she argued that scandals surrounding "the infernal Mrs. Woodhull" had contributed to the defeat of suffrage in the Iowa legislature in 1872. Livermore admitted to a friend that she had wept upon learning of the defeat in this western state, the first setback that truly discouraged her. When a suffrage amendment under consideration in Michigan also went down to defeat, activists there blamed negative publicity over the scandals. Lucy Stone, lamenting the failure of suffrage to prevail in the Massachusetts legislature in 1872, wrote to a friend, "The heaviest millstone we carry, is Free Love." Membership in suffrage organizations declined, including both the New England and the Massachusetts associations. The latter redefined what constituted a quorum in order to adjust to its diminished membership. Even Olympia Brown, who had once sympathized with the NWSA, now concluded that "the Beecher scandal, which Mrs. Woodhull precipitated by publications in her paper," had caused "great injury" to the suffrage cause. Suffrage opponents gained enough momentum to start a newspaper called *True Woman*.[53]

Although both wings of the suffrage movement survived the scandal, it created another layer of tensions between them. Throughout the 1870s and 1880s, the AWSA and NWSA continued as separate and competing organizations, at times creating painful and awkward situations. In Illinois the state suffrage organization that Livermore had founded in 1869 eventually affiliated with the NWSA, over the strenuous objections of James and Myra Bradwell, who supported the American Association. Elizabeth Boynton Harbert became president of the Illinois Woman Suffrage Association after moving to Evanston in 1874. Mary Livermore had known "Lizzie" Harbert since her teenage years in Crawfordsville, Indiana, when she had tried unsuccessfully to win admission to Wabash College. Later she launched a career as a suffrage lecturer, and Livermore had encouraged her efforts, believing that Lizzie had a bright career ahead of her. Livermore urged Harbert to *"Keep out of the quarrel,"* adding, "It would be unfortunate for you to break with New England for here are the elements of power, and your future requires you to keep with them." Evidently Harbert disagreed. When she moved to suburban Chicago a few years later, Harbert was actively recruited by Susan Anthony, who wrote that she must accept the IWSA presidency in order to save the organization from "being *run* in to the Boston Depot." Harbert did so.[54]

Livermore tried to mend fences with those among her friends who chose New York over Boston. To Harbert she wrote, "I have preferred identification with the Am. Wom. Suff. Assn., for local reasons, and because, in the outset, we foresaw something of the trouble that has come to society through the affiliation of the other side with Tilton and Woodhull." Livermore then added: "But because I have cast my lot with the people whom I know best, and among whom I live, I have never had any hostility to the grand women who are working with the other wing–or are identified with it. I have thought and still think, it would be better if we could all pull together. But as we have ceased to pull apart, and as I am but one of a great host, who think differently from me, I assent, and do the best I can in my lot and place." Evidently James Bradwell did not share her charitable view of the situation in Illinois. When, several years later, Harbert wrote to him requesting that he speak at the NWSA's forthcoming meeting in Chicago, Judge Bradwell responded tersely that he would not speak, would not attend, and would not allow his name to be used in any way by those who did.[55]

In January 1872, after helping to organize a suffrage fair, Mary Livermore stepped down as *Woman's Journal* editor, a position she had held a year beyond her original commitment. To *Journal* readers she wrote, "Overburdened with work, I am compelled to relinquish some portion of it–and release from the editorship of the *Journal* has become a necessity to me." The newspaper she had helped to launch in 1870 would remain in continuous publication until women achieved the vote by constitutional amendment fifty years later and would be the undisputed leader among woman's rights newspapers during the entirety of its existence. Livermore promised to maintain a relationship with the paper and to contribute articles. For the rest of her life she would use the *Journal* offices as her Boston headquarters and frequently wrote letters on the newspaper's letterhead. Julia Ward Howe, Lucy Stone, and Harry Blackwell took over her editorial duties without salary, for the *Journal*'s finances were precarious. In later years they would be assisted by Alice Stone Blackwell. Livermore held the title "corresponding editor."[56]

With her popularity as a lyceum speaker now soaring, Livermore believed that her time was better spent pursuing the myriad opportunities the platform now afforded her. She had become the most famous woman orator in the nation and would use her voice in hundreds of speeches to advance the cause of woman's rights.

CHAPTER 10

❦•❦•❦

Queen of the Platform

B Y THE 1870s, Mary Livermore's name had become a household word. Giving 150 speeches a year and reaching thousands of people, she had become the most popular female orator in America, a civic educator to the nation widely known as "queen of the platform." William Lloyd Garrison, who had been listening to the country's most talented speakers for the better part of fifty years, said of Livermore, "I regard her as the ablest woman speaker in the land."[1] Although the American Woman Suffrage Association remained central to her career as reformer, Livermore now sought other avenues toward achieving rights for her gender and solutions to the country's ills.

While she continued to celebrate the Civil War for its twin accomplishments of national reunification and liberation of the slaves, Livermore realized that a new set of problems was now afflicting America. The war's military mobilization had been accompanied by economic mobilization on an unprecedented scale. Postwar economic growth had further transformed the nation. The America of Livermore's youth, one largely characterized by small farmers and artisans, was now increasingly dominated by propertyless workers on the one hand and a wealthy urban elite on the other. As entrepreneurs earned millions in an expanding economy largely unregulated by the government, workers crowded into America's burgeoning cities, some of them native-born country folk seeking steady employment in industry, but many of them recent immigrants whose very presence altered the traditional northern European and Protestant nature of American society. Economic downturns, including the devastating Panic of 1873, led to pay cuts for some and unemployment for many. Bleak winters, rampant crime, strikes, disease, and intense poverty came to characterize northern cities. Moreover, as the new elites began to translate their economic might into overarching political influence, they threatened the nation's claim to republican virtue. America was at another crossroads in the 1870s. Almost as much as the war itself, this period would define the nation's future.[2]

Livermore worried about that future. She deplored the greed of business-men who made millions at the expense of the laboring classes. "Mammon Worship has become intensified," she wrote. "The war crushed out the one gigantic evil of chattel slavery–but when that work was over, we bounded over into the sin of avarice." And yet she also held working people responsible for some of their own misfortunes. In her estimation, workingmen often fell prey to vice, including drunkenness, and manipulation by corrupt politicians.[3]

Like other Americans, Livermore searched for solutions to the problems of ethnic and class conflict. She continued to argue that female suffrage could improve the nation by adding women's moral sensibilities to the political sphere. She placed high hopes on public education. In a lecture titled "The Teacher as Moral Force," she extolled the virtues of the nation's teachers, such as hard work, honesty, and "moral excellence," as factors in shaping the values that would "maintain the integrity of the republic." Livermore also renewed her commitment to temperance during the 1870s. "Who can look without trembling on the growing enslavement of our people to strong drink," she told one audience, citing its accompanying sins of poverty, vice, and fam-ily disintegration.[4]

It was vital, she believed, for the nation to find leaders who represented the qualities of honesty, virtue, and egalitarianism once embodied by the martyred Abraham Lincoln. To Livermore, Lincoln had come to personify all that was good in America, the values of hard work and compassion, the virtues of abstinence from tobacco and alcohol, a reverence for God, and a commitment to serve the nation. Although the Republican Party was no longer guided by Lincoln's elevating hand, it nonetheless remained a bastion of virtue in Liv-ermore's eyes. In 1870 she served as a delegate to the state Republican con-vention along with Lucy Stone. Livermore presented a memorial to the convention asking that the state abolish voting distinctions based on gender just as it had abolished distinctions based on race. Although her proposal fell fifty-seven votes short of adoption in the party's platform, Henry Blackwell applauded the admission of the two women as delegates, writing in the *Woman's Journal*: "The *principle*, of Woman Suffrage was really recognized. For if a woman may represent one hundred Republican voters, why may she not represent herself?" Livermore presented a less rosy picture. In an editorial titled "Not Satisfied," she indicated her unwillingness to accept any gesture by the Republican Party short of its open support for woman suffrage. The Massachusetts Woman Suffrage Association made no endorsements in the fall elections but did remind its members that two of the three candidates for governor sympathized with their cause, including incumbent William Claflin, who won.[5]

Despite her dissatisfaction in 1870, Livermore campaigned for the Republican national ticket in 1872. Although she had criticized President Grant in the past, the Democrats' nomination of *New York Tribune* editor Horace Greeley left her with no alternative, for Greeley publicly opposed woman suffrage. Livermore freely admitted that she had an "unmistakable aversion" to the Democrats, a party she associated with slavery, rebellion, and patriarchy. Victoria Woodhull's campaign that year also aroused her ire. The Republicans' successful prosecution of the Civil War and their willingness to listen to suffragists' arguments gave them credibility in Livermore's estimation, and the party's choice of Senator Henry Wilson of Massachusetts as Grant's running mate impressed Livermore as well. Wilson's reputation as a statesman was matched by his devotion to temperance and woman suffrage. At their summer convention in Philadelphia, Republicans adopted a plank similar to one that had been debated in Massachusetts in the preceding years, acknowledging their "obligations to the loyal women of America" and promising to treat "with respectful consideration" women's call for "additional rights." In campaigning for the Republican Party, Livermore was joined by an array of leaders from both the AWSA and NWSA.[6]

Livermore hoped that women would become involved in the campaign, both to use their influence with their voting husbands, brothers, and male friends, and also to show their own readiness to become voters themselves. During the spring, summer, and fall of 1872, she campaigned for the Republican Party in New Hampshire, Massachusetts, and Pennsylvania and published a treatise, "The Presidential Campaign: A Word to Women," in the *New York Independent*. Time after time she lauded Grant for his patriotism and his successes as chief magistrate, which included paying down the public debt, building the transcontinental railroad, and creating respect for America abroad, and she condemned Greeley as an opponent of woman suffrage. Observing the large number of women in attendance at a speech she gave in Philadelphia on September 12, she declared that Greeley's "pathway to-day is barred by an army of women, who do not say much but exercise a quiet and all-powerful influence at home." She urged them to use their influence in winning votes for Grant. In a Boston rally later that month, she addressed the charge that the Republican platform had danced around the issue of woman suffrage, responding that Republicans' "flirtation" with suffrage might, as flirtation often does, lead to "happy marriage at last." She believed that such would be the case this time.[7]

When Grant won reelection in November, Harry Blackwell crowed that "the Women of America have won their first recognized political battle." He urged them to attend the forthcoming annual meeting of the AWSA, where vice president–elect Henry Wilson would become a vice president at large of the organization. Suffragists' ebullience was short-lived, however, for the Republican Party's flirtation with suffrage did not lead to marriage after all. In Massachusetts, Governor William Washburn, who had run on a platform that looked forward to a day when the "enlightened conscience of Woman will find direct expression at the ballot-box," failed to make any move toward the enactment of woman's rights. His only gender-related initiative was to recommend separate prisons for female offenders to house, as the *Woman's Journal* put it, the "bodies of those women who violate man-made laws," adding, "O Governor Washburn! you owed us and the platform of your party, something better than this." For the next fifty years Republican woman suffragists would experience disappointment as the party failed to reward their loyalty and campaign efforts with substantive support for female enfranchisement.[8]

While Mary Livermore never relinquished her "aversion" to the Democratic Party, she curtailed her support for the Republicans after Grant's reelection. In 1875 she told a group of suffragists that "she had been cheated once by the Republican party, and did not propose to be cheated again." To a friend she hinted that women might turn to third parties. "Old parties are disintegrating," she wrote, and "new parties are to be formed based on new issues. And I also *hope* that in the formation of new parties women may see the beginning of the end."[9]

Massachusetts suffragists moved forward, using a variety of tactics to pressure the state legislature. In January 1873 they presented two petitions to the lower house, signed by twenty-six eminent women and thirty-four eminent men of the state, including Mary and Daniel Livermore. These petitions called women's disfranchisement unjust and demanded that the state's constitution be amended to include women as voters. Their suffrage proposal failed to make headway in the legislature. Although Lucy Stone called for "persistent and more vigorous use of the instrumentalities we have all along employed," her husband noted that those suffragists who had supported the Greeley presidential ticket had begun to shout, "Served you right." Suffragists then launched a new initiative, the formation of political clubs around the state designed to act as pressure groups in local areas. On November 22, 1873, the *Woman's Journal* noted the formation of such clubs in Newburyport, Lynn, Andover, Salem, and Worcester.[10]

The following month, suffragists held a rally in commemoration of the Boston Tea Party's one hundredth anniversary. Livermore's friend Annie Fields had written asking her to attend Boston's official festivities in Faneuil Hall. Livermore expressed an interest in the event, but refused to speak since the occasion was to be celebratory and nonconfrontational. Reminding Fields that "the watch-word of the historical tea-party was 'Taxation without representation is tyranny,'" she declared that as a disfranchised taxpayer herself, "I should deserve universal contempt, were I to speak at the proposed Faneuil Hall party, without reminding all present that our government has not yet carried out its principles."[11]

Livermore had a chance to express her views at a protest rally, held on December 15, 1873, organized by the New England Woman Suffrage Association as an alternative to the city's official celebration. The *Woman's Journal* reported that "[Faneuil] Hall was literally packed solid with a dense mass of humanity." Chaired by Colonel Higginson, the dais crowded with Boston's abolitionist and feminist reformers, the meeting began with a speech by Wendell Phillips, who was followed immediately by Mary Livermore.[12] It was one of the finest speeches of her career, a combination history lesson, protest over Republican Party failure, legal discourse, economic analysis, and emotional call to action.

Boston audiences were accustomed to hearing orators quote Sam Adams and James Otis. Livermore quoted Mrs. Ames, a seamstress who had written verses for a Massachusetts newspaper in 1773 condemning British taxation. Then she refuted the old argument that women had political influence through their husbands, pointing out their legal disabilities in Massachusetts, which included lack of joint legal guardianship over their own children. She spoke of women in the state being compelled to seek their husband's consent in order to bequeath their own property in a last will and testament. She spoke of the plight of working-class women, an often forgotten group whose "pitiful stories" were almost unbearable to hear. She spoke of wage discrimination in the workforce, citing as one example women clerks in the U.S. Treasury Department who received an annual salary as much as 50 percent less than that of male colleagues. Livermore ended her speech by noting positive changes in the nation. She spoke of the elevation of black men, formerly enslaved and now voters with political clout. She had attended the 1872 Republican convention in Philadelphia and had seen the influence wielded by African American delegates. She spoke of the election of four Boston women to the city's school committee, establishing the principle that mothers "have a voice in the conduct of the schools in which their children are educated." She concluded by invoking principles of Judaic-Christian tradition, calling all humans "the sons and the daughters of God." She added, "You need us, gentlemen." While men might have physical strength, women had moral strength, and this moral strength was needed to enrich the nation. She closed by signaling a new interest in rights based on taxpaying instead of citizenship, telling legislators to "take the first step" of granting taxpaying women the franchise, thereby enlisting "an army of the best women in the country, immediately, in the service of Humanity."[13]

Increasingly Livermore contributed to the suffrage movement as an independent operator. Although she would always respond to requests from her friends to appear at woman's rights meetings and rallies, she began to devote less of her time to the American, New England, and Massachusetts suffrage organizations. She wrote to a friend: "I have almost dropped out from the Woman Suffrage *sects*—not from the cause, or the work. But the rows, and wrangles, and splits and divisions put me beyond expression. I rarely go to conventions, and doubt if I go again in a hurry." Stress sometimes affected her well-being. Although her general health remained excellent, Livermore suffered from a variety of complaints, including insomnia, headaches, and dyspepsia, which may have been exacerbated by the "rows and wrangles" to which she referred.[14]

The rows Livermore described included continued sniping with the NWSA, which Henry Blackwell alleged "never had any real strength, except the impressive personality of a few strong leaders," namely, Elizabeth Cady Stanton and Susan B. Anthony. By contrast, the AWSA had fourteen auxiliaries. When

Stanton and Anthony undertook to write and publish the history of the woman's movement through collected documents from both national and state organizations, Lucy Stone refused to cooperate with the venture and wrote indignantly to Stanton, "I cannot furnish a biographical sketch, and trust you will not try to make one," signing herself "Yours with ceaseless regret that any 'wing' of suffragists should attempt to write the history of the other." Livermore turned down a request from Elizabeth Boynton Harbert to assist in drafting a history of the suffrage movement in Illinois, contending, "The days are not long enough for the work I now have in hand," and adding: "I cannot see the sense of writing a history of woman suffrage now. It can be only a history of struggles with very few victorious results." The biases of Stanton and co-editor Anthony, coupled with a lack of cooperation from AWSA members, led to the production of a set of volumes that gave short shrift to the American Woman Suffrage Association. Livermore purchased the first two volumes for her personal library but told one correspondent that she had not read them because, at eight hundred pages per volume, "their bulkiness, and the fact that they do not seem well-edited, have hindered my investigating them." Given her appetite for books, Livermore's statement appears disingenuous.[15]

Livermore's lyceum career occupied an increasing amount of her time, as she made two lengthy cross-country trips each year, the first beginning in January and lasting until March or April, with a second trip commencing in September or October. At the end of each lecture season she gave a series of free lectures—nineteen, for example, in 1876. Susan Anthony, always Livermore's most vociferous critic, alleged that she had abandoned the suffrage cause in favor of pursuing lucrative speaking engagements. In a letter to Elizabeth Boynton Harbert, Anthony wrote, "A mere lecture of Mrs. Livermore to 3000 people & $100 *in her pocket*—The mischief is those women who can *make money* out talking or practising woman's rights, *don't give themselves nor* any of their money to help carry on the movement." Whether or not Livermore earned as much as Anthony supposed, there is no doubt that she earned a considerable income from her lyceum lectures. When she returned from a western tour in April 1874, the *Woman's Journal* described the trip as "one of the longest and most lucrative lecture tours ever made by an American woman." Livermore told Elizabeth Boynton Harbert that her booking agent, G. H. Hathaway of the Redpath Bureau, earned almost $1,000 a year in fees from handling her engagements. Since Redpath charged 10 percent in commission, Livermore must have earned nearly $10,000 that year. Despite Anthony's suppositions, Livermore gave generously to the suffrage cause, routinely contributing $100 at festivals and other fundraisers.[16]

As for abandoning suffrage, Livermore would have disagreed wholeheartedly if Anthony had publicly charged her with this. But the tenor of her lectures had changed. By the mid-1870s woman suffrage had ceased to be a new and exciting topic to the American public at large. As a result, and because of her own preoccupation with a variety of social issues, Livermore expanded her lecture repertoire to incorporate a broader range of themes. As she explained in a letter to a friend: "Lectures on Woman Suffrage, directly, do not pay—in fact, when free . . . will not command an audience. You must take some cognate topic, and so get at the heart of things, by a flank movement."[17]

Several of her speeches approached the topic of woman's rights through this kind of indirect route. In "Superfluous Women," she took issue with the notion that marriage was a woman's only path to fulfillment. As a practical matter, there were not enough marriageable men because of the Civil War's slaughter of thousands; hence the number of "superfluous" females in postwar America. Women who could not or chose not to be married needed to support themselves, and so she called on Americans to encourage expanded opportunities for single women to find the education and training they needed to survive in the working world. In "What Shall We Do with Our Daughters?"—a speech so popular that Livermore gave it eight hundred times in her career and reprinted it in *The Story of My Life*—she emphasized the importance of education and industrial training while at the same time highlighting the need to help recently married women learn the art of household management. This speech also focused on the health of women and girls through physical exercise, nutritious diet, and attention to dress. She disparaged tightly laced corsets and blamed their popularity on men's fondness for the hourglass figure. Corsets not only literally restrained women but also contributed to "dire diseases on whose treatment gynaecologists fatten." Livermore concluded with a subtle but distinctive statement of gender egalitarianism when she urged, "Let our sons and daughters be taught that they are children of god," and incorporated criticisms of both Amerians' religious doubts and their rampant materialism: "While the coldness of skepticism seems to be creeping over the age,—mainly, I believe, because of its great immersion in materialism . . . it is possible to train children to such a far-reaching, telescopic religious vision that they will overlook all fogs and mists of doubt."[18]

In the 1870s Livermore began speaking to a broader constituency of listeners on a wider range of social issues, including poverty. She often reached out to audiences by invoking the Civil War, especially the themes of individual sacrifice and national redemption. Because she spoke from personal experience about the conflict, since her nursing work had allowed her to see, hear, and feel its horrors, Americans found her both an empathetic figure and a credible interpreter of the postwar world. "Sympathy is capable of becoming, as act, a point of shared psychic experience that allows for entry into the position of the other," one scholar has written about Civil War caregivers.[19] If Livermore owed her reputation as a public speaker in part to her Civil War credentials, her success was also due to the popularity of her message, an appealing blend of wartime patriotism, analysis of social and economic issues, and optimism about the nation's future. While never underestimating America's social problems, she always included a message of hope about the possibility of solving them.

Her speech "The Battle of Life" illustrates these themes. Livermore condemned the "business dishonesty . . . [and] the insane and vulgar greed for riches that actuates corporations, monopolies, trusts, and other like organizations, whose tendency is to deprive the wage-earner of a fair share of the wealth that he helps create." Then she reminded her listeners of the honor, civility, and comradeship displayed by Union soldiers in wartime, relating an instance in which she had traveled with a group of men following a battle at Murfreesboro. On a long march in searing heat, many soldiers collapsed. Officers and enlisted men worked together to help those who had succumbed, determined to transport all men to safety before any fell prey to Confederate guerrillas reported in the area. Livermore drew parallels between the wartime army and the present situation when she spoke of working people and those who were physically or mentally weak deserving protection and help, not contempt. She closed with an uplifting message, declaring that "the distinguishing characteristic of our nineteenth century civilization is its intense humaneness." As an example of the "new spirit of helpfulness" in the nation, she spoke of the outpouring of financial support received by the city of Chicago in the aftermath of its famous fire. Then she emphasized two important goals: an end to war as an instrument of foreign policy and an end to alcohol consumption, which was a drain on the economy, the family, and the national character. Livermore promised that a "better day . . . is dawning."[20]

Her lectures resonated with listeners of both sexes. Livermore reached out specifically to men with a variety of lecture topics. For example, "Husbands" praised American men as "the best in the civilized world," while at the same time rejecting the notion that women should be considered merely the non-voting property of their spouses. When she presented this speech in Lincoln, Nebraska, in 1876, she incorporated a discussion of laws in the western states that discriminated against women including their disfranchisement, then softened her tone by interjecting doses of humor. Livermore's speech drew the largest crowd in Lincoln's history, and she held its attention for two hours and five minutes. Often she emphasized the theme that success in life was due to the virtues of honesty and integrity, not the accumulation of wealth. The most successful men of all were those who dedicated their lives to helping others. *"It is not possible to be a Christian unless actuated by this spirit of service to the world,"* she emphasized in a lecture called "The Highest Type of Manhood," adding, *"Those whose lives are actuated by this spirit of service to the world, best know God."*[21]

Nineteenth-century Americans had a love affair with oratory. In the days before television, radio, or even spectator sports on a mass scale, audiences flocked to hear orators and expected to sit for several hours each time. In many parts of the country that lacked cultural institutions and universities, lyceums represented an opportunity for lively entertainment along with intellectual stimulation unavailable otherwise. Consequently, Americans looked on orators as men and women of enormous stature and influence, capable of inspiring thousands of people with their words and their voices. Audiences especially admired those who spoke extemporaneously, as Livermore did. Although she often wrote out a new speech as a way of organizing her thoughts, she did not use text or notes when she addressed an audience. Her speeches lasted one and a half to two and a quarter hours on average.[22]

In the absence of any sound recording of Mary Livermore's voice, it is difficult to analyze the vocal power that contributed to her phenomenal success as a public speaker, but surviving accounts provide clues. In an era before microphone amplification, many speakers could not project their voices so that large audiences could hear them. Livermore could. With her tall stature, erect posture, and deep, clear, melodic speaking voice, Livermore made a strong visual and auditory impression. Her tasteful and conservative dress contributed to a ladylike appearance, and her celebrity status ensured that the newspapers would take note of what she wore. In Cincinnati during the winter of 1880, for example, she chose a black satin dress trimmed in velvet with touches of lace at the wrists, in her hair, and at her throat, along with a blue satin ribbon to add a dash of color. Her hair was tastefully pulled back in a "plain Grecian coil," observed a local newspaper, which praised her "manner and stage presence."[23]

In contrast with her formal appearance, Livermore's lecture persona revealed a relaxed demeanor and a lack of pretense such that she could address a crowded hall as if talking with an intimate group of acquaintances. Long before she became a public speaker, she had honed her communication skills by writing newspaper stories that shared family, household, church, and travel experiences in an effort to create a bond with her readership. She proved equally adept at establishing a bond with her lecture audiences. One observer put it this way: "She unites a great deal of dignity with an unusual degree of familiarity." A reporter covering Livermore's 1879 speech in Des Moines wrote: "No other lecturer upon the rostrum can greet her audience like Mrs. Livermore. She has a way of her own. She greets it as she would greet a very old friend, with that rare and pleasing frankness that warms every heart before her, and there is at once a bond of sympathy." Lilian Whiting, a journalist who became Livermore's friend after hearing her speak in Cincinnati, had a similar reaction. Livermore "appeals instantly and profoundly to her audience," Whiting believed, "and establishes a swift and direct relation between speaker and hearer. In this lies, perhaps the secret of her marvellous power."[24]

In addition to her powerful voice and soothing delivery, listeners frequently noted Livermore's intellect, use of logic, and effective arguments. J. R. Sage, the young divinity student who had resided with the Livermores in the 1850s, later recalled her "prodigious capacity for absorbing knowledge," adding that she also "knew how to impart it to others." A woman who heard her speak in Vermont described Livermore as "calm, self-possessed, . . . her positions . . . judiciously taken, her assertions so reasonably qualified, her illustrations so apt, her arguments so telling and her whole lecture so candid, sensible and forcible, that the most prejudiced cannot help feeling some conviction of the truth."[25]

Among her female contemporaries on the lecture circuit, only Anna Dickinson and Elizabeth Cady Stanton approached her success. All three women advocated an agenda that was both progressive and explicitly feminist, and all became celebrity orators. While Dickinson was renowned for her youth and oratorical acrobatics and Stanton for her erudition and sophistication, neither of them could connect with an audience the way Livermore could. Although all three had Unionist credentials, Livermore was the only one whose Civil War career involved working with soldiers in the field in addition to efforts on the home front. In contrast with Dickinson and Stanton, whose rhetoric and persona sometimes revealed their iconoclasm, Livermore projected an image of unassailable propriety and feminine virtue. She was a reformer but one who was also solid, maternal, and reassuring. Moreover, she had staying power. Long after Dickinson and Stanton had moved on to other interests, Livermore still spent months every year speaking to audiences from Maine to California.

It is impossible to know how many people Livermore converted to woman suffrage or to any other cause. But her sustained popularity as a speaker in the 1870s and 1880s is undeniable. She addressed thousands of men and women annually with speeches emphasizing patriotism, education, equality, and elevation of the national character. She constantly reminded audiences of the need to make the nation worthy of the sacrifices so many had made in the war of 1861–65. By the mid-1870s Livermore had clearly moved beyond the role of feminist agitator to also become a civic educator to the nation.

While she was away on lengthy speaking trips, Daniel Livermore sent her copies of the *Woman's Journal* so that she could keep abreast of issues concerning women. In turn she wrote articles for the *Journal* describing the vicissitudes of travel, characterizing her audiences, and addressing the mood of the nation. Often she discussed women's progress in becoming doctors, ministers, teachers, artists, notaries, railroad clerks, and postmasters. She also characterized setbacks, including the refusal of the Dartmouth College faculty to allow her on their campus, forcing her to relocate to a neighboring town. To her friend, publisher James T. Fields, she wrote, "The Dartmouth Faculty set their faces like flints against a woman lecturer." Instead she spoke to an audience of eight to nine hundred, including many students, in nearby Lebanon on the topic "Marriage versus Free Love."[26]

During the two to three months at a time when Livermore traveled the lyceum circuit, she adhered to a punishing schedule. She told Elizabeth Boynton Harbert that she had given 159 speeches during one "season," from October to June. She wrote to Henry Blackwell in 1874, "I am lecturing every night, even Saturdays, [and] I speak in somebody's pulpit every Sunday." Travel was uncomfortable. Trains could be crowded and often were either overheated or underheated. Moreover, she always had difficulty falling asleep in railway sleeping compartments, especially at the beginning of the fall season, when she was unaccustomed to it. She did allow herself one luxury. With her new affluence, she insisted on hotels with heated rooms, unlike the miserable accommodations of her first lecture tour in 1870, when she had shivered half the night in a crude establishment, unable to sleep. Hotel cuisine remained a source of annoyance. She wrote in the *Woman's Journal* in 1872 about "minced, hashed, mashed, fried, baked, boiled and stewed abominations, brought to the table as food." She remained upbeat, however, even about traveling through inclement weather in the dead of winter. "I have hired special trains–have ridden in box cars, mail cars, cabooses, in open sleighs across the country," she wrote in the *Journal* while lecturing in the winter of 1873, and even related one instance when she had ridden eighteen miles by sleigh while the thermometer registered ten below zero. Undeterred, she spoke glowingly of the "strong, healthy growth of what we call the 'Woman Movement.' "[27]

Women often approached Livermore after her speeches or in her hotel lobby. Sometimes they came to tell her their problems, hoping that she could help them. She admitted to Alice Stone Blackwell that these visits frequently depressed her: "I receive at my room at the hotels women, women, women, who steadily come to me for something, till my heart is saturated like the river sponge, with the passing streams of other women's sorrows." She helped those she could help. For example, when a medical student at Boston University had her pocket picked and lost all her tuition money, Livermore wrote an article for the *Journal* soliciting help for the devastated young woman. In a follow-up article, she noted with relief that generous donors had recouped the student's loss, enabling her to continue her medical education.[28]

Livermore also acted as mentor to a growing number of young women eager to emulate her success on the lecture platform. One was Anna Howard Shaw, who would become a leader of the suffrage movement in the late nineteenth century. In her teenage years Shaw had heard a female minister preach and determined to enter the ministry herself. Encountering virulent opposition from her parents and siblings, however, she felt beaten down in spirit and health. Then Mary Livermore came to her hometown of Big Rapids, Michigan, while on a lyceum visit. The entire town turned out to hear her speak. After the address, Shaw joined a group of people pressing forward to meet Livermore. Someone told Livermore that Shaw hoped to become a minister but had encountered family pressure to drop the notion. Taking Shaw's hand, Livermore said: "My dear . . . if you want to preach, go on and preach. Don't let anybody stop you." Too awestruck to respond at the time, Shaw later recalled the meeting as a transforming moment in her life: "I have always felt since then that without the inspiration of Mrs. Livermore's encouragement I might not have continued my fight. Her sanction was a shield, however, from which the criticisms of the world fell back."[29]

Livermore gave advice and assistance to women in a variety of circumstances. She supported the public career of Ann Eliza Young, one of the many wives of Mormon patriarch Brigham Young. After fleeing Utah territory to escape polygamy, Young wrote *Wife No. 19; or, The Story of a Life in Bondage.* In an introduction to the book, Livermore praised Young's "heroic" efforts. Livermore also counseled Alice Stone Blackwell on how to find a lecture bureau to represent her, and she did the same for a young reformer who would play a central role in Livermore's life during the 1870s and afterwards, temperance advocate Frances Willard.[30]

During the early 1870s Willard had worked with Jane Hoge in Chicago to found the Evanston College for Ladies, serving as its president until it merged with Northwestern University. In 1873 she met Livermore at a club-sponsored convention in New York, where she presented a paper related to higher education for women, a favorite topic of Livermore's. The following year, Willard experienced a revelation in which God directed her to devote her efforts toward the newly emerging temperance movement. Seeking the advice of friends and family members to supplement that of the deity, she heard a chorus of opposition to her new path from everyone she questioned, with the exception of Mary Livermore. In her autobiography Willard recalled that Livermore "sent me a letter full of enthusiasm for the new line of work and predicted success for me therein."[31]

As a way to support herself financially, Willard gave temperance speeches for pay. She also worked with the evangelist Dwight Moody, the charismatic lay minister who had clashed with Mary Livermore during and after the Civil War, when both resided in Chicago. Indirectly, Moody and Livermore now clashed again, since Moody vehemently objected to Willard's appearing on the same temperance lecture platform several times with Livermore, whose liberal Christianity offended him deeply. Ultimately Moody and Willard went their separate ways, but Livermore and Willard became close.[32]

The temperance movement that Livermore and Willard embraced began in 1873 with a series of spontaneous demonstrations by women in upstate New York and southern Ohio. Inspired by a lecture by Dr. Dio Lewis, urging greater temperance activism on the part of women, a group of women in Fredonia, New York, prayed and demonstrated in front of a saloon and then appealed to the proprietor to shut the place down. A similar occurrence happened in the town of Jamestown, New York. A short time later, women in Hillsboro, Ohio, staged a demonstration following Lewis's lecture in that community. From there the movement spread rapidly. Livermore participated in the Ohio crusade for eight weeks, lecturing, preaching, and joining groups of women praying in saloons. On the occasion of its tenth anniversary she recalled, "That phenomenal and exceptional uprising of women in southern Ohio . . . lifted them out of a subject condition . . . to a plateau where they saw that endurance had ceased to be a virtue." The uprising gave women the "moral courage" to work together in order to end the scourge of inebriety, an evil that had never before represented such a grave threat to the republic. A temperance advocate since the 1840s, Livermore now enthusiastically endorsed this new reform movement against alcohol initiated and led by women.[33]

The following year a group of women representing sixteen states met in Cleveland to found the National Woman's Christian Temperance Union. Mary Livermore sent a letter of support, which was read to the delegates. The organization's first president, Annie Wittenmyer, favored traditional approaches, including prayer and what had been known before the war as "moral suasion," but downplayed political activism or legal prohibition. Frances Willard, who quickly became an influential member of the Illinois chapter, challenged Wittenmyer by favoring "local option laws" that would allow votes on licensing saloons and could include women in a minimal type of suffrage at the local level. The National Union ultimately endorsed the notion. Nevertheless, at a Philadelphia convention where delegates founded the International Woman's Christian Temperance Union, Wittenmyer would not allow Willard to speak on the suffrage issue and refused to allow Livermore to speak at all. Willard later recalled, "I spoke, but not upon the theme I would have chosen, and Mrs. Mary A. Livermore who was present and to whom I offered to give my time, so greatly have I always honored and admired her, was not allowed to speak, because of her progressive views upon the woman question." Livermore and Wittenmyer had tangled before. During the Civil War, Wittenmyer had fought to maintain control over soldiers' aid efforts in Iowa, while Livermore had favored statewide support for the Sanitary Commission.[34]

In recognition of her myriad talents, Frances Willard won appointment as chair of the WCTU's publishing committee, charged with reviving a failing newspaper called *Our Union*. Livermore strongly advised Willard to cease publication, declaring bluntly that the newspaper "has always been dull, stupid, and heavily loaded with what I call 'pious blarney,' " then adding, "I believe in *you*, and your honesty and ability." Livermore backed Willard in her effort to unseat Wittenmyer as WCTU president. After failing in her first attempt, Willard was elected in 1879 and held the position until her death in 1898. Ignoring Livermore's publishing advice, Willard kept *Our Union* afloat.

Later renamed *Union Signal*, it would achieve a circulation of nearly 100,000 by 1890.[35]

Livermore's reference to "pious blarney" points to one potential source of friction between herself and the WCTU. In an organization that was overwhelmingly dominated by evangelicals, Livermore remained unequivocally a liberal Christian both by choice and by marriage to a minister in the Universalist Church. Willard's allusion to Livermore's "progressive views on the woman question" points to another, for in an organization that was tentative in its approach to woman suffrage, Livermore was one of its national champions. And yet Livermore was more in sympathy with the WCTU than she was against it. She shared with it a belief that consumption of alcohol in any quantity was unhealthy and could lead to chronic inebriety and family breakdown. She blamed much of the nation's poverty on drinking. She believed in the moral power of women to improve society, notably in this case by changing the behavior of men. Like other members of the WCTU, she believed in social purity, the concept of Victorian morality that emphasized monogamy and sexual restraint. And she shared with the WCTU a proclivity to disparage immigrants (the Union sponsored a Department for Temperance Work among Negroes and Foreigners), believing that they should model their lives on upright, non-drinking Protestants such as herself.[36]

The historian Ruth Bordin has suggested that the WCTU helped to make women's public activism respectable in the aftermath of the Woodhull-Beecher-Tilton scandals. Livermore never commented on this subject, but she certainly embraced with great enthusiasm the temperance movement on the local, state, and national levels. She supported the creation of a State Temperance Association in Massachusetts and gave dozens of speeches in which she upheld sobriety as a biblical mandate and a social necessity. In 1875 she was elected president of what was now being called the WCTU Massachusetts chapter, a position she would hold for most of the next decade.[37]

As state chapter president Livermore had to tread carefully so as not to alienate the evangelicals within her organization. She described her membership in one letter to a friend as "fiercely Orthodox," and added that these women "seem to regard nothing done, unless the persons they deal with 'become converted,' and you know what dreary human beings are made of the poor and the fallen by this business of 'conversion.' " Livermore did manage to stay in the good graces of her conservative constituents, and the Massachusetts Union climbed steadily in membership. When Dwight Moody suggested that the women change the name to Ladies' Evangelical Temperance Union, many objected on the grounds that liberals including Livermore might be excluded. Moody replied, "Let them all go, even your president, though she is a good woman." They declined.[38]

In 1877 Livermore led a delegation from the WCTU to confront the mayor of Boston, Frederick O. Prince. The group presented him with a manifesto demanding that "no intoxicating liquors shall be furnished at the expense of the city" at a forthcoming banquet to honor the president of the United States, Rutherford B. Hayes. The document further stated that "it is impossible to stop the intemperate use of liquor by the masses while moderate drinking is fashionable in the best society." At their meeting, widely reported in the local press, Livermore insisted that "[the president] never drinks wine." Politely but firmly, Mayor Prince responded that most Bostonians approved of moderate drinking of wine, and its use at the banquet was in keeping with appropriate etiquette on such occasions. Although their efforts were unsuccessful, Livermore and her comrades won commendation from the national WCTU for the "earnestness and vigor" with which they had attempted to curtail the use of alcohol at the Hayes banquet. The WTCU regarded the non-drinking first lady, Lucy Webb Hayes, as a heroine because of her policy of serving no alcohol in the White House.[39]

The Massachusetts chapter of the WCTU flourished under the leadership of president Mary Livermore, vice president Susan Gifford, and secretary Mrs. L. B. Barrett. By the late 1870s, the chapter had eight thousand members in sixty auxiliaries. Thirty-nine juvenile organizations contained an additional nine thousand members. The state chapter published a temperance cookbook, distributed pamphlets, collected signatures on petitions, and issued appeals that voters keep the temperance issue uppermost in their minds as they considered candidates in upcoming elections. On May 29, 1879, the Massachusetts Union sponsored a Children's Musical Temperance Festival at Tremont Temple in Boston. The audience of two to three thousand children marched into the Temple wearing badges and carrying banners. A "trained choir" of one thousand youthful voices sang, clergymen made addresses, and Mary Livermore presided. Like other members of the WCTU, she believed that "securing the attention and influence of the *young*" was integral to the effort to keep the nation sober, for with proper training of children, "*intemperance* soon *ceases.*"[40]

The following year, in October 1880, the WCTU met in Boston for its annual convention. Mary Livermore, who was reported to have given thirty temperance lectures in the state during the previous winter, served as chair of

the Committee on Resolutions. She read aloud a series of proposals calling
for a constitutional amendment outlawing liquor, establishing coffeehouses in
large cities to offset the social lure of saloons, and urging temperance women
to patronize doctors, pharmacists, grocers, hotels, restaurants, and other
businesses dedicated to the principle of total abstinence. That evening the
WCTU held a public reception at which Frances Willard presided and Mary
Livermore delivered the welcome on behalf of the local Union. As she often
did, Livermore revisited the Civil War, beginning with an anecdote recalling
the close cooperation among regiments that had helped to win the war. She
told the temperance supporters who had gathered from across the land, united
in purpose, "We are sisters all to-night—members of one common family,
soldiers of one army—held together by a sense of affectionate comradeship."
Although Unionist analogies worked well with suffrage audiences, the temperance movement, unlike the suffrage cause, had begun recruiting in significant numbers among southerners. Acknowledging this, Livermore launched
into a litany of the tragic consequences associated with alcohol abuse throughout the land. Nonetheless, she saw reason for optimism in President Hayes's
stand against alcohol.[41]

Although she did not mention it that night, Livermore also saw reason for
optimism on another front, for she had persuaded members of the Massachusetts Union to back limited suffrage for women. In 1877 she told Lucy Stone
that half the members of her state chapter favored municipal suffrage and
added that she had prevailed on its executive committee to endorse woman
suffrage by constitutional amendment. By 1879 she had won over the membership to support of the temperance ballot, or the right of women to vote on
local licensing of alcohol. Proud of these strides, she told a friend, "I have
accomplished so much with these women." Because of her commitment to
both temperance and suffrage, Livermore continued to serve as president of
the state Union until 1884. She recognized that the tens of thousands of
women who had joined the WCTU represented an important potential constituency for the suffrage movement. The historian Ann Firor Scott has estimated that the WCTU's membership included more suffragists than the
AWSA and NWSA combined.[42]

Livermore found another avenue through which to promote women's advancement and service to the disadvantaged in the club movement, an effort
that gained considerable momentum across the nation during the 1870s. She
viewed the movement as a venue through which women might contribute to
discussions about important issues of the day and at the same time improve

themselves intellectually, culturally, and socially. In a letter to Clara Barton, the Civil War nurse with whom she carried on a postwar correspondence, Livermore spoke of a broader issue, "the ideal womanhood to which the whole sex is moving." The club movement represented an important aspect of this phenomenon for her.[43]

Livermore began affiliating with women's clubs in the late 1860s. In Chicago she had joined the local branch of Sorosis, a literary organization whose disagreements over tactics and personnel ultimately led to permanent schism. In Boston she affiliated with the New England Women's Club, though she was never as active as her friend Julia Howe and was known to make occasional acid remarks about the very proper ladies of that association. The organization that won Livermore's greatest support was the Association for the Advancement of Women, an outgrowth of New York's Sorosis and its desire to spread its influence to a larger audience.[44]

The AAW represented an effort to unite old ideas about benevolence with new ideas about organization, science, and medicine—"feminist social science," as the historian William Leach put it. The organization never intended to have a broad-based membership; rather, its approximately four hundred members came from the ranks of educated women, many from clubs and the professions. According to the AAW constitution, members would "consider and present practical methods for securing to women higher intellectual, moral, and physical conditions, with a view to the improvement of all domestic and social relations."[45]

Mary Livermore presided at the AAW's first two conferences, called Woman's Congresses. At the second Woman's Congress in Chicago during October 1874, she both presided and spoke several times in response to lectures on women's employment. Presaging an argument that twentieth-century feminists would make, she decried society's undervaluation of women's work within the home. As she had on so many occasions in the past, she deplored the aimlessness of middle-class women's lives, winning applause when she declared that American girls had "nothing to do, or to look forward to, except to embroider little white dogs for the footstool cover, learn to play the piano very badly, go into the kitchen once in a while, and make a little indigestible cake, and then go in the parlor and sit with folded hands, waiting for the coming man." Instead, she urged, "mothers should say to their daughters: 'Be whatever you want to be.' " Indeed, a central tenet of the AAW was its emphasis on women entering professions, including medicine and public health. Livermore also focused on the tragic plight of the nation's seamstresses in her 1874 speech and argued for more industrial training for women. In the wake of the Panic of 1873, she had visited a sewing room in Boston where eleven women stitched red flannel shirts at six to fourteen cents per shirt, subsisting on a diet of tea, crackers, and toast. The AAW also advocated increased female presence as administrators of institutions serving the needy, including asylums and hospitals.[46]

The second Woman's Congress addressed the issue of women's restrictive clothing. The meeting was closed to men but reported in the newspapers, including the *Melrose Journal*, which ran a story titled "Corsets and Mrs. Livermore." Although Mary Livermore had long criticized women's uncomfortable footwear and tightly laced corsets, she nevertheless defended wearing a moderately laced corset herself as necessary support during long days of standing and speaking at the lecture podium. "Corsets seemed to be her only help for the all-gone feeling," the *Woman's Journal* reported her saying. Although Dr. Mary Safford Blake, a friend of Livermore's since the days when Blake treated soldiers in Cairo, Illinois, told her that such a feeling represented "Nature's demand for rest for an overtaxed system," Livermore continued to defend her decision to wear a corset. Once, to help her stamina, a physician had prescribed a mixture of egg and wine, but she had become violently ill, reaching the understandable conclusion that a corset was preferable to the unpalatable drink. Although Livermore's defense of corsets seems outmoded today, the fact that she chaired a meeting where women discussed undergarments in a public setting represents a new willingness to bring issues of health and hygiene to the public sphere. She continued to participate in Woman's Congresses during the ensuing years. After her term as president ended, she joined the Committee on Topics and Papers. In her travels around the country, she encouraged women to start new clubs and join existing ones.[47]

Like temperance activists, club women across the land formed a reservoir of potential woman suffragists, "feminists under the skin," as the historian Karen Blair puts it. Livermore certainly realized this. Speaking to the New England Woman Suffrage Association in 1879, she talked about her observations regarding women's public activism: "In the interior towns of Iowa, in Algona, for instance, you find women's clubs. . . . In Milwaukee they are studying political economy to such purpose that their gentlemen friends have asked them to change the hour of meeting from afternoon to evening, so that the men may join them. . . . At Indianapolis I heard of thirteen such clubs." Illinois women had recently sent a petition weighing fifty-six pounds and containing thousands of signatures of men and women demanding the temperance vote for women. Periodically Livermore felt discouraged about the failure of suffrage to win acceptance in state legislatures, but the temperance and club movements gave her hope for women's advancement in all manner of arenas. "The whole sex is moving," she told suffragists. "Yes, Woman will be free."[48]

Although Livermore told one friend in 1873 that she had "almost dropped out" of organized suffrage work and told Henry Blackwell the following year that she "*may absolutely refuse . . . ever,*" to become president of the AWSA, her friends evidently prevailed on her to change her mind, for she was elected president of the AWSA for the 1876–77 term and president of the New England Woman Suffrage Association the following year. Livermore's busy schedule as lyceum lecturer, temperance activist, and club woman left limited time for presidential duties. Moreover, she refused to attend the AWSA meeting held in conjunction with the U.S. Centenary festivities in Philadelphia during July 1876, declining to appear at a celebration of national freedom after the seizure of suffragist Abby Kelley Foster's home for nonpayment of taxes. She did preside at the AWSA and NEWSA annual conventions, and in each case gave an address that showcased her interest in both temperance and suffrage. In refutation of anti-suffragists' argument that the vast majority of American women had no significant interest in public affairs, she offered as "proof" the activism of women on the temperance question.[49]

After her presidential terms ended and she scaled back her work with the Massachusetts WCTU, Livermore allowed herself some time to relax and travel. During the second half of the 1870s, Mary and Daniel Livermore experienced another period of transition in their personal lives. As daughters Etta and Lizzie reached adulthood, their parents gained a new degree of freedom.

After the family moved to Melrose, Henrietta White Livermore, then age nineteen, applied to Amherst College. She was rejected because of her gender, thereby giving her mother a reason to lambaste Amherst along with all-male Harvard in the *Woman's Journal*. Instead, Etta enrolled at Chauncy Hall School, a coeducational private school located in an imposing Gothic Revival building on Boylston Street in Boston. She graduated from Chauncy Hall in 1873 at the top of her class of 264 students, 14 of whom were women. In addition, Etta won an award for writing the best compositions of the year. At the graduation ceremony she gave a speech. The *Woman's Journal*, quoting the *Boston Advertiser*, remarked that Etta "had inherited 'the same rhetorical power as her gifted mother,' " concluding, "and thus has Mrs. Livermore given a practical answer to her own question, 'What shall we do with our daughters?' "[50]

Very little is known about Mary Livermore's relationship with her own daughters. She does not even mention her children by name in her memoirs. Only on rare occasions did she mention Etta in public, in one instance describing her as "the light of her home" in a speech criticizing Harvard's exclusion of women. At the second Woman's Congress she praised female graduates of Chauncy Hall for winning so many prizes, and told the audience proudly that the first-prize winner "was my daughter." After graduating, Etta became a teacher. In April 1876 she married John O. Norris, a Dartmouth-educated teacher who served as head of Boy's English High School in Boston and later as master of Charlestown High School. The Livermores liked Etta's husband; Mary described him in letters to her friends as "a first-rate fellow" and a "grand man." Like his mother-in-law, Norris loved learning and read widely. Livermore paid him the ultimate compliment when she named him in her will as beneficiary of her personal library, or of such books as he might select.[51]

John Norris had one failing in the opinion of his in-laws: he was a member of the Unitarian Church. While the Livermores felt a bond with Unitarians as religious liberals, they also appear to have viewed them as rivals, and Mary Livermore occasionally made barbed remarks about the denomination in her correspondence. In a letter written in the 1880s, she referred to Norris's membership in the Unitarian church of Melrose with this backhanded compliment: "My son-in-law, J. O. Norris, Melrose, [is] the livest" in that "dead-and-alive organization." Norris took Etta with him to his church, where he served as Sunday school superintendent for twenty years.[52]

Etta Livermore Norris gave birth to five children, the first named Mary Livermore Norris for her famous grandmother. Little Mary was followed by two more girls, Marion and Ethel, and a son, John Oscar Norris Jr. Another child named Emma Ashton Norris died young. The senior Livermores found great satisfaction in their new role as grandparents. Mary filled her correspondence with commentary about the young Norrises, who lived only a ten-minute walk from their house. She described three-year-old Mary Norris as the "sweetest, brightest, dearest little girl alive. We have never loved anything as much." She would sometimes answer letters with a grandchild on her lap, as when, in the fall of 1880, she apologized to Annie Fields for her "wretched scrawl," adding, "My grand-baby is helping me today, and persists in sitting in my lap while I write letters. Behold the result in blots and scrawls!"[53]

The Livermores' younger daughter, Marcia Elizabeth, continued to reside with her parents. In 1871 Mary wrote to a friend in Chicago that Lizzie "cannot go to school, but suffers no pain, and is very happy." Writing ten years later to the same friend, she described her younger daughter as an "invalid, hopeless, incurable . . . familiar with death." It is impossible to know how Mary and Daniel Livermore coped emotionally with their daughter's apparent mental handicap. They never referred to their feelings in any surviving correspondence. Mary rarely mentioned Lizzie at all, and when she did, most often described her as an "invalid," a common term in the nineteenth century that might suggest a range of medical, emotional, or mental problems, or might simply refer to an aging relative in declining health. Many, perhaps most households, had an invalid among its members. Clearly, Lizzie's condition affected her parents' lives profoundly. During the first half of the 1870s Daniel and Mary Livermore never traveled together, except when they took their extended household to the White Mountains in the summertime, for they believed that one of them must always be at home with Lizzie. In the 1870s Mary told a friend in California that "an invalid daughter, who must be an invalid while she lives, and with whom one or the other of us must stay, renders it impossible for us to leave home together" for an extended trip. She spoke of her long-standing desire to make a trip to Europe, but the impossibility of doing so without Daniel, for their many "years of married life have unfitted us to enjoy a pleasure trip unless we are together."[54]

Difficult as it must have been to cope with their "hopeless" daughter, Daniel and Mary Livermore remained a close, loving, and mutually supportive couple. In addition to their children and their home, the Livermores shared a sense of humor, a commitment to reform, and a love of books and travel. Alice Stone Blackwell, who knew them well, wrote many years after Mary Livermore's death, "Her married life was exceedingly happy." Daniel, Mary wrote, was her lover, her confidant, her financial adviser, and above all her best friend. He supported her public activism, and he calmed her when the rows and wrangles of the suffrage and temperance movements upset her or the immensity of her workload overwhelmed her. Once, when she was editing the *Woman's Journal*, he insisted that she take a vacation. She retold the incident in humorous fashion, quoting Daniel: "Drop that everlasting paper on somebody's shoulders, for awhile—let Massachusetts elect Beelzebub for Governor if she chooses—send your Bazaar, conventions and lectures to the dogs—let the canning, pickling and housekeeping take care of themselves—and start with me to-morrow for the White Mountains." He added, "A big dose of out-doors is *my* prescription for your head-ache, dyspepsia, sleeplessness and nervous-ness—and that will make a new woman of you." Mary responded, using "we" to refer to herself, "We looked at the hearty fellow . . . listened, and—though we didn't promise to do so, in the beginning, some twenty-seven years ago—this time we obeyed."[55]

Mary supported Daniel, as she always had, by playing the role of minister's wife. She helped his Hingham congregation by arranging for her friends to appear at lyceum lectures and by giving fundraising lectures herself when the Universalist Church needed money. One of her lectures was attended by Anna Howard Shaw, the young woman inspired to pursue a public career by Liver-more's appearance in Big Rapids, Michigan. Now a minister in Hingham's Methodist church, Shaw became acquainted with both Livermores, describing them as a "charming couple." Shaw remembered an incident that says much about their relationship. Mary had taken the train to Hingham to give a lec-ture in Daniel's church. Seated in the front row, next to an unoccupied chair on which Mary had left her coat and bonnet, Daniel looked up at her with "adoring eyes," Shaw recalled. When the chair next to him was needed by a latecomer, he picked up Mary's garments and held them in his lap until she had finished speaking. After the lecture, a member of the congregation, who was offended by the Reverend Livermore's deference to his famous wife, won-dered aloud how it felt to be merely the husband to Mrs. Livermore. In re-sponse, Shaw later recalled, Daniel "flashed on him one of his charming smiles" and answered cheerfully: "Why, I'm very proud of it. . . . You see, I'm the only man in the world who has that distinction."[56]

In 1878, after the spring lyceum season had ended, the Livermores traveled to Europe, fulfilling their dream of taking a vacation alone and of seeing the great museums and historic sites of the Old World. Lizzie was nearly twenty-four when they sailed, and, presumably, they decided she was sufficiently mature to be left in the care of her aunts, Abby Coffin and Eliza Livermore. Unlike their friends, who sometimes stayed abroad for an entire year at a time, the Livermores limited their vacation to four months. "This visit has only whetted our appetite for more," Mary later confided to William Lloyd Garri-son, but "our family affairs forbade more than four months' absence at this time."[57]

They stayed in London for a month. Carrying letters of introduction from William Lloyd Garrison and Maria Weston Chapman, two Americans who were widely traveled and deeply admired in England for their antislavery activ-ism, the Livermores met dozens of reformers, and accepted a limited number of social invitations along the way, careful not to let too many engagements interfere with their freedom to sightsee. In London, Mary gave four lectures, one of them in the pulpit of Moncure Conway, an abolitionist with ties to American reformers. She also spoke at the home of Duncan McLaren, a member of Parliament, whose wife, Priscilla, was a sister of the famous statesman John Bright. At the latter event she addressed two hundred people on the topic of woman's rights in America, pointing out the serious way in which the subject was being treated at home and the progress women had made in winning admission to colleges nationwide. Livermore seemed to be captivated by the extended Bright family, along with other English reformers whom she met, among them Josephine Butler and Frances Power Cobb. The Livermores also visited Cambridge, Liverpool, Leeds, and Manchester. Of special meaning for her was their trip to the Lake Country, where they visited Ambleside, the former home of Harriet Martineau. Mary had admired this English writer since childhood and had prepared a lyceum lecture on Martineau, seeking the assistance of both Garrison and Chapman, who became her literary executor.[58]

At a whirlwind pace, the Livermores visited many famous sites on the Continent, beginning with Rome, where they hired a professional guide and toured the Colosseum, the Baths of Caracalla, and St. Peter's. The Catacombs, "to which we gave more time and study than to any other of the city's historic wonders," fascinated her. In Florence they reveled in the artistic treasures of the Uffizi and Pitti galleries before continuing on to historic Pompeii. Mary had nothing positive to say about Naples, which she described as "a city of noise, laziness, dirt, beggars, and of cruelty to animals," but she was captivated by Venice, with its marble palaces and gondola rides. In the Alps, the Livermores ascended La Flégère on mules, and reaching the summit beheld a stunning view of Mont Blanc, one of their favorite moments of the entire trip. After stops in Geneva, Cologne, and Antwerp, they made only a "flying visit to Brussels, Amsterdam, Rotterdam, and The Hague" so they could spend a longer time in Paris, a city Mary found to be "gay, bright, beautiful, and bewildering." The Livermores visited the Louvre and the Bastille and shopped at Bon Marché, the famous department store, where Mary purchased a camel's hair cape lined in silk. She attended a preliminary session of the International Women's Rights Congress before time constraints dictated their return to England, and then home.[59]

When they arrived, citizens of Melrose gathered at the town hall to offer a formal welcome to the town's most famous resident, complete with the presentation of flowers and a musical interlude from the girls' chorus of a local school. Samuel Sewall, a wealthy attorney, reformer, and friend of the Liver-mores, gave an address in which he declared that public receptions for return-ing statesmen had become commonplace, but he believed that "this was the first extended to a lady in private life by a municipal power."[60]

Mary Livermore gave a speech of her own to thank the people who had turned out to welcome them home. While they were away, Daniel Livermore had celebrated his sixtieth birthday, another milestone in their lives that prob-ably helps to explain why Mary's speech was uncharacteristically personal and philosophical. "The long dream in which my husband and myself had been indulging for nearly a quarter of a century, hardly expecting to be realized, has been fulfilled," she told the citizens of Melrose. A few days later she wrote to William Lloyd Garrison, "I am conscious of having enjoyed and learned more during this period than during any previous four months of my life."[61]

Having served as president of two suffrage organizations and the state tem-perance union, having given hundreds of lyceum lectures across the land, having met with presidents and senators and members of Parliament, and now having fulfilled her dream of visiting Europe, Mary Livermore seemed uncer-tain of what the future had in store for her. She did not hesitate for very long. "The general suffrage will not be given in your lifetime, nor mine," she told Lucy Stone in 1877. "Still we must continue to work for it." And so she would. After a short period of rest, she returned to her public career with as much enthusiasm as ever.[62]

CHAPTER 11

———◆◆◆◆———

Politics, Suffrage, and Socialism

Dᴜʀɪɴɢ ᴛʜᴇ 1880s Mary Livermore entered the political arena again by campaigning for the Republican Party, and she continued to promote the cause of woman suffrage as a lecturer and organizer. She also found new ways to act as a civic educator. She accepted the most prestigious speaking engagement of her career, addressing a vast audience at the centenary celebration of the Northwest Ordinance in Marietta, Ohio, giving a performance one newspaper called "polished and impressive."[1] And she championed a new reform, Christian Socialism, one that caused her to rethink basic assumptions about inequality and poverty. She urged others to do so as well.

In May 1881 the Livermores sailed again for Europe, a trip that would take them away from home for three months. As she had in 1878, Mary spent part of her time lecturing and part of her time traveling. In London she addressed members of the English Woman Suffrage Society meeting in St. George's Hall, choosing as her topic "The Duties of Women to the Nation." Mary and Daniel then traveled to Germany and Switzerland as tourists. They especially enjoyed visiting the Royal Library of Munich and the art museum at Dresden, where Mary realized a lifelong dream of seeing the original Raphael painting of the Sistine Madonna, one of her favorite works of art. Their trip to Europe was marred by a serious illness Mary suffered at some point during their travels.

She did not mention it to readers of the *Woman's Journal* but recalled the situation several years later in a letter to Henry Blackwell: "I was sure I should die in Europe when I last went there, and so was my physician." She had been ill the winter before their departure, complaining to Lucy Stone of sciatica, neuralgia, and respiratory problems. Perhaps owing to her ill health, this time there was no formal ceremony in Melrose welcoming the Livermores home. Although they talked about making another trip to Europe, Mary and Daniel Livermore never crossed the Atlantic again.[2]

Ultimately, Mary recovered her health and spirit and resumed her public career at a pace that would have exhausted a woman much younger than her sixty years. In addition to her work as a suffragist, temperance advocate, and public orator, she reentered the world of national politics, campaigning for the Republican presidential ticket headed by Senator James Blaine in 1884. After the reelection of Ulysses S. Grant in 1872, Livermore had become disenchanted with the Republicans because she believed that they had reneged on a campaign promise to consider seriously the issue of woman's rights. Although she had voiced her opposition to an anti-suffrage gubernatorial candidate in Massachusetts in 1882, it was the presidential election of 1884 that truly brought her back into fighting form in national politics, not so much because she admired Blaine and the Republicans but rather because she despised the Democratic nominee, Governor Grover Cleveland of New York.[3] Twelve years earlier, indignation with Horace Greeley had motivated her to campaign for Grant. Now anger with Cleveland motivated her to help Blaine.

This time the issue was not woman suffrage. She disliked Cleveland because of what she regarded as his low moral character and consequently his utter unworthiness to hold the office once occupied by the exalted Abraham Lincoln. One flaw was his admission that as a bachelor he had fathered a child. A second flaw was the allegation, which subsequently proved false, that he drank to excess.[4] In Livermore's view, a candidate who was sexually promiscuous and intemperate could not possibly serve the nation as an appropriate role model. She believed fervently in the social purity movement, speaking out against prostitution and a double standard that held women but not men to marital fidelity. On her personal calling cards Livermore often wrote the phrase "character is destiny." In a letter to William Clapp, editor of the *Boston Journal*, Livermore declared that "the nomination of Cleveland is such an insult to women, such a menace to the home, such an encouragement to licentiousness, such an ignoring of the laws of social purity" that she was determined to work for his defeat. She had little to say about Blaine.[5]

Livermore feared that the Prohibition Party might siphon off enough votes to throw the election to Cleveland. WCTU president Frances Willard had strong ties to the Prohibition Party, and might influence the WCTU's 200,000 members to support its candidate, former Kansas governor John P. St. John. In Massachusetts, Prohibitionists' strength made the Republicans especially vulnerable. Livermore had sympathized with the Prohibitionists in the 1870s, when they actively solicited support from woman suffragists in Massachusetts, but ultimately Prohibitionists had found their female allies to be expendable; since women could not vote, their usefulness was severely limited. When Prohibitionists refused to endorse woman's rights in 1884, Livermore struck back. In a letter printed in the *Woman's Journal* on January 5, she denounced Prohibitionists for seeking the cooperation of women, then refusing to endorse their political equality.[6]

In August 1884 Livermore published "A Word to Women" in the *Boston Journal* and the *Woman's Journal*, sending five hundred copies of her article to woman suffragists and temperance advocates around the nation, urging them to submit it to newspapers "from Maine to New Mexico." "I hope to stir up a great opposition to Cleveland," she wrote to William Clapp. Livermore began her article by invoking Elizabeth Cady Stanton and Susan B. Anthony, who had sent a circular titled "Stand by the Republican Party" to members of the NWSA. She reminded women that while they could not vote, "they exert a large political influence, which cannot be measured, but which is potent, felt, and recognized." In no recent election, she claimed, was that influence more urgently needed. She told women not to be swayed by the Prohibition Party, noting its nonexistent chance of success and its failure to give women "the recognition which was their due."[7]

Then she directed her attention to Grover Cleveland. "Women are not more the victims of man's drunkenness than of his consuming lust," she declared. "A liquor-seller is not a greater foe to the happiness of woman, or of the community, than is an habitual libertine." For the past twelve years Livermore had served as a member of the board of directors of the Magdalen asylum, and this experience had led her to conclude that "social impurity taints the whole being, and untones and depraves the intellectual character, as all of us know who have worked among the fallen of our own sex." Because Governor Cleveland had not denied the charges leveled against him, "he is wholly unfit to be the standard-bearer of the American people." Senator Blaine, by contrast, had a distinguished career of public service and was neither a drunkard nor a libertine.[8]

Late in the campaign, however, Democrats found a skeleton in Blaine's closet. They released evidence showing that the senator's marriage to Harriet Stanwood twenty-five years earlier had occurred just three months before the birth of their first child. Blaine further contributed to his electoral defeat when, late in the campaign, he hesitated before distancing himself from a Presbyterian minister who had railed against the Democrats as the party of "Rum, Romanism, and Rebellion." Livermore's reaction to all of this is not known. But as she feared, Prohibitionists siphoned votes away from the Republicans in several key states. Four years later, however, Livermore was leaning toward the Prohibition Party herself. Speaking before a meeting of the WCTU in 1888, she noted that the Republican leaders of the Civil War had given way to a new and by implication less virtuous generation. While two thirds of elected Republicans, she granted, were honorable men, the remaining third "leads them right around by the nose." In Massachusetts that meant granting "concessions" to the liquor interests in order to fund political campaigns. Livermore closed her speech by disavowing a piece of campaign literature disseminated by the Republican Woman's National Committee intended to prevent temperance men from defecting from the party. The literature had been stamped "With the compliments of Mary A. Livermore." She denounced the signature as a forgery. Obviously the forgery had been committed by someone who recognized Mary Livermore's political clout.[9]

The 1888 contest resulted in a Republican victory. Livermore must have gained some satisfaction from Cleveland's ouster, though the bachelor president had gained respectability in the view of many by marrying during his second year in office. Although Livermore told Henry Blackwell that "women will certainly stand by *any* party that enfranchises them," her sympathies now returned to the Republicans. She knew that suffrage was a legislative issue that could not succeed without the support of one or both major political parties, and she continued to regard the Republicans as both more sympathetic to women's issues and more virtuous than the Democrats. Regarding the surprising degree of loyalty that many suffragists showed for the GOP despite its equivocation on the issue of female enfranchisement, the historian Melanie Gustafson has concluded, "Individual loyalties and histories with the party that dominated national politics during the defining historical moment of the Civil War certainly played a part." Such was the case with Livermore. In every presidential contest save the one that Blaine lost, Republicans ran solid public servants who had fought in the Union Army, credentials that appealed to Livermore. The last of these Civil War veterans was William

McKinley, whose election in 1896 she privately applauded in letters to her friends.[10]

During the 1880s and 1890s Livermore became increasingly preoccupied by the issue of poverty. Concerns over the destitution of the nation's poorest citizens led her to conclude that questions of labor and capital deserved her attention to the same extent that woman's rights and temperance did. She spoke out against the monied corporations for exploiting workers and the U.S. government for providing subsidies of land and special legislation for their benefit. Through this "special and unrighteous legislation, the rich of the country are continually being made richer," she told an audience in 1880, singling out the railroads for particular condemnation. The railroads had come to symbolize both the technological wonder of the age and its extremes of wealth and poverty. Built by immigrant labor, they transported thousands of recent immigrants each year to America's interior cities, including Livermore's former home, Chicago. Yet the nation's greatest period of labor unrest to date, the Great Strike of 1877, was an uprising born of the desperation of rail workers to earn a living wage. Meanwhile, corporate leaders demanded and received protective tariffs and other forms of government aid, sometimes using bribery to achieve their ends. For Livermore, these problems threatened to erode the republican values that had been tested and redeemed by the war of 1861–65.[11]

Bellamy Nationalism and its corollary, Christian Socialism, provided her with what appeared to be a workable solution to the problems of economic inequality. Both movements were inspired by the publication of Edward Bellamy's utopian novel *Looking Backward* in 1888, a book that described the spiritual death of its central character, Julian West, and his awakening in the year 2000 into a nation without crime, poverty, and class warfare. Instead, he finds a country devoted to an "army of industry," in which all able-bodied men and women, twenty-one to forty-five years of age, work for the state as equal partners, giving their service in accordance with their abilities and preferences.[12] With its comprehensive rather than piecemeal view of reform, its emphasis on the equality and financial independence of women, and its sunny outlook for America's future at a time of pervasive urban unrest, Bellamy's vision appealed to many progressive Christian reformers, including Mary Livermore. For years she had been telling audiences what was wrong with America and proposing a patchwork of solutions. Now she gave this broad-based new movement her enthusiastic support.

Bellamy's novel spawned a series of Nationalist Clubs dedicated to imple-

menting his socialist vision, the first of them formed in Boston in December
1888. Encouraged by Frances Willard, Mary Livermore joined the organization and, owing to her stature, was quickly asked to become a vice president.
Many of her woman's rights friends also joined, including Lucy Stone and
Anne Whitney, the well-known sculptor. Livermore and Whitney first became
acquainted during the early 1880s, when Whitney was commissioned to create
a marble sculpture of Harriet Martineau, one of Livermore's literary heroines.
Livermore wrote about Whitney and the Martineau statue for the *Woman's
Journal.* They began corresponding and exchanging occasional visits during
this time. Livermore admired Whitney's artistic talent and described her as
"my semi-Christian, semi-pagan, but very much beloved friend." Whitney in
turn admired Livermore's commitment to public service, confiding to a relative, "Her sympathies are as large as her intelligence." For Livermore and for
her feminist friends, Bellamy Nationalism seemed to provide what Mary Jo
Buhle has called "a coherent intellectual framework for creating a comprehensive solution to the woman question."[13]

Christian Socialism also grew out of interest in *Looking Backward.* The
Society of Christian Socialists was founded by a minister, William D. P. Bliss,
and by Francis Bellamy, a relative of Edward. Mary Livermore joined this
movement in its early days, becoming a vice president and an associate editor
of its journal, the *Dawn.* Christian Socialists, some of whom found Nationalism too secular, nonetheless embraced a similar reform agenda. They advocated public ownership of utilities, an eight-hour workday, and woman suffrage. At last Livermore seemed to find a reform movement that combined
her interests in social and economic change without relegating women's issues to the margins. "No movement has ever before so taken possession of me
and filled me with such buoyant hope," she wrote in the July 1889 issue of the
Dawn.[14]

With her busy schedule of lectures, suffrage, and temperance activism,
Livermore had limited time to give to Boston's Nationalist Club and the Christian Socialists, but when time allowed, she spoke at their meetings. She also
wrote an editorial, titled "Along the Road," for the *Dawn* in which she explored the present state of the nation's economy. This essay reflects a transformation in her thinking about reform. In the past Livermore had criticized
industry but had also deplored the waves of immigrants from Europe whose
presence had so dramatically redefined the nation and, by implication, blamed
them for much of America's poverty, lawlessness, and political corruption.
Now, increasingly, she placed the blame for America's economic ills squarely

at the door of industrial monopolies. She called upon the U.S. government to nationalize telephone, telegraph, and rail service as a first step, hinting that "one great industry, and then another" might follow. "The audacity and extortions of the monopolies which now control them, are manufacturing the sentiment which shall eventually compel this result," she wrote, and cited England's nationalized telegraph service as a barometer of America's future. She concluded by stating boldly that "a new departure is called for" in order to stem the greed of corporations.[15]

Livermore became interested in cooperative efforts on both the national and the local levels. In an article published in a leading journal of opinion in 1891, titled "Cooperative Womanhood in the State," she examined the role of Civil War relief societies in propelling women toward cooperative action in the postwar period to fight poverty, drunkenness, and crime. Now there were almost sixty national cooperative societies founded by women, including the WCTU, the Women's Educational and Industrial Union, and the Women's Moral Education Association, to name a few. In another essay, she searched further back into history to examine early convents in Europe, and praised the work of nuns who had served the needs of the young, the sick, and the poor. Then she jumped forward to Massachusetts, where she looked at cooperative efforts of young women in Foxboro who had rented a house together and engaged in the manufacture of straw goods. She praised the lobbying efforts of women who had worked for more than a decade to convince the state to build a separate prison for women. Livermore believed that the Women's Reformatory Prison at Sherborn was a "model institution of its kind, unsurpassed in the world." She visited the facility on several occasions, dined with the inmates, and spoke to them. Late in her life Livermore met Jane Addams, whose work with immigrants at a Chicago settlement house impressed her greatly. Livermore noted approvingly that Addams supported woman suffrage.[16]

Mary Livermore also endorsed cooperative housekeeping efforts for women, a subject she had promoted in Chicago when she was publishing the *Agitator*. By creating communal kitchens and laundries, Livermore told an audience gathered for a meeting of the New England Woman Suffrage Association, women could save money and be emancipated from household drudgery. They would then have more time to read and pursue other interests to enrich their minds. As an example of a successful communal effort, she cited a student dining room at the University of Michigan that served 1,500 to 1,800 students daily. If thirty to forty families pooled their resources, a person might

eat for as little as $2.70 per week. Boston's Tremont House hotel charged
$4.00 a day. Livermore's speeches and articles emphasizing the practical na-
ture of cooperative housekeeping drew attention to the topic among a growing
number of suffragists, temperance advocates, and socialist groups.[17]

The Bellamy Nationalists appeared to gain momentum when, in 1891 the
Massachusetts legislature passed a law granting towns and cities the power to
own and regulate gas and electric companies. In spite of this victory, Livermore soon began to criticize the movement she had embraced so enthusiastically after Edward Bellamy united his urban-based Nationalist movement with
the agrarian Populist Party. Indeed, the Populist Party in Massachusetts consisted largely of Nationalists and Christian Socialists. In 1892 a delegation of
these reformers visited Livermore in Melrose to ask that she share the platform with Bellamy at a grand ratification rally in Boston's Faneuil Hall announcing the merger of Nationalism with Populism. Livermore refused. In a
letter to Anne Whitney she complained that the Populist platform failed to
recognize woman's rights "even to the degree that Nationalism does." Temperance had also been relegated to a "secondary" issue, while monetary concerns such as free coinage of silver held center stage. "Of course I would not
speak for the People's Party, as it is now," she concluded. Ultimately Bellamy's
reform movement, like the Republican Party, proved to be a disappointment.
Initial enthusiasm for woman's rights had given way to a preoccupation with
bimetalism. In 1889 Livermore had written to the editor of the *Dawn*, "I
endorse every word" it published. By the following year, however, her name
no longer appeared on a list of potential lecturers on Christian Socialism.
Ultimately she ceased to be associated with the *Dawn*, even though she sympathized with many of its goals and retained her interest in cooperative
efforts.[18]

As "queen of the platform," Livermore continued to make annual lyceum
trips to the West, admitting to a friend in 1885 that "I am as much intoxicated
with the West as when I was young." Nevertheless, as she aged, the vicissitudes of travel, especially in wintertime, began to catch up with her. Daniel
worried about her health and safety. If a lyceum tour took her away from home
for several months, he would pay her a visit every three weeks, bringing her
mail and back issues of the *Woman's Journal*, insisting that she take a few
days off for relaxation and recreation.[19]

During the winter of 1885, Mary Livermore faced her most harrowing experiences yet with winter travel. On a tour of Iowa and Nebraska she endured
the worst winter on record in forty years. "My powers of endurance have been

tested to the utmost," she wrote to Anne Whitney. For a period of three days and nights she had been trapped inside a train while a blizzard raged outside and snow drifted as high as the roofline. Finally rescued by a snowplow, Livermore and the other passengers watched in horror as a ghostly apparition passed them, a livestock car filled with sheep that had piled on top of one another seeking warmth but had frozen to death. "We forgot ourselves in our pity for the poor beasts," she recalled.[20]

In Cedar Rapids, Iowa, the temperature plunged to forty-two degrees below zero the night of her lecture. Although 800 people held season tickets, only 123 turned out. In Kansas City, 1,200 season ticket holders were reduced to a meager crowd of 150. Nonetheless, Livermore forged ahead, determined to fulfill her commitments. "Through it all . . . I have only missed three engagements, that fell due while I was 'snowed in' on the train," she told Anne Whitney proudly. Daniel was frantic. Rushing out from Melrose to meet her, he had been trapped in a blizzard himself. Finally catching up with her, he remained at her side until she arrived in St. Louis, away from the worst of the storms. Before returning to Melrose, he made her promise not to travel west of Chicago again in wintertime. She agreed.[21]

In 1888 Mary Livermore reached the pinnacle of her success as a public orator and civic educator when she was invited to speak at the week-long celebration in Marietta, Ohio, commemorating the one hundredth anniversary of the Northwest Ordinance, legislation that opened the West to settlement and outlawed slavery therein. Other invited speakers included Senators John Sherman of Ohio, William Evarts of New York, and John Daniel of Virginia, along with the governors of Ohio, Wisconsin, Indiana, Illinois, and Michigan.[22] Twenty years earlier Livermore had been pilloried by clergymen, politicians, and newspaper editors as a selfish and strong-minded woman because she dared to speak in public to demand rights for her sex. Now she was included among a select group of the nation's most eminent orators. By 1888 it had become de rigueur to put a woman on the platform at a time of civic celebration. Mary Livermore had helped to achieve this milestone. Charged with speaking about the first women pioneers who had traveled from Massachusetts with General Rufus Putnam to settle in the Northwest, Livermore understood the auspiciousness of the occasion and the honor bestowed upon her. She prepared carefully for the address. Hers would be the keynote speech for the second day's festivities.[23]

Monday, July 16, in Marietta began with "the roar of a hundred guns from the wooded hilltops" announcing the start of the day's events. Throughout the day, people arrived by train and boat. They were entertained with a street parade led by Ohio's governor and by a series of exhibits prepared by the Smithsonian Institution. At eight o'clock that evening in Centennial Auditorium, Mary Livermore rose to address a crowd estimated at six thousand. She opened by lamenting the absence of historical records about Marietta's first women settlers. Like so many women in history, they had become anonymous figures about whom little was known. Livermore suggested that they were women of "grace and refinement," devout in their religious views, dedicated to educating their children and realizing their families' hopes for a better life.[24]

After presenting this overview of pioneer days, Livermore moved seamlessly into a discussion of women's contributions to the Revolutionary War and the Civil War, accenting changes in the public perception of women's rightful sphere that resulted. She applauded the Northwest for its leadership role in women's advancement, especially in the realm of higher education, noting that sixty-eight of ninety-five colleges in the region admitted women. She concluded with an eloquent endorsement of woman's rights, suggesting that female enfranchisement was as logical a progression in America's legal development as the abolition of primogeniture a century earlier. This was precisely the kind of "flank attack" she had perfected in her lyceum career, a discussion of American progress through the ages followed by the introduction of woman suffrage as a logical next step toward national improvement:

> If women have proved themselves worthy of all trusts thus far committed to them, shall there be hesitancy in trusting them yet farther? If they can be safely given the care of estates, schools, prisons, charities and institutions, if they are faithful as wives, mothers, homekeepers, and co-workers with men, can there be doubt they will show equal fidelity in the wise use of the ballot, to which the largest interpretation of liberty entitles them? Shall not the principles formulated in the Declaration of Independence, and underlying the Ordinance of 1787–twin documents that heralded an hour for which the ages had waited, when, in the mortal throes of a great spiritual agony, a nation was born free–shall these not be applied to women as they have been to men, since they are but the two halves of the unit we call Humanity?[25]

This was Livermore at her finest, and she was greeted enthusiastically. Combining history and logic with a measured and forceful delivery, she was persuasive and convincing. How many converts to woman suffrage she made on this or any other occasion is impossible to gauge, but Mary Livermore was clearly one of the movement's most effective spokeswomen.

Although she affected a casual tone in a letter to Anne Whitney recounting her speech—"I am just home from Marietta, Ohio, where I went to deliver one of the addresses"—Livermore must have been thrilled with both the invitation and her reception. The *Springfield Republican* said of her speech, "Mrs. Livermore has always known how to mingle force, eloquence and sweetness in exactly the right proportion, but the Marietta speech is a notable example of all these attributes." The *New York Tribune*, hostile to woman suffrage, nevertheless praised her speech as "polished and impressive," receiving "hearty" applause, while declining to provide specifics of her argument in favor of female enfranchisement. The speech was followed by an elaborate display of fireworks on the Ohio River."[26]

During the 1880s Livermore continued to support the three suffrage organizations of which she had been a member for so many years: the American Woman Suffrage Association and the New England and Massachusetts societies. Given her reputation as an orator and her stature within the suffrage movement, she was always accorded a prominent role in their conventions. Livermore often told audiences that she did not expect to see suffrage enacted at the national level during her lifetime. And yet she would not give up the fight. She told an AWSA convention in Chicago during 1884, "I would not work for this cause another day if I did not believe that woman is eventually to lift this country up to a higher plane." She saw cause for optimism in the number of women graduating from college and in the growing ranks of female physicians. She told an audience in Brooklyn that she "was going out of life happier than she was when she stood on the threshold of womanhood" because of the vast opportunities now open to women.[27]

Massachusetts suffragists celebrated a victory in 1879 when women won the right to vote in elections for local school boards throughout the state. The New England Women's Club had disseminated a petition to grant women this right, and while suffragists favored unrestricted enfranchisement, limited voting was better than no voting. The state Republican Party backed the law in part because it hoped that the votes of middle-class women would counteract the increasing power of largely working-class Catholic men in local elections. Indeed, the nativist element in this new law was reflected in the eligibility requirements, which were clearly designed to exclude the poor. To be eligible, a voter had to be a resident of the state, twenty-one years of age, literate, and pay a poll tax of two dollars, lowered to fifty cents in 1881. Samuel Sewall, a wealthy lawyer, resident of Melrose, and friend of Mary Livermore, prepared a pamphlet of instructions for women as they experienced their first opportunity to cast a ballot. Mary Livermore wrote of joining a dozen friends in going to the assessor's office to put themselves on a tax list so as to be eligible to vote, but she missed her first school board election because of lecturing engagements in the West.[28]

After school suffrage had been achieved, the Massachusetts Woman Suffrage Association launched an initiative to win municipal suffrage as well. Beginning in 1881 the MWSA circulated petitions with endorsements from Mary Livermore, Lucy Stone, and Julia Ward Howe, collected thousands of signatures, and sent its leaders to speak before the legislature. They faced opposition not only from intransigent members of the state legislature, including Republicans who refused to back the bill, but also from women opposed to their own enfranchisement. As early as 1868 anti-suffragists in the state had begun to organize. With the municipal suffrage campaign gaining momentum during the 1880s, the "antis" challenged suffragists by appearing as "remonstrants" before the legislature. Kate Gannett Wells, Clara Leonard, and Francis Parkman were among their most articulate speakers. Parkman, the eminent historian, summarized the arguments of the "antis" when he told the legislature that most suffragists were "in mutiny against Providence because it made them women," and added that "if the ballot were granted to women it would be a burden so crushing that life would be a misery." Apparently the legislature agreed, since municipal suffrage failed to win approval in the Bay State.[29]

In order to assist the state suffrage society to recover financially from the municipal suffrage campaign, Mary Livermore agreed to organize a "festival and bazaar" to be held December 13–16, 1886, in Boston. Given the title of president, she launched into organizing the event with the same enthusiasm she had given to the Sanitary Commission fairs more than twenty years earlier, sending a flurry of letters to friends and acquaintances. She told one correspondent that "ten counties and forty [local suffrage] Leagues are united in working for it." Writing to another, she spoke of the "earnest women, who have been standing for the uplifting of our sex from the repression of ages, until our youth has departed." Livermore's letter-writing campaign paid off, as she lined up more than fifty vice presidents and other officers, including Abby Kelley Foster, Julia Howe, William Lloyd Garrison II, Annie Fields, Henry Blackwell, John Greenleaf Whittier, Louisa May Alcott, Anna Howard Shaw, and former governor John D. Long. Archibald H. Grimké, the mixed-race nephew of Sarah and Angelina Grimké, would serve as marshal. She also recruited family members. Abby Coffin contributed her best home-canned fruit, and Etta and John Norris donated furniture to the sale and urged their friends to help. Livermore characterized the fair volunteers as "the very best men and women among woman suffragists" in the state.[30]

The Woman Suffrage Festival and Bazaar began its four-day run on December 13, 1886, in Boston's Music Hall. Mary Livermore, Lucy Stone, and Henry Blackwell addressed the crowd, followed by a "grand chorus of 100 voices" from the New England Conservatory of Music. In keeping with the season, many items for sale had a Christmas theme. The Melrose table sported a white and gold banner bearing the sentiments of its leader: "Man and woman are two halves of the integer we call humanity, with equal rights and responsibilities." Etta Norris served as one of the attendants at the Melrose table. The *Woman's Journal* reported that "Mrs. Livermore's great personal popularity brought contributions to her table from outside the suffrage ranks," including an old school friend who made a donation out of fondness for her chum despite opposing suffrage for women, opposing the temperance movement, and drinking claret wine on a daily basis. Clearly Mary Livermore's powers of persuasion remained considerable when it came to organizing a fair. All told, the fair netted $6,000 for the MWSA and additional money for its fifty-one auxiliaries, money that would be used to help with municipal and presidential suffrage campaigns.[31]

In 1889 Livermore proposed a different kind of fundraiser to support the Massachusetts effort. Borrowing the idea from an event she had seen in Marietta during the centenary celebration, she organized a pageant to showcase American history, with special attention paid to women's advancement. Five hundred amateur thespians staged this drama to a sold-out audience in Boston's Hollis Street Theatre. Narrated by Livermore herself, the pageant lasted five hours and featured the role of Queen Isabella in Columbus's voyages, the banishment of Puritan religious dissenter Anne Hutchinson, the home life of Abigail and John Adams, and women's participation in the antislavery movement, the Sanitary Commission, and the temperance crusade. The final scene contrasted women's largely maternal role in 1800 with their contributions as scientists, doctors, lawyers, writers, and ministers in 1889. The fundraising pageant initiated by Livermore would become a staple of suffrage events for years to come.[32]

Despite these fundraising successes, the suffrage movement had reached a stalemate on the national level by the 1880s. In an effort to recruit new members, the American Woman Suffrage Association began holding its annual conventions in western cities, including Chicago, Minneapolis, and Topeka, while the National Woman Suffrage Association continued to hold its conventions in the seat of national power, Washington, D.C. Neither side generated the kind of enthusiasm it had once hoped for, although Susan Anthony's indefatigable organizing and the NWSA's decision to embrace state-by-state as well as national work led to its growth at the AWSA's expense. Nearly twenty years after the schism, enmity clearly remained within the suffrage ranks. Susan Anthony wrote to Elizabeth Boynton Harbert in 1885, "Boston can *never* be the *centre* of any National Movement." Among a new generation of young suffragists, however, pressure mounted to unite the two groups. Younger reformers, who had not witnessed the acrimonious events of 1869, now argued that a fragmented movement hurt the cause. Moreover, the issues that had once separated the two groups were no longer divisive. The National had ceased to discuss divorce reform at its meetings, nor was it still scandalizing the Boston group by showcasing notorious characters such as George Francis Train. Even Victoria Woodhull was now a distant memory.[33]

Alice Stone Blackwell, whom Livermore fondly called "daughter of the regiment," encouraged the merger. In 1887 Blackwell and her mother met for the first time with Susan Anthony and Rachel Foster of the NWSA. A committee representing both groups would meet for three years before an agreement acceptable to each could be achieved. The AWSA negotiating team included Julia Howe, Hannah Tracy Cutler, Anna Howard Shaw, and Henry Blackwell. They suggested that since Lucy Stone, Susan Anthony, and Elizabeth Cady Stanton had been the most controversial figures in the two organizations, all three should recuse themselves from the presidency of the combined group. They also suggested that Mary Livermore would be an appropriate choice to lead the new association.[34]

Livermore's views on this subject are not known, for she played no official role in negotiations and was absent from the proceedings. Nor did Livermore attend the first convention of the united suffrage organization, known as the National American Woman Suffrage Association, held in Washington, D.C., February 18–21, 1890. Her name was not entered into nomination as president of the organization, nor was that of any other member of the AWSA. The presidency went to seventy-four-year-old Elizabeth Cady Stanton, in recognition of her role in founding the woman's movement at Seneca Falls in 1848 and her many years of service to the cause. Members of the AWSA would have preferred Susan Anthony, but Anthony instructed delegates, "Don't you vote for any human being but Mrs. Stanton."[35]

When the American Woman Suffrage Association held a final executive session before dissolving the organization, Julia Howe admitted feeling a "pang" of regret about ending "our separate existence." Henry Blackwell, by contrast, pointed out the many ways in which the AWSA had prevailed philosophically in the merger. NAWSA conventions would give voting privileges to officially designated "delegates" from state organizations. Men would not be excluded from leadership positions. Efforts to win passage of suffrage laws would focus on both the state and the national levels. "Side issues" would be avoided in favor of "woman suffrage pure and simple." The AWSA would be represented in the leadership structure of the new organization through both Lucy Stone, who would serve as chairman of the executive committee, and Alice Stone Blackwell, who would become corresponding secretary.[36]

Mary Livermore did not play a leadership role in the NAWSA. She held no office and appears not to have attended meetings, yet in all likelihood she approved of the merger. In 1869 she had hoped to avoid the schism. Periodically she had supported the National Association by praising its efforts and signing its petitions. Two years before the merger, she had shown enough camaraderie with the NWSA to attend its International Council of Women, held in Washington, D.C., to commemorate the fortieth anniversary of the Seneca Falls Convention. She spoke on the topic "Woman's Industrial Gains during the Last Half Century." Her failure to attend meetings of the combined organization appears to have been the result of age and priorities, not unhappiness with the merger. In 1901 the *Woman's Journal* reprinted a letter in which she declined to attend a meeting of the NAWSA in Minneapolis, citing ill health. But she sent her greetings and added a note emphasizing the importance of unity: "God bless you all, and give you an enobling season together, harmonious and uplifting in its results."[37]

By the 1890s, Livermore preferred to focus her efforts closer to home. During the previous decade she had founded a local organization called the Melrose Non-Partisan Woman Suffrage League. Friends and neighbors quickly joined the group, which elected Livermore its president and her son-in-law, John O. Norris, its vice president. Eventually they gained a membership of 150. The group encouraged women to vote in school board elections and urged male voters who sympathized with woman suffrage to oppose legislative candidates who did not. In October 1885 the league hosted a rally in the town hall attended by two thousand citizens, who listened to speeches by Mary Livermore, former governor John D. Long, and the Reverend Anna Howard Shaw.[38]

Livermore also started a branch of the WCTU in her hometown. Organized in 1882, the Melrose branch won widespread support among local women, enrolling 362 members by 1893. Livermore did not serve as president, but she never hesitated to throw her weight around, especially when it came to demanding the resignation of Rebecca Hesseltine as head of the local children's department after Hesseltine refused to sign the WCTU's anti-alcohol pledge, presumably because she drank socially. *"There is but one course to take,"* Livermore wrote to Melrose WCTU president Abby Burr on July 19, 1887. "Our duty is clear. . . . Our Constitution *compels* us to decline to receive any woman who does *not* sign the pledge." Failure to do so would result in gossip within and outside Melrose, *"and that I cannot bear."* Because the city of Melrose was "dry," the local WCTU focused its efforts on running a temperance school for children.[39]

Mirroring the national organization, members of the Melrose WCTU tended to be evangelical Christians. In order to give these women an alternative to "another prayer-meeting," Livermore started an "Afternoon Lecture Course" and served as coordinator. During the 1886–87 season, the monthly series included speeches encompassing literary, historical, health, and reform topics. Livermore often cajoled her friends to speak, including Julia Ward Howe and Dr. Mary Safford Blake. Each lecture season closed with a social gathering, usually a picnic.[40]

By the 1890s, however, the Melrose Suffrage League had disbanded, the victim of the invalidism or death of many of its most prominent members, including Samuel Sewall, the wealthy attorney who had lent his time, money, and legal expertise to the woman suffrage cause for many years. "In my absence they voted to disband, and unite with the W.C.T.U.," Livermore wrote to Henry Blackwell in 1894. The local WCTU maintained a "franchise department," and its entire membership of almost four hundred members supported woman suffrage. The Melrose Suffrage League made a donation of $100 to the Massachusetts Woman Suffrage Association when it dissolved.[41]

Mary Livermore remained active in the state suffrage organization. She joined Lucy Stone and Julia Ward Howe in asking all newspaper editors in the state to publish a plea for woman suffrage and to offer their own support. Some did so. All three women appeared before the Massachusetts legislature when it held special hearings on February 1, 1893. Following addresses by

Howe and Stone, both of whom made the case for women's enfranchisement, Livermore took the platform and refuted the presentation of a Baptist minister's wife, rejecting her allegation that most women did not want to vote and would not show up at the polls if enfranchised.[42]

The presence of Livermore, Stone, and Howe at the statehouse in February 1893 was one of the last joint appearances for these three friends who had labored so long and so hard for the cause of women's enfranchisement. By the end of the year Lucy Stone would be dead of stomach cancer, a major blow to the movement and a terrible loss for her family and her friends. In August, aware that Stone was failing rapidly, Livermore wrote her a letter, attempting to be cheerful and upbeat on the occasion of Stone's seventy-fifth birthday. "If Gladstone at eighty-three years of age could say, 'I represent the youth and hope of England, and her advancement along ideal paths,' I am sure you and I, and all the other 'old girls' of the suffrage reform, can use similar language to America," she said. "We *do* represent the future, and although we shall 'die without the sight,' our rewards are coming in the future." Livermore added that she would look forward to writing Lucy a birthday letter one year hence.[43]

It was not to be. Summoned to Stone's deathbed in October, Livermore said good-bye in a meeting that was emotional for them both. At one point Stone covered her eyes with one hand as she fought back tears. With the other, she reached for Livermore's hand, saying, "I pledged you that I would keep up with the procession to the end, but I have dropped out, and you will go on without me." The two friends had planned to attend conventions together in the fall, but now Lucy told her, "you will go to the conventions alone." Livermore promised she would. At Stone's funeral, October 21, 1893, she eulogized her friend as "a heroic woman, such as I have never known in my life, who dared as a young girl [to] stand up and battle against all the united world for her ideal." She spoke of what Stone's friendship had meant to her, of the camaraderie of working side by side as suffragists, enduring "contumely and ostracism . . . receiving defeat together and sometimes victory." Since Mary and Daniel Livermore had been close to both Stone and Blackwell, she felt a special concern for Henry as he faced the future without his wife. "My heart aches for you," she told him a few days before the funeral. Although several of Livermore's good friends died during this period, including Jane Hoge in 1890 and Myra Bradwell in 1894, none of the other losses affected her as much as Lucy Stone's death. Stone had been her closest comrade in the woman's movement as well as an intimate friend.[44] No one could replace Lucy.

Stone's death created a leadership vacuum in the Massachusetts Woman Suffrage Association. A few months before her demise, Stone had taken over the presidency from Julia Howe. Now Livermore agreed to step in, probably to fulfill her promise to Lucy that she would carry on without her. She would remain president of the organization for the next decade.

Although age, health, and other commitments prevented Livermore from presiding at every function of the MWSA, she contributed when she could, especially in cultivating ties with the temperance and club movements. The association offered to send a speaker to any woman's club in the state that would consider suffrage as a topic for discussion. Thirty quickly accepted. The MWSA also continued its efforts to persuade newspaper editors to launch discussions of the issue in their newspapers, and, preferably, to endorse the vote for women.[45]

Livermore's most important contribution to the Massachusetts Woman Suffrage Association was her creation of the Fortnightly Club. At the annual meeting of the association in 1895, she had proposed the idea of holding meetings every two weeks in the "handsome" offices of the MWSA on Park Street. At each meeting a speaker would make a presentation on a topic related to reform, politics, literature, society, or education, not necessarily to suffrage. Discussion would follow the lecture. No doubt Livermore had in mind a series somewhat akin to her WCTU lecture series in Melrose, but on a larger scale and with speakers drawn from across New England. Men as well as women would attend the meetings. The Fortnightly Club offered Livermore a new format in which to act as civic educator and gave her more satisfaction than almost any other pursuit in public life during the 1890s. It combined gatherings of intellectual people, many of them reformers whom she jokingly called "the Saints"; a broad range of topics covering many aspects of American life, indicative of her lifelong pursuit of education; lively discussions in a club-like setting; and the possibility of converting some of the unconverted to support for woman suffrage by showing them how many of New England's finest thinkers favored this reform. Members of the MWSA or its auxiliaries were admitted free; their guests were charged an admission fee of ten cents. Refreshments were served after the meetings.[46]

The Fortnightly Club was a success from the beginning. Livermore almost always presided at the meetings, which were held during the fall and winter months. Topics covered a broad spectrum, including "The Education of the Deaf in Boston," "Bicycling for Women," "The Present Status of Arbitration," "Sociology as a Study for Women," and, at its first meeting in 1901,

"The Negro in the 20th Century." The *Woman's Journal* always made note of upcoming meetings of the club, and the fact that Livermore would be presiding, crediting her efforts with stimulating interest in suffrage and boosting membership in the MWSA.[47]

During the late 1880s and into the 1890s, Livermore still mustered the energy and initiative to travel long distances giving public speeches. She no longer commanded top dollar for her efforts, but money had never been her only motivator. When asked by friends or in response to a worthy cause such as suffrage or temperance, she often spoke without charge, and in other circumstances asked for only a nominal fee of fifteen or twenty dollars plus expenses. Livermore was clearly past her prime as an orator. She had always spoken extemporaneously, and in her heyday could hold the attention of an audience for several hours at a time. In some instances she could still do this, as when she spoke so eloquently at the Northwest Ordinance centenary in 1888. But she did not always execute a consistently fine performance. Agnes Garrison, the daughter of William Lloyd Garrison II, heard Livermore on one occasion and wrote in her diary that the speech was "very bright & racy" but also "rambling." Her father, who was Livermore's friend and sometime lecture companion, complained on one occasion that Livermore had been "egotistical & irrelevant" in remarks honoring Harry Blackwell's seventieth birthday, probably because she spoke in some detail about her own marriage as well as Blackwell's union with Lucy Stone.[48]

In addition to her speeches becoming uneven over time, Livermore grew less and less tolerant of the vicissitudes of railroad travel. She had always hated sleeping berths. Now she avoided them when possible, preferring to schedule a series of lectures that would allow her to spend her nights in hotels and travel during the day. On occasion she still managed a schedule of marathon appearances. During the spring of 1889, for example, she wrote to a friend about lecturing five nights in Maine, including one presentation for the WCTU. She was sixty-eight years old at the time. One of her favorite anecdotes, told and retold to her friends, involved a conversation with the Quaker poet John Greenleaf Whittier at a social or reform function in 1890. "Mary, how old art thou?" he asked her. "Sixty-nine, Greenleaf," she responded. "Get thee hence, get thee hence," he teased her, "thou'rt nothing but a giddy girl."[49]

More and more often she complained of being tired, burdened, and unhealthy, expressing these views in letters to her friends, including Anne Whitney. "I think I never before was conscious of so great fatigue," she wrote in

June 1888, turning down an invitation to visit Whitney at her summer home in Shelburne, Vermont. "All the burdens of two households, somehow, tumble to my back, and there have been not a few of them this last year." She did not provide specifics. In 1892 she appeared more upbeat when she told Whitney that she would soon depart for a lecture tour to Brooklyn, Providence, Pawtucket, Holliston, and Columbus, and quoting a humorous line of her granddaughter's, suggesting that she would return on Saturday "tired like 40 dogs." Later that year she seemed less optimistic. Writing from Indianapolis, where she lectured in December, she wrote of her desire to return to Melrose: "Then no more trips this season, only occasional small excursions near home. I shall be glad to get home, for although well, I haven't enjoyed this trip."[50]

By the mid-1890s Livermore had lost the desire to travel the lecture circuit. She loved presiding over the Fortnightly Club and working with the WCTU lecture series in Melrose, but she no longer cared to leave home for extended periods. On January 8, 1895, the *New York Times* announced that while she would retain the presidency of the Massachusetts Woman Suffrage Association, "Mrs. Mary Livermore is to partly retire from the lecture platform and from public life. This practically means the end of an active career of more than thirty years." In a follow-up article the *Times* noted that at the peak of her fame she was one of the four most popular speakers on the lyceum circuit, and the only woman. For many years she lectured five nights a week for as many as five months of the year and annually traveled 25,000 miles by rail. Livermore "does not intend to retire absolutely from the field," the *Times* reported; but would speak mostly in and around Boston and would devote an increasing amount of her time to literary work. The *Woman's Journal* was quick to clarify that she did not intend to retire, but would only restrict her schedule to speaking engagements that did not take her away from Melrose overnight.[51] While acknowledging to her family and herself that she no longer had the energy she once had, Mary Livermore had no intention of retiring.

CHAPTER 12

◄•◄•◄►•►•►

The Grand Old Woman

B Y THE 1890s Mary Livermore had become one of the most respected women in America, widely recognized as an orator, activist, and civic educator. One admirer, likening her to the English prime minister William Gladstone, often hailed as "the grand Old Man," introduced her to an audience in Maine as "the grand Old Woman." By now she had reached her seventies and was slowing down, nagged by health problems and a decline in her legendary energy. Nonetheless, she remained a vibrant, astute, and persuasive figure in American public life. As the author of two autobiographies and the editor of a biographical directory, she contributed substantially as a chronicler of her era.[1]

Although the Civil War had never been far from Livermore's thoughts, in the later years she reflected often on the period that had transformed her life and the nation's. She always tried to keep in touch with her Civil War friends, especially the Sanitary Commission women with whom she shared a special bond–a "holy comradeship," she once called it. Mary Bickerdyke remained a presence in her life. In 1886 she breezed in for a "flying visit" of a couple of days, spending most of her time searching the local jails for one of her favorite veterans, a man named Berry who had apparently been incarcerated for public drunkenness and rioting. "Wet, weary and footsore, she came to my house at night, mourning that she had not found Berry," Livermore wrote in a letter to a friend. "I remonstrated, 'Why do you waste yourself, a woman of 73, on such a worthless fellow as that Drunken Berry? I would not bother with him,' I said. Turning to me with a flash of her blue eyes, and a straightening of the curves of her yet beautiful mouth, she said, 'Mary Livermore, I've a commission from the Lord God Almighty to do all I can for every poor miserable wretch that comes in my way! He's always sure of two friends–God and me!' Isn't that characteristic?" Livermore noted with satisfaction that Bickerdyke had finally secured a small pension and a position in the San Francisco mint.[2]

In 1890 the city of Boston hosted a reunion of the Woman's Relief Corps, an organization consisting of women formerly involved in Civil War soldiers' aid work. Though founded several years earlier, the national organization did not win official auxiliary status to the leading veterans' group, the Grand Army of the Republic, until 1881. Mary Livermore was not officially connected to the WRC at either the national or the state level. The national president of the organization was Annie Wittenmyer, with whom Livermore had had a long and contentious history. Nonetheless, Livermore shared the WRC's interest in soldiers' homes and efforts to help children of those slain in the war. She welcomed the Woman's Relief Corps to Boston and served as hostess when the *Woman's Journal* organized a reception for the visitors at its offices on Park Street.[3]

In the 1880s and 1890s Livermore wrote two volumes of autobiography. The first was *My Story of the War*, published in 1887. She had lectured on the topic to a wide range of audiences, from children to college students to lyceum groups. She had also written articles for the *New Covenant* and *Ladies Repository*, which she pulled out and brushed off for incorporation into her work. By the 1880s many public figures of her generation had written memoirs, including Ulysses S. Grant, whose phenomenally successful posthumously published autobiography came out in two volumes during 1885–86. Livermore expressed her views on the subject of Civil War memoirs in a letter to Clara Barton. "There is a great demand today for autobiographies of people who have been helpers of the world," said Livermore. She thought it especially important that Civil War nurses record their thoughts "for the benefit of women," and she urged Barton to write "a *real* and *full* biography." In the preface to *My Story of the War*, Livermore spoke of the need to preserve the historical record of common soldiers and women volunteers. "Who has fully narrated the consecrated and organized work of women," she asked?[4]

Livermore's memoir celebrates the contributions of nurses and soldiers, typical of a late-nineteenth-century genre that the historian Jane Schultz has called the "triumphal narrative."[5] It begins with an essay on battle flags, and includes four chapters on the exploits of Mother Bickerdyke, a section on the "heroism of soldiers' wives," and a series of chapters excerpting letters from soldiers in the field that Livermore culled from her ubiquitous notebooks. Her own recollections are mixed in: her decision to work for the Sanitary Commission, descriptions of the commission offices in McVicker's Theatre, her fond memories of colleagues Jane Hoge and Mark Skinner, lengthy commentary on the first Sanitary Commission fair, and her trips down the Mississippi River.

In places the narrative is captivating. The story of her first exposure to seriously wounded men in a St. Louis hospital in 1862 is a chilling account of a nurse confronting her fears and conquering them. Her recollections of President Lincoln in 1862 and 1865 are equally compelling, revealing a chief executive who was melancholy and long-suffering yet compassionate and wise. Livermore's justifiable pride in the 1863 Sanitary Commission fair, what it meant to her personally as well as to the Sanitary Commission and the city of Chicago, represents the war's idealism at its best, while the relative lack of description of the 1865 fair speaks volumes about a nation in mourning and a divided country not ready to forgive and forget. Her book provides invaluable insights into the workings of the Sanitary Commission in the Midwest and the role of women in wartime.

In at least one instance Livermore appears to have collapsed several narratives into a single episode: her trip to Vicksburg in 1863, her meeting with Ulysses S. Grant, her rescue of the slave child Ben Morris, and her return to Chicago. To this already dramatic narrative she added a climactic depiction of her first public speech in Dubuque, Iowa. Livermore implies that all these events occurred within a short period of time during the spring of 1863. Neither of Dubuque's newspapers recorded Livermore's having spoken there at that time, however. Moreover, Livermore places governor-elect William Milo Stone at the scene urging a reluctant Livermore to give the oration in the name of patriotism and the need to inspire women to greater activism in the Union cause. But Stone was still a colonel in the army stationed at Vicksburg. He did not leave the army until May 1863 and won election as governor in October of that year.[6]

Livermore probably met Stone in Vicksburg during the spring of 1863, since she often visited midwestern regiments on her hospital inspection trips. She traveled to Iowa on at least two occasions during the war. She journeyed to Des Moines in December 1863 in an effort to bring about a resolution of the strife in that state between supporters of the Sanitary Commission and backers of Annie Wittenmyer's own state relief fund. Governor-elect William Milo Stone was present at that meeting. Although Livermore spoke briefly in Des Moines, she did not give a formal address. It is entirely possible that Stone, impressed by Livermore in Des Moines, urged her to speak in public before mixed audiences. In 1864 Livermore did speak in Dubuque in support of the Sanitary Commission. This speech, well documented in the local press, may have been her first solo public address before a sizable audience of men and women, although she had spoken briefly at the soldiers' banquet that concluded the 1863 sanitary fair.[7] What might appear as intentionally misleading to the modern reader would not have bothered Livermore herself. She wanted to tell a story in a way that was exciting and readable. If she manipulated chronology and combined her appearances in Des Moines during 1863 with those in Dubuque in 1864, she felt at liberty to do so.

"No one is more keenly alive than I to the defects of this volume," Livermore wrote, referring to the way she had pieced it together in a somewhat disorganized fashion from old letters returned by friends and articles written many years earlier for the *New Covenant*, collected and collated with Daniel's help. Nevertheless, the *New York Tribune* praised the work as "valuable," adding, "Livermore tells some stories which cut deep." The public liked her work. Published by A. D. Worthington of Hartford, it sold 64,000 copies, a reflection of both Livermore's popularity and a renewed interest in the war among the reading public. Livermore profited handsomely. She told Clara Barton that the book earned $10,000 in royalties. At a time when her lyceum career had begun to wind down, Livermore was now earning a sizable income from her writing.[8]

The following decade she wrote a second volume of autobiography, *The Story of My Life*, published in 1897. She dictated the book to a stenographer, then corrected proofs. Livermore wrote the second book at least in part to raise money for her grandchildren's college tuition. She was especially anxious that her granddaughters not be prevented from seeking the educational opportunities she had long advocated for girls and which had been denied to her own generation.[9]

For many years Livermore had considered writing an autobiography, urged by friends and family to do so. Her publisher also pressed her to write another memoir, warning, she said, that if she did not do so, "my decease would inevitably be the signal for the appearance of unauthorized, unreliable, and shabby biographies." She agreed. Several days after signing a contract, Livermore became ill and was confined to her bed for a period of convalescence. A woman came to call on her in Melrose. To Livermore's amazement, her unidentified guest announced that she had completed a "sketch" of the suffragist's life, which lacked only further elucidation about the early years. Would Livermore supply her with the missing information? Amused but also offended by the woman's opportunism, Livermore explained that "my publisher, my family, and myself had rights which she would infringe if she persisted in publishing" the manuscript, which Livermore characterized as "incorrect, badly written, and unauthorized."[10]

Again, Daniel helped her to assemble materials. They had done some of the legwork already, for Mary had published a series of essays about her Virginia experiences in *Worthington's Illustrated Magazine* during 1893. She devoted two hundred pages to this topic in *The Story of My Life*, explaining that it "presents a phase of society and civilization that has passed away forever, and, as such, may prove of value and interest to young readers." But she would protect the identity of her employers. Despite the fact that James and Helen Jones had died many years earlier, Livermore knew that their daughter Mary had married a public figure, Edward Cary Walthall, formerly a major general in the Confederate army and now a senator from Mississippi. Throughout her life Livermore felt strongly about protecting both her own private life and others'. She would not embarrass the Walthalls by revealing information about the family's past.[11]

Livermore's memoir reads very much like a manuscript dictated to a stenographer and edited lightly. The book follows a chronological format until the Civil War, when she switches to a topical approach, with individual chapters dedicated to the war, lecturing, the temperance crusade, and her trips to Europe. Transcripts of six of her speeches are appended at the end, including her phenomenally popular "What Shall We Do with Our Daughters?" Most of the book concerns Livermore's life before the Civil War, with disproportionate attention to the Virginia years. Consequently the book is unbalanced in its treatment of her life. Perhaps the experience of being visited by an unauthorized biographer convinced her that her life before 1860 should be explored in depth, since her later public life had been well documented in the *Woman's Journal* and elsewhere.

Her descriptions of childhood in 1820s Boston, the family's disastrous experiment with farming in upstate New York, and her religious upbringing, early education, and teaching career make interesting reading. Line drawings enliven the text. In places the book is very funny, as when Livermore pokes fun at herself as a failed cook during the early years of her marriage. What is left out of her autobiography, however, is as noteworthy as what is included. While devoting a chapter to the Woman's Christian Temperance Union, with detailed descriptions of the spontaneous uprisings that preceded its formation, Livermore has surprisingly little to say about woman suffrage. She calls it the most important issue she advocated during her public career, but never alludes to the 1869 schism in which she played such a pivotal role, never mentions the American Woman Suffrage Association, and does not even discuss her editorship of the *Woman's Journal*. Livermore always regretted the suffrage split and disliked the "rows and wrangles" that plagued the movement for so many years. At the end of her life, when she wrote this memoir, she wanted to focus instead on the remarkable people she had known. Beginning with Lucy Stone, she pays tribute to her friends in the suffrage movement and the Sanitary Commission, to the writers, educators, reformers, and politicians she had met. The chapter ends with a tribute to her husband: "To no other person am I so deeply indebted, as to him, who has been for more than fifty years my lover, friend, husband, housemate, and efficient helpmate." It includes his photograph.[12]

Livermore was well aware of her book's shortcomings. When her journalist friend Lilian Whiting requested a copy, Livermore agreed to send her one, although she warned Whiting that the book had been written not for intellectuals "such as you" but for the "general reading public" and "leaves out much that is vital to me, and fundamental." Livermore played at least a small role in marketing the book. Because her publisher was a Congregationalist who had "*no* acquaintance" with religious liberals, Livermore feared that he would include endorsements solely from among the ranks of the orthodox clergy. Livermore wrote to her friend Isabel Barrows asking that her husband, Samuel Barrows, editor of the *Christian Register*, write something positive about the volume "if he can conscientiously." He did so, responding to Livermore that he had been "greatly delighted with your book," which had engaged him so much he had stayed up late one night to finish it. He predicted that it would "sell like hot cakes." Although sales figures for the volume are not known, apparently it did well enough, for Livermore confided to Whiting, "I wrote it, to get money to send my granddaughter to college. It has done that, and much more, for I am now helping her with her trousseau." Livermore's namesake, Mary Livermore Norris, graduated from Wellesley College in 1898, fulfilling her grandmother's dream that the younger women in her family might achieve the higher education that had been impossible for her own generation and still difficult for Etta's.[13]

In 1893 Mary Livermore collaborated with Frances Willard in publishing a compendium of biographical sketches of women. Titled *A Woman of the Century: Leading American Women in All Walks of Life*, the book includes nearly fifteen hundred short sketches accompanied by line-drawing portraits.[14] Five years earlier, speaking at the Northwest Ordinance centenary, Livermore had noted that women were all too often left out of the history books. By writing her own memoir, encouraging others to do so, and now contributing to this collective biography, Livermore helped to preserve a record of the many and varied accomplishments of nineteenth-century women.

On the title page, under the names of Willard and Livermore as editors, is the phrase "assisted by a corps of able contributors." In all likelihood the able contributors did most of the actual research and writing of the sketches. Willard and Livermore wrote the introduction. In it they said that they intended the volume as a tribute to women's contributions both "in the humbler as in the higher walks of life," and they intended the volume to fill a void left by women's exclusion from other encyclopedias and biographical directories. They believed that "the nineteenth century is woman's century," for no other period had offered women so many opportunities. They hoped to provide women and girls with the inspiration to achieve their goals—educational, economic, and political.[15]

Livermore published articles in journals of opinion during the 1880s and 1890s, including *North American Review*, *Arena*, and *Chautauquan*. In several articles she supported woman suffrage, in one instance pointing out its success in Wyoming and in twelve states where women had won the right to vote in school elections. In "Centuries of Dishonor," she began by paraphrasing Helen Hunt Jackson in the "remarkable" book by that title, which traced the American government's unjust treatment of Native Americans during the previous one hundred years: "Whoever shall write of the wrongs of women must entitle the story, 'Centuries of Dishonor,' and the arraignment will not be confined to one nation."[16]

She then proceeded to answer the leading arguments made by anti-suffragists, including the notion that men voted on behalf of their entire families. "Men cannot represent women until women shall give their legal consent that they may," she responded. She countered the argument that enfranchised women would not bother to vote by noting the high turnout in

Kansas after women won the right to vote in municipal elections there. She rebutted the claim that women were not knowledgeable enough to vote by showing that in the nation as a whole, girls stayed in school longer than boys. Although Livermore's interest in Nationalism and Christian Socialism had tempered her nativist outlook, causing her to blame many of America's woes on trusts and monopolies, she never entirely overcame a tendency to view Catholics with suspicion and condescension. To anti-suffragists' claims that the votes of female immigrants would give the "foreign element" added political clout, Livermore replied that in every part of the nation, native-born Americans outnumbered immigrants. Although her views on race had always been progressive, in this instance she expressed a sentiment commonly offered by southern suffragists to allay fears that African American female voters would pose a threat to white supremacy, noting that the population of white women in the South was greater than the combined population of black men and women. As she always did, Livermore cautioned that female enfranchisement would not usher in the millennium but rather would represent a new era in which men and women would work together as equals to improve the nation.[17]

In 1890 Livermore wrote an article about divorce, a practice she had condemned years before in an article for the *New Covenant*, but one she had not dared to speak about in the ensuing decades, fearing its potential to damage the suffrage movement. Now she expressed disapproval of the national trend toward easing restrictions, insisting that divorce crippled family life and threatened the social welfare of the nation. Although she did not oppose divorce altogether, she decried laws that allowed legal proceedings to take place in secrecy, and even suggested that jury trials might bring appropriate public censure to "guilty parties." As a preventive to divorce, she suggested that women should be given equal status in the American legal system.[18]

Although she no longer played an active role in the Bellamy Nationalist movement, Livermore continued to lament what she saw as rampant greed among American industrialists. In 1894, when Pullman rail car workers went on strike after a series of wage cuts, she expressed her sympathy for the strikers and their families. In a letter to Anne Whitney she condemned the "colossal selfishness and brutal indifference and rapacious greed" of the Pullman Company and spoke of the "harrowing suffering" of the workers and their children. The strike failed after President Grover Cleveland ordered the army to Chicago to reopen the rail lines, though eventually the Illinois Supreme Court ordered Pullman's company town dismantled and sold. Livermore also criticized the big business trusts that had come to dominate the American economy. In a letter to a Melrose newspaper, reprinted in the *New York Times*, she advocated "strong Governmental control" in order to regulate them.[19]

When the United States went to war with Spain in 1898 over the issue of Cuban independence, Livermore opposed military intervention. Like many of her generation, she was adamant about the need to avoid bloodshed on the scale she had witnessed during the 1860s. Complaining about the " 'jingoism' that swept the country like a hurricane" and propelled the nation toward war, she suggested that if women had been making the decision, they would have opposed military intervention "by a large majority," and President William McKinley would have been forced to continue seeking a diplomatic resolution. She complained that this war, like all wars, had been declared without the consent of women, whose taxes paid for its armies. Once war was declared, however, though its "purpose is slaughter and conquest," Livermore did what she could to assist soldiers and sailors. Although she did not know President McKinley, she did know Secretary of the Navy John D. Long, a former Massachusetts governor, longtime woman suffragist, and a friend of Livermore's. His endorsement of the war effort no doubt helped change her mind. When a group called the Massachusetts Volunteer Aid Association asked Livermore to serve as a vice president, she agreed, and helped raise both money and supplies to be sent to Cuba. Because the war ended in a matter of weeks, the organization quickly became obsolete.[20]

In her later years Mary Livermore found increasing satisfaction outside the public sphere, by spending time with her family, especially her husband. In 1885 Daniel Livermore retired from his Hingham pastorate, ending a forty-five-year ministerial career. Thereafter he devoted more time to the woman suffrage movement, writing articles for the *Woman's Journal* and other publications in which he rebutted the views of leading anti-suffragists. He also published a book, *Woman Suffrage Defended by Irrefutable Arguments*, grounding his defense of enfranchising women in the "fundamental principle of universal suffrage, on which our government is based." Tall, portly, and affable, Daniel reminded one friend of an English squire who enjoyed a good joke and always looked on the bright side of life. He continued to manage the family finances, and "reads incessantly," his wife wrote to Anne Whitney. Both Livermores spoke to local audiences of the Roundabout Club, a literary society in Melrose. Daniel presented a series of lectures relating to their European travels, while Mary recycled her lyceum topics.[21]

The Livermores still enjoyed traveling. In the autumn of 1885 they vacationed on Lake Ontario and took a boat trip from Cape Vincent to Alexandria Bay, a cruise of twenty miles, watching the skiffs and yachts and enjoying the illuminations on shore. They chanced to meet the novelist William Dean Howells with his family, and Howells and Daniel Livermore struck up a friendship. The Livermores spent two consecutive winters in southern California during the late 1880s, enchanted by the climate, "majestic mountains," and the exotic vegetation. They went sightseeing during the daytime, and Mary lectured in the evenings. Their love affair with California continued during the 1890s. In 1898 Mary wrote to a friend that if California were closer to New England, "we would have a winter home there, and all hands would go down in Oct. and stay till June." By the 1890s, more often than not, they vacationed closer to home, including a trip to the Adirondacks for "a little general vagabondizing."[22]

Their home in suburban Melrose remained a refuge from city life and a place to welcome family and friends. Mary described it to writer James Parton in 1891 as a "house full of the souvenirs of a happy married life, and of extensive travel at home and abroad." Among her favorite souvenirs were the handmade mementos given to her by grateful soldiers she had nursed during the Civil War. Mary answered correspondence and wrote articles at a rolltop desk in her book-lined study on the first floor. In 1890 the Livermores hired a secretary named Adelaide Witherington to help with paperwork. She would remain their employee for the rest of Mary's life.[23]

In addition to Mary and Daniel Livermore, their household included daughter Lizzie, along with Daniel's sister Eliza and Mary's sister Abby. Although the Livermores had long since concluded that Lizzie would never live a normal life, she apparently learned how to write; her name, in a childlike scrawl, appears in the front of a book her mother gave her in 1899. Lizzie collected autographs of notable people and pasted them into scrapbooks, a popular pastime during the late nineteenth century. Her mother occasionally asked friends to send autographs for "my Lizzie." Eliza Livermore was the oldest member of the household, Daniel's senior by nearly a decade. A pious Methodist, she was described by her famous sister-in-law as "the original 'Aunt Ophelia,' " a not entirely kind reference to the prim New England spinster of Harriet Beecher Stowe's *Uncle Tom's Cabin*. Mary remained close to her sister Abby, who managed all domestic affairs in the household, relieving her sister of duties she had always despised.[24]

Etta and John Norris and their children continued to reside close by. Mary called the grandchildren "my delight," although she worried about their generation of young people. In a letter to an acquaintance she complained of the "aimlessness" of most youth, "their eternal demand for 'a good time,' their senseless search for fun.' " Indeed, Livermore sometimes feared that the new generation behaved much like the French, with their "tendency to regard life as a gala day from which one must extract all the fun and frolic possible, regardless of consequences." From time to time, Mary attended Unitarian services with the Norris family, despite her past tendency to complain about the denomination. Daniel remained a stalwart of the local Universalist church. Eliza attended Methodist services, while Abby visited yet another house of worship, possibly the Baptist church of her youth. Referring to the range of religious perspectives within her household, Mary told a group of suffragists, "We are a very independent family, and a very happy one."[25]

During the 1890s Mary Livermore received many honors and awards. Because of her decades of support for working women, Boffin's Bower, a settlement house in Boston, hung her portrait on the wall of its parlor. In recognition of her lifelong commitment to education, the city of Melrose built a public school in 1891 and named it for her. Tufts College, which had ties to the Universalist Church, made her an honorary doctor of laws in 1896. In her acceptance speech Livermore praised the "broad and liberal foundation" of schools such as Tufts which had made the commitment to educate women. The Woman's Christian Temperance Union commissioned Anne Whitney to do a marble bust of Livermore for its Massachusetts headquarters. Thanking Whitney for her effort, Livermore chided her friend gently for making the likeness too idealized. "While it resembles me, it is a glorified likeness," she wrote, "and is finer looking than I ever was." Daniel apparently liked the bust, for he donated a plaster cast of the piece to the local library in Melrose.[26]

No celebration in her later life pleased Mary Livermore more than her golden wedding anniversary, a joyous day filled with family and friends gathered to honor a couple renowned for their mutual love and respect. In an era in which life expectancy was barely fifty years, it was a rarity to be married for five decades. The Livermores invited their friends and townspeople to attend a reception in their home on Monday, May 6, 1895. "From 2 until 7 P.M., the house was thronged with guests," according to the account Harry Blackwell wrote for the *Woman's Journal*. Standing in front of the bay window in their parlor, surrounded by floral tributes, the Livermores greeted fifteen hundred guests, among them relatives, friends, and representatives of various organizations: the local high school, the Ulysses S. Grant Post of the Grand Army of the Republic, the Anti-Tobacco League, and the Beneficent Society of the New

England Conservatory of Music, an organization that assisted talented and needy students, for which Mary Livermore served as president. The Livermores received eight hundred telegrams, cablegrams, letters, and cards from friends all over the country.[27]

Their extended family assisted with the party. John and Etta Norris acted as master and mistress of ceremonies, introducing the afternoon's entertainments, including male and female vocalists. Granddaughters Mary and Marion, home from Wellesley, poured cocoa and coffee in the dining room. Sandwiches were served on the lawn. In the back parlor Abby Coffin and Eliza Livermore presided over the gift table displaying busts of Eros and Hermes, gold spoons and serving pieces, and fifty gold coins from the Melrose WCTU.[28]

The following week the Livermores celebrated again, when the Massachusetts Woman Suffrage Association hosted a reception in their honor at the Park Street offices. Several hundred of their friends turned out to honor them, including Julia Ward Howe, William Lloyd Garrison II and his brother Francis Jackson Garrison, Henry Blackwell and daughter Alice, Anne Whitney, and former governor William Claflin. At Mary's insistence, there were no speeches. Instead, guests enjoyed a social evening, with piano music playing in the background and lemonade and cookies as refreshments.[29]

Mary and Daniel would celebrate several more anniversaries together, but by May 1899, when they observed their fifty-fourth anniversary, it was clear that Daniel was dying. Like his wife, he had enjoyed robust health for most of his adult life, but in the months after his eightieth birthday in June 1898, he began to decline. His condition became critical in the spring of 1899, and on July 5 he died of "infirmities incident to old age." In making the sad announcement, the *Woman's Journal* added this statement: "Only those who know them intimately can realize how great a bereavement this will be to Mrs. Mary A. Livermore."[30]

Almost fifty years earlier she had written Daniel a letter while he was away on a business trip, telling him, "Life is not life without you." Now he was gone forever. In the final weeks she had rarely left his bedside, and when the end came, she suffered from "severe nervous strain." Etta and John Norris insisted she come up to Boothbay Harbor, Maine, where they had a summer house. She needed to get away from Melrose, and she did take some comfort in being surrounded by her extended family. But she mourned Daniel. "The sundering of a companionship of fifty-four years has left me sorrowing, depressed and lonely," she told Anne Whitney.[31]

For years she had comforted her bereaved friends by advising them to cope with widowhood by throwing themselves into their work. On his deathbed, she said, Daniel had told her to keep on working and "go on as I had been living," but he had also cautioned her, as he always did, not to "overdo." Without Daniel, she had lost her anchor. Work no longer brought the fulfillment it had always afforded her. She told Anne Whitney that she thought her useful life was over, and she spoke often to Julia Howe of wanting to join Daniel.[32]

Spiritualism brought her some solace. Although she had once disdained the practice, she now eagerly sought a spirit medium through whom she could communicate with Daniel. Less than a month after his death she wrote to her friend Lilian Whiting, a believer in spiritualism, about her plans to use a medium named Minnie Soule. Mary believed that Soule succeeded in helping her speak with Daniel. In a series of letters to Whiting she referred to conversations with Daniel, and on December 15, 1902, she told Whiting that Daniel was readying a place for her in the Beyond.[33]

Livermore did return to her literary work eventually, writing articles and answering letters. At times she mustered considerable energy. In 1899 and 1900 she published sketches of Louisa May Alcott and Ralph Waldo Emerson for *Perry Magazine*. She reread all of Emerson's collected works in recognition of the centenary of his birth in 1903, and never tired of rereading a volume by Emerson and others about Margaret Fuller, telling a friend that the book still "rivets my attention." Nor did Livermore ever lose her sense of humor even when old age and infirmities slowed her down. In 1904 she promised Alice Stone Blackwell that she would make every effort to attend a meeting in Faneuil Hall, since "all the old war horses [would be] brought out to 'shoulder their guns.' "[34]

The Fortnightly Club continued to hold its popular lecture series, with Livermore presiding. On those occasions in which she both presided and spoke, the MWSA rooms on Park Street were invariably packed to capacity. In 1900, for example, she gave a lecture titled "Eminent Men I Have Known," in which she recalled her conversations with Abraham Lincoln and Ulysses S. Grant during the Civil War and reached farther back in time to talk about her impressions of Henry Clay and Daniel Webster. By the turn of the century, Mary Livermore had become a Grand Old Woman among New England's reform community, a recognition with which she was not entirely comfortable. When Melrose threw a party at City Hall to celebrate her eightieth birthday, she insisted there be no gifts and no long speeches. Hosted by the Massachusetts WCTU, with decorations provided by the Massachusetts Woman

Suffrage Association, the reception attracted a thousand people. Thereafter she insisted on quieter birthday celebrations. She did allow herself one luxury. In 1901 she added a conservatory to her house. Sixty years earlier she had admired the winter flowers that Helen Jones grew in a conservatory at St. Leon plantation. Now she had her own. With the death of Eliza Livermore a few months after Daniel, Mary's household now included Abby and Lizzie, and her secretary Adelaide Witherington, who wed William Boynton in a ceremony held in Mary's Emerson Street home.[35]

In 1903 Livermore stepped down from the presidency of the Massachusetts Woman Suffrage Association and ceased to preside over the Fortnightly meetings. By now she suffered from a variety of health problems, including chronic indigestion, neuralgia, a weakened heart, and, most troubling to her, difficulty with her eyes. In 1902 the *New York Times* reported that Livermore was threatened by blindness and had to remain in a darkened room to retard a degenerative condition. In the fall of 1902 she wrote to Lilian Whiting that her eyesight had improved enough that she could work for two hours each day, but she also noted that she had been felled by bronchial pneumonia. A nurse now took charge of her care.[36]

The end came in the spring of 1905. On May 10 she appeared at Faneuil Hall for an annual festival sponsored by the New England and Massachusetts Woman Suffrage Associations, where she presented a silver pitcher to Henry Blackwell on the occasion of his eightieth birthday. Although her friend William Lloyd Garrison II feared that she was too frail to make the presentation, she was determined to give a short speech and did so, praising Blackwell's "brotherliness, [and] his fraternal spirit." She offered her best wishes for his continued good health and her earnest hope that he would "always be surrounded by friends as fond and proud of him, and as willing to stand by him, as he is to-night!" Garrison later wrote to his wife that "she has rarely spoken with more clearness and feeling."[37]

The following day Livermore appeared at the Melrose WCTU's annual meeting and spoke about her recent visit to the women's prison in Sherborn. She had a head cold that did not appear to be serious. It would be her last public appearance. The cold turned into bronchitis, and her heart began to weaken. The Boston newspapers took note of her illness on May 18, with the *Journal* announcing that "Mrs. Livermore has a slight illness." Two days later the *Post* reported she was that she was "critically ill." She died on Tuesday morning, May 23, 1905, at the age of eighty-four. It was fifty-two years to the day since the death of her daughter Mary Eliza.[38]

The funeral was held on May 25. Melrose honored its most famous resident by tolling bells and closing businesses, schools, and public buildings. Because of Livermore's renown, the Unitarian service was held at the local Congregational church, the largest house of worship in Melrose, the Reverend Edward A. Horton officiating. Mary's sister, children, grandchildren, and nieces gathered to pay their last respects. Julia Ward Howe came, as did Anne Whitney and Alice Stone Blackwell. Henry Blackwell, William Lloyd Garrison II, and his brother Francis were among the honorary pallbearers. Representatives of the WCTU, the Massachusetts Woman Suffrage Association, and various women's clubs sent representatives and floral arrangements. The service began with a quartet singing "Lead Kindly Light," after which the Reverend Horton read scripture and poetry. Then he spoke of Livermore's long and productive life. "There were three great sources that made that luminous personality," he said. "One was Sincerity, the other Sympathy, and the last Service." At the conclusion of the simple ceremony, pallbearers carried the coffin slowly out of the church, where they passed through a double row of Civil War veterans, some of whom had known Livermore during the 1860s. A hearse carried the coffin to Wyoming Cemetery, where the body was cremated and her ashes placed in the family vault next to Daniel.[39]

After her death, Mary's attorney issued a statement to the press asking that journalists refrain from posing questions about her estate. Always concerned about protecting the privacy of her daughter Lizzie, Livermore had not wanted the newspapers to get a copy of her will, which might arouse speculation about Lizzie's condition. In fact, the will created a trust fund that allowed Lizzie to live independently for the rest of her life, attended by a full-time guardian. With Mary's earnings and Daniel's careful investing, the Livermores left an estate of more than $30,000 for Lizzie's benefit. In the records of the Middlesex County Probate Court are carefully prepared annual reports of the financial adviser who administered the trust fund until Lizzie's death in 1928.[40]

Etta Livermore Norris suffered a double blow in the spring of 1905. In the same month that her mother died, her husband, John Norris, contracted pneumonia; he died June 14. Some of the floral tributes donated for Mary's memorial service were used at his funeral. In three weeks' time, Etta Norris had lost her mother and her husband. She continued to reside in Melrose, as did Mary's sister Abby Coffin, who died in 1911, a much-beloved figure known to her many friends and neighbors as Aunt Abby. Etta died in 1929 at the home of a daughter on Long Island.[41]

Mary Livermore did not live long enough to see her cherished reforms enacted. The Eighteenth Amendment, prohibiting the manufacture and sale of alcohol, became law in 1919. But Livermore, who well remembered the Maine liquor law crusades of the early 1850s, always believed that the temperance movement was better served by changing the hearts and minds of individuals through appealing to their moral and spiritual nature. Woman suffrage became law in 1920, fifteen years after her death. Massachusetts, with one of the best-organized anti-suffrage efforts in the nation, failed to enact a state law before adoption of the national constitutional amendment. None of her generation lived to see the triumph of the Nineteenth Amendment. Elizabeth Cady Stanton had preceded Livermore in death. Susan B. Anthony died in 1906, Henry Blackwell in 1909, and Julia Ward Howe in 1910. But Mary Livermore's indomitable spirit lived on through her granddaughter and namesake, Mary Livermore Norris. An 1898 graduate of Wellesley College, she married English teacher Malcolm Barrows, bore two sons, and then launched a political career. After being elected to the Melrose Board of Aldermen, she ran for a seat in the state legislature. In 1929 Mary Livermore Norris Barrows became the first woman ever elected to represent Melrose in the Massachusetts legislature. Her strong-minded grandmother would have been proud.[42]

NOTES

LC	Library of Congress, Washington, D.C.
Life	*The Story of My Life* by Mary A. Livermore
LS	Lucy Stone
MAL	Mary A. Livermore
MWSA	Massachusetts Woman Suffrage Association
MCC	Mecklenburg County Courthouse, Boydton, Va.
MWSA	Massachusetts Woman Suffrage Association
NYPL	New York Public Library
NAWSA	National American Woman Suffrage Association
NWSA	National Woman Suffrage Association
OB	Olympia Brown
SBA	Susan B. Anthony
SLR	Schlesinger Library, Radcliffe College
T&P Papers	Temperance and Prohibition Papers, University of Michigan
TWH	Thomas Wentworth Higginson
USCC	United States Christian Commission
USSC	United States Sanitary Commission
War	*My Story of the War* by Mary A. Livermore
WC	Wellesley College
WCTU	Woman's Christian Temperance Union
WLG	William Lloyd Garrison
WPA Inventory	Works Progress Administration of Virginia, Historical Inventory, Library of Virginia, Richmond

Prologue

1. *Boston Evening Transcript*, May 23, 1905; *New York Times*, Jan. 20, 1895.
2. Stephen B. Oates, *Woman of Valor: Clara Barton and the Civil War* (New York: Free Press, 1994); Ruth Bordin, *Frances Willard: A Biography* (Chapel Hill: University of North Carolina Press, 1986); Elisabeth Griffith, *In Her Own Right: The Life of Elizabeth Cady Stanton* (New York: Oxford University Press, 1984); Kathleen Barry, *Susan B. Anthony: A Singular Feminist* (New York: New York University Press, 1988).
3. L. P. Brockett and Mary C. Vaughan, *Woman's Work in the Civil War: A Record of Heroism, Patriotism, and Patience* (Philadelphia: Zeigler, McCurdy, 1867), 577; Phebe A. Hanaford, *Daughters of America; Or, Women of the Century* (Augusta, Me.: True, [1882]), 305-21; Lilian Whiting, *Women Who Have Enobled Life* (Phil-

adelphia: Union Press, 1915), 53-85; LaSalle Corbell Pickett, *Across My Path: Memories of People I Have Known* (New York: Brentano's, 1916); Grace Humphrey, *Women in American History* (1919; reprint, Freeport, N.Y.: Books for Libraries Press, 1968), 164-78.

4. Calvin Coolidge was scheduled to speak at the Livermore service but canceled at the last minute. A few weeks earlier he had been elected vice president of the United States. A copy of the program for the hundredth anniversary service, dated Dec. 19, 1920, may be found in the Woman's Rights Collection, SLR. See also untitled newspaper clipping of the same date, NAWSA Collection, reel 45, LC. *Melrose (Mass.) Free Press*, Dec. 24, 1920.

5. For a discussion of the World War II merchant marines, Liberty Ships, and the *Mary A. Livermore*, see *www.usmm.org/men_ships.html*. Samuel I. Rosenman, comp., *The Public Papers and Addresses of Franklin D. Roosevelt*, 13 vols. (New York: Harper and Brothers, 1950), 10:325-33; *New York Times*, Aug. 20, 1941. Livermore recounted her November 1862 visit with Lincoln in Mary A. Livermore, *My Story of the War: A Woman's Narrative of Four Years' Personal Experience* (1887; reprint, New York: Da Capo, 1995), 555-65. See also Carl Sandburg, *Abraham Lincoln: The War Years*, 4 vols. (New York: Harcourt, Brace and World, 1939), 1:553-55.

6. *Boston Herald*, Aug. 22, 1941.

7. Ken Burns, *The Civil War*, 1992; Stephen B. Oates, *Whirlwind of War: Voices of the Storm, 1861–1865* (New York: HarperCollins, 1998). Among academic histories citing Livermore, see Phillip Shaw Paludan, *"A People's Contest": The Union and Civil War, 1861–1865* (New York: Harper & Row, 1988). Recent studies of women in the Civil War Sanitary Commission include Jeanie Attie, *Patriotic Toil: Northern Women and the American Civil War* (Ithaca: Cornell University Press, 1998); Judith Ann Giesberg, *Civil War Sisterhood: The U.S. Sanitary Commission and Women's Politics in Transition* (Boston: Northeastern University Press, 2000).

8. MAL discussed the fire at her publisher's in an undated letter to Lilian Whiting reprinted in *Women Who Have Enobled Life*, 65. Although the term "feminist" was not used in MAL's lifetime, it is used in this book to refer to a women's rights advocate. There is no other one-word descriptor to replace it.

9. Anna Howard Shaw, *The Story of a Pioneer* (1915; reprint, Cleveland: Pilgrim Press, 1994), 95. MAL complained about Wilde and Whitman becoming popular among respectable people in a letter to Colonel Thomas Wentworth Higginson, Feb. 17, 1882, Livermore Collection, BPL. Susan Fessenden to Anna Gordon, June 27, 1893, T&P Papers, reel 19.

10. Livermore's fear of an "indiscreet biographer" and her decision to burn the scrapbooks are discussed in *Woman's Journal*, April 30, 1904. She wrote of "burning her past" twelve years earlier in a letter to Henry B. Blackwell, Oct. 30, 1893, NAWSA Collection, reel 12, LC. Regarding *My Story of the War*, she told "Mr. Goss" that she had "committed it [the manuscript] to the furnace" and suggested that he might want to "cremate" her second memoir in a letter on Nov. 30, 1896, Livermore Collection, BPL. In all likelihood, Livermore's fear of biographers was

grounded, at least in part, in her concern that her younger daughter's mental handicap would become public knowledge. See chapters 10-12. Josephine Mutti is quoted in *Melrose Free Press*, Sept. 16, 1991.

11. *Chicago Tribune*, Oct. 2, 22, 23, 1863, Feb. 28, March 28, Sept. 12, 1869; *Agitator*, Oct. 2, 1869.

12. *Woman's Journal*, Nov. 30. 1889.

1. BOSTON CHILDHOOD

1. *Life*, 42.
2. *Life*, 42, 47; *Agitator*, May 8, 1869.
3. *Life*, 38-39, 85, 106, 121-22; Hanaford, *Daughters of America*, 313. The 1850 federal census lists Timothy Rice as sixty-two years old, making his likely birth date 1788. He died in 1865. See Census Microfilm Records, Mass., 1850, disk 5, Suffolk County, sec. 1, roll 334.
4. *Life*, 39. The 1850 federal census lists Zebiah Rice as fifty-seven years old, making her likely birth date 1793. She died in 1869. Census Microfilm Records, Mass., 1850, disk 5, Suffolk County, sec. 1, roll 334.
5. *Life*, 39-40, 106.
6. *Life*, 38, 44, 71. See *Boston City Directories*, 1820-1832; David Ward, "Nineteenth-Century Boston: A Study in the Role of Antecedent and Adjacent Conditions in the Spatial Aspects of Urban Growth" (Ph.D. diss., University of Wisconsin, 1963), 26-28.
7. *Life*, 43-44.
8. *Life*, 45-50; "Eighty Years of Age" [1900], unidentified newspaper clipping, Melrose (Mass.) Public Library; J. S. Dennis, "Mrs. Mary Ashton Livermore," *Ladies Repository* 39 (Jan. 1868): 2.
9. *Life*, 40-42.
10. *Life*, 52-58; Hanaford, *Daughters of America*, 313; Dennis, "Mrs. Mary Ashton Livermore," 1; Nathan Wood, *The History of the First Baptist Church of Boston, 1665-1899* (Philadelphia: American Baptist Publication Society, 1899), 264, 311-25. Francis Wayland became pastor of First Baptist Church in 1821; in 1827 he became president of Brown University. See *Dictionary of American Biography*, 20 vols. (New York: Charles Scribner's Sons, 1936), 19:558-59.
11. MAL offered a tribute to her unidentified Sunday school teacher in *New Covenant*, Aug. 20, 1859.
12. *Life*, 52-56; "Eighty Years of Age."
13. *Life*, 58-59.
14. *Life*, 56.
15. MAL to "unknown," Oct. 12, 1888, Edward Levy Collection, SLR.
16. *Life*, 41.
17. *Life*, 65-70; Hanaford, *Daughters of America*, 312-13.
18. *Life*, 90-91.

19. *Life*, 84-85, 96-100. In *Life*, 98, MAL wrote, "I . . . cannot remember at what time my father decided to leave Boston for a residence in Western New York. I was between ten and twelve years of age at that time." Timothy Rice's name does not appear in *Boston City Directories* in 1833 and 1834.

20. *Life*, 99-104; Russell Bourne, *Floating West: The Erie and Other American Canals* (New York: W. W. Norton, 1992), 102, 162-69; Ronald E. Shaw, *Canals for a Nation: The Canal Era in the United States, 1790-1860* (Lexington: University of Kentucky Press, 1990), 29-30. Founded in 1792 by Dutch investors, the Holland Land Company owned millions of acres of land in New York and Pennsylvania. William Chazanof, *Joseph Ellicott and the Holland Land Company: The Opening of Western New York* (Syracuse: Syracuse University Press, 1970), 3, 17, 175-77.

21. *Life*, 104-5.

22. *Life*, 103-5; Donald H. Parkerson, *The Agricultural Transition in New York State: Markets and Migration in Mid-Nineteenth-Century America* (Ames: Iowa State University Press, 1995), 71.

23. *Life*, 105-6.

24. *Life*, 107-11.

25. *Life*, 111-13.

26. *Life*, 62-63; Dennis, "Mrs. Mary Ashton Livermore," 2; Wood, *History of the First Baptist Church of Boston*, 331-32, 339-40. Rollin Heber Neale (1808-1879) served as pastor of First Baptist from 1837-1877.

27. *Life*, 118-21. Livermore would remain an admirer of Harriet Martineau and later in life would write and speak about the British writer.

28. *Life*, 124.

29. *Life*, 124-26; Alice Kessler-Harris, *Out to Work: A History of Wage-Earning Women in the United States* (New York: Oxford University Press, 1982), 48.

30. *Life*, 126-27; Linda K. Kerber, *Women of the Republic: Intellect and Ideology in Revolutionary America* (Chapel Hill: University of North Carolina Press, 1980), 189-231.

31. *Life*, 127; Catharine N. Badger, *The Teacher's Last Lesson: A Memoir of Martha Whiting, Late of the Charlestown Seminary* (Boston: Gould and Lincoln, 1855), 13-17, 23-27, 33-34, 57-58, 101-5, 116. See also Hanaford, *Daughters of America*, 509.

32. *Life*, 127-29; "Mary A. Livermore," *The Leader: A Magazine of Modern Education* 1 (May 1903): 351.

33. *Life*, 127-29; Badger, *The Teacher's Last Lesson*, 15, 69, 108-9.

34. Badger, *The Teacher's Last Lesson*, 67, 114, 131, 160-63, 244.

35. *Life*, 232-35, 273-74.

36. *Life*, 130.

37. *Life*, 130-31.

38. *Life*, 114-17, 130-31.

39. *Life*, 132-35; Dennis, "Mrs. Mary Ashton Livermore," 3; MAL, "Two Years on a Virginia Plantation," *Ladies Repository* 41 (Feb. 1869): 129.

40. *Life*, 131-33.

41. *Life*, 135-41; *Boston Post*, May 18, 1905. In *Life*, 609, MAL relates that her parents adopted an orphan girl following the death of Rachel. They called her Annie.

42. *Life*, 141-42.

43. *Life*, 143-45; MAL, "Two Years on a Virginia Plantation," 129.

44. *Life*, 144-45.

2. VIRGINIA TEACHER

1. MAL, "In 'Old Virginny' Fifty Years Ago: First Paper," *Worthington's Illustrated Magazine* 1 (Jan. 1893): 17.

2. *Life*, x. Neither the Virginia journal nor the letters to her parents have survived.

3. MAL, "Two Years on a Virginia Plantation," 129-30; MAL, "In 'Old Virginny': First Paper," 17.

4. MAL, "Ten Years on a Virginia Plantation," 129-30; *Life*, 147.

5. *Life*, 147-48; MAL, "Two Years on a Virginia Plantation," 131. MAL recalled her meeting with Henry Clay more than forty years later in an article in *Woman's Journal*, March 3, 1900.

6. MAL, "Two Years on a Virginia Plantation," 131-32.

7. Ibid., 132-33; *Life*, 151-53. Major Rainey was probably Phillip Rainey, whom Mary's employer identified as a friend in his last will and testament.

8. *Life*, 153; MAL, "In 'Old Virginny' Fifty Years Ago: Second Paper," *Worthington's Illustrated Monthly* 1 (Feb. 1893): 119.

9. Paul Douglas Hardin, "Edward Cary Walthall: A Mississippi Conservative" (M.A. Thesis, Duke University, 1940), 17-18, 83.

10. The name Henderson does not appear in the Mecklenburg County federal census in 1840 or 1850. Although the name does appear frequently in neighboring Warren and Granville counties in North Carolina, there are no listings for James and Helen Henderson. On the identity of the Jones family, see *War*, 223, 262; *Life*, 151, 154, 175, 199, 205, 283, 309. See the description of St. Leon plantation and the Jones children in the will of James Y. Jones, dated April 5, 1843, Mecklenburg County Will Book, 15: 538-39, MCC. See also Munsey Adams and Margaret Moore, comps., *Cemetery and Tombstone Records of Mecklenburg County, Virginia*, 2 vols. (Chase City, Va: Munsey Moore Publications, 1987), 2:225. The only documented graves in the cemetery are those of James and Helen Jones, their two sons, three of their daughters, two sons-in-law, and three grandchildren. Today there are no surviving tombstones, although the cemetery is enclosed by a handsome brick wall. Much of what was once St. Leon plantation is underwater, flooded when the Army Corps of Engineers built the John H. Kerr Dam in the 1950s.

11. *Life*, 159; MAL, "Two Years on a Virginia Plantation," 134.

12. County records reveal the land purchases made by the Jones family during the 1840s and 1850s. See Mecklenburg County Deed Books, bk. 20, 337-38; bk. 33, 249; bk. 35, 193; bk. 36, 213, MCC; Mecklenburg County Order Book no. 21, 265, 270, MCC. See also WPA Inventory, "The St. Leon Site," June 10, 1837; federal

census of 1850; Auditor of Public Accounts, Personal Property Tax Books, Mecklenburg County, 1823-1840, Library of Virginia, Richmond. Regarding the number of slaves, in "Two Years on a Virginia Plantation," 134, MAL referred to "between two and three hundred persons," while in *Life*, 157, she reported that "five
hundred people, black and white, [lived] on the plantation." Both were exaggera-
tions. See U.S. Bureau of Census, *Population Schedules of the Fifth and Sixth
Census of the United States*, Mecklenburg County, Va., M19, roll 197, 001, and
M704, roll 565, 403.

13. *Life*, 160-61; codicil to will of James Y. Jones, April 6, 1843, Mecklenburg Will
Book, 15: 538-39, MCC.

14. *Life*, 159-60; MAL, "Two Years on a Virginia Plantation," 134.

15. *Life*, 153-58. St. Leon plantation may have been named for a novel of that title by
the radical freethinker William Godwin, published in 1799. According to WPA
Inventory, St. Leon burned in 1911. See also Mecklenburg County Department of
Taxation, Personal Property, James Y. Jones Estate, 1858, Library of Virginia.

16. *Life*, 165-67; MAL, "Two Years on a Virginia Plantation," 136-37.

17. *Life*, 157, 186, 205-7; MAL, "In 'Ole Virginny' Fifty Years Ago: Third Paper,"
Worthington's Illustrated Monthly 1 (March 1893): 223.

18. Susan L. Bracey, *Life by the Roaring Roanoke: A History of Mecklenburg County,
Virginia* (Richmond: Whittet and Shepperson, 1978), 260. According to historian
William G. Shade, Mecklenburg, Halifax, Pittsylvania, and Charlotte counties pro-
duced 36 percent of Virginia's tobacco crop in 1849; see his *Democraticizing the
Old Dominion: Virginia and the Second Party System, 1824-1861* (Charlottesville:
University Press of Virginia., 1996), 33. federal census, 1840.

19. Bracey, *Life by the Roaring Roanoke*, 129-30, 209, 265-66; William B. Hill, *Land
by the Roanoke: An Album of Mecklenburg County, Virginia* (Richmond: Whittet
and Shepperson, 1957), 46.

20. Bracey, *Life by the Roaring Roanoke*, 142; *Life*, 319. Census information for the
county in 1840 may be found at www.fisher.lib.virginia.edu/collections/stats/
histcensus.

21. *Life*, 253; Bracey, *Life by the Roaring Roanoke*, 235-36.

22. Jones described his daughters' intellect in his will, dated April 5, 1843, Mecklenburg Will Book, 15:538-39, MCC. Horace Greeley, *Recollections of a Busy Life*
(New York: J. B. Ford, 1869), 104-5; Glyndon G. Van Deusen, *Horace Greeley:
Nineteenth-Century Crusader* (Philadelphia: University of Pennsylvania Press,
1953), 35-36; Lizzie Wilson Montgomery, *Sketches of Old Warrenton, North Carolina* (Raleigh: Edwards & Broughton, 1924), 146-48.

23. Jan Lewis, *The Pursuit of Happiness: Family and Values in Jefferson's Virginia*
(New York: Cambridge University Press, 1983), 205.

24. *Life*, 189-201; MAL, "Two Years on a Virginia Plantation," 135; "In 'Ole Virginny':
First Paper," 22; and "In 'Ole Virginny': Third Paper," 215-24.

25. *Life*, 176-77, 198-99, 208, 317, 327, 360; MAL, "In 'Ole Virginny': Third Paper,"
221-22.

26. *Life*, 210-11.

27. *Life*, 168-70, 344, 362-64.

28. *Life*, 161; MAL, "Two Years on a Virginia Plantation," 135. Jan Lewis, *Pursuit of Happiness*, 52, notes that the religious skepticism that characterized the thinking of Enlightenment era Virginians swiftly became "socially unacceptable" in the nineteenth century. See wills of James Y. Jones, April 5, 1843, 15:538-39, and James Y. Jones Jr., April 28, 1861, 20:408-9, Mecklenburg Will Books, MCC; MAL, "In 'Ole Virginny' Fifty Years Ago: Fifth Paper," *Worthington's Illustrated Magazine* 1 (May 1893): 404.

29. *Life*, 314, 362-64; MAL, "Two Years on a Virginia Plantation," 135; "Mary A. Livermore," *The Leader: A Magazine of Modern Education* 1 (May 1903): 351.

30. *Richmond Enquirer*, Nov. 23, 1841; Bracey, *Life by the Roaring Roanoke*, 159-61; Hill, *Land by the Roanoke*, 50. William Goode pronounced his name as rhyming with "food." Goode and Baskerville, along with their homes, Wheatland and Buena Vista, are described in WPA Inventory.

31. Bracey, *Life by the Roaring Roanoke*, 159-64, 260; *Life*, 224-25, 236-38. Humberston Skipwith of Prestwould plantation was by far the wealthiest patriarch in Mecklenburg County, but his family situation, his lack of interest in politics, and the location of his home do not fit the profile of the Blackstocks and their manor; author's interview with Julian Hudson, director, Prestwould Foundation, July 1999. See also Jeffrey St. John and Kathryn St. John, *Landmarks, 1765-1990: A Brief History of Mecklenburg County, Virginia* (Boydton, Va.: Mecklenburg County Board of Supervisors, 1990), 34-42. The Blackstocks may have been the Goode family. While not the richest, they were among the oldest and wealthiest families in the country, and they built a new plantation called Rotherwood on family property that included an eighteenth-century mansion. Congressman William O. Goode may have been the recently elected "Senator Gordon" MAL referred to. Goode won election to Congress in 1840. See WPA Inventory, Rotherwood.

32. *Life*, 237, 239, 270.

33. *Life*, 268-70. Her confessed lack of interest in politics contrasts with the findings of Elizabeth R. Varon, who reports considerable interest among Virginia women during the 1840s in *We Mean to Be Counted: White Women and Politics in Antebellum Virginia* (Chapel Hill: University of North Carolina Press, 1998), 71-102.

34. *Life*, 271-74.

35. *Life*, 271, 274-76.

36. *Life*, 280-81, 293-310. WPA Inventory notes one instance of the mill burning. MAL, "In 'Ole Virginny' Fifty Years Ago: Seventh Paper," *Worthington's Illustrated Magazine* 2 (July 1893): 27-37.

37. In the *Agitator*, April 17, 1869, MAL described her father's outrage at attempts to use the Bible to support slavery. She called him "a firm believer in the Bible, but a terrible hater of slavery."

38. *Woman's Journal*, July 23, 1870. Celia Burleigh was a friend of MAL. It is interesting to note that MAL did not mention the Grimké speech in either of her two autobiographies, perhaps because she did not want to draw attention to the fact

that even after she had heard one of the antislavery movement's most compelling orators, she had accepted employment from a slaveholder anyway. She did mention having once heard Grimké speak in "Twenty-Five Years on the Lecture Platform," *Arena* 33 (Aug. 1892): 261.

39. Jane Turner Censer, *North Carolina Planters and Their Children, 1800–1860* (Baton Rouge: Louisiana State University Press, 1984), 48-54.

40. Catherine Clinton, *The Plantation Mistress: Woman's World in the Old South* (New York: Pantheon, 1982); Elizabeth Fox-Genovese, *Within the Plantation Household: Woman's World in the Old South* (Chapel Hill: University of North Carolina Press, 1988).

41. *Life*, 158, 260.

42. *Life*, 236.

43. *Life*, 228; Fox-Genovese, *Within the Plantation Household*, 30.

44. *Life*, 187, 220, 228, 362-63; *War*, 259-61; MAL, "In 'Ole Virginny': First Paper," 22; MAL, "In 'Ole Virginny': Second Paper," 120.

45. *Life*, 153, 166, 229, 332-41.

46. *Life*, 332-41, 346-47.

47. *Life*, 229-30. Fanny Kemble visited Georgia about the same time that Mary Rice lived in Virginia; see Frances Anne Kemble, *Journal of a Residence on a Georgian Plantation in 1838–1839* (Savannah: Beehive Press, 1992), 334-37.

48. *Life*, 187, 254-58, 328-30. For a discussion of slave weddings, see John W. Blassingame, *The Slave Community: Plantation Life in the Antebellum South*, rev. ed. (New York: Oxford University Press, 1979), 179-81.

49. *Life*, 327-30. See Harriet Beecher Stowe, *Uncle Tom's Cabin or Life Among the Lowly* (New York: Penguin, Putnam, 1998).

50. *Life*, 176, 214, 327.

51. *Life*, 182-87, 212-20; MAL, "In 'Old Virginny' Fifty Years Ago: Fourth Paper," *Worthington's Illustrated Magazine* 1 (April 1893): 312-20.

52. *Life*, 214, 227; Robert William Fogel, *Without Consent or Contract: The Rise and Fall of American Slavery* (New York: W. W. Norton, 1989), 68. See also Censer, *North Carolina Planters and Their Children*, 136.

53. *Life*, 231-35.

54. Years later, Mary Jones Walthall, wife of Senator Edward Walthall of Mississippi, recalled her early education at St. Leon with two private teachers, one for literature and the other for music. She identified her literary tutor as MAL. See Hardin, "Edward Cary Walthall," 17, citing an oral history interview with Blanche Winter, July 2, 1939. As a child, Winter had been a neighbor and close friend of the Walthalls. Mary Jones Walthall did not disclose the name of her music tutor. *Life*, 350-59.

55. *Life*, 359.

56. *Life*, 364-65.

57. *Life*, 359-60; obituary notice in *Richmond Enquirer*, July 21, 1843.

3. Minister's Wife

1. *Life*, 365-67. Although MAL did not describe her living arrangement in Duxbury, in all likelihood she rented a room with a family. In the nineteenth century, young unmarried teachers generally did not live alone.

2. *Life*, 368-69; *Boston Daily Standard*, July 5, 1895, in T&P Papers, reel 32.

3. *Life*, 369-74; *Boston Daily Standard*, July 5, 1895.

4. *Life*, 380-82.

5. *Life*, 374; Ian R. Tyrrell, *Sobering Up: From Temperance to Prohibition in Antebellum America, 1800–1860* (Westport, Conn.: Greenwood Press, 1979), 159-60; E. Waldo Long, ed., *The Story of Duxbury, 1637–1937* (Duxbury, Mass.: Norwood Press, 1937), 91, 114-15; Katherine H. Pillsbury et al., comps., *The Duxbury Book, 1637–1987* (Duxbury, Mass.: Duxbury Rural and Historical Society, 1987), 53.

6. Ian R. Tyrrell, "Women and Temperance in Antebellum America, 1830-1860," *Civil War History* 28 (June 1982): 129-31, 134; Tyrrell, *Sobering Up*, 181. For a discussion of definitions of women's sphere in the nineteenth century, see Barbara Welter, "The Culture of True Womanhood, 1820-1860," *American Quarterly* 18 (Summer 1966): 151-75; Kathryn Kish Sklar, *Catharine Beecher: A Study in American Domesticity* (New Haven: Yale University Press, 1973).

7. *Life*, 377-78.

8. *Life*, 384.

9. *Life*, 385-92.

10. *Life*, 392-393.

11. David Robinson, *The Unitarians and the Universalists* (Westport, Conn.: Greenwood Press, 1985), 3-5, 47-48, 56, 61-64. Although the Universalist Church united with the Unitarian faith in the mid-twentieth century, it remained independent and theologically more traditional in the nineteenth century.

12. *Life*, 394; MAL, "The Highest Types of Manhood," n.d., Livermore Collection, FLP.

13. Walter Eliot Thwing, *The Livermore Family of America* (Boston: W. B. Clarke, 1902), 194. MAL recalled that she met Daniel about two years after arriving in Duxbury, presumably in 1844; see *Life*, 391. On their wedding, see *Woman's Journal*, Sept. 2, 1871, and undated clipping in the Melrose Public Library titled "Fifty Years."

14. *Life*, 402; DPL obituary, *Woman's Journal*, July 15, 1899.

15. Thwing, *Livermore Family*, 194; DPL obituary, *Woman's Journal*, July 15, 1899. DPL's obituary in the *Melrose Reporter*, July 6, 1899, claims that he was ordained at the age of nineteen. If so, that would have been in 1837. See R. Tomlinson and D. P. Livermore, *Orthodoxy as It Is; Or, Its Mental Influence and Practical Inefficiency and Effects Illustrated by Philosophy and Facts* (Boston: A. Tompkins, 1846), 21-35.

16. Dennis, "Mrs. Mary Ashton Livermore," 5. The daguerreotype is reprinted in *Life*, 395.

17. MAL to DPL, July 29, [1852], Livermore Collection, FLP. See also MAL to Eliza

Livermore, May 1, 1846, ibid; MAL to Anne Whitney, Dec. 26, 1892, Whitney Collection, WC.

18. *Life*, 395-96; Lilian Whiting, *Boston Days* (Boston: Little, Brown, 1902), 457-58.

19. *Life*, 394.

20. *Life*, 398-99, 409.

21. *Life*, 399; MAL to Eliza Livermore, May 1, 1846, Livermore Collection, FLP; MAL to Lilian Whiting, Dec. 11, 1900, Livermore Collection, BPL.

22. MAL, "The Look of Prayer," *Ladies Repository* 13 (June 1845): 468; "Jesus," ibid. 15 (Nov. 1846): 182-83; "The Spirit-Mother," ibid. 15 (March 1847): 357. *Ladies Repository*, edited by the Reverend Henry Bacon, began publication in 1832. At one time it had the largest subscription list of any Universalist periodical. See Ann Lee Bessler, *The Universalist Movement in America, 1770–1880* (New York: Oxford University Press, 2001), 90, 95.

23. MAL, "Annie," *Ladies Repository* 13 (July 1845): 12; "The Picture Gallery of the Heart," ibid. 14 (May 1846): 421-22.

24. MAL, "The Present Age," *Ladies Repository* 15 (Feb. 1847): 306-7; Nancy Isenberg, *Sex and Citizenship in Antebellum America* (Chapel Hill: University of North Carolina Press, 1998), 44.

25. *Life*, 400-401. See also Elbridge Henry Goss, *The History of Melrose, County of Middlesex, Massachusetts* (Melrose, Mass.: A. W. Dunston, 1903), 374.

26. MAL, *Thirty Years Too Late, A True Story* (Boston: Lockwood, Brooks, & Co, 1878).

27. Mrs. Mary Livermore and Mrs. N. T. Munroe, *The Two Families; and The Duty That Lies Nearest: Prize Stories* (Boston: A. Tomkins, 1848), 2-55. MAL first called her story "A Mental Transformation." See *Life*, 401; MAL to Lilian Whiting, Dec. 11, 1900, Livermore Collection, BPL.

28. *Life*, 401-6.

29. *Life*, 406-9.

30. *Life*, 409-11. DPL is listed as pastor in church records beginning in 1847 and ending in April 1852. See Stafford First Universalist Church Records, vols. 2-3, CSL.

31. Connecticut Historical Commission, Historic Resources Inventory Form, "Universalist Church, Old Monson Road," Stafford Springs, Conn., Oct. 1983. The church was built next to the home and mill of Jasper Hyde, a member and benefactor. The church still stands.

32. Stafford First Universalist Church, "Constitution, Forms of Church Government," Stafford First Universalist Church Records, vol. 3, CSL. See also Maud Booth, *History of the First Universalist Church of Stafford, Connecticut, and Its Organizations* (Stafford, Conn., 1945), 9-11. DPL is called "our beloved pastor" on numerous occasions, such as in Records of Church Meetings, Jan. 9, 1848, Stafford First Universalist Church Records, vol. 3. See also Minutes of the Connecticut Convention of Universalists for 1850 and church records of the Universalist Church of the United States, Connecticut, RG 70:53, box 119, CSL.

33. Secretary's Record of the Stafford Ladies Benevolent Society and Treasurer's Rec-

ord of the Stafford Ladies Benevolent Society, vols. 6 and 9, respectively, of Stafford First Universalist Church Records, CSL. For a discussion of women's charitable associations, see Anne M. Boylan, *The Origins of Women's Activism: New York and Boston, 1797–1840* (Chapel Hill: University of North Carolina Press, 2002), 212.

34. "Excursion to New London," broadside of the Stafford Universalist Sabbath School, Aug. 14, 1850, Connecticut Historical Society, Hartford; *Life*, 414-15, 428-29; MAL, "Minister's Wife of Olden Times," *Cleveland Leader*, Dec. 15, 1901.

35. Secretary's Record of the Stafford Ladies Benevolent Society, vol. 6; *Life*, 430-34.

36. *Life*, 419-20.

37. *Life*, 420-24.

38. Thwing, *Livermore Family*, 107, 195. Mary ceased recording minutes after April 27, 1848. See Secretary's Record of the Stafford Ladies Benevolent Society, vol. 6. Although their first child was undoubtedly named at least in part for her mother, Mary was a common name on both sides of the family. Daniel had sisters named Mary and Eliza.

39. Thwing, *Livermore Family*, 107, 195; Carl Degler, *At Odds: Women and the Family in America from the Revolution to the Present* (New York: Oxford University Press, 1980), 181, 209.

40. MAL quoted in *New York Times*, April 28, 1903. Roosevelt had suggested that native-born women should have larger families in order to prevent immigrants from taking over the nation–the concept of "race suicide."

41. See Census Microfilm Records, Connecticut and Rhode Island, 1850, disk 3, Tolland Country, Conn., microfilm 50.

42. *Life*, 419. In the 1851 edition of the annual *Lily of the Valley* (Boston: James M. Usher), 315-17, MAL published seven short stories and poems, including "Trust in God": "When sudden darkness on my life-path falleth / Blotting the light . . . trust me to Thy guiding / My hand in Thine."

43. MAL, "Elliot Gray: Or, the Brave-Hearted Fireman," *Lily of the Valley* 21 (1853): 204-22; "The First Quarrel," ibid. 18 (1850): 5-10; see also "The Wife's Secret," *Rose of Sharon* (1856): 240-58. MAL did stray from domestic topics to write a fictional piece called "The Execution." It condemned the death penalty, corresponding to Universalist Church doctrine; see *Ladies Repository* 18 (July 1850), 45-49. Minutes of the Connecticut Convention of Universalists for 1849, Church Records of the Universalist Church in the United States, Connecticut, RG 70:53, box 119, CSL.

44. Tyrell, *Sobering Up*, 252-89; Minutes of the Connecticut Convention of Universalists for 1846, Church Records of the Universalist Church in the United States, Connecticut, RG 70:53, box 119, CSL.

45. *Life*, 415, 434-35; Albert E. Van Dusen, *Connecticut* (New York: Random House, 1964), 220; J. R. Cole, *History of Tolland County* (New York: W. W. Preston, 1885), 527-31.

46. *Life*, 435-43.

47. *Life*, 435, 444-45.

48. *Life*, 445-47; J. Robert Lane, "A Political History of Connecticut during the Civil War" (Ph.D diss., Catholic University, 1941), 17, 41; "An Act for the Suppression of Intemperance," *Public Acts Passed by the General Assembly of the State of Connecticut, July Session 1853* (Hartford: Alfred E. Burr, 1853), 54; Minutes of the Stafford First Universalist Church, April 20, 1852, Stafford First Universalist Church Records, vol. 2, CSL; DPL obituary, *Woman's Journal*, July 15, 1899.

49. Thwing, *Livermore Family*, 195; *Life*, 447. MAL spoke of her daughter having an eye infection in a letter to DPL, July 29, [1852], Livermore Collection, FLP. When the family moved to Melrose in 1870, the Livermores reinterred Mary Eliza in the family vault. See Wyoming Cemetery Records, Melrose, Mass.

50. Thwing, *Livermore Family*, 195. Articles in *Auburn Daily Advertiser*, Nov. 16, 1855, and April 13, 1857, note the arrival and departure of the Reverend Livermore. Mrs. M. A. Livermore, "They Are But Two," *Ladies Repository* 25 (July 1857): 22-23. Under the title is inscribed, "Written during the dangerous illness of little Lizzie," and the poem is dated "Auburn, N.Y., April 1856." See also MAL, "Dreams," *Rose of Sharon* (1857): 107-9.

51. MAL to Mr. Garrison [William Lloyd Garrison II], April 8, 1886, Garrison Family Correspondence, Smith College. William Lloyd Garrison II married Martha Wright's daughter Ellen. William Lloyd Garrison I referred to tensions in Auburn over the slavery issue in his obituary of Martha Wright; see *Woman's Journal*, Jan. 9, 1875. On Wright's activism, see Sherry H. Penney and James D. Livingston, "Expectant at Seneca Falls," *New York History* 84 (Winter 2003): 33-49. Lucretia Mott recalled meeting MAL in Auburn during the 1850s in a letter to Martha Wright on June 1, 1869, in *Selected Letters of Lucretia Coffin Mott*, ed. Beverly Wilson Palmer (Urbana: University of Illinois Press, 2002), 419. If the Livermores knew Auburn's most famous resident, the distinguished abolitionist Senator William H. Seward, they did not mention it.

52. *Woman's Journal*, Sept. 14, 1872; *Life*, 450. On the divisiveness of the slavery issue for America churches, see Julie Roy Jeffrey, *The Great Silent Army of Abolitionism: Ordinary Women in the Antislavery Movement* (Chapel Hill: University of North Carolina Press, 1998), 138.

53. The divinity student was J. R. Sage. He wrote an obituary of MAL in the *Des Moines Mail and Times*, June 3, 1905. *Dubuque (Iowa) Times*, March 12, 1864.

54. Amy Swerdlow, "Abolition's Conservative Sisters: The Ladies' New York City Anti-Slavery Societies, 1834-1840," in *The Abolitionist Sisterhood: Women's Political Culture in Antebellum America*, ed. Jean Fagan Yellin and John C. Van Horne (Ithaca: Cornell University Press, 1994), 44; Nancy A. Hewitt, *Women's Activism and Social Change: Rochester, New York, 1822-1872* (Ithaca: Cornell University Press, 1984), 22, 40. See also Boylan, *Origins of Women's Activism*, 2-3.

55. *Life*, 454-55; "The Slave Mother," *New York Tribune*, Feb. 8, 1856; MAL, "The Slave Tragedy at Cincinnati," *Auburn Daily Advertiser*, Feb. 9, 1856, and "Kansas," July 21, 1856. See also Isenberg, *Sex and Citizenship*, 118; and Andrea Moore Kerr, *Lucy Stone: Speaking Out for Equality* (New Brunswick, N.J.: Rutgers University Press, 1992), 93. In the Kansas-Nebraska Act of 1854, Congress decreed

that the majority of white settlers in these territories would decide whether slavery would be allowed. Both pro- and antislavery settlers rushed to settle Kansas, and a virtual civil war ensued. For a discussion of free labor ideology, see Eric Foner, *Free Soil, Free Labor, Free Men: The Ideology of the Republican Party before the Civil War* (New York: Oxford University Press, 1970), 11–72.

56. *Life*, 454–57. As early as 1846, DPL began to talk about moving West. MAL did not want to go. See MAL to Eliza Livermore, May 1, 1846, Livermore Collection, FLP.

4. EMERGENCE OF A PUBLIC WOMAN

1. *Life*, 454–55.
2. Ibid.; MAL to Eliza Livermore, May 1, 1846, Livermore Collection, FLP.
3. Cayuga was located near Atchison in northeastern Kansas. MAL recalled that "I met the colonists for the first time fifteen years after, and I visited their location some dozen years ago. See *Life*, 454–56. Kansas was admitted as a state, without slavery, in 1861.
4. Ibid., 456. David F. Wilcox, *Quincy and Adams County History and Representative Men* (Chicago: Lewis Publishing Company, 1919), 551; Wesley Norton, *Religious Newspapers in the Old Northwest to 1861: A History, Bibliography, and Record of Opinion* (Athens: Ohio University Press, 1977), 8.
5. *Life*, 455–56; Mrs. E. R. Hanson, *Our Women Workers: Biographical Sketches of Women Eminent in the Universalist Church for Literary, Philanthropic, and Christian Work* (Chicago: Star and Covenant Office, 1882), 128. The minister quoted in this passage was J. W. Hanson, who bought the *New Covenant* from DPL in 1869.
6. Frederick Francis Cook, *Bygone Days in Chicago: Recollections of the "Garden City" of the Sixties* (Chicago: A. C. McClurg, 1910), 107; A. T. Andreas, *History of Chicago from the Earliest Period to the Present Time*, 3 vols. (Chicago: A. T. Andreas, 1884), 2:441–42.
7. In the *New Covenant*, Jan. 15, 1859, DPL spoke of his travels in an article titled "Religious Famine." On Feb. 5, 1859, the *New Covenant* recorded DPL's appointments for the coming month: Bloomfield, Iowa; Buchanan, St. Joseph, and Dowagiac, Michigan; Ligoner, Indiana; and Niles and Plainfield, Illinois. For MAL's description of country meetings, see ibid., Oct. 10, 1863. See also DPL obituary, *Woman's Journal*, July 15, 1899, which uses the term "self-constituted missionary."
8. DPL obituary, *Melrose Reporter*, July 6, 1899; Dennis, "Mrs. Mary Ashton Livermore," 5. See *Chicago City Directories*, 1859-60, 1860-61, 1862-63, 1864-65, 1866-67, 1867-68, 1869-70. According to the 1859-60 directory, the *New Covenant* office was located at 172 South Clark Street. In 1863-64 the office was listed at 132 Clark Street. MAL refers to their farm in a letter to Miss [Phebe] Hanaford, April 25, 1869, Livermore Collection, SLR.
9. Andreas, *History of Chicago*, 2:52; G. P. A. Healy quoted in Emmett Dedmon, *Fabulous Chicago* (New York: Athenaeum, 1981), 10.
10. *Life*, 457–58; Andreas, *History of Chicago*, 2:65–67, 549–52.

11. *Life*, 460-61.

12. *Life*, 457. The 1860 census lists a live-in domestic, Mary Farrell, age twenty-three born in Ireland, as a member of the Livermore household. See United States Bureau of Census, *Population Schedules of the Eighth Census of the United States, 1860*, Cook County, Ill., M653, roll 116, 211.

13. *Life*, 457. See Lori D. Ginzberg, *Women and the Work of Benevolence: Morality, Politics, and Class in the Nineteenth-Century United States* (New Haven: Yale University Press, 1990).

14. *New Covenant*, Jan. 15, 1859, and Jan. 2, 1869; *War*, 98. For a discussion of Chicago's "Newspaper Row" on Clark Street, see Lloyd Wendt, *Chicago Tribune: The Rise of a Great American Newspaper* (Chicago: Rand McNally, 1979), 32, 319.

15. *New Covenant*, June 19, 1858, Feb. 5, 1859 (DPL), and March 29, 1862 (MAL). See also Norton, *Religious Newspapers in the Old Northwest*, 60.

16. *New Covenant*, Feb. 5, 1859; *Atlantic Monthly* 3 (Feb. 1859): 137-50.

17. *New Covenant*, Dec. 24, 1859.

18. MAL, *Pen Pictures or Sketches from Domestic Life* (Chicago: S. C. Griggs, 1862), 73-99.

19. *War*, 85-87, 90-91, 97. Timothy Rice would not die until the spring of 1865, shortly before the Civil War ended.

20. Ibid., 85; will of James Y. Jones, dated April 5, 1843, Mecklenburg Will Book, 15: 538-59, MCC.

21. *Tobacco Plant*, May 17, 1861; Hardin, "Edward Cary Walthall," 19-21.

22. *War*, 550; Theodore J. Karamanski, *Rally 'Round the Flag: Chicago and the Civil War* (Chicago: Nelson-Hall, 1993), 27.

23. *War*, 550-51; Wendt, *Chicago Tribune*, 80. The *Melrose Reporter*, April 21, 1899, reported the incident in similar fashion but claimed that MAL was attending the convention as a journalist representing ten newspapers.

24. *War*, 551-54. Presidential candidates did not appear in person at conventions in the mid-nineteenth century. Although she recalled this event as having taken place in February 1861, Lincoln did not appear in Chicago during that month. It must have been the previous November, when Lincoln did visit Chicago, holding several days of meetings with vice president-elect Hannibal Hamlin. See Earl Schenck Miers, ed., *Lincoln Day by Day: A Chronology, 1809-1865*, 4 vols. (Washington, D.C.: Lincoln Sesquicentennial Commission, 1960), 2:298-99.

25. Andreas, *History of Chicago*, 2:160; *Life*, 457. Owen Lovejoy would become a good friend of the Livermores during the war. His brother Elijah had been killed by a mob while trying to protect his antislavery press in southern Illinois in 1837.

26. *War*, 112-13; *Chicago Tribune*, April 24, 1861.

27. *War*, 121-22.

28. Attie, *Patriotic Toil*, 52-53; William Quentin Maxwell, *Lincoln's Fifth Wheel: The Political History of the United States Sanitary Commission* (New York: Longmans, Green, 1956), 1-3.

29. Maxwell, *Lincoln's Fifth Wheel*, 4-8. For the Sanitary Commission's "Plan of Organization" and approval by Cameron and Lincoln, see *Documents of the United*

States Sanitary Commission, 3 vols. (New York: United States Sanitary Commission, 1866-71), nos. 2 and 3. George M. Fredrickson's account of the USSC, *The Inner Civil War: Northern Intellectuals in the Crisis of the Union* (New York: Harper & Row, 1965), 98-112, is a classic.

30. Maxwell, *Lincoln's Fifth Wheel*, 8, 297; *War*, 157; Andreas, *History of Chicago*, 2: 315; Karamanski, *Rally 'Round the Flag*, 100; J. S. Newberry, *The U.S. Sanitary Commission in the Valley of the Mississippi during the War of the Rebellion, 1861–1866* (Cleveland: Fairbanks, Benedict, 1871), 219-20. For a list of commissioners, see United States Sanitary Commission, *Documents*, vol. 2.

31. Andreas, *History of Chicago*, 2:315; *War*, 136-37, 155.

32. Livermore and Hoge were assisted by Mrs. O. E. Hosmer. One reason for the fair's limited success was the failure of Madame Crevelli to draw a crowd. The *Chicago Tribune* offered a scathing review of Crevelli's voice, noted her less than enthusiastic audience, and also reported that when she gave a second concert for the benefit of the fair, only twenty-five people showed up, leading to cancellation. See *Tribune* stories relating to the fair and its proceeds on Dec. 16, 17, 19, 21, and 28, 1861.

33. *War*, 159-60. See Hoge obituary written by MAL, *Woman's Journal*, Sept. 20, 1890; Henry H. Forsyth, *In Memoriam: A Biographical Sketch* [of Jane Hoge] (Chicago: Illinois Printing and Binding, 1890); Brockett and Vaughan, *Woman's Work in the Civil War*, 562-63; Mrs. A. H. Hoge, *The Boys in Blue or Heroes of the "Rank and File"* (Chicago: C. W. Lilley, 1867), 35; Cook, *Bygone Days*, 108. One of Hoge's sons was colonel of the 113th Illinois Regiment, stationed at Camp Douglas. She wrote to both Abraham Lincoln and Ulysses S. Grant regarding her sons' commissions.

34. *New Covenant*, Dec. 10, 1864; Cook, *Bygone Days*, 108. The oyster supper was a fundraiser to assist a breakaway group from North Presbyterian Church who were angered when millionaire Cyrus McCormick attempted to use his influence to secure the appointment of the Reverend George Junkin as the congregation's new pastor. MAL incorrectly identified Junkin as the uncle of Confederate general Stonewall Jackson and a man with southern loyalties. Junkin was actually the father of Jackson's first wife. He left Virginia in 1861 because of his unwavering Unionism. *Dictionary of American Biography*, 5:248-49.

35. *New Covenant*, March 29, 1862, July 16, 1864. Brockett and Vaughn, *Woman's Work in the Civil War*, 578-80, includes a discussion of MAL's *New Covenant* article "Women and the War," dated May 18, 1861, and her discussion of the festival, dated Dec. 18, 1861.

36. *War*, 175-77, 181; Hoge, *Boys in Blue*, 45; *Chicago Tribune*, Feb. 17, 1862; Karamanski, *Rally 'Round the Flag*, 85-86.

37. *War*, 178-83.

38. *War*, 179-85; Andreas, *History of Chicago*, 2:316; Sarah Edwards Henshaw, *Our Branch and Its Tributaries: Being a History of the Work of the Northwestern Sanitary Commission and Its Auxiliaries during the War of the Rebellion* (Chicago:

Alfred L. Sewell, 1868), 74. Henshaw was a volunteer with the La Salle County Aid Society. She wrote the official history of the Chicago branch based on archival materials stored at the Chicago Historical Society's "fire-proof building." These materials burned along with the "fire-proof building" in 1871. See *Our Branch,* ix, 157.

39. *War,* 185, 197-98. On the phenomenon of "seeing the elephant," see James M. McPherson, *For Cause and Comrade: Why Men Fought in the Civil War* (New York: Oxford University Press, 1997), 32-36.

40. *War,* 187-88.

41. *War,* 188-97. For a discussion of nurses learning to cope with hospital life, see Jane E. Schultz, *Women at the Front: Hospital Workers in Civil War America* (Chapel Hill: University of North Carolina Press, 2004), 74-75.

42. *War,* 197-204.

43. *War,* 204, 218, 224; Jane E. Schultz, "The Inhospitable Hospital: Gender and Professionalism in Civil War Medicine," *Signs* 17 (Winter 1992): 367, 376.

44. MAL's correspondence relating to wounded and missing soldiers may be found in boxes 909 and 917, USSC Papers, Western Dept. [Louisville], NYPL. See also *War,* 223-29, 314-17.

45. *War,* 225-29. General Samuel Curtis (1805-1866) commanded the Department of the Missouri. See Stewart Sifakis, *Who Was Who in the Union* (New York: Oxford University Press, 1988), 99; Nina Silber, intro. to *War,* xi.

46. Andreas, *History of Chicago,* 2:316.

47. *War,* 219-21; *Chicago Tribune,* April 17, 1862; Karamanski, *Rally 'Round the Flag,* 88-92.

48. Andreas, *History of Chicago,* 2:317.

49. *War,* 232-35. See DPL, *Comfort in Sorrow: Token for the Bereaved* (Chicago: New Covenant Office, 1866). An earlier version of this book is advertised in the *New Covenant,* Sept. 20, 1862.

50. Robert J. Driver Jr. and Kevin C. Ruffner, *First Battalion Virginia Infantry, Thirty-ninth Battalion Virginia Cavalry, Twenty-fourth Battalion Virginia Partisan Rangers* (Lynchburg, Va: H. E. Howard, 1996), 5-7, 110. MAL noted a tendency toward braggadocio when James Jones Jr. was young: "His combativeness would have equipped half a dozen boys." See "In 'Old Virginny': Fifth Paper," 404.

51. Driver and Ruffner, *First Battalion Virginia Infantry,* 13; Combined Service Record of James Y. Jones, Library of Virginia; probate records of James Young Jones, Mecklenburg Will Book, 20:409, MCC. An inventory of James Young Jones's estate, dated Dec. 17, 1862, includes fifteen slaves, listed by name and age and all apparently women and children; two horses; a cavalry saddle and accouterments; books; dueling pistols; and a double-barreled gun. See Mecklenburg Will Book, 20:453. According to local legend Jones had seven written challenges for duels in his pocket when he died; see WPA Inventory. On Kernstown, see Herman Hattaway and Archer Jones, *How the North Won the War: A Military History of the Civil War* (Urbana: University of Illinois Press, 1983), 162.

52. *War*, 235.

53. *War*, 248; Hoge, *Boys in Blue*, 81–82; Attie, *Patriotic Toil*, 196; Andreas, *History of Chicago*, 2:318.

54. *War*, 555; Hoge, *Boys in Blue*, 82.

55. *War*, 241–42, 555–62; Hoge, *Boys in Blue*, 82–84.

56. *War*, 560–62.

57. *War*, 245; Andreas, *History of Chicago*, 2:314; Thomas J. Brown, *Dorothea Dix: New England Reformer* (Cambridge: Harvard University Press, 1998), 289–90. Later in the war, Dix gave James Yeatman of the Western Sanitary Commission in St. Louis authority over the appointment of nurses in the West. Henshaw, *Our Branch*, 167, provides no explanation for this change.

58. *War*, 247–48; MAL to Mr. [Robert] Thorne, April 23, 1865, box 913, USSC Papers, Western Dept., NYPL; Schultz, *Women at the Front*, 15.

59. *War*, 246; Brown, *Dorothea Dix*, 303–4.

60. *War*, 248–49; Hoge *Boys in Blue*, 84–89; Andreas *History of Chicago*, 2:310–13.

61. Henshaw, *Our Branch*, 94. Chicago branch president Mark Skinner discussed the employment of MAL and Hoge in a letter to the commission's general secretary, Frederick Law Olmsted, Dec. 11, 1862, box 953, USSC, NYPL. The *Chicago Times*, Oct. 19, 1863, mentions their salaries. Giesberg, *Civil War Sisterhood*, 99. By 1864 the USSC had 450 paid employees. See Robert H. Bremner, *The Public Good: Philanthropy and Welfare in the Civil War Era* (New York: Alfred A. Knopf, 1980), 54.

5. GOD'S MISSIONARY WORK

1. MAL to Lilian Whiting, May 18, 1890, Livermore Collection, BPL. MAL quoted Carroll D. Wright in using the term "God's missionary."

2. Paula Baker, "The Domestication of Politics: Women and American Political Society, 1790–1920," *American Historical Review* 89 (June 1984): 635–36.

3. MAL discussed hiring servants in *Life*, 471. Adelaide Livermore was the daughter of DPL's brother Lewis. Her death in 1865 caused the family considerable anguish. See *New Covenant*, April 8, 1865. MAL recalled her laundry endeavor in a speech titled "Co-Operative Housekeeping," n.d., Livermore Collection, FLP, and in an article, "The Story of a Co-Operative Laundry," *Boston Cooking School Magazine* 1 (June 1896): 5–7. The laundry is characterized as "her first venture in domestic cooperation" by Delores Hayden, *The Grand Domestic Revolution: A History of Feminist Designs for American Homes, Neighborhoods, and Cities* (Cambridge: MIT Press, 1981), 115–16. See also *Woman's Journal*, Nov. 20, 1880.

4. *Life*, 471; *New Covenant*, June 28, 1862; see also Sept. 19, 1863. In *Religious Newspapers in the Old Northwest*, 130, Wesley Norton wrote that editors of religious newspapers in the Midwest "varied in their early judgment of Lincoln's personality, [and] ability . . . but they were as one in rallying behind his decisions."

5. MAL to John S. Newberry, Jan. 27, 1863, box 914, USSC Papers, Western Dept. [Louisville], NYPL.
6. Ibid.; Jane Gray Swisshelm to Elizabeth Boynton Harbert, n.d., Harbert Collection, HL.
7. *Chicago Tribune*, Oct. 2, 1863; Henshaw, *Our Branch*, 153-55.
8. See lists of "items received by Chicago Branch," Nov. 10, 1863, box 925, USSC Papers, Western Dept., NYPL; Jane Hoge to John Newberry, Aug. 24, 1864, ibid., box 921.
9. *War*, 155-160; MAL to Caroline Healey Dall, April 28, 1865, Dall Collection, Massachusetts Historical Society, Boston.
10. Mary A. Livermore, "Western Scenes," *Bulletin*, March 1, 1864 (New York: U.S. Sanitary Commission, 1866), 273-75.
11. Ibid.; Henshaw, *Our Branch*, 103.
12. MAL, "Western Scenes," 273-75; *Life*, 170. MAL described Martha as "our stout, enduring Norwegian maiden" in *New Covenant*, Nov. 26, 1864. She paid her perhaps the ultimate compliment when she wrote that Martha "had for long years presided in the kitchen, with the neatness, and skill, and economy of one of my own New England country-women." See MAL, "Mother Bickerdyke," *Ladies Repository* 39 (June 1868): 450.
13. Henshaw, *Our Branch*, 208, 229, 277; *New Covenant*, March 29, 1862, March 21, 1863, July 16, 1864. MAL also handled internal accusations involving missing sanitary stores. See, for example, A. A. Dunseth to John Newberry, July 31, 1864; MAL to John Newberry, Oct. 3, 186[4]; MAL to Robert Thorne, Oct. 12 and 17, 1864, box 911, USSC Papers, Western Dept., NYPL.
14. Karamanski, *Rally 'Round the Flag*, 120-22; John Haynes Holmer, *The Life and Letters of Robert Collyer, 1823-1912*, 2 vols. (New York: Dodd, Mead, 1917), 1:271-73; Fredrickson, *Inner Civil War*, 107.
15. *War*, 331-32.
16. MAL to James A. Hardie, March 2, 1865, Record Group 94, Records of the Adjutant General's Office, Letters Received by the AGO, Main Series, File L-131 (AGO), 1865, National Archives, Washington, D.C. The Livermores discussed the missionary movement in the *New Covenant* on Jan. 30, April 30, Oct. 1, and Nov. 12, 1864.
17. Jane Hoge to John Newberry, Aug. 14, 1863, box 909; MAL to Robert T. Thorne, Oct. 12, 1864, box 912, USSC Papers, Western Dept., NYPL.
18. *War*, 282-84, 301, 328, 613-16. During one public lecture in Albion, Michigan, the mother of a dead soldier gave Livermore her daughter-in-law's wedding ring. It was the young woman's dying wish that Livermore should have the ring as a gesture of her appreciation, for Livermore had completed her dying husband's last letter from a Memphis hospital and sent it to her in Michigan. MAL's letters on behalf of individual nurses, soldiers, and family members may be found in boxes 909 and 917, USSC Papers, Western Dept., NYPL. She also wrote to Dorothea Dix reporting USSC news and supporting efforts of volunteer nurses to find employ-

ment. See, for example, MAL to Dorothea Dix, June 18, 1864, Jane Gay Dodge Collection, SLR. For a discussion of nurses' ability to have a "shared psychic experience" with their patients, see James Dawes, *The Language of War: Literature and Culture in the U.S. from the Civil War through World War II* (Cambridge: Harvard University Press, 2002), 46-47.

19. *War*, 301-3; George L. Andrew, "Account of His Work with the Sanitary Commission, c. 1884," Ida Husted Harper Collection, HL.

20. *War*, 487, 491, 499-500; MAL to Mary Ann Ball Bickerdyke, March 21, 1864, Bickerdyke Collection, LC.

21. *War*, 511-14; MAL to Mary Ann Ball Bickerdyke, Aug. 13, 1863, Bickerdyke Collection, LC.

22. *War*, 503-5; MAL, "Mother Bickerdyke," *Ladies Repository* 40 (July 1868): 52.

23. *War*, 506-7; MAL, "Mother Bickerdyke" (July 1868), 53.

24. *War*, 506-9; MAL, "Mother Bickerdyke" (July 1868), 53.

25. *War*, 348. For a discussion of reform women's use of deference, see Boylan, *Origins of Women's Activism*, 168.

26. *War*, 308-11; MAL, "Opposite Vicksburg," *Ladies Repository* 39 (March 1868): 209.

27. Ibid., 314-16; MAL, "Opposite Vicksburg," 210. For a discussion of nurses' roles as advocates for soldiers, see Schultz, *Women at the Front*, 109.

28. *War*, 316-17; MAL, "Opposite Vicksburg," 211.

29. *War*, 290-91; MAL, "A Trip Down the River," *Ladies Repository* 39 (Feb. 1868): 115-16.

30. *War*, 291-94; MAL, "A Trip Down the River," 116-17.

31. *War*, 294.

32. *War*, 300-302; MAL, "A Trip Down the River," 120. MAL recalled life in the Milliken's Bend shebang fondly in an article for the *New Covenant*, Sept. 9, 1865. Ann Douglas Wood, in "The War within a War: Women Nurses in the Union Army," *Civil War History* 18 (Sept. 1972): 201, has pointed out that "many of the boys in blue were just that–boys, and they missed their homes and sang their songs not about their sweethearts, but about their mothers."

33. *War*, 333-35, 339-40.

34. *War*, 341, 345, 349.

35. *War*, 351-53. The pre-Civil War abolitionism of H. Ford Douglass, including his advocacy of black migration to Haiti, is described in Leon F. Litwack, *North of Slavery: The Negro in the Free States, 1790-1860* (Chicago: University of Chicago Press, 1961), 259-60, 265-66, 275. Douglass was one of the first African Americans from Illinois to enlist in the army. He joined a majority-white unit, Company G, Ninety-fifth Illinois Volunteers. See Victor Hicken, "The Record of Illinois' Negro Soldiers in the Civil War," *Journal of the Illinois State Historical Society* 56 (Autumn 1963): 533. He later won a discharge from the Ninety-fifth Illinois and helped to organize an African American regiment, serving as a captain. Douglass died of malaria a few months after the war ended. See pension file of H. Ford Douglass in the National Archives.

36. *War*, 352. Illinois's Black Laws are outlined in *The Statutes of Illinois, Embracing All the General Laws of the State in Force December 1, 1857* (Chicago: D. B. Cooke, 1858), 820-22.

37. *War*, 354-62.

38. *War*, 362-68. In 1920 Etta Livermore Norris, Mary's daughter, related the story in a newspaper article commemorating the one hundredth anniversary of her mother's birth. See untitled newspaper clipping, Dec. 19, 1920, NAWSA Collection, reel 45, LC. MAL also accompanied two white orphans named Johnny and Lizzie, whose father had been a southern Unionist, and found adoptive parents for them.

39. *War*, 317-18, 363.

40. *War*, 131; Andreas, *History of Chicago*, 2:310-11; *Chicago Tribune*, July 5, 8, 9, 1863.

41. MAL to Anna Dickinson, Aug. 17, 1863, Dickinson Collection, LC; *New Covenant*, Oct. 17, 1863. On September 24, 1863, MAL wrote to Louisa Schuyler, "The Fair is my suggestion, and I am largely concerned with all its various departments." See Schuyler Collection, New-York Historical Society. In *Patriot Fires: Forging a New American Nationalism in the Civil War North* (Lawrence: University Press of Kansas, 2002), 16-18, Melinda Lawson suggests that the Chicago fair and others that followed it emphasized the unifying themes of martial courage and national identity but not the divisive issue of slavery.

42. Karamanski, *Rally 'Round the Flag*, 130.

43. *War*, 411-12; Hoge, *Boys in Blue*, 333.

44. Beverly Gordon, *Bazaars and Fair Ladies: The History of the American Fundraising Fair* (Knoxville: University of Tennessee Press, 1998), 7, 10-11, 49, 96.

45. Ibid., 11, 60. Lowell, Massachusetts, organized a Sanitary Commission fair in February 1863 that raised $5,000, but it did not attract attention outside the immediate community. According to Gordon, fairs organized in support of the commission added $5 million to its coffers.

46. *Chicago Tribune*, July 27 and 29, Sept. 2-3, 1863; *Chicago Times*, July 29, 1863; *War*, 411-12; Hoge, *Boys in Blue*, 333-34; *History of the Great North-Western Soldiers' Fair Held in Chicago* (Chicago: Dunlop, Sewell, & Spalding, 1864), 11. This last book may have been written by MAL; Henshaw, *Our Branch*, 222, refers to "History of the Fair, by Mrs. Livermore."

47. *War*, 411-15; Hoge, *Boys in Blue*, 333-35; *Chicago Tribune*, Oct. 4-5, 1863; *History of the North-Western Fair*, 14.

48. *Chicago Tribune*, Oct. 5, 1863; MAL to Anna Dickinson, Aug. 17 and Oct. 1, 1863, Dickinson Collection, LC. On Dickinson's early life and career during the Civil War, see Wendy Hamand Venet, *Neither Ballots Nor Bullets: Women Abolitionists and the Civil War* (Charlottesville: University Press of Virginia, 1991), 37-39, 45-51.

49. *Chicago Tribune*, Oct. 7 and 15, 1863. The "successful manufacturer" they referred to was probably Cyrus McCormick. The doctor's identity is not known.

50. *War*, 435.

51. *War*, 436. In *The Rise of Public Women: Woman's Power and Woman's Place in the United States, 1630–1970* (New York: Oxford University Press, 1992), 135-36, the historian Glenna Matthews has written regarding MAL and others, "Public women grew in self-confidence because of the scale on which some of them were carrying forward their activities."

52. *War*, 436; *Chicago Tribune*, Oct. 20, 1863.

6. Fair Mania

1. *Chicago Tribune*, Oct. 20, 1863.

2. MAL to Abraham Lincoln, Oct. 11, 1863, Robert Todd Lincoln Collection, LC, reprinted in *The Collected Works of Abraham Lincoln*, 10 vols., ed. Roy P. Basler (New Brunswick, N.J.: Rutgers University Press, 1953), 6:539-40.

3. Abraham Lincoln to MAL, Oct. 26, 1863, ibid.

4. *War*, 416; *Chicago Tribune*, Oct. 22-23, 1863; Karamanski, *Rally 'Round the Flag*, 174, 186. Cyrus McCormick was a native Virginian and former slave owner who opposed southern nationalism but advocated a negotiated end to the war. See William T. Hutchinson, *Cyrus Hall McCormick*, 2 vols. (New York: D. Appleton-Century, 1935), 2:4, 8, 99; *New Covenant*, Dec. 19, 1863. The *Volunteer* was published from October 27 to November 7, 1863.

5. *New Covenant*, Oct. 31, 1863.

6. *Chicago Tribune*, Oct. 27-28, 1863; *Chicago Times*, Oct. 28, 1863; Frank B. Goodrich, *The Tribute Book: A Record of the Munificence, Self-Sacrifice, and Patriotism of the American People during the War for the Union* (New York: Derby & Miller, 1865), 160-61.

7. *Chicago Tribune*, Oct. 28, 1863. In *War*, 425, MAL incorrectly identified Thomas B. Bryan as "the loyal and gifted nephew of the rebel general Robert Lee." Bryan (1828-1906) was born and raised in Alexandria, Virginia, where Lee also grew up. While Bryan may have been related to Lee through his wife, Jane Byrd Page Bryan, he was not the son or son-in-law of any of Lee's siblings, and Mrs. Robert E. Lee had no siblings. See Edmund Jennings Lee, *Lee of Virginia, 1642–1692: Biographical and Genealogical Sketches of the Descendants of Colonel Richard Lee* (Philadelphia: Franklin Printing, 1895).

8. *Sanitary Commission Bulletin*, Dec. 1, 1863; *Chicago Tribune*, Oct. 23 and 28, 1863; *Chicago Times*, Oct. 30-31, 1863; *Volunteer*, Oct. 28, 1863; *War*, 427-28; Hoge, *Boys in Blue*, 359. See also J. Christopher Schnell, "Mary Livermore and the Great Northwestern Fair," *Chicago History* 4 (Spring 1975): 34-43.

9. *Chicago Tribune*, Oct. 29, 31, Nov. 3, 6, 1863; *Volunteer*, Oct. 30, Nov. 4, 1863; "Chicago Northwestern Sanitary Fair, 1863, Record of Articles Donated," ledger kept by Martha I. Lamb, Chicago Historical Society.

10. *War*, 430-33, 439-42; *Chicago Tribune*, Oct. 29, 30, 31, Nov. 1, 3, 4, 1863; *Chicago Times*, Nov. 14, 1863; *Volunteer*, Oct. 28, Nov. 7, 1863.

11. *War*, 437-38; *Chicago Tribune*, Oct. 30, 1863.

12. The *Chicago Times*'s editor, Wilbur Storey, supported Lincoln early in the war but

turned against the president when he issued the preliminary Emancipation Proclamation, believing that Lincoln had become preoccupied with antislavery at the
expense of Unionism. At one point military authorities shut down the newspaper's
offices because of outrage over its editorial slant. See Karamanski, *Rally 'Round
the Flag*, 188–97. Articles critical of MAL and Hoge appeared in the *Times* on Sept.
2 and 3, Oct. 16, 19 (comparison with Sisters of Mercy),1863. See *Chicago Tribune*,
Oct. 20, 25, 1863.

13. *Chicago Times*, Nov. 2, 1863.

14. Ibid. The *Chicago Times* printed many articles alleging USSC secrecy and misap-
propriation of funds; see Nov. 4, 6, 7, 9, 10, 13, 1863.

15. *Chicago Tribune*, Nov. 7, 8, 1863; *Chicago Times*, Nov. 9, 1863. The discretionary
funds MAL used for the USSC came from a benefactor named Jonathan Burr, who
was visiting the USSC rooms on a day when MAL helped a soldier's wife who had
fainted. Moved by this episode, Burr donated $100 and made other donations later.
See Henshaw, *Our Branch*, 160.

16. MAL's comments in *New Covenant*, Nov. 14, 1863. DPL defended his wife and
condemned the *Times*, ibid., Dec. 19, 1863. See Matthews, *Rise of Public Women*,
136–37. Jane Schultz, *Women at the Front*, 116, notes the growing self-confidence
of nurses, writing, "The longer a worker stayed at the job, the more likely she was
to prove her mettle."

17. *Chicago Times*, Nov. 5, 7, 1863; *Chicago Tribune*, Nov. 5, 7, 1863. Other evening
entertainments at the fair included a concert by two hundred children and a tab-
leau by patriotic citizens of Detroit, including Mrs. R. S. Willis, who wore a striped
skirt and "Liberty cap." *War*, 445; *Chicago Tribune*, Oct. 28, 30, 1863.

18. *New Covenant*, Nov. 14, 1863; *Chicago Tribune*, Nov. 9, 1863; *Chicago Times*, Nov.
9, 1863; *War*, 450–53; Hoge, *Boys in Blue*, 361–62.

19. *Chicago Tribune*, Nov. 11, 1863.

20. Ibid., Nov. 15, 18, 1863. MAL also analyzed Dickinson's oratory in *New Covenant*,
Nov. 14, 1863. The *Chicago Evening Journal*, Nov. 9, 1863, complained about
Dickinson's pay while praising the fair as a "remarkable and wonderful event."

21. *Chicago Tribune*, Nov. 2, 7–9, 26, 30; *Volunteer*, Nov. 7, 1863; In *War*, 455, MAL
wrote that the fair's "net receipts were nearly eighty thousand dollars." *History of
the North-Western Soldiers' Fair*, 183–84, reported profits of $78,682.89, also cited
by Gordon, *Bazaars and Fair Ladies*, 66. Hoge, *Boys in Blue*, 367, uses the figure
$86,000, also cited by Andreas, *History of Chicago*, 2:321. Charles J. Stillé, *His-
tory of the United States Sanitary Commission* (Philadelphia: J. B. Lippincott,
1866), 483, noted that all the money stayed in the Chicago branch treasury. Abraham Lincoln received a gold watch courtesy of a Chicago jeweler for having donated the fair's most profitable item. A copy of MAL's letter to Lincoln presenting
him with the watch is in *History of the North-Western Soldiers' Fair*, 54. The
president acknowledged the gift in a letter to Livermore and Hoge dated Dec. 17,
1863; see Hoge, *Boys in Blue*, 358–59. Photographic reproductions of the Emancipation Proclamation were sold to benefit the Soldiers' Home. Lincoln's original
burned in the Great Chicago Fire of 1871. See Paul M. Angle, *The Chicago*

Historical Society, 1856–1956: An Unconventional Chronicle (New York: Rand McNally, 1956), 70–74. See also Henshaw, *Our Branch*, 210.

22. Hoge, *Boys in Blue*, 368; *War*, 455–56; Gordon, *Bazaars and Fair Ladies*, 65–71. MAL described the Cincinnati fair in *New Covenant*, Jan. 16, 1864.

23. For an extensive discussion of the Iowa situation, see Elizabeth D. Leonard, *Yankee Women: Gender Battles in the Civil War* (New York: W. W. Norton, 1994), 51–70, 87. See also *Iowa State Weekly Register* (Des Moines), Nov. 18, 1863.

24. *Iowa State Weekly Register*, Nov. 25, 1863; *Iowa Daily Statesman* (Des Moines), Nov. 19, 1863; *New Covenant*, Nov. 28, 1863. In the coming months, both Kynett and Wittenmyer would resign from the Sanitary Commission to pursue other interests. See Leonard, *Yankee Women*, 80. MAL to John Newberry, Nov. 25, 1863, box 910, USSC Papers, Western Dept. [Louisville], NYPL; MAL to John Newberry, n.d., quoted in Henshaw, *Our Branch*, 259.

25. *New Covenant*, Dec. 5, 1863; *Chicago Times*, Jan. 4, 1864; *Chicago Tribune*, Dec. 7, 1863.

26. *Chicago Tribune*, Dec. 14, 20, 21, 27, 29, 1863. The *Chicago Times* attacked Daniel Livermore as well, printing a letter ostensibly from a man in Milwaukee which characterized him as "an itinerant preacher" who made no effort to hide the "large salary" that the woman he called his "superior half" received, $100 per month plus expenses. *Chicago Times*, Jan. 25, 1864; Henshaw, *Our Branch*, 201–2.

27. *Chicago Tribune*, Dec. 14, 20, 21, 27, 29, 1863; Henshaw, *Our Branch*, 201–2. The society was sometimes called the Society for Providing for Soldiers' Families or Soldiers' Relief Society.

28. "Mary A. Livermore," *The Leader: A Magazine of Modern Education* 1 (May 1903): 381.

29. *War*, 591–600. Charles Cardwell McCabe (1836–1906), once an army chaplain, became active with the United States Christian Commission. See Frank Milton Bristol, *The Life of Chaplain McCabe: Bishop of the Methodist Episcopal Church* (New York: Eaton & Mains, 1908), 146–49, 163–65.

30. *New Covenant*, Feb. 18, 1865.

31. See ibid., Jan. 30, March 19, May 21, 1864, for adoptions and March 12, 1864, for the discussion of "painful scenes."

32. Ibid., April 23, 1864.

33. Ibid., March 12, 1864.

34. *Dubuque Times*, March 12, 1864. Dubuque's Democratic newspaper was the *Herald*.

35. Ibid. MAL later claimed that her speech ultimately raised pledges to the USSC totaling $8,000. See *War*, 609; Gordon, *Bazaars and Fair Ladies*, 70.

36. *New Covenant*, Aug. 27, 1864.

37. Ibid., April 9, Aug. 20, 1864, Nov. 26, 1864; Jane Hoge to John Newberry, Sept. 16, 1864, box 911, USSC Papers, Western Dept., NYPL.

38. Rural children also organized fairs, with MAL noting receipt of $75 from children in Lemont, Illinois. See *New Covenant*, April 9, Aug. 20, 1864, and *War*, 152–54. James Marten discusses children's fundraising efforts in *The Children's Civil War* (Chapel Hill: University of North Carolina Press, 1998), 180–83.

39. *New Covenant*, Jan. 21, Feb. 18, 1865; *Voice of the Fair*, April 27, 1865 (the official organ of the fair); Record of Meetings of the Executive Committee of the North-western Sanitary Fair (hereafter Record of Meetings), Nov. 4, Dec. 30, 1864, Newberry Library, Chicago; Gordon, *Bazaars and Fair Ladies*, 70-71.

40. *New Covenant*, March 11, April 1, 1865; MAL to John Newberry, Feb. 20, 1865, box 913, USSC Papers, Western Dept., NYPL; Hoge, *Boys in Blue*, 404-5.

41. *New Covenant*, March 11, May 6, 1865; Hoge, *Boys in Blue*, 405.

42. *New Covenant*, March 11, April 1, 1865.

43. Ibid., April 1, 8, 1865. See *The Diary of George Templeton Strong*, 4 vols., ed. Allan Nevins and Milton Halsey Thomas (New York: Macmillan, 1952), 1:562. The diary entry is dated March 9, 1865.

44. *New Covenant*, March 4, 1865; Record of Meetings, Nov. 22, 1865.

45. *New Covenant*, April 15, 1865.

46. Because of financial problems, DPL discussed selling the *New Covenant* on Nov. 21 and 28, 1863, and Jan. 9, 1864. MAL and Hoge imply that their trip to the contraband camp occurred in conjunction with their trip to Washington for the Woman's Council. That would date it November, 1862. See *War*, 251-52, 257-62; Hoge, *Boys in Blue*, 93-94.

47. *War*, 257-62.

48. Driver, *First Battalion Virginia Infantry*, 110, 112; Hardin, "Edward Cary Walthall," 19-48. Robert Jones, the elder of the Jones sons, died before the war.

49. Mecklenburg Will Book, 22: 356; Mecklenburg County Deed Book, 41: 201, MCC; WPA Inventory; United States Bureau of Census, *Population Schedules of the Ninth Census of the United States, 1870*, Mecklenburg Co., Va., M593, roll 1663, 430. Aggy Jones is listed as "insane." It is not known whether MAL had any contact with the Jones family after the war.

7. Emergence of a Suffragist

1. *Boston Post*, n.d. [1890], newspaper clipping, Melrose Public Library, Melrose, Mass.

2. *Chicago Tribune*, April 14-15, 1865.

3. *New Covenant*, May 6, 1865. Lincoln's funeral procession in Chicago is described by Karamanski, *Rally 'Round the Flag*, 245-49.

4. Record of Meetings, Dec. 20, 1864, Jan. 9 and 23, March 29, 1865. By this time Ezra McCagg had replaced Mark Skinner as president of the Chicago branch. Much to MAL's regret, Skinner was forced to leave the position because of poor health. See Hoge, *Boys in Blue*, 420-21. For General Hooker's role at the fair, see "North-Western Fair Military Circular," Kantor Collection, Wichita State University, Wichita, Kansas.

5. *Chicago Times*, May 30, 1865; *Chicago Tribune*, May 8, 1865; *New Covenant*, July 18, 1865.

6. *New Covenant*, Sept. 24, 1864, Jan. 7, 14, 21, 1865.

7. Ibid., May 20, 1865; MAL to John Newberry, April 10, 1865, USSC Papers, box 913, Western Dept. [Louisville], NYPL.

8. *Chicago Tribune*, May 23, 1865; *Chicago Times*, May 1, 1865.

9. *Chicago Tribune, Chicago Times, Voice of the Fair*, May 31, 1865. The *Tribune*, June 15, 1865, reported that a "colored citizen" ran a shoeshine shop in Union Hall.

10. *Voice of the Fair*, May 30, 31, 1865; *Chicago Tribune* and *Chicago Times*, May 31, 1865; *Harper's Weekly*, June 17, 1865.

11. *Chicago Tribune*, May 30, 31, June 6, 1865; *Chicago Times*, May 1, June 2, 1865; *Voice of the Fair*, May 25, 30, 1865.

12. *Chicago Tribune*, June 2, 3, 24, 1865; *Chicago Times*, June 1, 1865; *Voice of the Fair*, June 1, 1865.

13. Correspondence relating to MAL's request for "Jefferson Davis's petticoats" may be found in Records of the Office of the Secretary of War, Record Group 107, Letters Received, file L672 (WD)1865, National Archives. See also *Chicago Tribune*, May 20, 1865. On Davis's capture, see Michael B. Ballard, *A Long Shadow: Jefferson Davis and the Final Days of the Confederacy* (Jackson: University of Mississippi Press, 1986), 141–43 and Felicity Allen, *Jefferson Davis, Unconquerable Heart* (Columbia: University of Missouri Press, 1999), 16–19, 412–13.

14. *Voice of the Fair*, May 11, June 3, 1865; *Chicago Tribune*, May 30–31, June 1 and 4, 1865. Jane Hoge, *Boys in Blue*, 417, recalled that soldiers enjoyed the Davis pistol "above all other sights" at the fair. Lincoln's cousins John and Dennis Hanks are described in Douglas L. Wilson and Rodney O. Davis, eds., *Herndon's Informants: Letters, Interviews, and Statements about Lincoln* (Urbana: University of Illinois Press 1998), 752.

15. *Chicago Tribune* and *Chicago Times*, June 10, 1865.

16. *Chicago Tribune, Chicago Times*, and *Voice of the Fair*, June 9, 1865. In April, Sherman had written to Judge James Bradwell that his wife, Ellen, "seems deeply interested in your Fair." Mrs. Sherman would preside over a booth in Union Hall that sported an enormous portrait of her husband painted by G. P. A. Healy and draped in American flags. Sherman's letter to Bradwell, dated April 20, 1865, was reprinted in *Voice of the Fair*, May 4, 1865; see also May 11, 1865.

17. MAL quoted from her letter to Ulysses S. Grant in *New Covenant*, April 1, 1865. Grant's response, dated March 14, 1865, is in *The Papers of Ulysses S. Grant*, 25 vols., ed. John Y. Simon (Carbondale, Southern Illinois University Press, 1985), 14:166.

18. *Chicago Tribune*, June 11 and 13, 1865. Ellen Sherman persuaded Grant to contribute his horse to the fair. His letter to her on this subject, dated May 31, 1865, is reprinted ibid., June 10, 1865. *Voice of the Fair*, June 12, 13, 1865, *War*, 621–22.

19. MAL to John Newberry, Feb. 20, 1865, USSC Papers, box 913, Western Dept., NYPL. See MAL's description of the fair, including a discussion of "Andersonville, Libby," and other southern prisons, *New Covenant*, July 18, 1865. On the fair's earnings, see Gordon, *Bazaars and Fair Ladies*, 70. With proceeds from the fair, a permanent Soldiers' Home was constructed at Thirty-fifth Street and Lake Avenue on Chicago's South Side. The building still stands today. See Andreas, *History of Chicago*, 2:312–13.

20. *New Covenant*, Jan. 16, 1864; *Chicago Tribune*, June 27, 1865. Lincoln's message to Congress endorsing the abolition of slavery in the District of Columbia brought

a high bid of $50, while a page from his final message to Congress yielded no bid "worthy of consideration" and was withdrawn. These items had been donated by the president's son, Robert Todd Lincoln. *Chicago Times*, June 16, 19, 1865.

21. *War*, 620-28; "Boys and Girls Circular" relating to "Old Abe," Kantor Collection, Wichita State University. By the time MAL published her memoir, Jefferson Davis had ceased to be the focus of widespread hatred in the North. Many southerners admired his fortitude during more than two years of incarceration and resented the federal government for its failure either to release him or to bring formal charges against him. In her memoir *Boys in Blue*, 420, Jane Hoge discussed the fair in greater detail than MAL did and praised the festival as a *"peace jubilee"* that welcomed returning veterans.

22. *Life*, 471. Sarah Henshaw, *Our Branch*, 302, 306, 314, says that MAL and Jane Hoge ended their connection with the USSC in July 1865. During its four years the northwestern branch sent out 77,660 packages and disbursed $405,792.66 from its treasury. More than three thousand aid societies with an estimated membership of thirty thousand had contributed to the branch.

23. *War*, 7. The superintendent of the Home for the Friendless, Mrs. Grant, had served under Bickerdyke in Memphis during the war, and Bickerdyke did not like the role reversal. She left her post after one year. See Nina Brown Baker, *Cyclone in Calico: The Story of Mary Ann Bickerdyke* (Boston: Little, Brown, 1952), 222-24. On Jane Hoge's memoir, see *New Covenant*, Nov. 9, 1867. On Hoge's postwar life, see Forsyth, *In Memoriam*, and James et al., *Notable American Women*, 2:200-201. In MAL's obituary of Hoge in *Woman's Journal*, Sept. 20, 1890, she wrote that her friendship with Hoge "has enriched and blessed my life."

24. *New Covenant*, May 5, 1866, Feb. 2, 1867, Jan. 26, 1869 (religion); Jan. 2, 1869 (Dubuque).

25. Ibid., Jan. 5, 1867.

26. Ibid., April 7, 18, Sept. 15, Oct. 13, 1866, Jan. 5, 1867, Feb. 29, 1868. For a discussion of Radical Reconstruction, including the civil rights bill and Johnson's impeachment, see Eric Foner, *Reconstruction: America's Unfinished Revolution, 1863-1877* (New York: Harper & Row, 1988), 239-51, 333-45.

27. *New Covenant*, Oct. 13, 1866, Jan. 5, 1867.

28. Ibid., Feb. 8, 1868. MAL's objection to the "election of another drunkard" probably referred to the fact that President Johnson, ill at the time of his inauguration as vice president, was believed to have imbibed heavily on that day.

29. *Life*, 479; MAL to Lilian Whiting, May 18, 1890, Livermore Collection, BPL; MAL, "Address for Lake Pleasant," July 5, 1880, Livermore Collection, FLP.

30. MAL to Isabella Beecher Hooker, Nov. 9, 1869, Hooker Collection, Stowe-Day Library, Hartford, Conn.

31. *New Covenant*, Aug. 12, Nov. 11, Nov. 25, 1865. The other two women were Mrs. H. B. Manford of Chicago and the Reverend Augusta J. Chapin of Portland, Michigan.

32. Ibid., Nov. 25, Dec. 23, 1865, Jan. 20, May 19, 1866; MAL to OB, May 15, 1867, Brown Collection, SLR.

33. *New Covenant*, Jan. 27, 1866, Feb. 15, 1868.

NOTES TO PAGES 139-144

34. Ibid., Jan. 20, 1866. Augusta Jane Chapin (1836-1905) attended Olivet College, began preaching in Michigan as an itinerant minister in 1859, was ordained a minister in the Universalist faith in 1863, and served a variety of pastorates, retiring in 1901. She was one of Universalism's first preachers. See Bessler, *Universalist Movement in America*, 90, and James et al., *Notable American Women*, 1:320-21.

35. MAL to OB, June 13, 1867, Dec. 24, 1868, Feb. 3, 1869, Brown Collection, SLR; *New Covenant*, June 1, 8, 1867. Olympia Brown (1835-1926) was ordained six months before Augusta Chapin. In 1878 Brown left Bridgeport to accept a position in Racine, Wisconsin. See Bessler, *Universalist Movement in America*, 90, and James et al., *Notable American Women*, 1:256-68. Pastor T. E. St. John's departure from MAL's church is noted in Andreas, *History of Chicago*, 2:441-42.

36. MAL to OB, April 28, 1868, Brown Collection, SLR; *New Covenant*, July 11, 1868.

37. *New Covenant*, June 13, Oct. 2, 1868.

38. J. S. Dennis, "Mrs. Mary Ashton Livermore," *Ladies Repository*, 39 (Jan. 1868): 1-7.

39. MAL's articles in *Ladies Repository* in 1868-69 are "Personal Recollections of President Lincoln" 39 (Jan. 1868): 40-52; "A Trip Down the River" 39 (Feb. 1868): 112-21; "Opposite Vicksburg" 39 (March 1868): 209-18; "Up the River" 39 (April 1868): 292-302; "After the Battle of Fort Donelson" 39 (May 1868): 371-81; "Mother Bickerdyke" 39 (June 1868): 450-56 and 40 (July 1868): 50-63; "Our Battery Boys" 40 (Oct. 1868): 290-302; "Two Years on a Virginia Plantation" 41 (Feb. 1869): 129-37.

40. *New Covenant*, April 24, 1869. In "An Explanation," *Ladies Repository* 43 (Jan. 1870): 73, the editor suggested that MAL had been too busy to finish her Virginia series but would do so. Phebe Hanaford (1829-1921) left the Quaker faith first for the Baptist Church and then for Universalism, preaching for the first time in 1865. See James et al., *Notable American Women*, 2:126-27.

41. Margaret Fuller, *Woman in the Nineteenth Century* (1855; reprint, New York: W. W. Norton, 1971), 175. After the publication of Fuller's book, MAL wrote her a "note of thankfulness," and Fuller responded with a letter that "enriched me as did no other of my possessions." See MAL, "Some Noble Women I Have Known," *Golden Rule*, July 14, 1892, 740-41.

42. *New Covenant*, Feb. 24, April 12, 1866 (working women); April 12, 24, 1866, Aug. 8, 1868 (typesetters); Sept. 2, 1865, and Aug. 8, 1868 (working women's homes).

43. Lyde Cullen Sizer, *The Political Work of Northern Women Writers and the Civil War, 1850-1872* (Chapel Hill: University of North Carolina Press, 2000), 4; Ellen Carol DuBois, *Feminism and Suffrage: The Emergence of an Independent Women's Movement in America, 1848-1869* (Ithaca: Cornell University Press, 1978), 53-104; MAL to SBA, March 22, 1867, Papers of Elizabeth Cady Stanton and Susan B. Anthony, reel 12, LC; *New Covenant*, April 13, May 1, 1867; MAL to OB, May 15, 1867, Brown Collection, SLR.

44. DuBois, *Feminism and Suffrage*, 53-104.

45. *Chicago Tribune*, June 19, 1868; Steven M. Buechler, *The Transformation of the Woman Suffrage Movement: The Case of Illinois, 1850-1920* (New Brunswick, N.J.: Rutgers University Press, 1986), 67-68.

46. *Chicago Tribune*, Feb. 5 and 8, 1869; *Chicago Times*, Feb. 7, 1869; Buechler, *Transformation of the Woman Suffrage Movement*, 68–70; MAL to OB, Feb. 3, 1869, Brown Collection, SLR.

47. *New Covenant*, Nov. 30, 1867; Elizabeth Cady Stanton, Susan B. Anthony, and Matilda Joslyn Gage, eds., *History of Woman Suffrage*, 6 vols. (1886; reprint, New York: Arno, 1969), 3:564–70 (hereafter *HWS*); Jane M. Friedman, *America's First Woman Lawyer: A Biography of Myra Bradwell* (Buffalo: Prometheus Books, 1993), 177.

48. *Chicago Tribune*, Feb. 12, 1869.

49. *Chicago Tribune* and *Chicago Times*, Feb. 12, 13, 1869; *HWS*, 3:569; Rosalyn Terborg-Penn, *African American Women in the Struggle for the Vote* (Bloomington: Indiana University Press, 1998), 49–50.

50. *Chicago Tribune*, Feb. 12–13, 1869; *HWS*, 3:569. Dickinson's debate opponent was the Reverend Robert Laird Collier.

51. *Chicago Tribune*, Feb. 13, 1869; *HWS*, 3:569.

52. *Chicago Evening Journal*, Feb. 15, 1869; *New Covenant*, Feb. 20, 1869; *Burlington Hawkeye*, n.d., quoted in Louise R. Noun, *Strong-Minded Women: The Emergence of the Woman-Suffrage Movement in Iowa* (Ames: Iowa State University Press, 1969), 107.

53. Buechler, *Transformation of the Woman Suffrage Movement*, 74–75. Women won the presidential ballot in Illinois in 1913.

54. MAL to OB, March 3, 1869, Brown Collection, SLR.

8. The Agitator

1. *New Covenant*, May 2, 1869.

2. Ibid. J. R. Sage obituary of MAL, *Des Moines Mail and Times*, June 3, 1905; DPL obituary, *Woman's Journal*, July 15, 1899.

3. *New Covenant*, Jan. 2, May 2, 1869; *Newspapers and Periodicals of Illinois, 1814–1879* (Springfield: Illinois State Historical Society, 1910), 62. Although it is not known how much Daniel Livermore paid for the *New Covenant* in 1857, Mary told Frances Willard that he sold the newspaper, presumably with the equipment needed to publish it, for $25,000. MAL to Frances Willard, Nov. 20, 1876, T&P Papers, reel 11.

4. *Agitator*, March 13, 1869. Elizabeth Cady Stanton discussed MAL's suggestions for a newspaper title in her own newspaper, the *Revolution*, March 18, 1869, reprinted in *The Selected Papers of Elizabeth Cady Stanton and Susan B. Anthony*, 2 vols., ed. Ann D. Gordon (New Brunswick, N.J.: Rutgers University Press, 2000), 2:226.

5. See advertisements in *Agitator*, Oct. 9, 1869. MAL discussed subscribers in a letter to Lucy Stone, Aug. 24, 1869, NAWSA Collection, reel 12, LC. The *Boston Journal's* obituary of MAL, May 24, 1905, mentioned her financial investment in the newspaper.

6. *Agitator*, Oct. 2, Nov. 6, 1869.

7. Ibid., July 24, 1869. MAL to OB, April 25, 1869, Brown Collection, SLR; MAL to Elizabeth Boynton, Aug. 14, 1869, Harbert Collection, HL.

8. *HWS*, 3:570; *Agitator*, March 20, 1869; Amy Dru Stanley, *From Bondage to Contract: Wage Labor, Marriage, and the Market in the Age of Slave Emancipation* (New York: Cambridge University Press, 1998), 174-217.

9. *Agitator* (all citations 1869): May 22 (Harvard); March 20 (Wabash); April 3 (Wisconsin); May 1 (Michigan); May 1 (Mass.); April 10 (Vassar).

10. Ibid., April 3, 10, 1869; Bonnie J. Dow, "The *Revolution*, 1868-1870: Expanding the Woman Suffrage Agenda," in *A Voice of Their Own: The Woman Suffrage Press, 1840-1910*, ed. Martha M. Solomon (Tuscaloosa: University of Alabama Press, 1991), 61-86.

11. *Agitator*, March 13, March 20, April 10, 1869.

12. Ibid., March 13, 1869.

13. Ibid., March 20, 1869. MAL evidently traveled to Washington, for she spoke of riding in "the cars" with several King opponents and discussing the issue at length with them. Ibid., May 1, 1869. ECS also championed the cause of Angie King. See Genevieve G. McBride, *On Wisconsin Women: Working for Their Rights from Settlement to Suffrage* (Madison: University of Wisconsin Press, 1993), 48.

14. *Agitator*, April 17, 1869. Grant had appointed Elizabeth Van Lew postmaster of Richmond. During the war, Van Lew had spied for the Union. See Elizabeth D. Leonard, *All the Daring of the Soldier: Women of the Civil War Armies* (New York: W. W. Norton, 1999), 56-57, and Elizabeth R. Varon, *Southern Lady, Yankee Spy: The True Story of Elizabeth Van Lew, a Union Agent in the Heart of the Confederacy* (New York: Oxford University Press, 2003), 216-38. Thomas Howard Ruger, breveted a major general of volunteers after his performance at the battle of Franklin, Tennessee, in 1864, served as colonel of the Thirty-third Infantry and later the Eighteenth Infantry in 1869. See *Dictionary of American Biography*, 16:219-20.

15. *Agitator*, May 1, 15, 29, 1869. After losing her job at the post office, King found employment as librarian of the Young Men's Association of Janesville. See *Woman's Journal*, April 2, 1870. Ten years after the imbroglio, she was admitted to the bar in Wisconsin, one of the state's first female attorneys. See McBride, *On Wisconsin Women*, 93-94.

16. *Agitator*, April 17, 24, May 8, 1869. MAL wrote about international issues on March 13, May 1, 8, June 26, Aug. 7, Sept. 25, and Nov. 6, 1869.

17. Ibid., March 20, April 24, 1869.

18. Ibid., April 24, May 1, 1869.

19. Ibid., May 22, 1869.

20. Ibid., March 20 (Madison); April 10 (Janesville); April 24 (Dubuque); May 15 (Mendota); May 1 ("Word to Women"); May 1, 15, 22, 1869 (other states). See also McBride, *On Wisconsin Women*, 47, and Noun, *Strong-Minded Women*, 112-39.

21. *Des Moines Bulletin* and *Centralia (Illinois) Sentinel* quoted in *Agitator*, June 26, 1869, and *Detroit Herald* quoted May 1, 1869.

22. *Agitator*, May 15, 1869 (Minneapolis). MAL's three articles, April 10, 17, and 24, 1869, were a response to the *Pantagraph*'s editorial of March 16, rejecting women's enfranchisement titled "Will the *Agitator* Answer."

23. Wendt, *Chicago Tribune*, 191-92, 224; George P. Upton, *Letters of Peregrine Pickle* (Chicago: Western News Company, 1869).

24. *Chicago Tribune*, Feb. 21, 28 (Peregrine Pickle), March 28, 1869 (Vic). In *Woman's Journal*, Feb. 19, 1870, MAL identified Vic as Mrs. M. A. Rayne.

25. *Chicago Tribune*, March 9, Sept. 12, 1869. In two additional editorials on Sept. 11, and 12, 1869, the *Tribune* condemned the woman's rights movement, in one article using the word "humbug" to describe the notion that by voting, women would "purify" politics, and in the other affirming its support for women's elevation in all realms other than agriculture, the military, and politics.

26. *Agitator*, March 13, April 3, July 17, 1869.

27. Ibid., July 10, 24, 1869. In rejecting Hanson's advice to speak in "a low sweet voice," MAL asked that he refrain from offering advice about how to edit her newspaper, especially in that his own success as an editor "is acknowledged on all hands" as "indifferent." Anti-feminist articles appeared in the *New Covenant* regularly. See, for example, Oct 16, Nov. 6, Dec. 11, 1869, Jan. 15, 29, 1870.

28. MAL spoke at a banquet in Boston honoring the seventieth birthday of Henry Blackwell. Her speech is quoted in *Woman's Journal*, May 11, 1895.

29. *Agitator*, May 22, 1869.

30. MAL to William Lloyd Garrison, Aug. 16, 1869, Livermore Collection, BPL.

31. MAL's stature described in an article "by a Westerner" and *Evening Post* quoted in the *Agitator*, May 22, 1869; audience characterized ibid., May 29, 1869; MAL's voice described by *Worcester (Massachusetts) Spy*, quoted ibid., June 5, 1869. MAL had to pay a former *Chicago Tribune* editor $100 to handle her duties at the *Agitator* while she was in the East, since DPL was "overwhelmed with business, and cannot give up the time"; see MAL to Phebe Hanaford, April 25, 1869, Hanaford Collection, SLR.

32. *Agitator*, May 29, 1869; *HWS*, 2:379-83, 397-98. MAL believed that Stanton and Anthony had made an enormous tactical blunder in accepting financial support from Train. Two years earlier, when he had accompanied the women on a lecture tour that included Chicago, Livermore heard all three speak. She denounced Train in the *New Covenant* (Nov. 30, 1867) as egotistical, incoherent, and "not the sort of man whose influence will help them."

33. *HWS*, 2:389-90.

34. *Agitator*, May 22, 1869. Lucretia Mott to Martha Wright, June 6, 1869, in Palmer, *Selected Letters of Lucretia Coffin Mott*, 419.

35. *Agitator*, May 29, 1869.

36. Ibid., June 5, 12, 1869. Garrison's praise for MAL printed in *Cincinnati Commercial* and reprinted June 12, 1869. Harriet H. Robinson, in *Massachusetts in the Woman Suffrage Movement* (Boston: Roberts Brothers, 1881), 52, wrote that MAL "made her *debut* in Boston, as a platform orator. . . . The newspapers said that this lady spoke even better than she had done at a recent meeting in New York city."

37. Eleanor Flexner, *Century of Struggle: The Woman's Rights Movement in the United States* (New York: Atheneum, 1974), 152; Kerr, *Lucy Stone*, 140-41. Ann Gordon, in *Selected Papers of Elizabeth Cady Stanton and Susan B. Anthony*, 2:242n, suggests that "Livermore, though she could not stay, knew that talk would turn to organization."

38. Ida Husted Harper, *Life and Work of Susan B. Anthony*, 2 vols. (1898; reprint, New York: Arno Press, 1969), 1:327-28; MAL to LS, Aug. 9, 1869, NAWSA Collection, reel 12, LC.

39. *Chicago Tribune*, June 23, 1869. In *Civil War Sisterhood*, 167, Judith Giesberg discusses the influence of the war in propelling MAL, Louisa Schuyler, and Abby May toward postwar public careers.

40. *Agitator*, June 19, July 3, 10, 1869. MAL met with SBA in Buffalo on July 25, 1869; See Gordon, *Selected Papers of Elizabeth Cady Stanton and Susan B. Anthony*, 2: 252n. MAL to LS, Aug. 9, 1869, NAWSA Collection, reel 12, LC.

41. MAL to Mathilda Anneke, Sept. 6, 1869, Fritz and Mathilda Anneke Collection, State Historical Society of Wisconsin, Madison. MAL told Anneke that she had hired a German translator in anticipation of Anneke's participation in the convention. *Agitator*, Aug. 28, Sept. 18, 1869.

42. WLG's letter to the convention reprinted in *Agitator*, Oct. 9. 1969. *Chicago Tribune*, Sept. 10-11, 1869.

43. *Chicago Tribune*, March 9, Sept. 11-12, 1869; *Agitator*, Sept. 18, 1869. During the September convention, someone in the audience shouted at MAL, "The *Times.*" She responded by noting that the Democratic newspaper "had been so long on the wrong side that she would be uneasy if it was not barking at her heels . . . and if it endorsed anything she did would begin to believe she was wrong." According to the *Tribune*, Sept. 11, 1869, her remarks elicited laughter and loud applause. In the *Agitator*, MAL ignored the *Times*.

44. In a letter to LS, Aug. 24, 1869, NAWSA Collection, reel 12, LC, MAL had discussed selling the *Agitator* to New England suffragists for $750 and becoming its western editor. HBB to MAL, Oct. 6, 1869, Blackwell Family Collection, LC. MAL's letter to HBB, which he says was written on Oct. 1, has not survived.

45. In *Life*, 482-83, MAL recalled: "There were associated with me as 'editorial contributors,' Mrs. Lucy Stone, Mrs. Julia Ward Howe, Colonel Thomas W. Higginson, William Lloyd Garrison, and Henry B. Blackwell,—so brilliant a coterie of men and women, as caused me to doubt my fitness for the editorship, notwithstanding my large experience in newspaper work."

46. Robinson, *Massachusetts in the Woman Suffrage Movement*, 62-63; Kerr, *Lucy Stone*, 145. See also Lois Bannister Merk, "Massachusetts and the Woman-Suffrage Movement" (Ph.D. diss., Radcliffe College, 1956).

47. MAL to Miss [Phebe] Hanaford, April 25, 1869, Hanaford Collection, SLR; Thwing, *Livermore Family*, 107. In *New Covenant*, Sept. 26, 1868, MAL recalled visiting her father-in-law in Leicester the year before his death, noting his declining health and the realization that they would have to sell the farm that had been in the Livermore family for seventy years.

48. *Chicago Tribune*, Sept. 11, 1869.

49. MAL to OB, April 28, 1868, Brown Collection, SLR; MAL to Laura [Hubbard], Dec. 17, 1871, Livermore Collection, Chicago Historical Society; United States Bureau of the Census, *Population Schedules of the Eighth Census of the United States, 1860*, Cook County, Ill., M653, roll 116, 211.

50. *HWS*, 2:756-66; *New York Tribune*, Nov. 25, 1869; Kerr, *Lucy Stone*, 146-47.

51. SBA to Mathilda F. Anneke, n.d. and Nov. 8, 1869, Fritz and Mathilda Anneke Collection, State Historical Society of Wisconsin; Harper, *Life and Work of Susan B. Anthony*, 1:335; DPL to SBA, Jan. 20, 1870, and SBA to DPL, Jan. 25, 1870 (copies), Hooker Collection, Stowe-Day Library, Hartford, Conn.

52. Barry, *Susan B. Anthony*, 225; Jean V. Matthews, *Women's Struggle for Equality: The First Phase, 1828–1876* (Chicago: Ivan R. Dee, 1997), 142-43; Kerr, *Lucy Stone*, 148.

53. *Life*, 482.

54. MAL to EBH, April 4, 1869, Harbert Collection, HL; MAL to LS, Aug. 9, 1869, NAWSA Collection, reel 12, LC.

55. Matilda Anneke to Fritz Anneke, Dec. 2, 1869, trans. from German by Henriette M. Heinzen, Fritz and Mathilda Anneke Collection, State Historical Society of Wisconsin; Buechler, *Transformation of the Woman Suffrage Movement*, 221.

56. DuBois, *Feminism and Suffrage*, 162-202.

57. Matthews, *Women's Struggle for Equality*, 142-44.

58. DuBois, *Feminism and Suffrage*, 197, 201, argues that the schism resulted in a positive outcome, because, with the creation of the NAWA, suffragists were liberated from their reliance on both the Republican Party and other reform movements. Now they had to "look to women themselves . . . to provide the solution to women's oppression." The AWSA, by contrast, "was designed to concentrate solely on the demand for woman suffrage." Matthews, *Women's Struggle for Equality*, 144-47, argues that the NWSA and AWSA successfully recruited from among different constituent groups but acknowledges that the split also weakened the movement by separating Stanton and Anthony from the Boston group.

59. *Agitator*, Aug. 7, 1869. The last surviving issue of the *Agitator* is Nov. 6, 1869. MAL offered no valedictory, a possible indication that the paper ceased publication on short notice.

60. Ibid., Oct. 2, 1869.

61. *Life*, 483; *Woman's Journal*, Jan. 15, 1870. As a professional courtesy the *New Covenant* continued to print DPL's preaching schedule, despite the editor's falling-out with the former editor's wife. See, for example, Dec. 11, 1869. MAL returned to Illinois in February 1870 to attend a convention of the Illinois Woman Suffrage Association being held in the state capital in conjunction with Illinois's constitutional convention. At that time Judge James Bradwell assumed the presidency of the IWSA. *Woman's Journal*, Feb. 19, 1870.

62. *New Covenant*, Oct. 21, Nov. 4, 14, 1871; *Woman's Journal*, Nov. 4, 1871; Andreas, *History of Chicago*, 2:441. SBA discussed the destruction of IWSA records in a letter to EBH, Nov. 12, 1876, Harbert Collection, HL.

63. *Woman's Journal*, Oct. 14, Nov. 11, Dec. 16, 1871; MAL to Laura [Hubbard], Dec. 17, 1871, Livermore Collection, Chicago Historical Society. It is not known whether the Livermores owned any real estate in Chicago at the time of the fire.

9. Two Newspapers and a Scandal

1. MAL to HBB, April 25, 1870, NAWSA Collection, reel 12, LC.
2. MAL to EBH, May 9, 1870, Harbert Collection, HL; *Woman's Journal*, Jan. 8, 1870. On Julia Ward Howe's early life and conversion to woman's rights, see Deborah Pickman Clifford, *Mine Eyes Have Seen the Glory: A Biography of Julia Ward Howe* (Boston: Little, Brown, 1979), 170-88.
3. Kerr, *Lucy Stone*, 8-95; *Life*, 586.
4. "Three Old Crows," 1870, SLR; Julia Ward Howe, *Reminiscences, 1819-1899* (1899; reprint, New York: Negro Universities Press, 1969), 380.
5. *Woman's Journal*, Jan. 21, 1871; Howe, *Reminiscences*, 381.
6. Clifford, *Mine Eyes Have Seen the Glory*, 203-4; Kerr, *Lucy Stone*, 144; MAL to HBB, April 25, 1870, NAWSA Collection, reel 12, LC.
7. William Lloyd Garrison rebuffed SBA's efforts to interest him in NWSA activities in a letter dated Jan. 4, 1877, Harper Collection, HL. James W. Tuttleton, *Thomas Wentworth Higginson* (Boston: Twayne, 1978), 41.
8. *Woman's Journal*, Aug. 20, 1870.
9. Ibid. DPL held the pastorate in Hingham for fifteen years, from 1870 to 1885. See *Life*, 596. On September 16, 1873, MAL wrote to James T. Fields: "I am trying to help the people of Hingham in their effort to arrange for a course of lectures. . . . My husband goes there every Sunday to preach to a Universalist Church." James T. Fields Collection, HL.
10. *Woman's Journal*, Aug. 20, 1870; Hanaford, *Daughters of America*, 309-17.
11. *Ladies Repository* 43 (March 1870): 228-30 and 44 (Nov. 1870): 388-95; Hanson, *Our Women Workers*, 131; Bessler, *Universalist Movement in America*, 95.
12. *Woman's Journal*, Jan. 8, 15, 1870, July 29, 1871. For a time Sarah Grimké Weld served as a clerk in the newspaper office; She was the daughter of Angelina Grimké and Theodore Weld. See ibid., Aug. 20, 1870.
13. Ibid., May 20, 1871. The newspaper reported 4,500 subscribers on Feb. 22, 1873.
14. *Woman's Journal*, Jan. 8, 1870.
15. Sharon Hartman Strom complains of scholars treating Boston as "the capital of stuffy feminism" in "Leadership and Tactics in the American Woman Suffrage Movement: A New Perspective from Massachusetts," *Journal of American History* 62 (Sept. 1975): 298. Ellen Carol DuBois, *Feminism and Suffrage*, 197, has written, "The American Association was designed to concentrate solely on the demand for woman suffrage." More recently, Suzanne M. Marilley, in *Woman Suffrage and the Origins of Liberal Feminism in the United States, 1820-1920* (Cambridge: Harvard University Press, 1996), 12, has written, "Reconstruction forced woman's rights reformers into narrower and narrower paths toward 'equal rights'–rewards or benefits tailored to fit particular groups, not equal rights to all groups without regard to race, ethnicity, or sex." See MAL's comments to Mr. [Franklin] Sanborn, Jan. 5, 1870, Mary Livermore Collection, University of Virginia, and, for MAL's editorials on education, *Woman's Journal*, March 5 and June 11, 1870.
16. *Woman's Journal*, Jan. 22, April 16, July 9, 16, 1870; Jan 14, 21, April 29, Nov. 4,

Dec. 9, 1871. In 1876 MAL told Annie Fields, wife of Boston publisher James T. Fields, that as a teenager she had accompanied five other girls to the office of Harvard's president, requesting admission to the college. He had replied, " 'We never allow girls at Harvard; you know, the place for girls is at home." Livermore told Fields she had responded, "I wish I were God for one instant, that I might kill every woman from Eve down and let you have a masculine world all to yourself and see how you would like that." Fields recorded this conversation in her diary. See Rita K. Gollin, *Annie Adams Fields: Woman of Letters* (Amherst: University of Massachusetts Press, 2002), 178–80. Although MAL spoke often of her adolescent resentment over Harvard's discriminatory admissions policy, she did not relate the story quite the way Fields recorded it.

17. *Woman's Journal*, June 4, Aug. 13, 1870, May 6, 1871.

18. Ibid., Aug. 20, Sept. 3, 1870 (teaching); June 25, 1870, Sept. 30, 1871 (doctors); Feb. 19, 1870, Aug. 5, 1871 (lawyers); July 8, 1871 (justices of the peace); July 30, 1870, Oct. 14, 28, 1871 (religion). See also Jan. 8, 1870, and July 22, 1871.

19. Ibid., June 17, Aug. 19, 1871.

20. Ibid., July 30, 1870 (Mrs. Flynt); July 8 and 22, 1871 (residences); Aug. 27, Oct. 15, 1870 (teachers and principals).

21. Ibid., March 26, 1870, and Sept. 23, 1871 (horticulturalists and shorthand reporters); Dec. 30, 1871 (telegraphy); April 2, 1870, and Feb. 25, 1871 (typesetters). MAL still promoted the appointment of women as postmistresses, despite the Angie King debacle; see March 18, 1871. She engaged in editorial debates over women's economic and political rights with writers for the *Nation*, *Scribner's Monthly*, and the *Hartford Courant*, among others. See *Woman's Journal*, March 19, 1870, June 24, Dec. 16, 1871.

22. *Woman's Journal*, July 9, 1870, Sept. 16, 1871. MAL acknowledged Myra Bradwell's help in educating her about spousal abuse in an article on Aug. 12, 1871.

23. Ibid., July 16, 1870.

24. Ibid., Jan. 8, March 26, April 2, July 23, 1870.

25. Ibid., May 7, 1870; MAL to EBH, May 9, 1870, Harbert Collection, HL.

26. *Woman's Journal*, Oct. 22, 1870; Howe, *Reminiscences*, 380-81; *HWS*, 3:388-89.

27. *Woman's Journal*, May 21, 1870; Aileen S. Kraditor, *Ideas of the Woman Suffrage Movement, 1890–1920* (New York: Columbia University Press, 1965).

28. *Woman's Journal*, May 7, 1870 (SBA); Jan. 22, 1870 (*Revolution*).

29. Walter M. Merrill and Louis Ruchames, eds., *The Papers of William Lloyd Garrison*, vol. 6, *To Rouse the Slumbering Land, 1868–1879* (Cambridge: Belknap Press, 1981), 167-72; *Woman's Journal*, April, 2, 9, 16, 23, 1870; *New York Tribune*, April 9, 1870. After the AWSA voted down the merger proposal, HBB wrote in the *Journal*, Dec. 3, 1870, "This settles the question of fusion for the coming year and, we hope, forever."

30. *Woman's Journal*, Aug. 6, 13, 20, Sept. 3, Dec. 10, 1870. On the Massachusetts Woman Suffrage Association, see Robinson, *Massachusetts in the Woman Suffrage Movement*, 55, and Strom, "Leadership and Tactics in the American Woman Suffrage Movement," 300.

31. *Woman's Journal*, Jan. 7, 1871.

32. Ibid., Jan. 14, Feb. 18, 1871. MAL described her relationship with James Redpath and his Boston Lyceum Bureau in a letter to Frances Willard, Nov. 20, 1876, T&P Papers, reel 11.

33. *Woman's Journal*, Jan. 21, April 15, 1871.

34. Ibid., Jan. 21, 28, 1871.

35. Ibid., Jan. 28, 1871. The *Woman's Journal* quoted the *Cleveland Daily Herald* in concluding that MAL "got the best of the Judge at every point."

36. *Woman's Journal*, Feb. 18, 1871. MAL recounted a similar occurrence in St. Joseph, Missouri. See ibid., Feb. 4, 1871. *Dubuque Herald* quoted in Noun, *Strong-Minded Women*, 163.

37. *Woman's Journal*, Feb. 11, 1871.

38. Ibid., Jan. 21, 1871.

39. Alice Stone Blackwell, *Lucy Stone* (1930; reprint, New York: Kraus, 1971), 226. Although she wished to avoid confrontations with the NWSA, MAL did editorialize against ECS's stand on divorce reform in the *Woman's Journal*, Nov. 5, 1870.

40. Barbara Goldsmith, *Other Powers: The Age of Suffrage, Spiritualism, and the Scandalous Victoria Woodhull* (New York: Alfred A. Knopf, 1998), 18-27, 50-52, 63-71, 104-9.

41. Ibid., 190-95, 210-12; James et al., *Notable American Women*, 3:652-53.

42. *Woman's Journal*, April 16, 1870, Feb. 11, 1871. Richard Wrightman Fox, *Trials of Intimacy: Love and Loss in the Beecher-Tilton Scandal* (Chicago: University of Chicago Press, 1999),153. See also Flexner, *Century of Struggle*, 153. For a full explanation of the origins of the "new departure" relating to the Fourteenth and Fifteenth Amendments, see Ellen Carol DuBois, "Taking the Law into Our Own Hands: *Bradwell*, *Minor*, and Suffrage Militance in the 1870s," in *Visible Women: New Essays on American Activism*, ed. Nancy A. Hewitt and Suzanne Lebsock (Urbana: University of Illinois Press, 1993), 19-40.

43. *Woman's Journal*, March 25, 1871. MAL's criticism of Woodhull's position represented a change from the previous month, when the *Journal*, Feb. 11, 1871, published an article titled "XIVth and XVth Amendments–Right of Suffrage under Them." It began, "Mrs. Woodhull's memorial to Congress . . . has perhaps received less attention than it deserves from the friends of Woman Suffrage," and concludes, "We are glad, then, to see the subject brought to the attention of Congress." The article is unsigned.

44. *Woodhull and Claflin's Weekly*, April 1, 1871; *Woman's Journal*, April 15, 1871.

45. *Woodhull and Claflin's Weekly*, May 27, 1871; Goldsmith, *Other Powers*, 272-75.

46. *Woman's Journal*, May 13, 1871.

47. SBA to Martha Wright, May 20, 1871, quoted in Goldsmith, *Other Powers*, 285; see also 282; Harper, *Life and Work of Susan B. Anthony*, 1:379; *Woodhull and Claflin's Weekly*, June 17, 1871. Evidently Anna Dickinson was the source reporting on the alleged marital travails of Phebe Hanaford and MAL. See Gordon, *Selected Papers of Elizabeth Cady Stanton and Susan B. Anthony*, 2:513n.

48. Goldsmith, *Other Powers*, 316-19; Griffith, *In Her Own Right*, 152-57; Melanie Susan Gustafson, *Women and the Republican Party, 1854-1924* (Urbana: University of Illinois Press, 2001), 46-47.

49. *Woodhull and Claflin's Weekly*, Nov. 2, Dec. 28, 1872; *Boston Journal*, n.d., quoted in Goldsmith, *Other Powers*, 335; Fox, *Trials of Intimacy*, 156-57. Another treatment of the subject is Altina L. Waller, *Reverend Beecher and Mrs. Tilton: Sex and Class in Victorian America* (Amherst: University of Massachusetts Press, 1982), 1-12.

50. Fox, *Trials of Intimacy*, 301.

51. *Woman's Journal*, Nov. 12, 1870, April 29, Sept. 2, Nov. 25, 1871; MAL to HBB, [1874], NAWSA Collection, reel 12, LC. In *Trials of Intimacy*, 298, Richard Wrightman Fox concluded "We will never know whether Elizabeth Tilton and Henry Ward Beecher slept together."

52. Goldsmith, *Other Powers*, 344-46, 440-41; Fox, *Trials of Intimacy*, 11-13, MAL to EBH, 187-, Mary Earhart Dillon Collection, SLR. Helen Lefkowitz Horowitz, "Victoria Woodhull, Anthony Comstock, and the Conflict over Sex in the United States in the 1870s," *Journal of American History* 87 (Sept. 2000): 431-34.

53. Blackwell, *Lucy Stone*, 225, 251; MAL to EBH, 187-, Mary Earhart Dillon Collection, SLR. On the defeat in Iowa, see *HWS*, 3:619-20, and Noun, *Strong-Minded Women*, 217-21. LS to EBH, April 12, 1872, Harbert Collection, HL; Olympia Brown, *Acquaintances, Old and New, among Reformers* (Milwaukee: S. E. Tate, 1911), 91. Historians debate the impact of the scandal on the suffrage movement. Andrea Moore Kerr has written that "the Woodhull misalliance did incalculable harm." See her essay "White Women's Rights, Black Men's Wrongs: Free Love, Blackmail, and the Formation of the American Woman Suffrage Association," in *One Woman, One Vote: Rediscovering the Woman Suffrage Movement*, ed. Marjorie Spruill Wheeler (Troutdale, Ore.: NewSage Press, 1995), 76-77. Eleanor Flexner, however, has argued that the scandal did little to damage the AWSA; see *Century of Struggle*, 154. In "The *Woman's Journal*," 96, Susan Huxman notes that the *Journal* adopted a "posture of dignified silence on the scandal." Andrea Frisken, "Sex in Politics: Victoria Woodhull as an American Public Woman, 1870-1876," *Journal of Women's History* 12 (Spring 2000): 89, 100, has written that "Woodhull served as a scapegoat for opponents of suffrage and other Reconstruction Era political and legal challenges."

54. *Woman's Journal*, Nov. 19, 1870; MAL to EBH, May 9, 1870, and SBA to EBH, March 15, 1875, Harbert Collection, HL; Buechler, *Transformation of the Woman Suffrage Movement*, 104.

55. MAL to EBH, April 20, 1876, and James Bradwell to EBH, SBA, and others, May 28, 1880, Harbert Collection, HL.

56. *HWS*, 3:274-75; *Woman's Journal*, Jan. 6, 1872; Huxman, "The *Woman's Journal*," 90-91.

10. QUEEN OF THE PLATFORM

1. For "queen of the platform," see, for example, ASB, reminiscence in *Boston Post*, Jan. 22, 1941 (copy in Woman's Rights Collection, SLR). WLG's characterization of MAL in a letter to Oliver Johnson, June 2, 1872, Garrison Collection, BPL. On the number of lectures MAL gave annually, see MAL to EBH, 187–, Mary Earhart Dillon Collection, SLR.

2. Richard Slotkin, *The Fatal Environment: The Myth of the Frontier in the Age of Industrialization, 1800–1890* (New York: Atheneum, 1985), 284–90; David Quigley, *Second Founding: New York City, Reconstruction, and the Making of American Democracy* (New York: Hill and Wang, 2004), ix–xi. David Montgomery analyzes issues of labor and capital in *Beyond Equality: Labor and the Radical Republicans, 1862–1872* (New York: Alfred A. Knopf, 1967).

3. MAL, "Address for Lake Pleasant," July 5, 1880, Livermore Collection, FLP.

4. Ibid. and MAL, "The Teacher as Moral Force," n.d., Livermore Collection, FLP.

5. MAL, "Abraham Lincoln," n.d., Livermore Collection, FLP; *Woman's Journal*, Oct. 8, 15, 22, 1870; Robinson, *Massachusetts in the Woman Suffrage Movement*, 69–74, 103.

6. MAL described her "unmistakable aversion" in a letter to Whitlaw Reid, Oct. 24, 1870, Whitlaw Reid Collection, LC; *Woman's Journal*, Sept. 21, 28, 1872; Rebecca Edwards, *Angels in the Machinery: Gender in American Party Politics from the Civil War to the Progressive Era* (New York: Oxford University Press, 1997), 5, 38. LS and JWH campaigned for Grant, as did ECS and SBA. The decision of the New Yorkers to work for the Republicans represented a shift from their earlier opposition to a party that refused to include women in legislation granting political rights to black men and ECS's earlier support for Victoria Woodhull. Anna Dickinson supported Greeley, creating tension with other NWSA leaders, notably ECS and SBA. See Gustafson, *Women and the Republican Party*, 47–51.

7. *Woman's Journal*, March 16, Sept. 14, Sept. 28, Oct. 12, Nov. 9, 1872; *Philadelphia Inquirer*, Sept. 13, 1872. MAL spoke of her Philadelphia appearance in a letter to Mr. Pugh, Sept. 9, 1872, Miscellaneous Manuscripts, New-York Historical Society.

8. *Woman's Journal* Nov. 9, 30, 1872 (election), Jan. 18, 1873 (Washburn). When Horace Greeley died shortly after the election, the *Journal* eulogized him on Dec. 7, 1872: "It was not that we loved Mr. Greeley less, but Woman Suffrage more." See also Robinson, *Massachusetts in the Woman Suffrage Movement*, 78–79. When Ulysses S. Grant died in 1885, the *Journal* praised his patriotism and character but also spoke of his "intellectual limitations" when it came to women's issues; see July 25, 1885. On women's struggles with the Republican Party over time, see Gustafson, *Women and the Republican Party*, 10.

9. MAL spoke to the a suffrage gathering in Boston, as reported in *Woman's Journal*, Oct. 16, 1875; MAL to Jeanne C. (Smith) Carr, Sept. 17, 1874, Carr Collection, HL.

10. *Woman's Journal*, Feb. 1, March 22, April 5, Nov. 22, 1873, Jan. 3, 1874.

11. MAL to Annie Fields, Dec. 4, 1873, Fields Collection, HL.

12. *Woman's Journal*, Dec. 20, 1873.

13. Ibid. The shift from arguments based on citizenship to arguments based on taxpaying is discussed by Mary P. Ryan, *Women in Public: Between Banners and Ballots, 1825–1880* (Baltimore: Johns Hopkins University Press, 1990), 155.

14. MAL to Jeanne C. Carr, July 26, [1873?], Carr Collection, HL.

15. *Woman's Journal*, Feb. 22, 1873; LS to ECS, Aug. 30, 1876, Harper Collection, HL; MAL to EBH, 187–, Mary Earhart Dillon Collection, SLR; MAL to James T. Colby, July 23, 1883, Alma Lutz Collection, Vassar College.

16. *Woman's Journal*, April 18, 1874; SBA to EBH, Dec. 23, 1876, Harbert Collection, HL. MAL described her lecturing career to a Mrs. Smith, Aug. 21, 1876, NAWSA Collection, reel 12, LC (free lectures); to EBH, 187–, Mary Earhart Dillon Collection, SLR (fees to booking agents); to Frances Willard, Nov. 20, 1876, T&P Papers, reel 12 (fees to booking agents); to Mr. Strickland, Aug. 11, 1874, Livermore Collection, SLR; to Mrs. Claflin, Nov. 2, 1877, Livermore Collection, BPL.

17. MAL to Jeanne C. Carr, July 22, 1877, Carr Collection, HL.

18. *Life*, 615–29. For the text of "Superfluous Women," see *Woman's Journal*, Nov. 13, 1875, and a report of her giving the speech, April 29, 1876. For reports of her giving "What Shall We Do with Our Daughters?" see April 6, 1872, March 1, 1873.

19. Dawes, *Language of War*, 47.

20. MAL, "The Battle of Life," reprinted in *Life*, 677–97.

21. MAL to Harriet Hanson Robinson, July 23, 1875, Robinson Collection, SLR; *Woman's Journal*, May 27, 1876; MAL, "Success in Life" and "The Highest Type of Manhood," Livermore Collection, FLP.

22. *Life*, 614. Fox discusses nineteenth-century attitudes toward oratory in *Trials of Intimacy*, 20–21.

23. *Cincinnati Commercial*, quoted in *Woman's Journal*, Jan. 24, 1880.

24. *Woman's Journal*, Nov. 28, 1874; *Des Moines State Register*, quoted ibid., March 1, 1879; Lilian Whiting, *Boston Days* (Boston: Little, Brown, 1902), 457.

25. J. R. Sage, obituary of MAL, *Des Moines Mail and Times*, June 3, 1905; *Woman's Journal*, Nov. 21, 1874.

26. *Woman's Journal*, Feb. 24, 1872, March 18, 1876; MAL to James T. Fields, Oct. 13, 1873, Fields Collection, HL. The *Journal* reported the speech on May 17, 1873, noting an audience of eight to nine hundred.

27. MAL to EBH, 187–, Mary Earhart Dillon Collection, and MAL to Mr. Strickland, Jan. 14, 1877, Livermore Collection, SLR; MAL to HBB, Jan. 20, 1874 and [1874], NAWSA Collection, reel 12, LC; *Woman's Journal*, Feb. 24, 1872, March 29, 1873.

28. MAL to ASB, Jan. 20, 1874, Livermore Collection, SLR; *Woman's Journal*, Oct. 23, Nov. 27, 1875.

29. This episode occurred before 1873, when Shaw entered Albion College. Shaw later approached Anna Dickinson after a lecture. "I thought all great women were like [Livermore]," she later recalled, "but I was now to experience a bitter disillusionment." Dickinson regarded her "icily, and turned away." Shaw expressed gratitude that fate had sent Livermore to her before Dickinson. Shaw, *Story of a Pioneer*, 54–66.

30. Ann Eliza Young, *Wife No. 19; or, The Story of a Life in Bondage* (Hartford: Dustin,

Gilman, 1876). The national sensation caused by this book and by Young's lyceum career helped lead to federal laws against polygamy. See James et al., *Notable American Women*, 3:696-97; MAL to ASB, Nov. 30, 1879, Livermore Papers, SLR; MAL to FW, Nov. 20, 1876, T&P Papers, reel 11.

31. Frances E. Willard, *Glimpses of Fifty Years: The Autobiography of an American Woman* (1889; reprint, New York: Source Books, 1970), 338; Bordin, *Frances Willard*, 71-72.

32. Bordin, *Frances Willard*, 88-89.

33. MAL described the origins of the temperance movement on its tenth anniversary in *Union Signal*, Dec. 20, 1883. Her participation is described in *Woman's Journal*, June 6, 1874. The origins of the crusade are analyzed in Ruth Bordin, *Woman and Temperance: The Quest for Power and Liberty, 1873–1900* (Philadelphia: Temple University Press, 1981), 15-26, and Anne Firor Scott, *Natural Allies: Women's Associations in American History* (Urbana: University of Illinois Press, 1991), 93-94.

34. Willard, *Glimpses of Fifty Years*, 351. MAL's letter to the WCTU convention is discussed in *Woman's Journal*, Dec. 5, 1874. See also Barbara Leslie Epstein, *The Politics of Domesticity: Women, Evangelism, and Temperance in Nineteenth-Century America* (Middletown, Conn.: Wesleyan University Press, 1981), 117-19.

35. MAL to FW, Nov. 20, 1876, T&P Papers, reel 11. *Union Signal* is discussed in Bordin, *Woman and Temperance*, 90. See Epstein, *The Politics of Domesticity*, 119. MAL discussed FW's defeat for the presidency in a letter to LS, Nov. 11, 1877, Livermore Collection, SLR.

36. Epstein, *Politics of Domesticity*, 124, 128.

37. Bordin, *Woman and Temperance*, 60; *Woman's Journal*, Nov. 13, Dec. 18, 1875; MAL, "Temperance," Livermore Collection, FLP. See also *Life*, 578-83.

38. MAL to Annie Fields, Dec. 1, 1879, Fields Collection, HL; *Woman's Journal*, June 30, 1877.

39. *Boston Post* and *Boston Journal*, June 23, 1877; *Woman's Journal*, June 30, 1877. Mayor Prince told MAL that ten years earlier as a state legislator he had voted for statewide prohibition. The mayor was defeated for reelection in 1878. Melvin G. Holli and Peter d'A. Jones, eds., *Biographical Dictionary of American Mayors, 1820–1980: Big City Mayors* (Westport, Conn.: Greenwood Press, 1981), 296. WCTU Annual Meeting Minutes, Chicago, 1877, 184-85, T&P Papers, reel 1. In 1880 MAL spearheaded an effort within the WCTU to commission a painting of Lucy Hayes. See *Chicago Inter Ocean*, Nov. 6, 1880 (copy in T&P Papers, reel 32).

40. *Woman's Journal*, Aug. 31, 1878, June 7, 1879; MAL, "Temperance," Livermore Collection, FLP; Massachusetts WCTU, *Cuisine: A Compilation of Valuable Recipes Known to Be Reliable* (Boston: E. B. Stillings, 1878); minutes of the National WCTU Convention in Indianapolis, 1879, 30-31, T&P Papers, reel 1; Bordin, *Woman and Temperance*, 52.

41. Minutes of the National WCTU Convention in Boston, 1880, 34-35, 77-78, 102-104, 148-51, T&P Papers, reel 1.

42. MAL to LS, Nov. 11, 1877, NAWSA Collection, reel 12, LC; MAL to Annie Fields, Dec. 1, 1879, Fields Collection, HL; MAL to Caroline Severance, May 23, 1882, Severance Collection, HL; *Life*, 578–83; Scott, *Natural Allies*, 103. After MAL's retirement as Massachusetts WCTU president, the state chapter focused its attention on license suffrage instead of municipal suffrage. See Merk, "Massachusetts and the Woman-Suffrage Movement," 141.

43. MAL to Clara Barton, Aug. 30, 1877, Barton Collection, LC. MAL appears not to have known Barton except by reputation during the Civil War.

44. MAL made fun of the ladies of the New England Woman's Club in a letter to ASB, Jan. 20, 1874, Livermore Collection, SLR. Karen J. Blair, *The Clubwoman as Feminist: True Womanhood Redefined, 1868–1914* (New York: Holmes & Meier, 1980), 45.

45. *Woman's Journal*, Nov. 8, 1873, Nov. 7, 1874; Blair, *Clubwoman as Feminist*, 45; William Leach, *True Love and Perfect Union: The Feminist Reform of Sex and Society* (New York: Basic Books, 1980), 15, 185–89.

46. *Woman's Journal*, Nov. 14, 1874; Leach, *True Love and Perfect Union*, 185–89.

47. *Woman's Journal*, Nov. 21, 1874; *Melrose (Mass.) Journal*, Dec. 26, 1874. On club activism, see *Woman's Journal*, Oct. 2, 23, 30, 1875, April 15, 1876.

48. *Woman's Journal*, June 7, 1879; Blair, *Clubwoman as Feminist*, 1.

49. MAL to Jeanne C, Carr, July 26, [1873?], Carr Collection, HL; MAL to HBB, n.d., [1874], NAWSA Collection; reel 12, LC. For MAL's decision not to attend the centennial festivities, see *Woman's Journal*, March 21, 1874; "Call" for festivities signed by MAL as AWSA president, June 10, 1876; and coverage of activities, July 8, 1876. Abby Kelley Foster had refused to pay taxes as a protest over women's exclusion from political rights. LS and HBB represented the AWSA in Philadelphia. The assembled delegates passed resolutions protesting a political system that both governed women and taxed them without their consent. For MAL's presidential addresses, see *Woman's Journal*, Nov. 27, 1875, Oct. 7, 1876, and June 2, 16, 1877.

50. *Woman's Journal*, Feb. 8, 1873. MAL mentioned Etta applying to Amherst in a letter to Laura Hubbard, Dec. 17, 1871, Livermore Collection, Chicago Historical Society. She complained about Amherst in *Woman's Journal*, Oct. 28, 1871. Thomas Cushing, *Historical Sketch of Chauncy-Hall School with Catalogue of Teachers and Pupils, 1828–1894* (Boston: David Clapp and Son, 1895), 135.

51. *Woman's Journal*, May 17, 1873 ("light of her home"); Nov. 28, 1874 (first prize and teacher); April 15, 1876 (wedding). The wedding is also mentioned in *Melrose Record*, April 8, 1876, and MAL to EBH, April 20, 1876, Harbert Collection, HL. MAL's praise for her son-in-law in letters to James T. Fields, Jan. 1, 1878, Fields Collection, HL, and Laura Hubbard, Aug. 24, 1880, Livermore Collection, Chicago Historical Society. For additional information about John and Etta Norris, see their obituaries: *Woman's Journal*, July 1, 1905 (John), and *Melrose Free Press*, Nov. 8, 1929 (Etta). There is no surviving correspondence between MAL and her daughters in public archives.

52. MAL to Mr. Cooke, Sept. 28, 1889, Livermore Collection, BPL; John Norris obituary, *Woman's Journal*, July 1, 1905, and Etta Norris obituary, *Melrose Free Press*, Nov. 8, 1929.

53. MAL to Laura Hubbard, Aug. 24, 1880, Livermore Collection, Chicago Historical Society; MAL to Annie Fields, Nov. 2, 1880, Fields Collection, HL; Thwing, *Livermore Family*, 195. The death of Emma Ashton Norris, age one year, eight months, is announced in *Woman's Journal*, April 19, 1884.

54. MAL to Laura Hubbard, Dec. 17, 1871, and Aug. 24, 1880, Livermore Collection, Chicago Historical Society; MAL to Jeanne C. Carr, July 26, [1873?], Carr Collection, HL.

55. ASB quoted in *Boston Post*, Jan. 22, 1941 (copy in Woman's Rights Collection, SLR); *Woman's Journal*, Sept. 2, 1871.

56. MAL to James T. Fields, Sept. 16, 1873, Fields Collection, HL; Shaw, *Story of a Pioneer*, 94–95.

57. MAL to William Lloyd Garrison, Sept. 8. 1878, Livermore Collection, BPL. See also *Life*, 519.

58. MAL to William Lloyd Garrison, Sept, 8, 1878; MAL to Mary A. Estlin, July 22, 1878; and William Lloyd Garrison to Frank J. Garrison, Sept. 13, 1878 (describing MAL's trip), MAL Collection, BPL. *Woman's Journal*, Aug. 10, 1878, discussed her speech in the McLaren home.

59. *Life*, 523–54. See also undated memoranda book MAL kept of their European trip in Livermore Collection, FLP.

60. *Woman's Journal*, Sept. 7, 1878.

61. Ibid., Sept. 14, 1878; MAL to William Lloyd Garrison, Sept. 8, 1878, Livermore Collection, BPL.

62. MAL to LS, Nov. 11, 1877, Blackwell Family Collection, LC.

11. POLITICS, SUFFRAGE, AND SOCIALISM

1. *New York Tribune*, July 17, 1888.

2. *Woman's Journal*, July 9 and Aug. 20, 1881; MAL to HBB, Oct. 30, 1893, and MAL to LS, May 9, 1881, NAWSA Collection, reel 12, LC.

3. MAL discussed the 1882 Massachusetts gubernatorial election in *Woman's Journal*, Aug. 19, 1882.

4. Mark Wahlgren Summers, *Rum, Romanism, and Rebellion: The Making of a President, 1884* (Chapel Hill: University North Carolina Press, 2000), 179–83. Richard Welch has concluded that the accusations against Cleveland ultimately failed to affect the election's outcome because they were made early in the campaign, in July, and because of Cleveland's candor in defusing the scandal by admitting paternity and paying child support. See Richard E. Welch Jr., *The Presidencies of Grover Cleveland* (Lawrence: University of Kansas Press, 1988), 36–41.

5. MAL to Mr. [William Warfield] Clapp, Sept. 6, 1884, Livermore Collection, HLH. A copy of MAL's calling card may be found in the Livermore Collection, SLR. Evidently Livermore had a falling out with Thomas Wentworth Higginson over the

issue of Cleveland's morality, for she complained in a letter to Anne Whitney of September 8, 1884, that Higginson regarded chastity as a secondary virtue. See Whitney Collection, WC.

6. *Woman's Journal*, Jan. 15, 1884; MAL to Mr. [William Warfield] Clapp, Sept. 6, 1884, Livermore Collection, HLH; *HWS*, 3:280-82. MAL's fears regarding the Prohibitionists were well founded. They won 150,000 votes in 1884, up from 10,000 in 1880. See Jack S. Blocker Jr., *Retreat from Reform: The Prohibition Movement in the U.S., 1890-1913* (Westport, Conn.: Greenwood Press, 1976), 36n, 139. Robinson, *Massachusetts in the Woman Suffrage Movement*, 81, noted that the Prohibition Party "sometimes holds the balance of political power in Massachusetts."

7. MAL to William Warfield Clapp, Aug. 11,[1884], Livermore Collection, HLH. Her editorial "A Word to Women" appeared in the *Boston Journal* on Aug. 8, 1884, and the *Woman's Journal* the following day.

8. MAL, "A Word to Women," *Boston Journal*, Aug. 8, 1884, and *Woman's Journal*, Aug. 9, 1884.

9. Wahlgren, *Rum, Romanism, and Rebellion*, 186, 279-85, 294-95. For MAL's speech to the WCTU, see *New York Times*, Oct. 15, 1888. The *Woman's Journal* called Cleveland's 1884 election a "shameful result" in its Nov. 8, 1884, edition. MAL no doubt agreed. See also Edwards, *Angels in the Machinery*, 41-42, 46-47.

10. MAL to HBB, Jan. 1, 1892, NAWSA Collection, reel 12, LC. MAL discussed the election of McKinley in a letter to Mrs. [Isabel Chapin] Barrows, Nov. 7, 1896, Livermore Collection, HLH. See Gustafson, *Women and the Republican Party*, 58, and Edwards, *Angels in the Machinery*, 52-54.

11. MAL, "Speech at Mount Pleasant," July 5, 1880; see also "The Teacher as Moral Force," n.d., Livermore Collection, FLP. For a discussion of railroads, see Slotkin, *Fatal Environment*, 6, 478-79.

12. *Dawn*, Sept. 15, 1889; Arthur E. Morgan, *Edward Bellamy* (New York: Columbia University Press, 1944), 229-32; John L. Thomas, *Alternative America: Henry George, Edward Bellamy, Henry Demarest Lloyd, and the Adversary Tradition* (Cambridge: Harvard University Press, 1983), 237-40; Mari Jo Buhle, *Women and American Socialism, 1870-1920* (Urbana: University of Illinois Press, 1981), 75-80.

13. Morgan, *Edward Bellamy*, 249-51. MAL discussed the Martineau sculpture in *Woman's Journal*, May 20, 1882. She described Whitney in a letter to AW, Sept. 15, 1892, Whitney Collection, WC. See also Whitney to Sarah Whitney, describing MAL, Aug. 28, 1884, Whitney Collection, WC; Buhle, *Women and American Socialism*, 79.

14. *Dawn*, July 15, 1889. The May 15, 1889, issue lists MAL as vice president of the Society of Christian Socialists. The October 1890 issue announced the creation of a department titled "Socialism and Women," edited by Anna R. Weeks of Chicago. See Morgan, *Edward Bellamy*, 285; Buhle, *Women and American Socialism*, 79; and Giesberg, *Civil War Sisterhood*, 165-66. See also Charles Howard Hopkins, *The Rise of the Social Gospel in American Protestantism, 1865-1915* (New Haven: Yale University Press, 1940), 173-81.

15. *Dawn*, July 15, 1889. MAL's speeches and appearances are discussed ibid., Feb., April, July–Aug. 1890.

16. MAL, "Cooperative Womanhood in the State," *North American Review* 153 (1891): 283–95. See as well her two-part article "Homes Built by Women," *Chautauquan* 7 (1887): 408–10 and 473–74. MAL spoke of her visit to the Sherborn prison in a letter to AW, June 13, 1884, Whitney Collection, WC. She spoke of meeting Jane Addams in *Woman's Journal*, Feb. 20, 1897. See also MAL, "Woman as a Home-Maker: The American Woman in Action," *Frank Leslie's Popular Monthly* 59 (Dec. 1899): 213–17.

17. *Woman's Journal*, May 29, 1880, Nov. 22, 1902; "Co-Operative Housekeeping," undated manuscript, Livermore Collection, FLP. In *The Grand Domestic Revolution*, 115–31, Delores Hayden contrasts Livermore's practicality with the more utopian cooperative housekeeping visions of reformers such as Marie Howland and Melusina Peirce.

18. Thomas, *Alternative America*, 315; Morgan, *Edward Bellamy*, 276; MAL to AW, Sept. 15, 1892, Whitney Collection, WC; *Dawn*, June 15, 1889. It is uncertain when MAL stopped being associated with the *Dawn*. There are no extant issues from 1893. Her name does not appear in 1894 issues.

19. *Life*, 596–97; MAL to Mrs. Burr, Nov. 30, 1885, Livermore Collection, Smith College. MAL discussed a visit by DPL in a letter to Mr. Fairchild, Jan. 22, 1882, Livermore Collection, SLR.

20. MAL to AW, Feb. 27, 1885, Whitney Collection, WC.

21. Ibid.

22. *Woman's Journal*, June 30, 1888; MAL to AW, July 25, 1888, Whitney Collection, WC.

23. *Report of the Commissioners of the National Centennial Celebration of the Early Settlement of the Territory North West of the River Ohio and of the Establishment of Civil Government Therein, Held at Marietta, Ohio, July 15–19, Inclusive, 1888* (Columbus, Ohio: Westbote, 1889), 70, 123–27.

24. Ibid.; *New York Tribune*, July 17, 1888.

25. *Report of the Commissioners of the National Centennial Celebration*, 123–37; *Woman's Journal*, June 30, July 21, 1888.

26. *Springfield Republican*, quoted in *Woman's Journal*, Aug. 4, 1888; *New York Tribune*, July 17, 1888; MAL to AW, July 25, 1888, Whitney Collection, WC.

27. *Woman's Journal*, Oct. 20, 1883, Nov. 29, 1884, May 30, 1885.

28. The Massachusetts school suffrage law is discussed in Robinson, *Massachusetts in the Woman Suffrage Movement*, 57–58, 104–7, 239–41, and Strom, "Leadership and Tactics in the American Woman Suffrage Movement," 299. MAL discussed going to the assessor's office in a letter to Mr. Dearborn, June 11, [no year], Livermore Collection, Smith College, and she mentioned missing her first vote in a letter to Miss [Abigail] May, April 13, 1880, May-Goddard Collection, SLR. See also *HWS*, 3:288 and 4:745–47.

29. Solicitation for municipal suffrage petitions signed by MAL, 1884, in MWSA Collection, SLR. A discussion of anti-suffragists and their rhetoric is in *HWS*, 4:721–

24. See also Robinson, *Massachusetts in the Woman Suffrage Movement*, 122-24, and Strom, "Leadership and Tactics in the American Woman Suffrage Movement," 299.

30. A broadside advertising the fair appeared in *Woman's Journal*, Dec. 11, 1886; see also Dec. 4, 1886. MAL discussed the fair in letters to Mr. Austin, Nov. 25, 1886, Livermore Collection, SLR; to Mr. [Phillips] Brooks, Dec. 10, 1886, MAL Collection, HLH; and to AW, June 24 [1886], Whitney Collection, WC.

31. *Woman's Journal*, Dec. 18, 1886, and June 11, 1887. The *Journal* did not reprint MAL's speech.

32. *Woman's Journal*, Jan. 26, Feb. 2, March 9 and 23, April 27, May 4 and 18, 1889; Merk, "Massachusetts and the Woman-Suffrage Movement," 128-29.

33. SBA to EBH, Nov. 2, 1885, Harbert Collection, HL; Blackwell, *Lucy Stone*, 227-29; Kerr, "White Women's Rights, Black Men's Wrongs," 77.

34. Rachel G. Foster, ed., *Negotiations between the American and National Woman Suffrage Associations in Regard to Union* (n.p., 1888). MAL referred to ASB as "daughter of the regiment" in her eulogy of LS in *Woman's Journal*, Oct. 28, 1893. See SBA to LS, Dec. 13, 1887, on their first meeting; Blackwell Family Collection, LC; Flexner, *Century of Struggle*, 220.

35. *Woman's Journal*, March 1, 1890.

36. A cold prevented Stone from attending the convention, but she sent a letter stating, "The time is full of encouragement for us." Ibid.

37. A copy of the program for the International Council of Women may be found in the Barton Collection, LC. *Woman's Journal*, June 8, 1901; *HWS*, 4:426.

38. *Woman's Journal*, Sept. 26, Oct. 17, 24, 1885. Membership figure discussed ibid., Dec. 10, 1892. Anna Howard Shaw would later serve as president of the NAWSA.

39. MAL to Mrs. [Ednah] Cheney, Sept. 28, 1885, and to Mrs. [Abby] Burr, Jan. 22, 1893 (WCTU), July 19, 1887 (Hesseltine), Livermore Collection, Smith College; MAL to Annie Fields, April 19, 1886 (Melrose school), Fields Collection, HL.

40. MAL to Mrs. (Isabel Chapin) Barrows, July 31, 1889, Livermore Collection, HLH; Melrose WCTU flyer for 1886-87 and discussion of "social gathering" in MAL to Mrs. (Abby) Burr, April 3, 1886, Livermore Collection, Smith College.

41. MAL to LS, Aug. 10, 1891, and to HBB, Jan. 15, 1894, NAWSA Collection, reel 12, LC. When Samuel Sewell died, MAL, LS, and JWH all served as honorary pallbearers. See *Woman's Journal*, Dec. 29, 1888.

42. *Woman's Journal*, Feb. 4, 1893, Jan. 12, 1895.

43. MAL to LS, Aug. 13, 1893, NAWSA Collection, reel 12, LC.

44. *Woman's Journal*, Oct. 28, 1893; MAL to HBB, Oct. 19, 1893, NAWSA Collection, reel 12, LC. Stone was one of the few people with whom Livermore used first names in her correspondence.

45. *Woman's Journal*, Jan. 12, 1895, Jan. 25, 1896.

46. Ibid., Jan. 12, Feb. 9, 1895. MAL described the meeting of the "Saints" at Frank Garrison's house in a letter to AW, Sept. 15, 1886, Whitney Collection, WC. MAL discussed literary topics with Edna Cheney on Nov. 14, 1896, New England Hospital Collection, Smith College.

47. *Woman's Journal*, Feb. 20, April 17, 1897, Oct 6, 27, Nov. 17, Dec. 15, 1900, Jan. 12, 1901. MAL's role boosting suffrage membership is discussed on Jan. 25, 1896.
48. MAL to Mrs. [Adelaide] Johnson, July 7, 11, 1891, Livermore Collection, BPL; Agnes Garrison diary, May 25, 1885, and William Lloyd Garrison II to Ellie, May 5, 1895, Garrison Family Collection, Smith College.
49. MAL to Mrs. [Adelaide] Johnson, May 19, 1889, Livermore Collection, BPL; Whittier anecdote in Lillian Whiting, "Some Personal Reminiscences of Mary A. Livermore," *New York Times*, May 28, 1905.
50. MAL to AW, June 10, 1888, Oct. 17, 1892, Dec. 22, [1892], Whitney Collection, WC.
51. *New York Times*, Jan. 8, 20, 1895; *Woman's Journal*, Jan. 12, 1895.

12. THE GRAND OLD WOMAN

1. Untitled newspaper clipping, n.d. [1893], T&P Papers, reel 32.
2. MAL to [Julia Annah Smith] Clark, Sept. 15, 1886, Clark Collection, HL. On the "holy comradeship," see MAL, "Some Notable Women I Have Known," *Golden Rule*, July 14, 1892. See also E. W. Blatchford to MAL, July 12, 1899, Livermore Collection, FLP.
3. *Woman's Journal*, Aug. 9, 16, 1890; Stuart McConnell, *Glorious Contentment: The Grand Army of the Republic, 1865-1900* (Chapel Hill: University of North Carolina Press, 1992), 218.
4. MAL to Clara Barton, Sept. 14, 1897, Barton Collection, LC; *War*, 9. MAL discussed her speech on "The Women of the War" to students at Wellesley College in a letter to Hannah E. Gilman, Nov. 9, 1896, Gilman Family Collection, Massachusetts Historical Society, Boston. MAL also wrote about women's wartime record in her native state; see "Massachusetts Women in the Civil War," in Thomas Wentworth Higginson, *Massachusetts in the Army and Navy During the War of 1861-65* (Boston: Wright & Potter, 1895-96), 586-603.
5. Schultz, *Women at the Front*, 212-45.
6. MAL uses the date April 1863 to describe both her exploits with the Sanitary Commission in Mississippi and her subsequent speech in Dubuque; see *War*, 295-368, 601-12. Stone was wounded at Vicksburg on May 22, 1863. See A. A. Stuart, *Iowa Colonels and Regiments: Being a History of Iowa Regiments in the War of the Rebellion* (Des Moines: Mills, 1865), 14-15. For Stone's election as governor, see *Dubuque (Iowa) Times*, Oct. 14, 1863. Dubuque's newspapers do not record his presence in that city in the spring or summer of 1863.
7. MAL's remarks at the soldiers' banquet, her visit to Des Moines, and her speech in Dubuque are discussed in chapter 6.
8. *New York Tribune*, July 19, 1889. MAL admitted that "my own tendency is to destroy the records of my past, as soon as an event or experience has ended"; see *War*, 9, 11. MAL to Clara Barton, Sept. 14, 1897, Barton Collection, LC. For a discussion of the popularity of Civil War books at the end of the century, see Alice Fahs, *The Imagined Civil War: Popular Literature of the North and South, 1861-*

1865 (Chapel Hill: University of North Carolina Press, 2001), 313-14.

9. MAL to Clara Barton, Sept. 14, 1897, Barton Collection, LC.

10. *Life*, ix-x.

11. *Life*, x. The series titled "In 'Old Virginny' Fifty Years Ago" was published in monthly installments in *Worthington's Illustrated Magazine* beginning in January 1893. Senator Walthall died the year after Livermore published this book. See Hardin, "Edward Cary Walthall," 30. It is not known whether MAL had any contact with the Walthall or Jones families after the Civil War.

12. *Life*, 583, 597.

13. MAL to Lilian Whiting, Nov. 20, 1899, Livermore Collection, BPL; MAL to Mrs. [Isabel Chapin] Barrows, Aug. 7, 1897, and Samuel J. Barrows to MAL, Nov. 1, 1897, Livermore Collection, HLH.

14. Frances E. Willard and Mary A. Livermore, eds., *A Woman of the Century: Leading American Women in All Walks of Life* (1893; reprint, Detroit: Gale, 1967).

15. Ibid., intro.

16. MAL, "Woman Suffrage," *North American Review* 143 (1886): 371-81; MAL, "Centuries of Dishonor," *Arena* 1 (1889): 82-92. The latter was reprinted as a pamphlet titled "Mrs. Livermore on Equal Rights" (Boston: Woman's Journal, 1890).

17. MAL, "Centuries of Dishonor," 82-92.

18. MAL et al., "Women's Views of Divorce," *North American Review* 150 (1890): 110-17. Her article condemning divorce appeared in the *New Covenant*, Feb. 8, 1868.

19. MAL to AW, Sept. 10, 1894, Whitney Collection, WC; *New York Times*, Jan. 5, 1903.

20. MAL's views on the Spanish-American War come from an undated manuscript, possibly the draft of a letter to the editor, NAWSA Collection, reel 45, LC. See also her letter on Massachusetts Volunteer Aid Association letterhead, Aug. 20, 1898, ibid. On John D. Long and MAL, see *HWS*, 4:719-20.

21. DPL, *Woman Suffrage Defended by Irrefutable Arguments: and All Objections to Woman's Enfranchisement Carefully Examined and Completely Answered* (Boston: Lee & Shepard, 1885), v. DPL's suffrage articles in the *Woman's Journal* include March 1, April 26, 1884, March 17, 1888. His other publications include "Female Warriors," in *The Ballot and the Bullet*, comp. Carrie Chapman Catt (Philadelphia: Alfred J. Ferris, 1897), 11-35. Phebe Hanaford described DPL in *Daughters of America*, 311. MAL spoke of DPL reading in a letter to AW, Sept. 10, 1885, Whitney Collection, WC. Roundabout Club in *Melrose Free Press*, Dec. 24, 1920. See also DPL obituary, *Woman's Journal*, July 15, 1899, and *Life*, 596.

22. MAL described the Alexandria Bay vacation in a letter to AW, Sept. 10, 1885, Whitney Collection, WC. California winters are discussed in *Woman's Journal* articles on April 20 and 27, 1889; DPL obituary, July 15, 1899; and MAL to Kate Sanborn, Feb. 15, 1898, Livermore Collection, Smith College. See also MAL to HBB, [1890], NAWSA Collection, reel 12, LC.

23. MAL to James P[arton], May 6, 1891, manuscript letter tipped into James Parton,

Eminent Women of the Age (Hartford: S. M. Betts, 1868), Rare Books, HL. Discussion of mementos in *Life*, 477–78. Description of MAL's study in Whiting, *Boston Days*, 459. Witherington described in MAL obituary in *Boston Journal*, May 24, 1905.

24. Lizzie's handwriting appears in the book *Comfort in Sorrow* written by DPL and published during the Civil War. The book also contains these words in MAL's handwriting: "Lizzie, from Father, July 1899." DPL died that month. This copy is in the Illinois State Historical Library. MAL requested autographs for Lizzie in letters to ASB, Nov. 6, 1888, and HBB, Oct. 30, 1893, NAWSA Collection, reel 12, LC. Eliza Livermore is described by MAL in a letter to AW, Sept. 15, 1886, Whitney Collection, WC. Abby Coffin's role in the household is characterized in newspaper articles from *Boston Post* [1890] and *Melrose Free Press*, May 25, 1905, Melrose Public Library.

25. MAL to "Dear Sir," Oct. 27, 1891, manuscript letter tipped into a copy of *Life*, Livermore Collection, BPL. Four different churches mentioned in *Woman's Journal*, Jan. 12, 1895, and MAL identified as Unitarian, May 11, 1895. JWH believed that MAL had no "strong denominational bias." See JWH to Mr. Horner, April 26, 1906, Howe Collection, SLR.

26. Buhle, *Women and American Socialism*, 79 (Boffin's Bower); *Melrose Free Press*, Sept. 7, 1867 (Livermore school); *Melrose Reporter*, June 20, 1896, and *HWS*, 4: 717 (Tufts); MAL to AW, Dec. 3, 1897, Whitney Collection, WC (MAL bust). See also *Melrose Reporter*, April 15, 1898, and undated clipping for donation of the bust to the Melrose Public Library.

27. *Woman's Journal*, May 11, 1895; *New York Times*, May 7, 1895; *Life*, 604–8.

28. Ibid.

29. *Woman's Journal*, May 18, 1895; *HWS*, 4:715. The reception took place on May 14, 1895.

30. *Woman's Journal*, July 8, 15, 1899; *New York Tribune*, July 19, 1899.

31. MAL to DPL, July 29, [1852], Livermore Collection, FLP ("Life is not life without you"); MAL to Mrs. Powell, July 23, 1899, Livermore Collection, SLR (deathbed vigil); MAL to ASB, July 9, 1899, NAWSA Collection, reel 12, LC (nervous strain); MAL to AW, Aug. 19, 1899, Whitney Collection, WC (bereavement).

32. Lilian Whiting, "Some Personal Reminiscences of Mary A. Livermore," *New York Times*, May 28, 1905 (citing DPL); MAL to AW, Aug. 19, 1899, Whitney Collection, WC; *Boston Journal*, May 25, 1905 (citing JWH).

33. MAL to Lilian Whiting, Aug. 4, 1899; see also Dec. 11, 1900, Dec. 31, 1901, Dec. 15, 1902, Livermore Collection, BPL. As MAL lay dying, the *Boston Journal* ran a story about her life reporting that she had announced her belief in spiritualism in November 1899. The *Journal*, May 20, 1905, noted, however, that she did not join any spiritualist "circles" and "did not believe much of what is accepted by the members. In fact she has been more of a Spiritist."

34. *Perry Magazine* 2 (Nov. 1899): 98–102 and 2 (Feb. 1900): 256–60. MAL discussed her views about Emerson and Fuller in letters to Mr. Cooke, June 8, 1903, ms. letter tipped into a copy of *Life*, and to Lilian Whiting, Dec. 4, 1899, Livermore Collection, BPL. MAL to ASB, May 9, 1904, NAWSA Collection, reel 12, LC.

35. *Woman's Journal*, March 3, 1900. The following week MAL spoke on "Eminent Women," but the *Journal* did not record her remarks. For a discussion of her eightieth birthday, see ibid., Dec. 22, 1900. Her conservatory is described in *New York Times*, Dec. 20, 1901, as is the marriage of Adelaide Witherington to William Boynton, Dec. 20, 1903.

36. MAL discussed her decision to step down from the Fortnightly in a letter to Miss Turner, Sept. 21, 1903, NAWSA Collection, reel 12, LC. *Woman's Journal* made the announcement on Oct. 17, 1903. Discussions of her failing eyesight may be found in: MAL to [Henry Nehemiah] Dodge, Oct. 16, 1900, Dodge Collection, Andover-Harvard Theological Library, *New York Times*, May 7, 1902, and MAL to Lilian Whiting, Sept. 8, 1902, Livermore Collection, BPL.

37. William Lloyd Garrison II to Ellen Wright Garrison, May 11, 1905, Garrison Family Collection, Smith College. MAL's speech was reprinted in *Woman's Journal*, May 20, 1905.

38. *Melrose Journal*, May 26, 1905, described the progression of her illness. *Boston Journal*, May 18 and 24, 1905; *Boston Post*, May 20, 1905; *Boston Transcript*, May 23, 1905; *Woman's Journal*, May 27, 1905. Wyoming Cemetery records, Melrose, Mass. include the death date for Mary Eliza Livermore.

39. *Boston Post*, May 24, 1905; *Boston Journal*, May 26, 1905; *Melrose Journal*, May 26, 1905; *Melrose Free Press*, May 26, 1905.

40. MAL wrote her will by hand on January 26, 1900. She bequeathed $3,000 to her sister Abby, but the bulk of the estate, including her home, which was to be sold, would go to pay for Lizzie's upkeep. MAL asked that her secretary Adelaide Witherington Boynton act as Lizzie's companion, and Boynton appears to have done so. On May 27, 1905, Charles C. Barry, executor of MAL's estate, released a statement to reporters asking that "you refrain from publishing any portion of her will. As there are no bequests of a public nature, and the details are of such a private and personal character . . . [the family] feel[s] sure that they may rely upon your proverbial courtesy and kindness." With Lizzie's death in 1928, Etta Livermore Norris inherited the estate of $33,740.51 as residuary legatee. See will and fiduciary materials relating to MAL's estate, case no. 68123, Middlesex Probate Court, Middlesex County, Cambridge, Mass.

41. *Woman's Journal*, July 1, 1905 (John Norris obituary); *Melrose Free Press*, April 14, 1911 (Abby Coffin obituary), and Nov, 8, 1929 (Etta Norris obituary).

42. Anti-suffragism in Massachusetts is described in Strom, "Leadership and Tactics in the American Woman Suffrage Movement," 296. Edwin C. Kemp, *Melrose, Massachusetts, 1900-1950* (Melrose: Fiftieth Anniversary Committee, 1950), 152-53. Mary Livermore Norris Barrows joined the crew team and the College Equal Suffrage League at Wellesley. During World War I she was chairwoman of the War Savings effort in Melrose. A Republican, she served on the Melrose Board of Aldermen, 1926-28, and in the legislature, 1929-39, where she was the only woman to chair a committee, the Pensions Committee. In 1939 she was appointed to the State Civil Service Commission, serving until 1945. She retired in 1946 and died in 1955. See Wellesley Alumnae Biographical Files, WC.

INDEX

Wendy Hamand Venet was born in Arkansas, raised in Illinois, and educated at the University of Illinois Urbana-Champaign (Ph.D., 1985). She taught for a decade at Eastern Illinois University before moving to Georgia State University in Atlanta, where she is currently associate professor of history. Her publications include *Neither Ballots nor Bullets: Women Abolitionists and the Civil War* (1991) and two coedited books, *Midwestern Women: Work, Community, and Leadership at the Crossroads* with Lucy Eldersveld Murphy (1997) and *Union in Crisis* with Robert W. Johannsen (2003). She lives in Decatur, Georgia, with her husband and two sons.